UNGENTLE GOODNIGHTS

UNGENTLE GOODNIGHTS

*Life in a Home for Elderly and Disabled
Naval Sailors and Marines and the Perilous
Seafaring Careers That Brought Them There*

————— ❧❧ —————

CHRISTOPHER McKEE

Naval Institute Press
Annapolis, Maryland

This book has been brought to publication with the generous assistance of Marguerite and Gerry Lenfest.

Naval Institute Press
291 Wood Road
Annapolis, MD 21402

Maps by Caitlin Campbell Scarborough and Chris Robinson. Building plans by Chris Robinson.

Library of Congress Cataloging-in-Publication Data
Names: McKee, Christopher, date, author.
Title: Ungentle goodnights : life in a home for elderly and disabled naval sailors and Marines and the perilous seafaring careers that brought them there / Christopher McKee.
Other titles: Life in a home for elderly and disabled naval sailors and Marines and the perilous seafaring careers that brought them there
Description: Annapolis, MD : Naval Institute Press, [2018] | Includes bibliographical references and index.
Identifiers: LCCN 2018025727 (print) | LCCN 2018026407 (ebook) | ISBN 9781682473672 (ePDF) | ISBN 9781682473672 (ePub) | ISBN 9781591145738 (hardcover : alk. paper) | ISBN 9781682473672 (ebook)
Subjects: LCSH: United States. Naval Asylum—History. | Sailors—United States—History—19th century. | Veterans—United States—History—19th century. | Older people—Care—United States—History—19th century. | United States. Navy—Sea life—History—19th century. | United States. Navy—Biography.
Classification: LCC VB293.P4 (ebook) | LCC VB293.P4 M34 2018 (print) | DDC 362.4086/970973—dc23
LC record available at https://lccn.loc.gov/2018025727

Printed in the United States of America.
26 25 24 23 22 21 20 19 18   9 8 7 6 5 4 3 2 1
First printing

Book interior design and layout by Stephen Tiano, Book Designer

Endpapers: The Asylum's still-rural setting is well captured in this 1847 watercolor by Augustus Köllner—that is, assuming that the artist represented the foreground landscape on the southeast side of Gray's Ferry Road accurately and did not romanticize the scene. Presumably for simplicity, Köllner has omitted the southwest gate, the lodge, and the surgeon's residence, all of which should be visible to left of the Asylum building. The ghostly image between the Asylum and the governor's residence (at the right) is the portico of Blockley, Philadelphia's alms house. The Library Company of Philadelphia

Being a Navy sailor or a Marine could be a deadly job in the nineteenth century. Battle was only the most dramatic danger. More common were fatal illnesses from strange diseases encountered in remote ports of the world, or accidental deaths—perhaps a fall from the yardarm into a stormy sea from which rescue was impossible. But if a Marine or a sailor was lucky enough to avoid all these and other dangers, eventually he met a peril he could not escape—old age. Ungentle Goodnights *is the story of that final encounter as experienced by U.S. Marines and sailors, and of the eventful lives that preceded it.*

CONTENTS

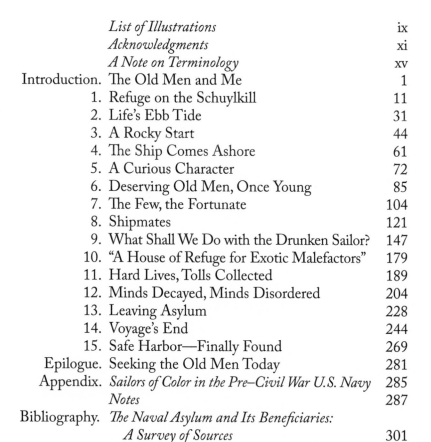

ILLUSTRATIONS

ACKNOWLEDGMENTS

More than was the case with my previous books, *Ungentle Good-nights* has been a team effort. Foremost among those team members, I recognize the nine Grinnell College students who worked so creatively as my research associates—Allison Amphlett, Grace Hazeltine Bartman, Caitlin Campbell Scarborough, Gretel Carlson, Megan Dimitt Merritt, Kathryn Ellefson, Ashley Morehead Erickson, Andrea Leiser, and Sophie Lobanov-Rostovsky. Ms. Amphlett moved to Washington following her graduation from Grinnell; she continued to work for the project, conducting research at the National Archives in time off from her day jobs. Nor must I fail to acknowledge four Grinnell students who labored hard and effectively on an earlier, but failed, attempt at enlisted history—Laura Chavanothai Darnielle, Laura Davis Juliano, Anna Embree, and Jennifer Wheeler Rothschild. Fortunately, much of the work they accomplished eventually found its way into this book.

Kevin Engel, Grinnell's science librarian, guided me to several health-related sources without which this would have been a deficient book.

My research involved a lot of ground time in Washington and Philadelphia. Even with the generous financial support that my work has enjoyed, I could never have afforded that kind of time if I had been required to add the cost of hotels to the other travel expenses. Fortunately, I was not. My friends Ellen and Norman Plummer own an apartment in northwest Washington that they visit only occasionally; they generously allowed me to use these comfortable accommodations whenever my research trail led to the National Archives. I was equally lucky that my daughter, Sharon McKee, had the unconscious foresight to join a Philadelphia law firm well before I began this book and was able to provide a base during my trips to that city.

Closer to home, the University of Iowa's Obermann Center for Advanced Studies provided me with office space for the initial four years that I was able to give my full-time attention to research for *Ungentle Goodnights*. Director Jay Semel and administrators Carolyn Frisbie and Neda Barrett were wonderfully supportive. They did anything they could to help, and then stepped aside unobtrusively as work proceeded in an atmosphere of friendship among scholarly colleagues. When the Center lost its spacious rural setting (and I lost my office there), Professor Constance Berman came to the rescue, helping me find alternate space in which I was able to continue my work.

Almost the entire text of this book was written at the Newberry Library, Chicago, an extraordinarily welcoming home for scholars. Officers and staff members there were the gold standard in their friendly and tireless assistance to researchers. My gratitude is immense to Sarah Alger, Martha Briggs, Keelin Burke, Margaret Cusick, Jo Ellen McKillop Dickie, Diane Dillon, Grace Dumelle, Kristin Emery, Ginger Frere, Jill Gage, Catherine Gass, Will Hansen, D. Bradford Hunt, Peter Nekola, John Powell, Matthew Rutherford, Martina Schenone, Jason Ulane, Andrea Villasenor, and Jessica Weller.

Money—whether used for extended stays at remote archives, to purchase microfilm, or to hire student research associates—is the mother's milk of historical scholarship. I am keenly grateful for the generous support that I have received while working on this volume. Besides the Secretary of the Navy's year-long Research Chair in Naval History, the Naval Historical Center awarded me two Vice Admiral Edwin B. Hooper Research Grants at different stages in my work. Grinnell College's annual research-support grants (associated with my Samuel R. and Marie-Louise Rosenthal chair), along with Grinnell's subsequent competitive research grants, were absolutely essential. At the Naval Historical Center, I acknowledge with much gratitude its successive directors Ronald H. Spector, Dean C. Allard, and William S. Dudley. Closer to home, I extend equally enthusiastic thanks to four of Grinnell College's vice presidents for academic affairs—Charles Duke, James Swartz, Paula Smith, and Michael Latham.

At a late point in my research, two groups of Asylum-related manuscripts became available for purchase from the archive of Rear Admiral George W. Storer, one of the institution's governors. Thanks to the alertness and effective action of Michael Crawford of the Naval History and Heritage Command; Vice Admiral George Emery, USN (Ret.); Captain Charles T. Creekman, USN (Ret.), executive director of the Naval Historical Foundation, and the cash contributions of three donors, these important records were secured for the Navy Department Library. Absent the information in the Storer manuscripts, the book would have told a sketchier story of the Asylum's early residents.

Throughout the many years that I have been working on *Ungentle Goodnights*, I have keenly appreciated the friendship, support, and active assistance of Charles Brodine, Michael Crawford, and Christine Hughes of the Naval History and Heritage Command. At the National Archives in Washington, I enthusiastically acknowledge the many years of assistance that I have received from Dennis Edelin, the late Charles Johnson, Chris Killillay, Rebecca Livingston, and Mark Mollan. These trusty guides to the Navy's records welcomed my repeated visits with expert knowledge, exemplary helpfulness, and unfailing courtesy.

My daughter, Sharon, has helped me in so many ways that I cannot enumerate them all. She has been my number-one cheerleader at moments of discouragement, accompanied me on research trips, searched and copied paper files, photographed the Naval Asylum's grounds and the Asylum plot at Mount Moriah Cemetery, and employed her expertise with online historical and genealogical resources to find many a crucial fact or essential news item about the Naval Asylum and its residents.

One person who has been associated with my Naval Asylum project almost as long as I have deserves particular notice and gratitude. When I first met Gail Farr, in 1990, she was working for the Philadelphia Maritime Museum (now the Independence Seaport Museum). She drove me on my first visits to the abandoned Naval Asylum—then in a sad state of disrepair—and to Mount Moriah Cemetery, a site of even greater neglect and decay. By the time I resumed work on the Naval Asylum project some ten years later, Gail had moved professionally to the National Archives at Philadelphia, where she has been my primary contact during numerous research visits to the United States Naval Asylum records housed there.

David, my son, and his wife, Jennifer, joined the team for the proofreading process, bringing needed reinforcements at just the right moment.

My spouse has been unfailingly supportive during long years of living with this story of the Asylum and its elderly and eccentric residents. Thank you, Ann, so very much.

A Note on Terminology

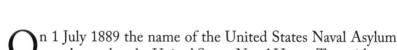

On 1 July 1889 the name of the United States Naval Asylum was changed to the United States Naval Home. To avoid confusion for readers, this change will be ignored and the institution will be referred to throughout the text as the United States Naval Asylum—or simply as the Asylum.

Before July 1851 residents of the Asylum were known as *pensioners*. This, too, can create some confusion. Not all Navy and Marine Corps veterans who drew pensions for injuries were residents of the Asylum, and not all residents had been granted pensions for such injuries, either. After July 1851 all Asylum residents were referred to as *beneficiaries*. Again, to prevent confusion, this book will refer to anyone who lived at the Naval Asylum as a beneficiary, whether he did so before or after July 1851.

In 1854 the City of Philadelphia and Philadelphia County were consolidated into a single governmental entity. Before that, the Asylum was legally in Passyunk Township, which was part of Philadelphia County. Because the distinction has no direct bearing on the narrative here, the Asylum will be described throughout the book as located in Philadelphia.

The name of Cedar Street, running between the Delaware and Schuykill Rivers, was changed in 1853 to *South Street*. The latter is the name by which it is usually called in the Naval Asylum's records, and that is the one that is used uniformly in this book.

THE OLD MEN AND ME: A SEARCH FOR ENLISTED HISTORY

This book had a long and difficult gestation. In 1990–91 I was awarded the Secretary of the Navy's Research Chair at the Naval Historical Center (now the Naval History and Heritage Command) in Washington. In my proposal for the fellowship I described my desire to write a history comparing U.S. Navy enlisted men during the first half of the nineteenth century and Royal Navy ratings from 1900 through 1945.

My year in Washington was spent in research at the United States National Archives. The most exciting aspect of that year was the discovery of the records of the United States Naval Asylum (later the United States Naval Home)—an institutional home that the Navy had established for elderly and disabled sailors and Marines—which opened its doors for its first residents, or beneficiaries as they were called, in 1831. I might never have known about these records had it not been for a colleague at the Naval Historical Center, Gordon Bowen-Hassell, a man with an impressively comprehensive and accurate knowledge of the manuscript archives of the U.S. Navy. Gordon said, in effect, if you are interested in Navy enlisted men, you need to look at the records of the Naval Asylum. He was right. Gordon had directed me to a splendid archive of information about the early Navy men of the lower deck.

Although I briefly considered writing a book about the Naval Asylum, I soon abandoned the idea. At that time, I saw the Asylum and its records as part of a larger book about the Navy's nineteenth-century enlisted force. At the end of my year in Washington, I returned to my home institution, Grinnell College, and set about writing that book. For a while, things seemed to go well. I wrote a chapter about the demographics of the Navy's enlisted force. The sources appeared more than adequate—British prisoner-of-war records from the War of 1812; scattered recruiting returns through the 1820s, 1830s, and 1840s; and the Navy's completely preserved recruiting rendezvous reports beginning in the 1850s. There, on record in tidy columns, was a mass of data on hundreds and hundreds of sailors—ages, places of birth, physical descriptions, years of previous service in the Navy, and years of experience at sea. It all went into the computer, and out came a chapter with which I was so pleased that I considered submitting it for publication as an article.

Fortunately, I did not. My subsequent work with the residents of the Asylum led to the discovery that these solid-looking data actually were like a castle built on sand. The problem was that individual sailors typically appeared but once in my data set. Only later, as I began to work with the Asylum's archives and encountered multiple recordings of data about the same beneficiary did I realize what I should have known all along—that sailors do not always tell the truth and observers are fallible. The Navy had no established means of tracking a sailor from one enlistment to another, or any way of verifying the answers that a sailor gave to a recruiting officer's questions. As a consequence, when it is possible to compare an individual's successive enlistments with other records of his life, it is common to discover that the man has reported wildly inconsistent ages. Sailors known from other records to have been born in a variety of European countries often asserted that they were born in one of the U.S. states—and not always the same state each time. Then there is the problem of the recruiting officer's subjectivity. Is this recruit's complexion fair or dark? Are his eyes blue or brown? I have reluctantly come to realize that about the only absolutely reliable data in the Navy's early recruiting returns are the sailors' heights.

Bad data were hardly the end of the problems. Once I had finished my demographic chapter, I could not find a satisfactory narrative thread on which I could proceed with my story. After struggling with this for a large part of a sabbatical year in the late 1990s, I decided to turn my full attention to the British side of my story, where my research and writing were proceeding in a much more satisfying manner. The outcome of that refocusing was *Sober Men and True: Sailor Lives in the Royal Navy, 1900–1945*, which was published by the Harvard University Press in 2002.

When I returned to American sailors about a year later, it was with a possibly risky determination: I would try to use the records of the Naval Asylum and its residents to tell the story of the nineteenth-century U.S. Navy enlisted men. The group on which I chose to focus was the five hundred forty-one men who were admitted to the Asylum between 1831 and the end of 1865. These include veterans of all the young republic's major wars: the Quasi-War with France (1798–1801), the Tripolitan War (1801–05), the War of 1812–15, the Mexican War (1846–48), and the Civil War (1861–65), as well as of the Navy's lesser hostilities, its commerce protection, its exploring expeditions, and its diplomatic missions in the years between the major wars. One could argue about whether these five hundred forty-one men represent a cross-section of the entire nineteenth-century enlisted corps. Certainly in terms of length of commitment to the Navy they do not. Most sailors signed on, served an enlistment or two or three, and left for other lives. The Asylum's beneficiaries were the minority long-service core of the organization. But this limitation was outweighed by one big advantage: the archives created by the Naval Asylum and related documents, such as pension application files, make the Asylum beneficiaries the only group of sailors whose lives one often can follow from their teenage years to their deaths. For almost all other enlisted men in the Navy of 1798–1865, the historian has to settle for snapshots at this or that point in their lives.

But wait: what about all those published autobiographies that have so long been the staple source for life on the Navy's lower deck? I have come to regard them as highly questionable sources for authentic enlisted history. For one thing, all such autobiographies were written to be sold to the reading public. This presented the purported sailor-authors—who probably had the seafarer's legendary penchant for embroidering the truth—with the temptation to include stories and adventures that usually are impossible to cross-check with other records. Moreover, many of the published lower-deck autobiographies appear to have been written with the assistance of unknown persons who were far more literate than the sailor whose name appears on the title page. How much is really the author's own story? How much is the embroidery of a hidden ghost-writer? Then there was opportunity to appeal to the middle-class audience's prurient interests—with sailors presenting themselves as repentant for their sinful ways. But, of course, this penitence would only be convincing if the sailors had catalogued their sins—with a certain degree of pre-Victorian discretion.

Finally, the genre was popular enough with the nineteenth-century reading public that a bumper crop of fake lower-deck autobiographies found their way into print. Many of these appear to have been written by non-lower-deck types with an insider's knowledge of the Navy and the sea. Some are so cleverly done that they have deceived scholars who have accepted them as authentic sources even though they ought to have known better. Lower-deck autobiography has been brilliantly analyzed—and the hidden meanings these stories contain insightfully decoded—by Myra Glenn in *Jack Tar's Story: The Autobiographies and Memoirs of Sailors in Antebellum America* (Cambridge University Press, 2010). I refer those with an interest in this literature to Professor Glenn's eminently trustworthy work. For myself, I have preferred to look elsewhere for reliable insights into lower-deck sailor life. In doing so, I have been guided in part by the fundamental observation that Alain Corbin offers in the first pages of *The Life of an Unknown: The Rediscovered World of a Clog Maker in Nineteenth-Century France* (Columbia University Press, 2001)—the simple fact that a non-elite, or working-class, person wrote an autobiography in the early nineteenth century automatically made him or her atypical of the mass of illiterate or silent contemporaries.

As I worked along on my project, I encountered a surprise that changed what I was doing in a major way. When I began my research, I assumed that I could more or less ignore the U.S. Marines among the Asylum's five hundred forty-one residents and focus on the sailors alone. Among other advantages, this would significantly reduce the number of persons on whom I would need to compile biographical profiles. I soon discovered how wrong I was. A surprising number of the Asylum's beneficiaries had served enlistments in both the Navy and the Marine Corps. More fundamentally, once these men entered the Asylum, the distinction between sailors and Marines vanished as far as I could discover in the historical record. Now they were all beneficiaries, sharing a common home. Almost all American naval historians have tended to ignore the Marines, at least until the Pacific campaigns of World War II, even though the Navy and the Marine Corps were both part of the naval establishment reporting to the Secretary of the Navy. The story of the Marine Corps has been left to a small, if dedicated, body of historians who study the Corps exclusively. But the historian who looks at the nineteenth-century naval establishment from the well-tended grounds of the Asylum cannot see either force in isolation. Clearly, this book was going to have to be about sailors and Marines.

The Asylum was only one of several institutions established in the nineteenth-century United States to provide old-age homes or temporary shelters to professional seafarers. Sailors' Snug Harbor on Staten Island is the best-known (and was the best-financed) of these. A comprehensive book about these institutions would be a valuable addition to our knowledge of American maritime history. I did learn a certain amount about those Asylum beneficiaries who also spent time at Sailors' Snug Harbor. That research aside, I made no attempt to explore the surviving records and the histories of the other sailor-supporting institutions of the nineteenth-century United States. My aim has been to exploit the rich records of the Asylum to enhance knowledge of the Navy's sailors and Marines; I have focused on that effort. The task has been challenging enough for this historian. I keenly hope that *Ungentle Goodnights* will provoke historical interest in exploring and recording the work of the Asylum's peer institutions, so that ultimately we will have a wider and better understanding of this network of safe harbors for those who spent their working years at sea.

At the end of the day I have to admit that my original plan to write a single-volume comparative history of U.S. Navy enlisted men of the first half of the nineteenth century and British naval ratings of the first half of the twentieth century was one that I could not execute. Weapons technology aside, in terms of shipboard culture and routines men from either nation or era soon would have adjusted if they had been time-traveled to the earlier or the later force. That commonality apart, they were men from different historical and social times, with different personal concerns and outlooks on life. Comparisons are not made as easily as I once naively assumed. Consequently, I present individual portraits of those who served on the lower decks of the two forces—*Sober Men and True: Sailor Lives in the Royal Navy, 1900–1914* in 2002 and now *Ungentle Goodnights*—and leave readers to discover for themselves whatever comparisons may have significance for them.

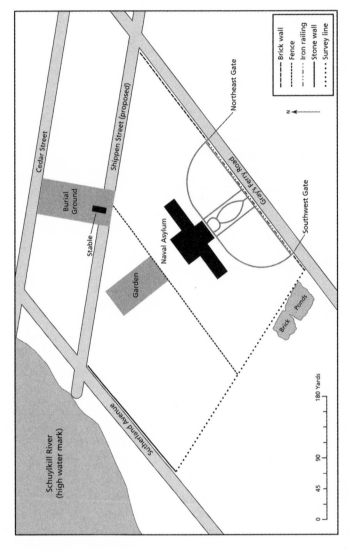

Naval Asylum Grounds, 1836. United States National Archives at College Park, MD, Record Group 71, Records of the Bureau of Yards and Docks, "Plan of the United States Naval Asylum with the land belonging thereto," Randal H. Rickey, Surveyor, 6 October 1836 (427-3-1); detail of brick ponds from sketch enclosed in U.S. National Archives in Washington, DC, Record Group 52, Records of the Bureau of Medicine and Surgery, Letters Received from Officers Not Medical: Charles W. Morgan to Thomas Harris, 14 April 1845

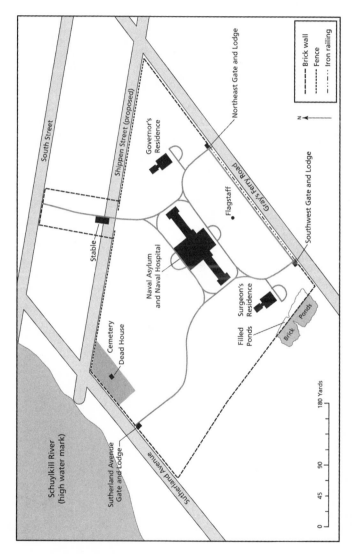

Naval Asylum Grounds, 1849. UNITED STATES NATIONAL ARCHIVES AT COLLEGE PARK, MD, RECORD GROUP 71, RECORDS OF THE BUREAU OF YARDS AND DOCKS, FRANCIS W. STRICKLAND, "SURVEY OF THE GROUND AND PLAN OF THE BUILDINGS OF THE UNITED STATES NAVAL ASYLUM, PHILADELPHIA," CIRCA 1844–1845 (427-3-2) AND SKETCH PLAN ENCLOSED IN U.S. NATIONAL ARCHIVES IN WASHINGTON, DC, RECORD GROUP 71, LETTERS RECEIVED BY THE CHIEF OF THE BUREAU OF YARDS AND DOCKS FROM THE GOVERNOR OF THE NAVAL ASYLUM: JOHN P. GILLIS TO WILLIAM BALLARD PRESTON, 21 MAY 1849

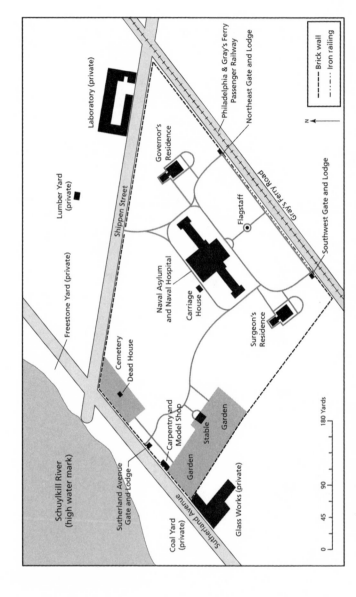

Naval Asylum Grounds, 1860. Smedley's Atlas of the City of Philadelphia (Philadelphia: Lippincott, 1862), Plate 2

Within the map:

Laboratory (private)

Philadelphia & Gray's Ferry Passenger Railway

Northeast Gate and Lodge

Governor's Residence

Lumber Yard (private)

Shippen Street

Gray's Ferry Road

Flagstaff

Southwest Gate and Lodge

Naval Asylum and Naval Hospital

Carriage House

Freestone Yard (private)

Surgeon's Residence

Cemetery Dead House

Carpentry and Model Shop

Stable

Garden

Garden

Schuylkill River (high water mark)

Sutherland Avenue Gate and Lodge

Coal Yard (private)

Sutherland Avenue

Glass Works (private)

N

Brick wall

Iron railing

0   45   90   180 Yards

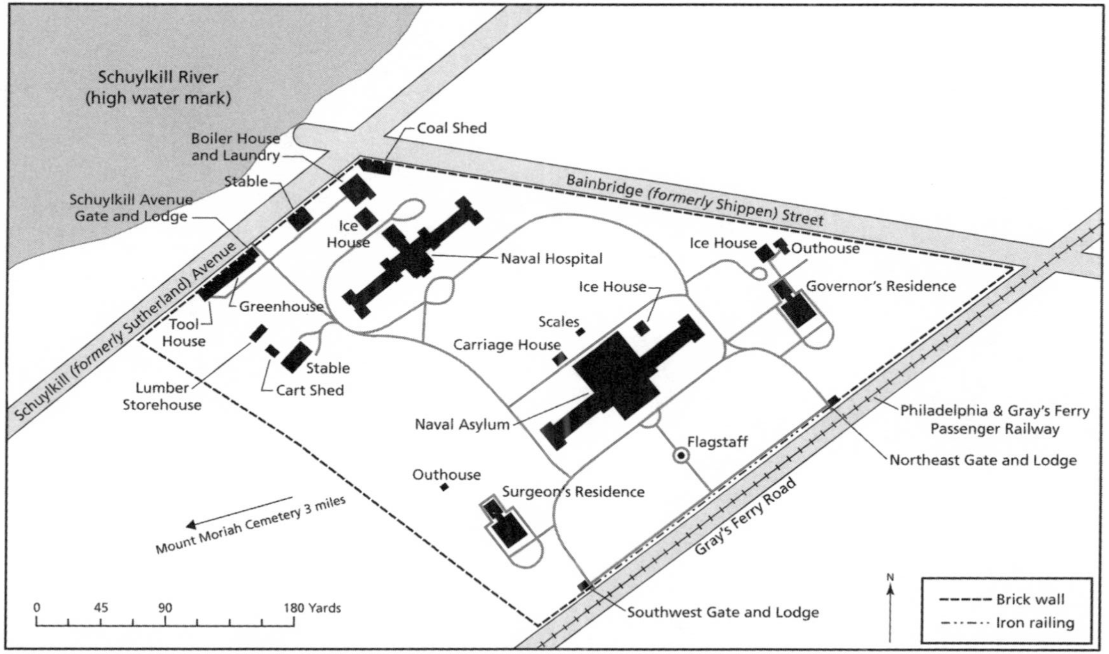

Schuylkill River
(high water mark)
Coal Shed
Boiler House
and Laundry
Stable
Schuylkill Avenue
Gate and Lodge
Ice
House
Bainbridge (formerly Shippen) Street
Naval Hospital
Ice House
Outhouse
Governor's Residence
Schuylkill (formerly Sutherland) Avenue
Greenhouse
Tool
House
Ice House
Scales
Carriage House
Stable
Lumber
Storehouse
Cart Shed
Naval Asylum
Philadelphia & Gray's Ferry
Passenger Railway
Flagstaff
Northeast Gate and Lodge
Outhouse
Surgeon's Residence
Mount Moriah Cemetery 3 miles
Gray's Ferry Road
N
0
45
90
180 Yards
Southwest Gate and Lodge
Brick wall
Iron railing

Naval Asylum Grounds, 1878. United States National Archives at College Park, MD, Record Group 71, Records of the Bureau of Yards and Docks, "Plan of the United States Naval Asylum, Philadelphia, Pa., Showing Boundary Lines and Improvements to Jan. 1st 1878"

ONE

REFUGE ON THE SCHUYLKILL

William Thompson was a hero. He held the Medal of Honor to prove it. Not that Thompson was the kind of man who would talk much about that sort of thing. A quiet, modest person—one officer who knew him well even called him taciturn—he was an exemplary naval sailor, one who did his duty, stayed out of trouble, and minded his own business. Thompson was around fifty years of age in 1861, five feet, ten inches tall, his hair still a dark brown, with dark gray eyes and a florid complexion. Although born in Cape May County, New Jersey, he called Philadelphia his home and sometimes stated that city to be his birthplace. An occasional misspelled word notwithstanding, he was fully literate. Place of birth and literacy aside, nothing is known about William Thompson's life until he joined the ship-of-the-line *Ohio*, flying the pennant of Commodore Isaac Hull, in October 1838 for a three-year cruise to the Mediterranean. Given Thompson's age when he first enlisted in the Navy, one can safely guess that he already possessed a number of years' experience in the merchant service or the coasting trade. But on that the record is silent. Naval service took Thompson to the Mediterranean again, to Brazil, and to China. Twenty-one years after he joined *Ohio* Thompson reenlisted for the last time in the steam sloop-of-war *Mohican*, bound for an anti-slaving patrol on the west coast of Africa.

Following the outbreak of the Civil War, *Mohican* was recalled to home waters, refitted at Boston, and steamed south to join Flag Officer Samuel F. Du Pont's South Atlantic Blockading Squadron. Du Pont was intent on capturing South Carolina's Port Royal

Sound as a base for his operations. During the squadron's massive
and successful 7 November 1861 naval attack on the two Confederate forts guarding the entrance to the sound, Thompson, a quartermaster, was stationed at *Mohican*'s wheel, steering the ship. As
the ships-versus-forts battle intensified, six Confederate shot struck
Mohican, killing one man and wounding seven others. One of the
seven was William Thompson. A 32-pound shot hit and shattered
his right leg above the knee. Immediately a nearby seaman jumped
to replace the wounded Thompson at the helm. But Thompson
was having none of that; he waved him away. Pulling out his knife,
Thompson cut the remaining ligaments that held the shattered leg
to his body, presumably fashioned some kind of temporary tourni-
quet, and continued to steer *Mohican* until he grew faint from
shock and loss of blood and was carried below.

Mohican's surgeons amputated the mangled stump of Thompson's
leg, and he was invalided on 14 November to the hospital at the
New York (Brooklyn) Navy Yard to recuperate. Thompson, obviously incapacitated for further active duty in the Navy, was granted
a full pension of eight dollars per month, and moved to the Sailor's
Home at 190 Cherry Street in New York City after his 22 July
1862 discharge from the hospital. He was cured of his wound, as
far as he could be, but William Thompson's problems were not
over. The stump of his amputated leg was only four inches long.
He tried to use a prosthetic leg and hoped that he would soon be
able to walk sufficiently to find shoreside employment to supplement his pension. But the artificial leg did not work satisfactorily
at all; the stump was just too short; getting about was difficult and
painful; and Thompson never did learn to walk well enough to hope
to hold a job. He could not remain at the Sailor's Home indefinitely; it was intended only as a transient residence for seamen.
What was a disabled sailor to do?

Rear Admiral Hiram Paulding, the commandant of the New
York Navy Yard, had followed Thompson's recovery with close interest since the latter's arrival at the hospital, because, said Paulding,
"No seaman ever behaved with more heroism in battle than
Thompson. . . . He is, in fact, the very type of a splendid American
seaman for whom the nation cannot do too much." Paulding had
a suggestion, and he would help Thompson make that suggestion
a reality: the incapacitated hero should apply to be admitted to the
United States Naval Asylum at Philadelphia.

THE WALLED ENCLAVE

The institution to which William Thompson applied, and to which he was eventually admitted on 7 January 1863, had been serving elderly and disabled sailors and Marines for something more than thirty-two years when the disabled ex-quartermaster presented himself, admission permit in hand, at the Naval Asylum's main gate. Why and how the United States Navy came to establish the Asylum—the first effort by the young federal government to provide long-term or lifetime residential care for any part of the country's population—may be left to the next chapter. A better introduction to the institution that William Thompson and five hundred forty of his fellow Navy and Marine Corps veterans would enter before the end of 1865—some of them to reside for a while, others to spend the remainder of their lives—is to examine what would have been these veterans' initial and continuing impressions of the United States Naval Asylum: its grounds, its buildings, its surrounding neighborhood. These physical realities of place would shape the lives of the men who would reside there.

The gate, called the *northeast gate*, through which William Thompson and his fellow beneficiaries were required to enter and leave the Naval Asylum grounds, fronted on Gray's Ferry Road (now Gray's Ferry Avenue), the principal highway by which one approached Philadelphia from the south and the way a road-using traveler would have left the city when heading for Baltimore or Washington. The Asylum's grounds were on the west side of the road and sloped in a northwesterly direction down to the banks of the Schuylkill River. At the foot of this slope, and close to the river's edge, Sutherland Avenue (now Schuylkill Avenue) ran parallel to the northeast-southwest line of Gray's Ferry Road. Although the Asylum's property extended across Sutherland Avenue to the river, the southeast side of the avenue was functionally the boundary of the Asylum proper. Land between Sutherland Avenue and the Schuylkill formed no part of the working institution. Under a congressional authorization of 3 March 1857, it was divided into lots and eventually sold off.

The Asylum's northern boundary was defined by the line of Shippen Street (today's Bainbridge Street). Although the bird's-eye perspective of the Naval Asylum in the maps of the grounds suggests to the unwary that the viewer is looking at flat land, such was far from the reality. The grade of Shippen Street was as much as nineteen and a half feet below the adjacent Asylum property. While Shippen Street was being cut through in the 1850s, the Asylum's land on the south side was terraced back from the grade of the street. The pedestrian passing along Shippen Street's sidewalk would have had the feeling of the Asylum's grounds and any buildings visible on them looming overhead. A peculiar feature of this northern side of the Asylum grounds was a kind of narrow peninsula of land, part of the original Asylum property, which extended to South Street. Once Shippen Street was completed this tract became a cut off and dysfunctional part of the property, isolated by the deep cut of the street. Under the just-mentioned congressional authorization of March 1857, this isolated tract was divided into lots and sold between 1857 and 1870.

The remaining boundary of the Asylum property, on the southwest side, originally had only a surveyor's line to define it—a line that ran straight from Sutherland Avenue to Gray's Ferry Road. This straight surveyor's line was slightly modified in 1844, when a narrow pie-shaped piece of land 60 feet by 660 feet was purchased and added to the Asylum grounds, creating a slight jog to the southwest in the property line. By the time William Thompson came through the gate in 1863, the Naval Asylum had settled into what were to be its functional boundaries for the balance of its Philadelphia existence; the outlying lots had either been sold or were authorized for sale. A handwritten note on the detailed survey of the Asylum grounds carried out in 1878 calculated the land within these boundaries to be 20.68 acres.

By the 1860s the institution's boundaries were all delineated by sturdy brick walls about eleven and a half feet high, resting on stone foundations and capped with limestone slabs. In earlier years the southwest and northern (Shippen Street) boundaries had been enclosed with ten-foot-tall board fences. The wooden fence along the southwest line was replaced with a wall in 1845, shortly after the pie slice–shaped addition to the property was purchased. On the north side of the grounds the board fence remained in place until 1857, when Shippen Street—the construction of which had been sporadically promised and delayed—was finally opened between Sutherland Avenue and Gray's Ferry Road. The wooden fence along the northern side of the Asylum property could be climbed by a man in reasonably good physical condition—recall here that even sailors in their forties and fifties routinely climbed rigging as part of their shipboard duties—and provided a clandestine route out of, and back into, the Asylum grounds when one wished to escape the attention of those in authority.

The only gap in the tall brick walls was some 620 feet along Gray's Ferry Road, where a low stone foundation topped with an ornamental iron fence permitted a view into the Asylum's grounds. This particular 620 feet of iron fence did not please Commodore Charles W. Morgan, one of the Asylum's early governors. (The governor was the senior naval officer in command at the Asylum, a role about which more will be said in chapter 4.) In November 1845 Morgan complained to Secretary of the Navy George Bancroft that the construction of the fence was such that beneficiaries—"even those who are the least active"—could climb over it. Worse yet, *women*—Asylum employees and others—were able to climb the fence! The idea of a woman having easy and inappropriate access to, and egress from, the grounds was especially irritating to Morgan, a man with more than a touch of misogyny in his psychic makeup. To remedy this situation, the commodore proposed to top the fence with a series of sharp iron points, alternately 12 inches and 20 inches tall, and about 3 inches apart.

Presumably Secretary Bancroft found the prospect of elderly beneficiaries, let alone fugitive women employees or members of the world's oldest profession, impaling themselves on the lethal-looking iron spikes distasteful or worse; he filed the proposal without comment or reply, and the plan was never implemented.

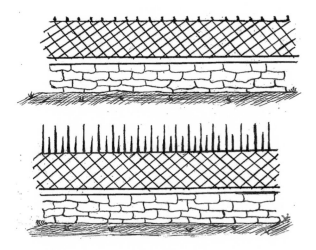

Top: Drawing of existing fence. Bottom: Proposed addition of spikes to fence. UNITED STATES NATIONAL ARCHIVES AT PHILADELPHIA, PA

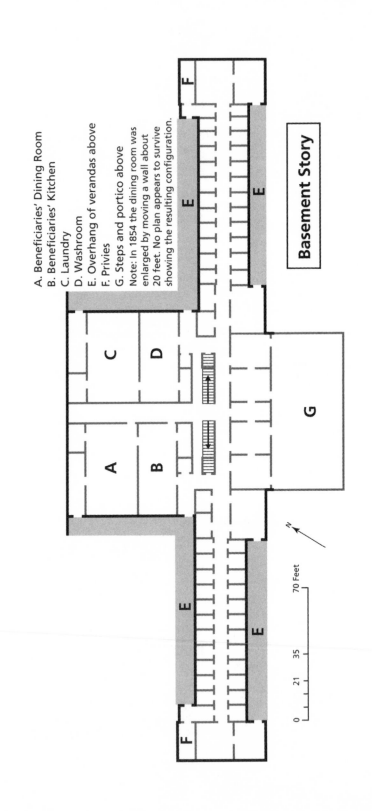

A. Beneficiaries' Dining Room
B. Beneficiaries' Kitchen
C. Laundry
D. Washroom
E. Overhang of verandas above
F. Privies
G. Steps and portico above

Note: In 1854 the dining room was enlarged by moving a wall about 20 feet. No plan appears to survive showing the resulting configuration.

Basement Story

A

B

C

D

E

E

E

E

F

F

G

N

0   21   35   70 Feet

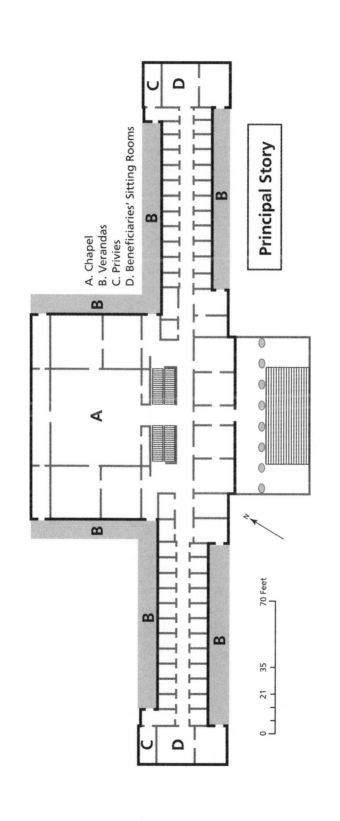

A. Chapel
B. Verandas
C. Privies
D. Beneficiaries' Sitting Rooms

Principal Story

0   21   35   70 Feet

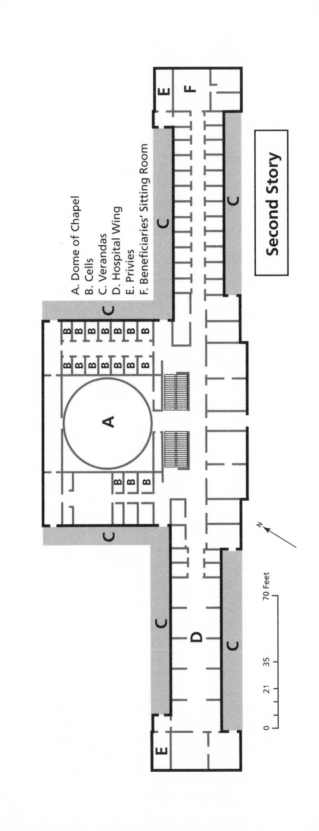

A. Dome of Chapel
B. Cells
C. Verandas
D. Hospital Wing
E. Privies
F. Beneficiaries' Sitting Room

Second Story

0   21   35   70 Feet

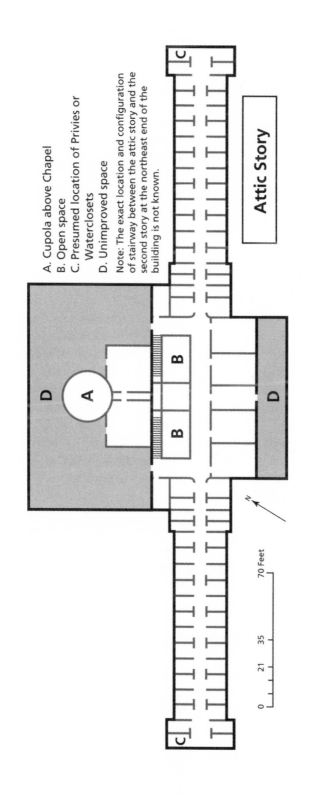

A. Cupola above Chapel
B. Open space
C. Presumed location of Privies or
   Waterclosets
D. Unimproved space

Note: The exact location and configuration
of stairway between the attic story and the
second story at the northeast end of the
building is not known.

Attic Story

0   21   35   70 Feet

The northeast gate through which William Thompson would have arrived at the Naval Asylum was the principal entrance to the institution, but not the only one. Another, the *southwest gate*, as it was known, was some six hundred feet farther along Gray's Ferry Road. It was used primarily for deliveries of goods to the Asylum and for the removal of rubbish. A third gate on Sutherland Avenue gave access to the western part of the grounds. Next to each gate there stood a small house, referred to as a *lodge*, in which two of the more active and responsible beneficiaries lived and alternately served as guards for the entrances to the Asylum enclave.

The grounds protected by these walls, gates, and lodges had, by the 1860s, attained the well maintained and almost park-like appearance one associates with a mature shore establishment of the U.S. Navy. That tidy and inviting ambience reflected the ongoing enthusiasm of the Asylum's successive governors, who had made a conscious and sustained effort to achieve it. The grounds had not always looked this good. In the 1840s the southwestern segment of the property was rough terrain. The portion of a disused brick pond acquired as part of the slice-of-pie addition to the grounds in 1844 required about 6 feet of fill dirt to level it with the Asylum grounds; a small hill, intersected by the southwestern brick wall, needed to be leveled off and the dirt therefrom used to fill an adjacent gravel pit that was 100 feet across and between 10 feet and 15 feet deep. Nothing could be done to eliminate a close-by lime kiln that rose over the Asylum's southwest wall; that was on private property. It could, however, be hidden behind trees, and the governors were enthusiastic tree planters. They favored elm, oak, and silver maple, purchasing and tending hundreds of saplings, until parts of the grounds, especially along the southwest and western boundaries, were forests of still-maturing trees. Open spaces not shaded by trees were sown to grass—grass that was kept mowed in the publicly visible space behind the iron fence along Gray's Ferry Road, but was otherwise left to grow until it could be harvested as hay for the Asylum's working horses or sold.

THE MONUMENTAL HOME

A newly arrived beneficiary, as was William Thompson, could not immediately have been aware of all these features of the Asylum precinct. That was knowledge to be gained through time and exploration. But off to his right, as he came through the gate on Gray's Ferry Road, Thompson would surely have noticed a substantial private residence, the official home of the Asylum's governor. Then his vision would quickly have moved to, and been dominated by, the massive granite and marble building that rose before him—the United States Naval Asylum itself. The aspect of the building that would most immediately have caught his attention was the central portico with its eight towering columns, approached by a broad flight of nineteen stone steps. Two wings extended on either side of the central portico to make the building about 385 feet long. In practical sailor terms, assuming Thompson paused to rest his leg and reflect, the Asylum was roughly twice as long as either *Ohio* or *Mohican*, two of the ships in which he had served. At first glance the building would have appeared to be three stories in height, but when he got to know the place better Thompson would have learned that this appearance was deceptive. He could hardly have missed the verandas or piazzas that stretched along the fronts of the second and third above-ground stories of the two wings. So much for initial impressions. As a pragmatic man, Thompson may have spent less time taking in the classically inspired architecture before him than in wondering how a one-legged man was going to climb that long and broad flight of stone stairs leading to the Asylum's main entrance.

History does not record how Thompson met the challenge, but once he was up the stairs, through the columns, and into the building it is safe to assume he would have been met by the beneficiary on duty inside the doors, who would have directed or escorted him to the office of the executive officer, the Naval Asylum's second-in-command. There he would have presented his admission permit from the Navy Department. The formalities of admission completed, one might imagine that the executive officer would have detailed a resident beneficiary to show the newly arrived man around the building. For a beneficiary as disabled as Thompson, that tour might have been abbreviated, but with a more able-bodied new man there would have been many spaces to cover.

Immediately ahead as one entered the Asylum's front door, and surely the space first pointed out on any tour, was a square room, 56 feet by 56 feet, surmounted by a spectacular rotunda that extended through the second floor of the building. It was the Asylum's chapel,

VIEW OF THE BUILDING AND GROUNDS.

Under the title, "A Home for Old Sailors," Harper's Weekly of 23 February 1878 presented its readers with this view of the Asylum. The tree-planting efforts of successive governors made the once-barren grounds pictured by John C. Wild a shaded and welcoming oasis in rapidly urbanizing southwestern Philadelphia. Unlike the images of Wild and Augustus Köllner, artists who were intent on placing the building's architecture and presence in the foreground, Harper's portrayed an Asylum alive with activity. Beneficiaries (Asylum residents) stroll the grounds in pairs, climb the long front stair, or congregate on the verandas. A pet dog joins two beneficiaries for a walk.   THE NEWBERRY LIBRARY

where Sunday religious services were held, and where the beneficiaries assembled for weekly and special musters. If the tour guide
was in a mood to grouse about the building's shortcomings—and
being an old sailor, he probably was—he might have complained
that, although the chapel was a handsome space, its acoustics left
a lot to be desired. Complaints included an annoying echo or
reverberation. As for the rotunda dome itself, unless the preacher
or the governor or the executive officer who was addressing the
assembled audience had a truly stentorian voice, his words soared
up into the dome and could not be heard by the beneficiaries,
many—if not most—of whom would have had hearing impaired
by years of naval gunfire experienced in drills, salutes, and combat.

Next, the tour guide would probably have pointed out that
the large rooms to the left and right of the entrance were the
quarters of the officers, other than the governor, and their families.
The Asylum was a pleasant shoreside assignment where lieutenants or commanders could at once be on active duty and full pay
and still have their families with them. Because the rooms assigned
to a particular officer were not necessarily a continuous suite, there
was a good deal of family-life traffic in and through the hallways
near the chapel—wives visiting, children running and playing, servants busy with their daily tasks. As is typical in any large, actively
used building, the purposes and assignments of particular areas
within the structure were always evolving. What had been the executive officer's office might become the lieutenant's parlor. The governor's secretary might find his assigned workspace remote from
the governor. Change-of-space assignments were constant and occasionally contentious, as officers jockeyed for the rooms they preferred or to which they thought they were entitled.

Halfway between the Asylum's front entrance and the chapel,
long hallways extended to the left and right. Off these were the
beneficiaries' rooms. Each man had a room—his own private space,
11 by 9 feet, almost certainly larger than any space he had all to
himself on shipboard. The Asylum furnished each room with a
white-painted pine wardrobe; a pine table and chair; a bedstead
with mattress, pillow, blankets, sheets, pillow cases and bedspread;
a mirror; a basin for washing; and a chamber pot. The bedsteads
were originally designed with wooden slats to support the mattress, but the wood had proved an excellent place for "vermin"—
not otherwise identified, but presumably bedbugs—to hide and

breed, and the slats were replaced in 1845 with a heavy wire mesh to support the mattress. Over and above those furnishings, each beneficiary was free to bring in additional furniture, hang pictures on the walls, or make the room his own with personal belongings—mementoes of his life at sea.

On the building's main floor—always referred to as the *principal story*—and on the floor above, the *second story*, the windows looked out onto the verandas or piazzas that ran along the southeast and northwest faces of the building. No doors led directly from the beneficiaries' rooms to the verandas; the latter were only accessible through entrances at their ends. As to whether beneficiaries occasionally climbed through the windows to gain access to the verandas, the record is silent. The windows were certainly big enough for an able-bodied man to do that, as architect William Strickland

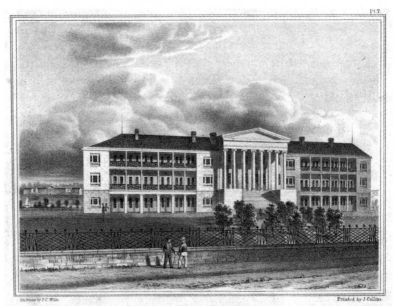

U. S. NAVAL ASYLUM.
PHILADELPHIA.

William Strickland's Naval Asylum is a long building, difficult to capture in a single image. One solution is to picture it from a distance, but in that case much interesting detail is lost. To solve this problem, John Caspar Wild chose to make the building appear shorter in length and taller than meets the human eye. That distortion aside, Wild's picture is an accurate record of the Asylum as it appeared in 1838, about the time James Biddle became governor. Note the elaborate iron railing along Gray's Ferry Road, the absence of mature trees on the grounds, and, to the left, a view of Blockley across the Schuylkill River.
THE LIBRARY COMPANY OF PHILADELPHIA

had deliberately designed the Asylum building to be filled with light and fresh air from the outside world. How successful Strickland had been in meeting his goal was a matter of opinion. At least one governor described the first three floors as rather dark and deficient in the cheerfulness imparted by sunlight.

At the end of each hall the guide would have pointed out a large common space, the beneficiaries' sitting rooms, where the residents could chat, smoke, read the day's newspapers, play games, or perhaps doze in a comfortable chair. These sitting rooms were privileged beneficiary turf, a tradition that the Asylum's officers tried to respect by intruding on them as little as possible.

Next to the sitting rooms, but accessible only through a corridor outside the sitting rooms, were the beneficiaries' privies or water closets. Originally, these had been traditional privies—simple seats with the human waste falling through brick flues into deep pits or wells below the Asylum building. Trouble was that brick is porous. By 1846 the brick flues had become saturated with human waste, which was by then leaching through and staining the exterior walls of the building behind the privies. Then there was the odor! It was pervasive, inside and outside the building. Commodore Morgan—the governor who proposed the fence topped with the lethal spikes—decided that something had to be done, and done immediately. He enlisted the imagination and design skill of a Philadelphia carpenter-mechanic, Oscar C. M. Caines, who devised an ingenious system of pipes and primitive flush toilets that largely solved the problems of eye and nose. It was the newest and best in institutional indoor plumbing circa 1846, and it is unfortunate that Caines' beautifully detailed drawings do not appear to have survived into the twenty-first century, so that one could have a better visual understanding of how this big improvement worked. Governor Morgan and the beneficiaries under his supervision were, for all the record shows, equally happy with the result.

Scattered among the building's water closets were five cast-iron bathtubs. These had been added to the Asylum's amenities for its residents only in the summer of 1849. Before then the beneficiaries had to get clean as best they could with the washbasins in their rooms—but even that was probably an improvement over the facilities for cleanliness they had experienced at sea. That nearly twenty years elapsed between the opening of the Naval Asylum and the installation of the bathtubs should not be interpreted as evidence that the U.S. naval establishment looked down on its former enlisted sailors and Marines or lacked concern for their cleanliness and hygiene. Rather, the new bathtubs of 1849 point to the emergence in American society of rising expectations of personal cleanliness—and the simultaneous development of technologies, such as city water services, that supported those rising expectations. The pre–Civil War United States was witnessing the beginnings of a long, slowly rising curve in its standards of personal cleanliness (again, supported by new technologies that made such higher standards possible) that reached its apogee in the middle of the twentieth century.[1] With five indoor bathtubs in addition to their new water-flush toilet system, the Asylum's residents were not far behind the cutting edge of then-contemporary hygienic and sanitary practice.

With his tour of the principal story completed, the guide had a choice. At the grand double staircase at the middle of the building, he could either head up or down. Assuming he chose to go up, he would have commented that the northeast wing of that story was identical with the wing below—beneficiary rooms, a sitting room, privies. But the southwest wing was different turf. This was assigned to the Philadelphia Naval Hospital, which reported to the Navy's Bureau of Medicine and Surgery, but existed in usually friendly cohabitation with the Asylum—the latter the home for the well elderly and the partially disabled. It was to the hospital that a beneficiary would be moved to be under the care of the medical staff if he became ill or seriously injured himself. By the time of William Thompson's arrival in 1863, the naval hospital's days of cohabitation with the Asylum were numbered. Wounded and sick Civil War sailors and Marines had strained the building's capacity to and beyond its limits. A separate hospital building was authorized in 1864, constructed on ground behind the Asylum building, and opened for use in 1868.

On a more ominous note, the guide almost certainly indicated that down a hall that extended to the north from the head of the stairs was a group of fourteen cells to which beneficiaries guilty of serious and repeated violations of the rules might be consigned to sober up and perhaps contemplate the desirability of behavioral change. He probably added that how frequently these cells were used as a punishment varied with the strictness or benevolence of the different governors and executive officers. A smaller group of cells in the hospital wing was apparently intended for the tempo- rary detention of insane patients before they were transferred else- where, as neither the Philadelphia Naval Hospital nor the Naval Asylum was equipped or intended to house the seriously mentally ill on a long-term basis.

From this point another double flight of stairs led to the build- ing's highest floor, the *attic story*. Originally, this floor had been just that—the building's attic, full of the usual stuff that accumu- lates in attics. But in 1846, Commodore Morgan, the most enthu- siastic builder among the Asylum's early governors, discovered that he was running out of rooms to house additional beneficiaries, and requested the Navy Department's permission to build more rooms in this space, admitting light by means of dormers or, as he called them, *skylights*. By Morgan's count, this development added eighty- one new rooms to the Asylum building, of which two—one at each end—were set aside as water closets, soon to be served by the new toilet system. Morgan was enthusiastic about the outcome, assert- ing that "this improvement has made the attic story much the most beautiful portion of the Asylum. The admission of the light from above exhibits the whole arrangement to a very great advan- tage and gives it a cheerful appearance which is not to be found in any other part of the house. It is much more comfortable, too, than any of the stories below—possesses a fine, free circulation of air in summer and during the winter will be close and warm." Others, including presumably the new beneficiary's hypothetical guide, did not share Morgan's enthusiasm, and the guide probably cautioned the newcomer to hope that he was *not* assigned a room up here. Not only were there all those stairs to climb, Commodore Morgan had been far too optimistic about the floor's habitability. Dormers or no, it was much too hot for comfortable living or sleeping in the sum- mer months; the rooms were often assigned to the Asylum's civil- ian employees or to the most recently arrived beneficiaries until they could move to a vacated room on one of the lower floors.

From the attic the tour guide would, one might imagine, have descended three floors to the *basement story*. He probably would have explained that this story, which was at ground level, was not the lowest space in the building. Below the basement story was the cellar, a utilitarian space with furnaces and receiving pits for the water-flush toilets. But that was terrain into which beneficiaries rarely ventured, leaving it to the tradesmen and laborers employed about the Asylum. Much of the layout of the basement story would already have been familiar from the floors above—the same two wings of beneficiary rooms. But, the guide might have explained, these rooms were not as desirable as those on the principal and second stories. This was because the soil on which the Asylum building stood was clay. That had been the area's attraction as a site for brickmaking, but clay retained water and the basement story and the cellar suffered from chronic drainage and dampness problems that—in spite of many well-planned efforts at solving the problem—resisted a completely successful resolution. Rooms in the basement story were desirable only for the beneficiaries who were so disabled that it was difficult for them to use the stairs to the upper stories, so a room here might have appealed to William Thompson. When the number of beneficiaries was small enough so that the basement rooms were not all in demand, many of these spaces were reassigned to other uses. The space under the chapel housed the laundry, where civilian women employees kept the beneficiaries' clothing and bedding clean and in good order. Just across the hall from the laundry was a space of keen interest to any old sailor or Marine—the kitchen and dining room where meals were prepared for, and served to, the beneficiaries. Here one might imagine the tour ending for a new beneficiary. A bell had just rung. Beneficiaries were assembling for supper. The new man spotted, and was eagerly welcomed by, an old shipmate or two or three. Off he went to join them for the evening meal.

THE BIGGER CITY
The United States Naval Asylum was a home, not a prison. Except for those residents who were confined to the grounds for serious infractions of the rules or because they were too incapacitated to leave, beneficiaries were allowed to depart the premises during the day so long as they were back through the gate by sunset. Once out on Gray's Ferry Road, they were free to explore the Asylum's immediate surroundings, more distant central Philadelphia, or the neighborhoods in between.

When the Naval Asylum admitted its first beneficiaries in the 1830s, the institution was surrounded by open country. That was not long to be, as the streets of future urban growth in the neighborhood were already platted, even if they were only surveyor's lines on a map. By 1840 the built-up portion of Philadelphia was still principally east of Broad Street. A scattering of developed blocks was advancing urbanization toward the Schuylkill, but the Naval Asylum remained a country retreat. Fifteen years later urban Philadelphia had arrived at the river and extended downstream in the Asylum's direction as far as South Street. The city was in sight, but it had not quite reached the Asylum. In the 1860s, when William Thompson took up residence there, urbanization had surrounded the Naval Asylum, which remained a green and peaceful refuge within its sturdy brick walls. Outside the walls it was another matter. The Asylum's immediate neighbors on the north, northwest, and southwest sides were manufacturing plants and other businesses, some ugly, some dangerous, some toxic: a glassworks, a coal yard, a stone yard, a lumber yard, and a chemical laboratory. The last-named business burned in a spectacular fire during the night of 29–30 January 1877. Only the absence of any wind and the prompt arrival of Philadelphia fire companies kept the blaze from spreading to—or at least endangering—the buildings of the Naval Asylum complex. Environmental quality in the neighborhood is best suggested by a Naval Asylum report of 1872 that described how the fumes emitted by a nearby carbolic acid factory had eaten away the mortar between the bricks of the southwest wall, leaving that section of the barrier in urgent need of immediate repair. The effect of those fumes on the throats and lungs of the beneficiaries was not reported, but can easily be imagined.

If a beneficiary turned southwest on Gray's Ferry Road after he exited the Asylum's northwest gate, he would have reached another federal facility, the Schuylkill Arsenal, in sight less than half a mile away. As far as the surviving record shows, there was little interaction between the two institutions, and the Arsenal had no known role in, or psychic impact on, the lives of the beneficiaries. But to look west, past the southwest corner of the Asylum's main building and across the Schuylkill, was to have a clear view of an institution that loomed large on any beneficiary's psychic horizon. There stood the five buildings of Philadelphia's alms house—Blockley—the likely next stop for misbehaving beneficiaries expelled from the Naval Asylum. Blockley, with its crowded wards, was a far cry from the Asylum's individual rooms, appealing meals served to the residents in the dining room, and smoking rooms where a man could relax over the day's newspaper. Even a quick glance over the river should have been enough to remind any beneficiary that it was in his best interest to be well behaved and more or less follow the Asylum's fairly lenient rules.

By William Thompson's time the area north and east of the Naval Asylum had developed into a mixed business, manufacturing, and residential neighborhood popularly known as Ramcat. The neighborhood's principal residents were recently arrived Irish immigrants, and the Asylum's many Irish-born beneficiaries must have found a warm welcome with their fellow expatriates as they walked the streets or dropped into one of Ramcat's many taverns for a spot of liquid refreshment. If a beneficiary wanted to explore farther afield than Ramcat, he walked a short distance northeast up Gray's Ferry Road until he came to South Street. If he turned east on South Street and walked about two miles, he reached a familiar maritime world at Front, Water, and Wharf streets along the Delaware River. But the typical beneficiary would probably not have gone that far, as his desires could be satisfied much closer to the Asylum at many places along the South Street corridor—that is, South Street itself and the blocks on either side of it. Before Philadelphia city and county consolidation in 1854 an imaginary line down the middle of South Street marked the southern boundary of the city. But South Street was marginal in more senses than that. It was an ethnically mixed neighborhood of native-born black and white Americans and of recent European immigrants, predominately Irish. Occupationally, the residents ranged from skilled artisans—watchmakers, tailors, typefounders, and silversmiths—down to day-laborers and others at the bottom of the social ladder. The South Street corridor offered ample opportunities for a beneficiary to satisfy his needs for alcohol at its taverns and sex in its brothels. Why go any farther?[2]

TWO

LIFE'S EBB TIDE

On 3 April 1827 a small crowd gathered at the site of the future United States Naval Asylum to witness the setting of the cornerstone of architect William Strickland's building. The stone in place, Commodore William Bainbridge, the president of the Board of Navy Commissioners, which held immediate responsibility for the Navy's shore establishments, rose to make a short dedicatory address. "A home will [here] be established," said Bainbridge, as he came to the heart of his remarks, "for the faithful tar who has been either worn out or maimed in fighting the battles of his country—a comfortable harbor will be secured where he may safely moor and ride out the ebb of life, free from the cares and storms by which he has been previously surrounded. He will here cheerfully and proudly live with his own messmates, with the companions of his former sports, toils and dangers, and where they will animate each other by recounting the pleasures which they enjoyed, the perils which they escaped, and the battles which they fought."[1]

Did Bainbridge write the address, with its flowery prose, himself? Or did he perhaps depend on the facile pen of the secretary to the Board of Navy Commissioners, Charles Washington Goldsborough? There will probably never be a definite answer to those questions, though the style sounds more like Goldsborough than Bainbridge. If Goldsborough was the real author, that was truly appropriate, for he had been a key player when the idea of a naval asylum was first broached some seventeen years earlier. That proposal had its roots in a report by the House of Representatives Committee on the Naval Establishment, "Navy Hospitals," dated

26 February 1810. This report incorporated a lengthy letter, signed by Secretary of the Navy Paul Hamilton, to Burwell Bassett, the committee's chair, advocating the establishment of hospitals specifically intended for members of the U.S. Navy. Goldsborough later asserted that he, Charles W. Goldsborough, then chief clerk in the Navy Department, was the real author of the letter to Congressman Bassett; he had written it "entirely by myself without even any previous instruction or direction from the Secretary of the Navy."[2]

Whoever its author may have been, the Hamilton-Goldsborough letter made no direct mention of a separate institution for elderly and disabled sailors and Marines, such as the United States Naval Asylum would later become, although the idea was implicit in the letter that such veterans would find permanent homes in the proposed naval hospitals. As the bill that resulted from the committee report worked its way through the legislative process it evolved into "An Act Establishing Navy Hospitals," approved 26 February 1811. This authorized the acquisition of an unspecified number of sites for naval hospitals and, if suitable buildings could not be purchased on the sites, the construction of appropriate structures, with the proviso that "one of the establishments [is] to provide a permanent asylum for disabled and decrepit Navy officers, seamen, and Marines." These seventeen words are the legislative basis on which the United States Naval Asylum was eventually created. How the Navy Department's proposal came to be modified to include the specific provision for a single "permanent asylum" does not appear in the record of Congress' action on the proposal. Because the young U.S. Navy looked to Britain's Royal Navy as its role model in all matters, one can assume that the aim here was to emulate Britain's Greenwich Hospital for naval pensioners—though how much anyone in the U.S. naval establishment knew about the actual operation of Greenwich is an open question.

Since 1 September 1799 the United States had deducted twenty cents per month from the pay of each naval officer, seaman, or Marine. This was added to a similar deduction, authorized 16 July 1798, from members of the merchant marine to create a fund, under the direction of the Secretary of the Treasury, to care for sick and disabled seamen and for the erection of marine hospitals in the various customs districts of the United States. The one combined fund was expected to provide medical treatment and accommodation for both merchant seamen and naval personnel. By an act of 26 February 1811, the naval contributions were segregated from those of merchant mariners to create a separate fund, which came to be called the Navy Hospital Fund, administered by three commissioners—the Secretaries of the Navy, the Treasury, and War. It was from these deducted funds alone that the sites, the naval hospitals and the "permanent asylum" authorized by the act of 26 February 1811 were to be purchased and erected. No congressional appropriation was required or anticipated; that probably accounts for the bill's easy and uncontroversial passage through Congress.

The commissioners of the Navy Hospital Fund (not to be confused with the Board of Navy Commissioners, a body of senior officers created in 1815 and subordinate to the Secretary of the Navy) soon got down to their task. Records of their proceedings are scanty. Most of the actual work of planning naturally fell to Secretary of the Navy Paul Hamilton and his office staff, with the three commissioners meeting only to review progress and make major policy decisions. The first project selected was to be a combined naval hospital and asylum in Washington. That choice should cause no surprise. In pre–War of 1812 days the capital city was seen as the vital center of United States naval activity. In addition to the Navy Department itself (the "Navy Office"), the city was also the site of the nation's most elaborate navy yard and of the Marine Corps headquarters at the Marine Barracks. To these the proposed hospital and asylum would add a fourth major naval facility.

In 1811 the Navy Department's architect of choice, Benjamin Henry Latrobe, submitted to the commissioners his ideas for the hospital and asylum, as did Navy surgeons Edward Cutbush and Samuel R. Marshall. The details of none of these three plans are known, but in 1812 Latrobe produced a new set of plans that may have incorporated some of Cutbush's and Marshall's ideas as well. By that time the commissioners had confronted the hard fiscal reality that they had less than sixty thousand dollars to invest in the project. Consequently, Latrobe's new plan proposed a building that could be constructed in phases. The initial phase accommodated only one hundred patients, but the plan called for monumental future expansion, approaching the Greenwich ideal, as funds became available. Latrobe was maturing his final drawings in May and June of 1812, but they were overtaken by the War of 1812. The naval establishment's attention and energies were necessarily absorbed by the demands of combat at sea and on the northern lakes. Latrobe's plans were laid aside, while the Navy's medical corps fought its War of 1812, not with new purpose-built hospitals, but on ship-board or in make-do shoreside facilities.[3]

Interest in naval hospitals revived slowly with the return of peace in 1815, but the proposed facilities had to compete for atten-tion with commerce protection, new and bigger ships, and enlarged navy yards that engrossed the attention of the confident, expan-sionist, and muscle-flexing naval establishment that emerged from the War of 1812. Then there was the money problem. Where was the Navy Hospital Fund? To tell a complicated administrative, accounting, and legislative story in its simplest terms, it appeared that the fifty thousand dollars that Congress had authorized by the act of 26 February 1811 to be moved from the combined Marine Hospital Fund to the new Navy Hospital Fund had never actually been transferred. Then, during the War of 1812, the twenty cents per man per month deducted from pay had been used by the finan-cially strapped United States to pay for wartime naval expenses rather than being segregated in a dedicated and protected fund. Even with the return of peace in 1815 this misappropriation was allowed to continue until Secretary of the Navy Samuel L. South-ard ordered that, effective 1 January 1824, funds from the twenty cents per person per month deduction were to be segregated in a separate fund. At that point Southard calculated that the govern-ment owed the fund $195,352 that had been used for other pur-poses. The House Committee on Naval Affairs had its own (of course lower) number of $167,759. In 1828 Congress appropriated $46,217, the balance apparently due on the never-transferred $50,000, and another $125,000 in 1829, making a total reimburse-ment of $171,217. Congress declined to repay the interest that would have accrued had the contributions to the Navy Hospital Fund been properly invested. And, by inaction on a proposal to appropriate additional funds for naval hospitals, Congress also reaf-firmed the principle that these should be built at the sole expense of the Navy's people—a point that was not lost on the sailors and Marines who used the facilities and who did not hesitate to assert their rights to the benefits for which they had paid.[4]

Meanwhile, the commissioners of the Navy Hospital Fund had managed to collect sufficient money to purchase in 1826 the Gray's

Ferry Road site for a combined naval hospital and naval asylum. By this time Benjamin Henry Latrobe had fallen from favor as a federal architect and died; his 1811–12 plans were collecting dust in the Navy Office's archives. For the new building, the commissioners turned to prominent Philadelphia architect William Strickland, who had the advantage of being on site to oversee construction. Although both the Naval Asylum and the contemporaneous naval hospital at Norfolk (designed by John Haviland) conformed to best practice in hospital design, the structures were monumental as well as functional—a reflection of the exuberant self-confidence of the 1820s United States and of the Navy's sense of its now-well-established role in the nation's life and its ambitions for the future. Funding shortfalls delayed until late 1833 completion of the Philadelphia project to a point at which the building, still lacking some interior finishing, could be occupied. In the interim, the Philadelphia Naval Hospital and one or two naval pensioners occupied a spacious country house, formerly a residence of the Pemberton family, that had been acquired with the land purchase.

It had required nearly twenty-three years, but the "permanent asylum" decreed in the law of 26 February 1811 was finally in place. Its institutional life was about to begin.

INTENTIONS

William Bainbridge's cornerstone-setting address may have proposed a romantically tinged picture of life at the new United States Naval Asylum, but behind those words the naval establishment of the country held a realistic and consistent vision of the institution's mission.

An enlisted sailor's pay was comparatively small. There was little opportunity for him to save a nest egg in anticipation of illness and old age. The life a sailor led—voyages to sickly climates, storms, battles—was one fraught with the possibility of illness and injury, and it aged him prematurely. For many, long absences militated against the formation of a family life to which the Marine or sailor could retreat in his final years. All such reasons argued, in the words Secretary of the Navy Southard wrote in 1827, "that the disabled and aged seaman, who has worthily served the country until his strength is exhausted, should have an asylum where a comfortable subsistence may be found for his last days." In 1829

Southard's successor, John Branch, expanded the roster of proposed Asylum beneficiaries beyond the aged and the disabled to "such as, though not disabled, may have merited, by their bravery or long and faithful services, the gratitude of their country." Two decades later, in his annual report for 1858, that mission was eloquently reaffirmed by Commodore Joseph Smith, chief of the Bureau of Yards and Docks, who wrote: "No class of the community is more destitute, and at the same time so deserving, as the old worn-out sailor. His young and vigorous years are devoted to the interests and advancement of the Navy, and the spirit of patriotism as well as humanity has established [the Naval Asylum] as a *home* for his decrepitude and old age. It is fitting that a beneficent government should thus reward faithful services with the necessary comforts of life and provide for the wants of the last hours of these veteran servants of our country."

It is important to quote these words at some length. Yes, they do reveal that the deference-stewardship relationship—the idea that God or Nature had placed some men higher on the social scale, who were thereby owed respect and obedience, but also that those higher on the social scale had a responsibility for individuals on the lower strata of the social order—was still deeply ingrained in the world view of the Navy, its civilian leaders, and its officers. But, just as significantly, the words and the generous spirit in which they were carried into effect argue strongly against the popular view that a deep chasm of indifference, if not contempt, separated the senior naval establishment from the men of the Navy's lower deck. Concern for the welfare of the long-service sailor and Marine was real and sincere, as will be amply documented by the story of the Naval Asylum as it rolls out through the nineteenth century.

There was another reason behind the Navy's concern for its long-service men that is never mentioned in the records but that surely must have been present in the minds of those who established the Naval Asylum. At the time the Asylum came into being the nation was shifting from a social philosophy that held local communities responsible for the care of society's less fortunate or anti-social members: the poor, the orphaned, the chronically ill, the insane, the aged, and the criminal. Driven in part by the growing tide of immigrants and by geographical mobility within the nation, the old system of locally based welfare was disintegrating and being replaced by city, county, state and even national institutions, with

the Naval Asylum one of the earliest examples of the latter category. The Navy's leadership was well aware that, although it said
officially that it was building a fighting force of American-born
seafarers, the reality was that a high proportion of the Navy's lower
deck were men who had begun life in northern Europe—England,
Ireland, France, Germany, Denmark, Norway, or Sweden. Once
arrived in the United States, these men would typically spend the
remainder of their lives in the country, though how many of them
went through the formal process of acquiring legal citizenship no
one knows. When asked by the recruiting officer "Where were
you born?" the savvy sailor from Königsberg in East Prussia knew
to say "Lancaster, Pennsylvania, Sir." The recruiter, eager to fill his
quota, was happy to write the would-be recruit with the heavy
German accent down as a native of that German-speaking portion of the nation. And so it went, lie after convenient lie, with the
Navy winking its agreement. In short, for sailors born abroad—
many of them the Navy's most capable and experienced petty officers—there was no local United States community to which they
could return to spend their old age. Only a new national institution, the Naval Asylum, could meet that need.

Foreign birth aside, the experience of beneficiary Robert Chase
captures well this transition from community to broader-based care
of the disabled. Chase, a man with brown hair, hazel eyes, and a
dark complexion, five feet, seven inches tall, was born in Camden,
Maine, in September 1813. His father, also named Robert, was a
master blacksmith who ranked high enough on Camden's social
scale to be elected one of the town's selectmen for a total of nineteen years and to represent the town in the state legislature in
1837 and 1838.[5] Robert, the son, the third of eight Chase children, first enlisted in the naval service in 1841, at which time he
would have been around twenty-seven or twenty-eight years old,
which suggests that he had pursued some other career or sailed in
the merchant service before turning to the Navy.

Although the names of the ships in which Robert Chase
served and the dates of that service are known, he seems to have
been a routinely competent sailor with nothing remarkable about
his career—that is, until the early years of the Civil War. Chase
was serving in the frigate *Cumberland* at Hampton Roads when
she was attacked and sunk by the Confederate ironclad *Virginia*
on 8 March 1862. Chase spent about an hour in the water before

he was rescued and later asserted that the exposure and his struggles to stay alive triggered a decline in his health. That, however, was his retrospective assertion. He was well enough to be transferred to the frigate *St. Lawrence* and thence to the screw steamer *South Carolina*. In the latter ship, he served as captain of the hold until the night of 3–4 February 1864, when he suffered a stroke (the same medical condition that killed his father); it left one side of his body completely paralyzed.[6] The paralysis was assessed as permanent; Robert Chase was discharged from the Navy and sent home to Camden.

Because the stroke was not diagnosed to be a result of Chase's naval service, he was not eligible for a pension. His father and mother were both dead, and he asserted that he had "no relatives or friends able to support me." This was a carefully worded statement that was close to, but not quite, the truth. The telltale word is *able*. After his return to Camden, Robert Chase moved in with one of his sisters, but her financial situation made his care and support a burden she could ill afford. In an earlier time, Chase would probably have been on the town's relief rolls for the balance of his life. But this was another day, and there was a national institution to which the town fathers could shift the impending expense—the United States Naval Asylum. In February 1865 Robert Chase applied to Secretary of the Navy Gideon Welles for admission to the Asylum. Chase's family still commanded enough respect in Camden that he was able to enlist the assistance of Ephraim K. Smart, former congressman and former collector of customs at Belfast, Maine, who in turn rallied the support of Maine's Senator Nathan A. Farwell for the application. This application initially encountered a rough passage through the Asylum's admission process, because Chase's stroke had left his mind cloudy; he had difficulty in recalling accurately the ships in which he had served, the names of his commanding officers, and the dates of his enlistments and discharges—documentation essential to verifying his right to admission. After some back-and-forth correspondence between the Navy Department and Chase's supporters, the required data were eventually assembled, and Chase was admitted to the Naval Asylum on 9 May 1865—no doubt to the relief of Camden's town treasurer. Because of his condition, Robert Chase was sent straight to the Asylum's hospital. There he remained, more or less bedridden, until his death from congestion of the lungs on 19 September 1874.

GETTING IN

As Robert Chase and his supporters discovered, being admitted to the United States Naval Asylum required the knowledgeable navigation of administrative waters strewn with a number of protruding regulations and some submerged variants waiting to snag the unwary. What was more, the Navy moved the navigational aids—the published rules for admission—three times in the years between 1831 and 1865.

The earliest set of regulations was issued by Secretary of the Navy Levi Woodbury in May 1834, based in part on suggestions from the Board of Navy Commissioners. It was also the most elaborate, promulgating four criteria for admission: (1) any former sailor or Marine who held a Navy pension, but was so incapacitated by injury or age that he could not "contribute materially" to his support through his own labor, might surrender his pension in return for admission to the Asylum; (2) an individual who had served in the Navy or Marine Corps for not less than twenty years and who was incapable of further service because of age or "infirmities which are not the effect of vice, intemperance, or other misconduct" was entitled to admission; (3) a man who had served for less than twenty years but was now physically incapable of further service, "and who shall have claims upon the country in consequence of distinguished gallantry in action or other highly meritorious conduct in the public naval service" could be admitted, presumably at the discretion of the Secretary of the Navy; (4) *but*, desertion from the Navy or conviction by a court martial of "any mutinous or disgraceful conduct" barred a man from admission.

Several matters in these regulations are worthy of note. With wording such as "contribute materially" much room was left for judgment, discretion—and conflicting interpretations. The provision that permitted exchanging a pension for a residence at the Asylum was, as will shortly appear, the fertile seedbed of ongoing problems. As for the "infirmities which are . . . the effect of vice, intemperance, or other misconduct"—presumably alcoholism and sexually transmitted diseases—these were never, so far as the record shows, actually invoked to bar a sailor or a Marine's admission. Finally, the provision that excluded from the Asylum a man convicted by a court martial of "any mutinous or disgraceful conduct" also proved to be a dead letter. Unless someone along the application's paper trail happened to remember that Seaman So-and-So had been convicted of such an offense (and that never happened) no one at the Navy Office had the time or interest to dredge through the unindexed files of old courts-martial to see if Seaman So-and-So might be there. Absent such a check, several individuals with serious courts-martial in their pasts were admitted—some to become model beneficiaries and others behavior problems.

The next iteration of the rules, issued by Secretary Abel P. Upshur in March 1843, reduced the requirements for admission to twenty-nine words: "No pensioner [as beneficiaries were then called] shall be admitted unless he shall produce satisfactory proof of general good character and that he has served *faithfully* at least fifteen years in the naval service."With the words *general good character* and *faithfully* there was still ample room for administrative or applicant interpretation. As to why the required length of service was reduced from twenty to fifteen years, no evidence survives; in any event it was a change that did not long endure.

When the management of the Naval Asylum was transferred to the Navy's Bureau of Yards and Docks in 1849—of that transfer more shortly—Commodore Joseph Smith, the bureau chief, promptly issued his own set of "Regulations for the U.S. Naval Asylum," with only one requirement for admission stated—twenty years' service in the Navy, although a shorter period of service could qualify "under extraordinary circumstances" at the discretion of the Secretary of the Navy. Two years' experience administering the Naval Asylum convinced Commodore Smith that he needed admission requirements with more teeth. Accordingly, a new set, issued 1 July 1851, specified: (1) applicants for admission had to prove twenty years of service in the Navy and/or Marine Corps; (2) the application was to state age, place of birth, physical condition, names of the ships in which the applicant had served, the ships' captains, and the dates of service; (3) an applicant must also supply a certificate from a naval surgeon stating that the sailor or Marine "is not able to support himself by manual labor"; (4) exchange of a pension for a place at the Asylum required a naval surgeon's certificate to the same effect; and (5) potential applicants were warned that these regulations would not be waived or modified "except under extraordinary circumstances" or by the written permission of the Secretary of the Navy. The 1851 requirements remained in effect for all beneficiaries admitted to the Asylum through 31 December 1865 who are the subject of *Ungentle Goodnights*.

There are rules, and then there are the implementation and the interpretation of the rules—where requirement meets reality. The method of verifying twenty years of naval service was to send the sailor's statement of service to the office of the Fourth Auditor of the Treasury—the official who approved all Navy accounts for settlement—where the clerks would check the applicant's statement of service against the muster and pay rolls on file. (Marine Corps service was verified by the office of the adjutant of the Corps.) In a perfect world, a sailor would have kept all his discharges and these could quickly be verified against the rolls. That happened rarely. Some men had lost their discharges through carelessness, pawning, theft, shipwreck, or fire. Others, also lacking discharges, could not remember the dates of their service on particular ships, the names of the captains, or even the correct order of their service. All this demanded extra work at the Fourth Auditor's office, although eventually—with the clerks' assiduous searching, the sailor's jogged memory, and an occasional assist by a former officer—a more or less complete record of twenty or more years of naval service could be worked up. Not that the Fourth Auditor's records were infallible either: some ships' rolls could not be found, only to resurface years later. This situation required a judgment call by the examining clerks, based on the perceived accuracy of the sailor's memory of his seagoing career: if the missing rolls *could* be found, the sailor *should* be there, too.

The biggest administrative headaches, from Commodore Smith's perspective, were the men holding naval pensions who wanted to exchange or *commute* these pensions for admission permits to the Naval Asylum. In the pre–Civil War years pensions were awarded only for injuries or disabilities incurred during active naval service—not for length of service. There were more men drawing pensions than there were places for them at the Asylum. Commodore Smith's ongoing anxiety was that, should commutation of pensions be routinely permitted, the Asylum would run out of space for those in dire need of admission. Add to that, pensions were granted based on the degree of disability. This meant, as Commodore Smith saw the matter, that a pensioner who was only partially disabled—say, by the loss of two or three fingers on his left hand—would have equal right to admission with an elderly man who might have lost an arm or a leg and was fully disabled from work. Smith tried to convince Secretary of the Navy William Ballard Preston that a man who had been awarded a pension had received all to which he was entitled from the government and should be denied admission to the Asylum. Preston referred the matter to A. O. Dayton, the Fourth Auditor of the Treasury, for a legal opinion. Dayton ruled against Smith's interpretation of the law, arguing that the act of 26 February 1811 clearly anticipated situations in which pensioners would be admitted to the Asylum and thereby forfeit their pensions.[7] The best Smith could do was to be rigorous in enforcing the rule that a naval surgeon *must* certify that a pensioner was incapacitated from functioning in the outside world and unable to subsist on his pension before he could commute it. The result: an ongoing struggle between Smith's determination to be firm and pensioners' always-sad stories of their need for Asylum admission.

Smith's other headache was the twenty-years-of-service rule. Here again, it was fear of relaxing this rule and filling the available space at the Asylum that drove his insistence on nothing less than twenty years, no matter how convincing was the case presented by the applicant and his backers. If rejected under this rule, however, the applicant had another recourse: he could appeal to the Secretary of the Navy, who had the power to make exceptions. This usually worked. If an applicant almost, but not quite, met the twenty-year rule—say he could only prove eighteen years of service but asserted more that he blamed on lost records—the secretary would typically, but not always, grant the exception.

A handful of other, more rarely occurring, situations could also scuttle an application. Correct wording in supporting documents was essential: if the examining naval surgeon merely certified that the applicant was not eligible for reenlistment in the Navy because of a disability, but failed to state that he could not earn his living shoreside by manual labor, the application would be denied. Likewise, if the surgeon reported that a sailor had, say, incurred a hernia, but could still perform duty on shipboard with the aid of a truss, that was grounds for refusing Asylum admission. Marine applicants who wanted to count one or more Army enlistments toward their twenty years of service were told: No, it has to be *naval* service. Finally, applicants who said they had served under two or more names—an assertion that raised the suspicion that the name changes concealed desertions or that an identity theft might be under way—were in real trouble. The only reprieve was for the sailor to find an officer who could certify that he personally knew that the sailor had served under both names and was not hiding a desertion. Even then the sailor might expect a scolding from Joseph Smith: "It is dangerous and jeopardizes a man's interest and reputation to change his name."

If the would-be beneficiary navigated these hazards successfully he soon received the desired document:

PERMIT
FOR ADMISSION INTO THE NAVAL ASYLUM.

————◇————

NAVY DEPARTMENT,
Bureau of Yards and Docks,
10th May, *1865*

John Smith, *late* Seaman *in the Navy, is entitled to the privileges of the Naval Asylum at* Philadelphia. *The Governor is accordingly authorized to admit and allow him the prescribed supplies during his continuance therein, on condition that the said* John Smith *conform in all respects to the rules and regulations which now are or hereafter may be established for the government of the Institution.*

By order of the Secretary of the Navy:

Jos: Smith
CHIEF OF BUREAU

THREE

A ROCKY START

It did not have to turn out as well as it did. Looking back from the perspective of a century and a half of the United States Naval Home's well-managed and respected existence, it would be easy to assume that this successful outcome had been inevitable from its beginnings as the United States Naval Asylum in the 1830s. That assumption would be wrong. The institution only haltingly and with some public embarrassment found its way through the first decade of its existence.

Although William Bainbridge's 1827 address at the cornerstone-setting ceremony for the William Strickland building saw the new facility primarily as one intended for the disabled and the elderly, the basic legislation on which the Asylum was founded, the act of 26 February 1811, only provided that one of the authorized naval hospitals was to be "a permanent asylum for disabled and decrepit Navy officers, seamen, and Marines." Elaboration of this requirement was left to the administrative discretion of the naval establishment. Because the Philadelphia building would accommodate both the asylum and the hospital functions, there was ample room for ambiguity and friction in this dual mission.

Not until late in 1833 was the new building sufficiently completed to permit occupancy, even if significant interior work remained to done. Meanwhile, the Philadelphia Naval Hospital continued to operate in the old Pemberton country home on the Asylum site. The hospital came under the jurisdiction of the commandant of the Philadelphia Navy Yard, but the Navy Yard was some two miles away from the hospital; members of the medical staff, eager to enhance their professional identity within the Navy, must have been glad to have the commandant far enough away to ensure a high degree of day-to-day autonomy.

It was to the Pemberton house facility that the Naval Asylum's first beneficiary was dispatched on 4 December 1831. He was a pensioner named Daniel Kleiss. On 6 May 1829, Kleiss, then an ordinary seaman in the frigate *Guerriere*, fell from aloft, fracturing his cranium and injuring his side and shoulder so seriously that his left arm was paralyzed. Kleiss' admission was atypical, for no other beneficiary was admitted until 2 August 1834. He was admitted to the hospital, on his own application, in the hope that he might recover the use of his paralyzed arm through treatment there. Kleiss messed with the other patients at the hospital and was allowed to continue to draw his pension so that he could purchase his own clothing. Dr. Thomas Harris, the hospital's senior surgeon, seems to have been happy enough to have Kleiss—a young man of about twenty-seven when he was admitted—on board, employing him as a part-time gatekeeper and, in 1832, as a nurse during the cholera outbreak of that year in Philadelphia. In September 1833 Kleiss' pension was terminated and he was transferred to the Asylum's rolls as a beneficiary, receiving one ration per day and his clothing, as did all future beneficiaries.[1]

Before then, in the summer of 1833, with the new asylum building approaching a condition in which it could be occupied, Secretary of the Navy Levi Woodbury began to give serious attention to the facility's organization by asking the Board of Navy Commissioners for their advice—advice that he substantially incorporated in his May 1834 "Regulations for the Government of the Naval Asylum." Before he issued the regulations, Secretary Woodbury visited the Asylum site early in 1834 and consulted with Commodore James Barron, the commandant of the Philadelphia Navy Yard, to whom the Asylum would report. Despite all this consultation, the regulations were pregnant with the seeds of future trouble: one commissioned officer and two warrant officers were to "reside" at the Naval Asylum, with preference for those appointments being given to individuals who had been wounded in action or incapacitated by service-incurred injuries. While it might be inferred that these officers were to have an administrative role at the Asylum, that was not specified—only that they were to "reside" there. In addition, the regulations required that, because the Asylum and the naval hospital occupied the same building, the hospital's surgeon was to attend both the hospital's patients and the Asylum's beneficiaries. Finally, the commandant of the Philadelphia Navy Yard was to have "general superintendence" of the establishment, and "the asylum and hospital buildings and their inmates shall be under the general government of the officers placed over them, and all be subject to the laws and rules for the government of the naval service at the different navy yards and such other rules as may be, from time to time, prepared and published for the asylum and hospital."

Now it was time to pick the wounded or injury-incapacitated officers who were to "reside" at the Naval Asylum. Commodore Barron suggested that, for the present, one lieutenant in addition to a warrant officer would be sufficient "for all the purposes of yielding to the establishment the necessary protection"—note again: no stated expectation of command authority vested in the two officers. (Barron later asserted orally that Lieutenant James B. Cooper—of whom more shortly—had the entire charge of the physical facilities at the Gray's Ferry Road site and was accountable for the behavior of the beneficiaries, but whether he ever put that charge in writing is not now known.) Woodbury's choice for the warrant officer was Sailing Master John Carlton, on the grounds that he was old, infirm, unfit for active duty, and had served in the War of 1812.

For the Asylum's lieutenant, Secretary Woodbury selected Lieutenant Cooper, a veteran officer from New Jersey, now seventy-two or seventy-three years old, whose service to his country ran back to the latter days of the American Revolution. Cooper came from a pacifist Quaker family, but when he was seventeen or eighteen he enlisted, in February 1779, as a private under Major (later Lieutenant Colonel) Henry Lee, in what eventually became a composite force of three troops of cavalry and three companies of infantry commonly known as "Lee's Legion." Quaker though he may have been, Cooper proved to be a skilled and natural soldier, with ample and creditable combat experience in the battles of Paulus Hook and Stony Point (1779), Springfield (1780), Guilford Courthouse and Eutaw Springs (1781), as well as a number of other actions in which Lee's Legion fought with reputation and success. He was also a lucky young cavalryman; later in life, Cooper reported that he had had four horses shot from under him in combat, but was never himself wounded. At the end of the war, Cooper turned his attention from land to the sea, entering the merchant service, in which he eventually rose to command vessels and achieved a degree of financial success. Upon the declaration of war in June 1812, he quickly offered his services to Secretary of the Navy Paul Hamilton, was warranted as a sailing master on 9 July of that year, and was assigned to gunboat service in coastal waters.

Following this, his second war, Cooper chose to remain in military service. He was granted an appointment as an acting lieutenant in May 1815 and ordered to the Philadelphia Navy Yard in August 1816. There he remained on duty until he was formally commissioned as a lieutenant in April 1822. About this time, Cooper, now in his early sixties, began to experience declining health, and was allowed to retire to his home in Haddonfield, New Jersey. Although on leave from active duty, he was permitted to continue to draw his full pay as a lieutenant. The concession was certainly welcome, as he had a large family, which his ability to support was a source of ongoing anxiety. Except for a brief tour of active duty at the New York Navy Yard, this situation continued until the fall of 1833 when Secretary of the Navy Woodbury discovered that, contrary to law, Cooper had been drawing his full pay for the eleven years during which he had not been on active duty. That, Woodbury decided, could not be allowed to continue. "Feeling anxious to befriend you and requite in some degree your Revolutionary services," Woodbury offered Cooper the appointment as the invalid lieutenant attached to the Naval Asylum; this would restore him to full-pay status. Cooper jumped at the chance, and duly received an appointment as an "invalid officer" at the Naval Asylum under the date of 23 May 1834.

With the building fit for occupancy, the institution's basic regulations in place, and the veteran officers appointed, the Navy Department began dispatching additional beneficiaries to the Naval Asylum: five in 1834, seven in 1835, four in 1836, eleven in 1837. All the elements, except one, were now in place for trouble.

COOPER VS. THE BENEFICIARIES

If Secretary Woodbury thought that having an elderly veteran officer supervise a group of disabled and aging sailors and Marines would create a harmonious bond of shared age and disability between them, he was sadly mistaken—at least in the choice of Lieutenant Cooper.

When Cooper assumed his duties, in early June 1834, there was still only one beneficiary assigned to the Asylum. It was the previously mentioned Daniel Kleiss, a native of Germany, about thirty years old, and still partially disabled by the persistent paralysis of his left arm, which the surgeons had not been able to alleviate. He was not to be around for long. On 27 June Kleiss was arrested by the civil authorities on a charge of theft. The report detailing what Kleiss was accused of stealing and other pertinent facts seems to have disappeared from—or is deeply buried in— the archives. As it turned out, the charges against Kleiss were dropped in early October on the grounds of lack of evidence on which to convict him, but this was not until he had been held in jail for a bit longer than three months. By 17 October 1834 he was back at the Asylum.

A few days earlier Cooper had received the Asylum's second beneficiary, one William Williams. Although Williams officially asserted that he was a native of New York City, he had in fact been born in England around 1806. He came to the United States in 1817; whether he was alone or with his parents is not part of the record. Williams apprenticed as a chair painter; whether this was in England or more probably in the United States is also unknown. In September 1827, at the age of twenty-one, Williams gave up chair painting for an altogether different line of work—he enlisted in the Marine Corps. As he faced the recruiter, Williams stood five feet, eight inches tall, a handsome young man with black hair, black eyes, and a ruddy complexion. Alas for the Corps, this promising recruit's active-duty career lasted less than a year. On 9 July 1828, while he was serving in the 74-gun *Delaware* in the Mediterranean, Williams fell down the main hatch, breaking his left leg so badly that it required amputation. This serious disability entitled Williams to a pension of six dollars per month, which he supplemented through civilian employment at the Norfolk (Gosport) Navy Yard. By 1834 he had decided that surrendering his pension for an appointment as a beneficiary at the Naval Asylum was a better deal, and he was officially admitted on 2 August of that year.

Williams was followed by a trickle of other newly appointed beneficiaries. They did not receive a warm, caring welcome from Lieutenant Cooper. By mid-June 1835 the lieutenant was complaining that "all the inmates placed here on the Asylum basis are habitual and incorrigible drunkards, taking every advantage of my absence to leave the premises to get drunk and bring in rum so that, on my return, I frequently find in the Asylum a scene of riot, drunkenness, and confusion." Because Sailing Master Carlton was so ill that he could do little or nothing to help Cooper maintain order, the lieutenant-superintendent asked that an additional officer or petty officer be ordered to the Asylum to aid him. Then, almost as an afterthought, he added to his appeal a request that Daniel Kleiss be dismissed from the Asylum as an incorrigible thief and drunkard. Secretary of the Navy Mahlon Dickerson was happy enough to send Kleiss on his way, but he rejected Cooper's request for additional help. At that time there were only five beneficiaries, and the number would drop to four once Kleiss was expelled. Although he did not say so explicitly, Dickerson must have judged that an officer of Cooper's experience should be able to manage four or five unruly men by himself.

So matters rocked along until the final crisis of March 1838. In the interim, a blind carpenter's mate named Cornelius Butler—the third beneficiary admitted to the Asylum—had complained orally to Commodore Barron about Lieutenant Cooper. Butler's litany of complaints against Cooper does not survive, but Barron came to the Asylum to check out Butler's story, which he labeled "a vile fabrication." What real basis there may have been for Butler's complaints cannot be known, but Barron was apparently determined to sustain and reinforce Cooper's authority over the beneficiaries, whatever the truth might be. There was bad blood between Lieutenant Cooper and the beneficiaries, but only Cooper's side of the story remains on the record. No question about it—there was a lack of respect for Cooper on the part of the beneficiaries. He was elderly; he was irritable; and he was only a lieutenant—a rank the beneficiaries apparently viewed less obediently than that of captain or commodore.

For his part, Cooper argued that sailors and Marines, while on active duty, had always been subject to strict discipline. Their "dissolute habits," which they had acquired during their seagoing careers, demanded strict surveillance when they became Asylum beneficiaries. Cooper, one man alone, could not provide that without subordinates to assist him. The only disciplinary measure available to him, asserted Cooper, was to forward a recommendation for dismissal from the Asylum to the Secretary of the Navy through the commandant of the Philadelphia Navy Yard. That was not entirely true, since on at least one occasion Cooper did imply that he used the building's cells to confine the most violent of the drinkers. From a legal perspective Asylum beneficiaries were no longer serving Marines or sailors and consequently were not subject to standard naval discipline. Even if this had not been so, any Secretary of the Navy would surely have been appalled at the idea of an elderly or disabled veteran being flogged, however much Lieutenant Cooper may have secretly fantasized about applying the wholesome and effective discipline of the lash to his most serious troublemakers.

As of the first of March 1838 twenty-eight beneficiaries had been admitted to the Naval Asylum; two of them had died; and fourteen were still present. The other twelve men had either been dismissed—including Daniel Kleiss, banished for the third time in November 1837 for drunkenness—or had simply walked away. Two fairly recent arrivals of September and October 1837—Thomas Barber and Charles W. White—were the primary instigators of the disciplinary crisis of March 1838. They were abetted to some unknown extent by the previously mentioned Beneficiary Number 2, William Williams, the one-legged Marine. Barber, like Williams, had only one leg. A former ordinary seaman, his left leg was caught in the machinery of the U.S. steamer *Lieutenant Lynch* at Pensacola on 6 July 1836, crushing his ankle, breaking his tibia, and damaging his knee as well. The steamer's commander, Lieutenant George M. Bache, who also held a degree as Doctor of Medicine from the University of Pennsylvania, decided that an immediate amputation was required and performed the operation himself. Barber subsequently obtained a job at the Washington Navy Yard, but apparently commuted his five-dollar-a-month pension for an appointment as a beneficiary in September 1837. White, the third perpetrator, had been an ordinary seaman, too. A recent recruit to the Navy, he had his right thigh badly fractured in a railroad accident on 29 June 1836, when a Providence-to-Boston train collided with a Boston-to-Dedham train in Roxbury, Massachusetts. Most of the damage was sustained by the two forward cars of the Providence train in which White, with 124 other naval recruits and their escorting officers, were traveling from New York to the Boston (Charlestown) Navy Yard. According to one newspaper report the two cars "were literally smashed to pieces; not one stick is left standing." Amazingly, only a small number of the recruits were injured, four of them—including White—so seriously as to be precluded from further naval service and, consequently, entitled to pensions.[2] White quickly exchanged his pension for admission to the Naval Asylum.

The root cause of the events about to unfold would seem to lie in the ages of the three troublemakers, who were—like Daniel Kleiss—relatively young men in their late twenties or early thirties. Williams was about thirty-two; the ages of Barber and White are not on record, but because they were both pensioned as ordinary seamen, it is safe to assume that they were younger men early in their naval careers. Although they may have been incapacitated for manual labor or for further naval service, they were still energetic adults, each provided by the government with his own room, clothing, three hearty meals—and no meaningful activity to occupy idle days. Alcohol filled the vacuum and inflamed disagreements with the septuagenarian Lieutenant Cooper, who apparently made no effort to conceal his dislike of them.

The exact chronology of what happened is not totally clear. Apparently Barber, White, and Williams were leading some likeminded followers among the beneficiaries in frequent debauches, which Cooper felt powerless to control. Commodore Charles Stewart, who had replaced James Barron as commandant of the Philadelphia Navy Yard, complained to Secretary of the Navy Mahlon Dickerson that the Asylum was "becoming a nuisance to its vicinity and [to] the passersby on the public highways. The outrageous conduct of those men, their violence and noise, induced many of those passing on the road to stop and, some of them, to scale the walls lest extreme violence might be committed." Matters reached their climax on 24 March, when Barber, White, and Williams beat Edward Barker, an elderly beneficiary with more than forty-four years of combined service in the Army, Navy, and Marine Corps. Barker had procured off-premises liquor for the other three, whereupon the fight erupted, probably caused by a dispute over payment—1838's version of the drug deal gone bad. Cooper and some invalid officers who were being treated at the hospital were able to rescue Barker, but, finding it impossible to get the three drunken men under control, they retreated to Cooper's quarters and locked themselves in. Barber and White, drunk as skunks, tried to break down the door, shouting threats to maim or murder Cooper if they could get their hands on him. This may have been more theatre-of-the-alcohol than real danger, but it must have alarmed the members of Cooper's family who shared his quarters.

Amidst all this uproar Cooper somehow managed to dispatch a messenger to the Navy Yard with a note to Lieutenant William W. McKean, reporting—perhaps a bit overdramatically—that some of the beneficiaries were "in a state of mutiny, and I fear that murder will be committed." McKean immediately dispatched an officer with a squad of Marines to the Asylum. The leathernecks took a deeply intoxicated Thomas Barber and Charles White into custody and escorted them back to the Navy Yard, entertained along the way by White's and Barber's threats to kill Lieutenant Cooper just as soon as they returned to the Asylum. Lieutenant McKean had a different destination in mind for the pair—the receiving ship *Sea Gull*, where he confined them, probably in irons.

When all of this was officially reported to Secretary Dickerson, he immediately dismissed Barber, White, and Williams from the Asylum—possibly influenced by a grossly exaggerated newspaper report of the incident.[3] The dismissal was accompanied by a stern warning that, if any of the three caused a post-dismissal riot or personal injury at the Asylum, Commodore Stewart was to have the offender or offenders turned over to the civil authorities for trial and punishment. In less than two weeks the trio, released from *Sea Gull*, had sobered up, stated (however insincerely) that they repented the error of their ways, and begged the Secretary of the Navy to readmit them to the Asylum. Dickerson passed the readmission decision to Commodore Stewart, who turned it down unequivocally. Barber and White disappear from the Asylum's history, Barber to die by 1845 and White to an as-yet-undiscovered fate. William Williams was able to gain readmission to the Asylum in November 1838 under Cooper's successor. He apparently behaved himself well enough to avoid additional negative reports and died in July 1840, at the early age of thirty-five.

COOPER VS. THE DOCTORS

There is a second strand to the story of James B. Cooper's years at the Naval Asylum. Chronologically that strand is braided with his problems with the beneficiaries, but it is best narrated separately, although the events of both strands contributed to his downfall.

The hospital (under its surgeon, Waters Smith) and the Asylum's beneficiary function (under Cooper) were, as mentioned earlier, both housed in William Strickland's building and both reported to Commodore James Barron, the commandant of the Philadelphia

Navy Yard, two miles to the east on the Delaware River. How often Barron visited his satellite command on Gray's Ferry Road is not known, but the busy navy yard, immediately under his eye, must have demanded a high proportion of his attention. This created a potentially explosive situation, with two conflicting centers of authority (Smith and Cooper) in the same physical space. It could have worked smoothly if the two individuals had been friendly and cooperative people, reasonably free of status anxiety. With Dr. Smith and Lieutenant Cooper, that was far from the case. When the first dispute occurred between them—an argument of which no record survives—Barron might have issued an order sharply delineating the responsibilities of each man. This would, however, have been difficult for even the most adept regulation-drafter to do, as the two functions were so intertwined—or at least dangerously contiguous—in the daily reality of life on Gray's Ferry Road. Instead, Barron tried counseling and conciliation: "I used such arguments as I had a hope would have induced the doctor to consider Lieutenant Cooper as having the entire charge of the house and also of his being accountable for the good order and deportment of its inmates—not supposing that any two officers could occupy a house so capacious as the Asylum without finding room enough for all the purposes of both without coming into collision with each other."

Wrong. In late May 1835 Lieutenant Cooper and Dr. Smith collided again. A barrel of pickled mackerel, stored in a room on the Asylum's second story, sprang a leak and the pickling seeped through the floor and dripped down into the principal story. Cooper sent for the hospital steward, William Anderson, who was responsible for all food supplies at the Asylum, with the intent of directing Anderson to have the leaking barrel dealt with and the mess cleaned up. Anderson, who considered himself a member of the hospital department and under the authority of Dr. Smith, asserted in no uncertain terms that Cooper could not issue an order to him, and a hot oral dispute was on. As is typical with such confrontations, each participant later proclaimed his complete innocence and blamed the whole conflict on the other. The level of invective flying between the two can be gauged by Anderson's assertion that Cooper "abused and cursed me as if I had been one of his slaves," and Cooper's threat, "Any more of your insolence and I will box your ears"—a threat backed up by Cooper's clenched and raised fist. How and by whom the fishy mess got cleaned up is not part of the record, but the whole dispute—with Dr. Smith stoutly defending Steward Anderson and casting all the blame on Lieutenant Cooper—was reported in tedious detail to Acting Secretary of the Navy John Boyle. He passed the responsibility back to Barron: the commodore should define for the doctor and the lieutenant their respective responsibilities and require a strict observance of the rules he laid down. If Commodore Barron ever issued such a directive, no record of it survives. The ambiguities of responsibility at Gray's Ferry Road simmered on.

Underlying this personal confrontation a more fundamental tension can be detected. The Navy's medical men were, by the 1830s, vigorously asserting their professional status, backed by an increased level of formal medical education and exemplified by their newly constructed and physically pretentious hospitals. This fed an ill-concealed resentment of the right of the Navy's sea-officers—its lieutenants, commanders, and captains—to issue orders to the doctors. For their part, the veteran sea-officers, such as Lieutenant Cooper, often responded with hostility when their right of command was challenged by the self-conscious medical professionals. It was a relative-status quarrel that would not soon nor easily be resolved by the U.S. Navy.

Perhaps orally admonished by Commodore Barron, Lieutenant Cooper and the medical staff of the hospital apparently maintained reasonably calm relations until October 1837, when a prominent naval person arrived at the Asylum to set in motion events that led to the next—and for Lieutenant Cooper, the terminal—interpersonal explosion. That prominent naval person was none other than the Navy's senior officer and dominating figure for three decades, Commodore John Rodgers. The commodore had suffered an attack of cholera in September 1832. Although the disease did not kill him, it took a heavy toll; he never regained his former formidable energy and his memory began to show signs of deterioration. Rodgers remained president of the Board of Navy Commissioners, but his colleagues, commodores Isaac Chauncey and Charles Morris, had to shoulder more of the board's work. Add to that, the board's highly competent secretary, Charles W. Goldsborough, was a thoroughly experienced drafter of letters and reports that could go out over Rodgers' signature. To all except those able to observe the inner workings of the Navy Department at close range, the Board of Navy Commissioners' responsibilities appeared to be executed normally.

But behind this façade John Rodgers was slowly descending into dementia. He resigned from the board in May 1837. A summer trip to England made no improvement to his physical or mental health. As his dementia worsened, a family decision was made in the fall of 1837 to move Rodgers, accompanied by his longtime and extremely loyal African American manservant, Henry Butler, to Philadelphia and the Naval Asylum. There he could be under the immediate care of the Navy's leading surgeon, Dr. Thomas Harris. At least in the early days of his residence at the Asylum, Rodgers could still recognize some old acquaintances, including Lieutenant John R. Goldsborough, son of the board's secretary; but he was basically hallucinatory. Rodgers thought the Asylum was a hotel; that he was the president of the United States; and that the government had made him a grant of 2 million dollars on which he was constantly writing (of course, worthless) checks that he gave to those around him. In his imagined reality as president of the United States, Rodgers proposed to commission newly fledged Lieutenant Goldsborough a captain in the Navy immediately, offered to lend him $35,000, and told Goldsborough that Mrs. Rodgers, in her husband-imagined role as the nation's first lady, would be giving a fashionable reception at the White House next week. Lieutenant Goldsborough simply *must* attend.[4]

Building tensions finally detonated in June 1838 in a wordy and tedious paper war between Assistant Surgeon Ninian Pinkney and Surgeon Mordecai Morgan on one side and Lieutenant Cooper on the other. As is usual in such paper wars, both sides emerged from the conflict with diminished reputations. The battle began when Pinkney asserted that Cooper found the manifestations of Rodgers' terminally deteriorating condition personally repugnant and made life difficult for both the commodore and Henry Butler. Pinkney's assertions turned out to be based only on his own perceptions of the situation, although Lieutenant Goldsborough supported Pinkney's opinions. When the charges were referred to Commodore Charles Stewart, he replied with some annoyance that he had asked for the *facts* concerning disrespect to, or mistreatment of, Commodore Rodgers and his caregiver, but had gotten only opinions—on which, of course, he could not take action.

Dr. Morgan subsequently weighed into the battle with a five-page letter to the Secretary of the Navy. He complained that Lieutenant Cooper held "an appointment of undefined authority"; gave his version of yet one more dispute about the hospital stewardship, the most recent incumbent of which post Cooper had fired; and charged that all those who knew Cooper recognized "how utterly unqualified he is for such a place [superintendent of the Naval Asylum] from want of knowledge, the infirmities of age, but above all from the infirmities of his temper," which resulted in Cooper's "unreasonable and impertinent interference" in the business of the hospital. Cooper replied at equal length with his side of the story, laying all the blame on the arrogance of the medical men.

Cooper made his final and fatal error of judgment on 5 June 1838. Henry Butler, Rodgers' primary caregiver in his rapidly deteriorating condition, had developed an accurate perception that Cooper found the deranged commodore's presence and behavior distasteful or worse. Cooper objected to Rodgers' and Butler's using the stairway adjacent to his quarters when they left the building for walks or carriage rides. More insensitively yet, Cooper told Butler that he "intended to call the Commodore to account for spitting on the walks and the floor." Butler owned a dog of which Rodgers had been particularly fond when they lived in Washington. In hopes that the dog would give Rodgers some company and pleasure, Butler brought him to the Naval Asylum. Rodgers appeared to recognize the dog and enjoyed having him visit his room. When not with Rodgers, the dog was kept tethered behind the building. This situation greatly displeased Cooper, who had a no-dogs policy at the Asylum, and who appears to have been a dog-hater. He told Butler that, if the dog was not removed by a certain day and time, "By God, he would shoot him." Butler probably calculated that, given Commodore Rodgers' exalted place in the Navy, Cooper—however much he blustered—would not have the temerity to shoot the dog. This opinion was reinforced in Butler's mind by the fact that Cooper owned ten or twelve hogs that roamed the Asylum grounds at will and whose pen sent an offensive stench about the premises and inside the building. Cooper's daughter, who lived with him at the Asylum, tried to warn Butler that her father was serious. However, Butler dug his heels in and insisted that this was the commodore's and his home, and he was standing on their rights. On the day of the appointed deadline Lieutenant Cooper got his double-barreled gun and shot the dog.

Butler responded in a fury, swearing with many an oath that he would get even with Cooper if it took twenty years and cost him his life—that he would shoot Cooper's horse and his cow—

and much more in the same vein. Here was a fully literate black man telling off a white officer in the plainest and most colloquial English. (History does not record whether there were any spectators of color observing the confrontation; if there were, they were surely silently cheering for Henry Butler.) However much Cooper may have ached to strike Butler or expel him from the Asylum, he had sense enough to know, even in this moment of extreme provocation, that Butler was under the protection of Rodgers and his family—untouchable, literally and figuratively.

Rodgers' physician, Surgeon Thomas Harris, visited the Asylum and his patient about an hour after the dog's death, and found the building's residents in a state of uproar and outrage over Cooper's "brutal and uncalled for" behavior. Harris confronted Cooper, who retreated into silence. Later Harris wrote an epitaph for the whole sorry affair: "I considered the conduct of Lieutenant Cooper in this affair as harsh and ungenerous and as highly offensive and disrespectful to the eminent and afflicted officer, whose condition ought to demand, not contumely, but kindness of every heart not deadened to generous sympathies."

JAMES BIDDLE TO THE RESCUE

The new Secretary of the Navy, James K. Paulding, who took office on 1 July 1838, had served as secretary to the Board of Navy Commissioners from 1815 until 1823. He was thoroughly familiar with how the Navy Department operated, knew most of the Navy's senior officers personally, and was, consequently, able to hit the ground running upon appointment. When a thick packet of papers—charges and countercharges among Henry Butler, James B. Cooper, and Mordecai Morgan, with Thomas Harris' commentary on the whole business—arrived on his desk Paulding was in no mood to tolerate the shenanigans at the Naval Asylum.

In mid-July Paulding had a conversation with Commodore Charles Morris. Morris had apparently received a private letter from, or had a personal conversation with, Commodore James Biddle. Philadelphia native and resident Biddle deplored the state of affairs at the Asylum, about which there was no shortage of negative commentary, printed and oral, in the city. Under its "present inferior management" the institution was unattractive to elderly and disabled naval veterans; active-duty officers and enlisted men were largely unaware of the home; and its public image was far from an

attractive one. What was needed to sort things out was one of the
Navy's senior officers in command, and Biddle let Morris know that
he was ready to take on the job. So informed by Morris, Paulding
enthusiastically accepted Biddle's offer. He created the position of
governor of the Naval Asylum, an independent command no longer under the supervision of the commandant of the Philadelphia
Navy Yard, and extended it to Biddle. He—of course—accepted.
Without question Biddle was disgusted with the Cooper regime
at the Asylum and eager to put things right, but the job had for
him the added advantage that it was a shoreside assignment, at
full pay, right in his hometown.

Let it be noted that Biddle took charge under exactly the same
set of "Regulations for the Government of the Naval Asylum,"
which had been in force during Cooper's term of office, but with
totally different results. Secretary Paulding urged Biddle to con-
vene a group of senior officers, command and medical, to propose
a better set of regulations for the Asylum, but Biddle persisted in
finding reasons to evade this task. Probably he was one of those
administrators who are temperamentally disposed to operate with
as few restricting rules as possible, because this situation gave him
more freedom to act as he, James Biddle, saw fit. And, because
Biddle was the right man for the job, that approach worked well.

It came down to rank and personality. Biddle's career went back
almost to the earliest days of the Navy. He was a protégé of the
legendary Commodore Thomas Truxtun; had commanded *Hornet*
in her defeat of *Penguin* during the War of 1812, winning a gold
medal from Congress; been sent to the Columbia River in 1817 to
assert the United States' claim to the Oregon territory; combatted
pirates (successfully) and yellow fever (unsuccessfully) in the West
Indies; and served with distinction as commodore of the Brazil and
Mediterranean squadrons, 1826–32. Over and above the prestige of
rank and accomplishment, Biddle brought to the position appropriate assets of personality. A member of Philadelphia's elite, Biddle
exuded an easy and natural air of hauteur and command—personality traits perfectly captured in Thomas Sully's portrait painted during
Biddle's tenure as governor of the Naval Asylum—that argued strongly
for a "Yes, Sir, Commodore," attitude among his subordinates.

With Biddle's appointment, Secretary Paulding retired James B.
Cooper from his active-duty assignment and returned him to "waiting orders" status. Under the circumstances, Cooper was naturally

eager for an exoneration of his four years at the Naval Asylum. Paulding passed the task of investigation to the new governor. When Biddle assumed command at the Asylum on 9 August 1838 he assembled the beneficiaries, addressed them, then asked the beneficiaries whether they had any complaints to make about Cooper's treatment of them. Perhaps intimidated by Biddle's presence—or recognizing that Cooper was an old man on his way out to whom they could extend the courtesy of kindness—all the beneficiaries said that they were satisfied with Lieutenant Cooper's management. Vindicated, at least in his own mind, Cooper retired to his home in Haddonfield, New Jersey. Although promoted to commander in 1841, Cooper never held another active-duty assignment. He died on 5 February 1854, ninety-two or ninety-three years old. The less-than-happy period at the Naval Asylum long forgotten, Cooper lived out his final years honored for his heroic service in the Revolution and as the last surviving member of Lee's Legion.[5] The story has it that, to the dismay of his Quaker neighbors, Cooper's body was escorted to its burial site in the Haddonfield Friends Cemetery with full military honors.

RETROSPECT

On 16 September 1842 an anonymous article, "United States Naval Asylum," appeared in Philadelphia's *Public Ledger*. The piece, by a well-informed but now unknown author, had several axes to grind. One of them was an assessment, not entirely unkind, of James B. Cooper's management of the Naval Asylum. The author made four points. First, Cooper was fond of agriculture and his primary emphasis at the Asylum was on improving the "broken and wild" character of the grounds. Second, absorbed as he was with his landscaping projects, Cooper paid little attention to the comfort of the beneficiaries or to the internal organization of the institution. Third, Cooper seemed more interested in decreasing the number of beneficiaries than in encouraging new residents. Fourth, he displayed "a distaste for mingling with the aged and decrepit," which led him to keep beneficiary amenities at the Asylum to a minimum and may have motivated his desire to hold down the number of beneficiaries under his charge.

Ungentle Goodnights has seen no evidence to substantiate or deny Cooper's absorption with landscaping the grounds, although it can be assumed that the *Public Ledger*'s contemporary observer knew whereof he wrote. All his other points are congruent with the surviving record. The frequency with which Cooper recommended dismissals—often of men who were able to return to the Asylum under later and more sympathetic regimes—can certainly be interpreted as a wish to hold down the number of beneficiaries under his supervision. As for Cooper's distaste for being surrounded by the disabled and the elderly, one need look no farther for evidence than his behavior toward Commodore Rodgers (who died in Butler's arms on 1 August 1838) and his caregiver. Does this seem a strange attitude for a man in his seventies? Perhaps not, if Cooper was motivated by a conscious or unconscious unhappiness about growing old himself and a fear of his eventual death. That proposed explanation can only be presented as psychological speculation, but it is consistent with Cooper's known behavior.

To the *Public Ledger's* analysis three other conclusions can be added from the surviving documentary record. First, James B. Cooper had no respect for the beneficiaries nor they for him. Unfortunately, the beneficiaries' side of the story is not on record, but the level of accumulated enmity can be gauged by the events and the rhetoric of the "mutiny" of March 1838. Second, if Cooper had ever possessed good command and leadership skills—and there is no evidence one way or the other on that—he had lost them by the time that he accepted the Naval Asylum appointment. And, third, Cooper was an ill-tempered man, abrasive in his relations with his peers, dominating and abusive to those he perceived as his inferiors or subordinates.

"Upon the whole," said James Biddle not long after he took over the command, "it is manifest that there has not been one head to this establishment and that the collisions between Lieutenant Cooper and the medical officers have been injurious and discreditable to the public service." Luckily for the United States Naval Asylum and its residents, a better era was about to begin.

FOUR

THE SHIP COMES ASHORE

W hen he replaced the "invalid officer" James B. Cooper with Commodore James Biddle, Secretary of the Navy James K. Paulding altered course to a management model for the Asylum with which every one of the residents was thoroughly familiar—the social and command structure of a ship-of-war. And it was as a land-based ship-of-war that the institution operated thereafter.

At the top of a ship's command structure—admired, respected, feared, or some combination thereof—was a ship's ultimate authority figure: the captain. At the Asylum he was called the governor. With the exception of one brief period (23 February 1843–15 May 1844) when Commander William W. McKean served as governor, that post was typically filled by a senior captain, commodore, or admiral, often as the last active-duty command of his career. Commodore Jacob Jones, the victorious commander in the *Wasp-Frolic* battle during the War of 1812, became governor on 1 July 1847, at the age of seventy-nine, and died shortly after transferring the command to his successor on 17 June 1850. Rear Admiral George C. Read, *Constitution*'s third lieutenant when she defeated *Guerriere* in 1812, died in office as governor on 22 August 1862.

The governor held ultimate responsibility for the institution, made the final decisions, and reported up the line to the Navy Department. As on shipboard, he was assisted by his next-in-command, the executive officer, who directed the day-to-day operations of the Asylum. In the early years the executive officer was typically a senior lieutenant; by the 1850s the post tended to be filled by commanders; still later, in the 1860s and 1870s, the incumbents were retired commanders, captains, or commodores. The names of

all of these men would be recognized by specialists in the history
of the nineteenth-century U.S. Navy, but only one executive officer achieved more general fame. That was Andrew Hull Foote, the
admiral well known by any Civil War enthusiast for his victories
on the western rivers. He served twice as the Asylum's executive
officer—22 November 1841–26 August 1843 and 9 March 1854–
2 June 1855. The relative roles of governor and executive officer
varied with the personalities and energies of the different governors, though these variations can only be dimly perceived. Because
reports from the Naval Asylum were always signed by the governor, whoever may have drafted them, detecting the relative inputs
of governor and executive officer in any situation is more a matter
of historian's intuition than archival record. Jacob Jones was old, in
poor health, and seems to have been content to leave the heavy lifting to his ambitious and pushy executive officer, Lieutenant John P.
Gillis. Jones' predecessor, Commodore Charles W. Morgan, who
served from 15 May 1844 until 1 July 1847, had been a more activ-
ist governor, busy with many construction and remodeling projects
around the institution. Early in his second term as executive officer Foote became concerned about the newly nominated governor,
Commodore George W. Storer, whom he did not know. Foote's
friend, Commodore Joseph Smith, Chief of the Bureau of Yards
and Docks, to which the Asylum reported, reassured him in an
off-the-record letter. "I gave [Storer] a hint to *let you go* ahead and
not to trouble you, only to sign his name." Tongue-in-cheek? Or
Smith's experience-based view of the respective roles of governor
and executive officer?

In the 1840s and 1850s, when the needs of the Navy did not
demand that every able-bodied officer be employed elsewhere, as
was the case during the Civil War years, an additional lieutenant
was often stationed at the Asylum to assist the executive officer.
The governor's immediate assistant was the Asylum's secretary, who
handled all of the governor's and the executive officer's paperwork.
Picking his secretary was the governor's prerogative; the post was
typically filled by one of his sons or by a friend. The Philadelphia
Navy Yard's purser (later *paymaster*) was accountable for the issues
of food and clothing at the Asylum; he had an on-site clerk or
steward who handled the daily responsibilities.

That was it as far as the Asylum's command structure went.
(The other officer stationed at the Asylum, the chaplain, will be

one of the subjects of chapter 8, as will the civilian household staff.)
Compared to a ship-of-war with a crew equal in number to the
Asylum's beneficiaries, the Asylum's officer complement was small.
Years of service had socialized the elderly and disabled sailors and
Marines, except when badly intoxicated, to be respectful and obe-
dient to officers. The Asylum ran quite smoothly with few authority figures, its orderly life resting primarily on the respect in which
the veteran governor was held and the extent to which the executive officer was seen to be genuinely concerned with the welfare of
the beneficiaries. (Andrew Hull Foote scored high on the latter
scale.) Contrary to the popular historical misperception, ships-of-
war of the nineteenth-century U.S. Navy were not managed by
terror of corporal punishment (though this was used in appropriate cases), but by the men of quarterdeck and lower deck—all of
whom served voluntarily—filling well-understood traditional roles
and respecting custom-defined social boundaries that were not to
be crossed with impunity. The same was true at the United States
Naval Asylum.

Until 1 July 1849 the governor of the Naval Asylum reported
directly to the Secretary of the Navy, who, with the aid of his
experienced senior office staff, appointed the governors and the
executive officers, decided the admission or dismissal of beneficiaries, approved or disapproved proposed expenditures, and occasionally visited the Asylum itself on tours of inspection. By an act
of Congress of 31 August 1842, the old Board of Navy Commissioners was abolished and replaced by five bureaus—Construction, Equipment, and Repair; Medicine and Surgery; Ordnance
and Hydrography; Provisions and Clothing; and Yards and Docks.
The Secretary retained direct control of policy, operations, and personnel. This change did not immediately affect the Naval Asylum,
as the Secretary explicitly reserved to his office the supervision of
that institution in a regulation issued on 26 November 1842.

That the Asylum building also housed the Philadelphia Naval
Hospital resulted in a triangle of communication and command
among the Secretary of the Navy, the Chief of the Bureau of Medicine and Surgery, and the Governor of the Naval Asylum. While
Dr. William P. C. Barton was Chief of Medicine and Surgery (September 1842–March 1844), this arrangement worked rather badly.
Barton, a naval surgeon with a much-commented-upon aversion to
sea duty and great skill at avoiding it, was intellectually brilliant,

but arrogant and overbearing. Conflict with him led directly to the premature resignation of Commodore James Barron as the Asylum's second governor. In one especially resented (and soon repealed) exercise in medical empire-building, Barton persuaded Secretary of the Navy Abel P. Upshur to allocate half the space in the Asylum building to the hospital function—even though the hospital's patient load in no way justified that much space—and to crowd the Asylum function into the other half of the building. When, in April 1844, Barton was replaced as bureau chief by Dr. Thomas Harris, equally capable but much more adept at human relations, the three-way administration of the Asylum worked smoothly enough. The governors interacted amicably with Harris about the Asylum's shared physical facilities and their improvement. This situation continued until 20 April 1849, when Secretary of the Navy William Ballard Preston decreed that, effective 1 July of that year, "the United States Naval Asylum at Philadelphia shall be under the control and supervision of the Bureau of Medicine and Surgery so far as relates to the treatment of the sick and their supplies and under the Bureau of Yards and Docks in all other respects."

No evidence survives as to why Secretary Preston made this decision at this time, but neither is there any as to why Secretary Upshur had earlier decided to retain the Asylum under his personal direction. Given the absence of evidence, speculation about motivations would be an exercise in historical fantasy. The important point is that Preston's decision placed oversight of the Asylum with a man who would take keen personal interest in, and have great influence on, the institution for the next twenty years—Commodore (later Rear Admiral) Joseph Smith, Chief of the Bureau of Yards and Docks from 25 May 1846 until 30 April 1869.[1]

A FRIEND TO OLD SAILORS

One of the more underappreciated officers in the history of the nineteenth-century U.S. Navy, Joseph Smith was born on 30 March 1790 in Hanover, Massachusetts. His father, Albert, was a prosperous shipbuilder whose rank among Hanover's elite can be gauged by his selection as moderator of the annual town meeting thirteen times between 1806 and 1822 and by his election three times to the lower house of the Massachusetts legislature and twice to the state senate.[2]

Young Joseph entered the Navy as a midshipman in 1809. He came to prominence, and assured his future career, as first lieutenant of the brig *Eagle* during the battle of Lake Champlain on 11 September 1814. In his official report on the battle, *Eagle's* commanding officer, Master Commandant Robert Henley, cited him as "that excellent officer," who "went into action in that cool and deliberate manner which marks the truly brave man."[3] The details behind that encomium became the basis of an oft-repeated and rather distorted legend. The real story, as told by Smith himself, was this: before the battle began Smith had placed springs on *Eagle's* cables as she lay at single anchor, intending to use them to adjust the brig's broadside to match that of her opponent, the British brig *Linnet*. However, this device failed its purpose, as it only forced *Eagle* ahead instead of correcting her broadside. In the heat of the action Smith quickly decided to send a boat with a kedge anchor and hawser off the port (unengaged) side of *Eagle* to accomplish the same objective. While Lieutenant Smith was standing on one of the guns, directing the men in the boat, an enemy shot passed close enough to him to strip off his jacket, belt pistols, and sword, knock him down, and cause his head to strike some part of a gun carriage. When Smith recovered consciousness, he found that he had been carried below with the other wounded and that the battle was still raging. Access to the main hatch was blocked, so Smith crept along the berth deck amid the dead and wounded, then regained the upper deck via the fore-scuttle. Once there, he found that *Eagle* had cut her cable and drifted down the line to a position just astern of Commodore Thomas Macdonough's *Saratoga*, where her guns could bear on *Saratoga's* opponent and help bring the battle to its victorious conclusion.[4]

Capable and always reliable performance in a variety of commands brought Smith to the rank of captain in 1837. From 1838 to 1840 he was captain of the ship-of-the-line *Ohio*, flagship of the Mediterranean squadron under Commodore Isaac Hull. In her, Smith sustained the reputation of a tough disciplinarian, not hesitant to award the lash to maintain his notions of naval discipline. Between 1843 and 1845 he returned to the Mediterranean as squadron commodore, hoisting his pennant in the frigate *Cumberland*. This was Smith's last seagoing command, quickly followed by his appointment as Chief of the Bureau of Yards and Docks. In Civil War history Smith is best remembered as the ranking naval officer and dominant figure on the Ironclad Board that selected, from among competing designs, John Ericsson's *Monitor* for construction. Secretary of the Navy Gideon Welles later asserted that Smith, in whose ability and intelligence he had complete confidence, "in addition to great nautical and civil experience, possessed a singularly mechanical and practical mind. On him devolved, ultimately, the chief responsibility and supervision of the execution of the plans adopted [for *Monitor*]. . . . Beyond any other person, [he] is deserving of credit, if credit be due to anyone connected with the Navy Department, for this vessel."[5]

As chief of Yards and Docks, Joseph Smith was a hardworking and efficient administrator, who kept his bureau functioning to the highest standards of public service. Even as he was busy bearing the bureau's heavy burdens during the Civil War, he made certain that less-urgent matters, such as routine letters from the Naval Asylum—Smith read every incoming letter to the bureau himself and noted how it should be answered—were dealt with promptly by his able staff. He always took a keen interest in the Asylum. "The letters of [Admiral Smith] show a very searching study of the details of [the Asylum's] administration" was the way one of the institution's early historians put it. The present historian is tempted to say that Smith had something of the micromanager in his psychic make-up and required the governors to refer to him matters that might

Joseph Smith. In this photograph, the caring and forgiving side of the "friend to old sailors" almost peeps out from behind the gruff exterior that Smith prefers to project. AUTHOR'S COLLECTION

have been left to their own discretion. (History, on the other hand, is in Smith's debt for this aspect of his personality; it created a rich documentary record of the Asylum and its beneficiaries during his tenure.) Micromanager or not, Smith never was deflected from the biggest matters under the bureau's responsibility, as the success of the Civil War ironclad program amply attests. Apparently responding to the adage, "If you want a job done well, get a busy person to do it," Smith, a lifelong Episcopalian, was elected by his fellow parishioners to the responsible and challenging post of senior warden at Saint John's Church on Lafayette Square in Washington for twenty years, serving from 3 April 1856 until 3 May 1876.[6]

It was at St. John's on Sunday, 9 March 1862, that Smith received word of one of the devastating personal losses in his life. Earlier that morning Secretary Welles learned that the ironclad CSS *Virginia* had, the previous day, attacked and sunk the frigate *Congress*—commanded by Smith's son, Lieutenant Joseph B. Smith—and the frigate *Cumberland* in Hampton Roads. After attending an emergency cabinet meeting at the White House about this disturbing news, Welles decided to stop by St. John's, where he knew that Commodore Smith—they had been good friends ever since Smith and Welles were appointed bureau chiefs at the Navy Department in 1846—would be at the late-morning service. Welles asked an usher to request Smith to step outside, so that Welles could tell Smith that *Congress* was lost. Mustering all the self-control he had developed from years of command and responsibility, Smith slowly and calmly buttoned up his coat and said, "The *Congress* sunk! Then Joe is dead." Not necessarily, replied Welles. *Congress* had gone down close to shore; surely many of the officers and crew must have escaped. "You don't know Joe as well as I do," Smith replied. "He would not survive his ship." And so it was. Mortally wounded, Lieutenant Joseph B. Smith had perished with *Congress*.[7]

It was neither the first nor the last heavy loss Joseph Smith would have to sustain in his life and keep on working. On 29 August 1855 his wife, Harriet, was seriously injured in a grisly and lethal railroad accident near Burlington, New Jersey. (The commodore, who was with her, was also injured, but not so seriously.) Following initial treatment in Burlington, Harriet Smith was moved to Governor Storer's residence at the Naval Asylum, but hopes for her eventual recovery there were in vain; she died at the Asylum on 2 September.[8] "My bereavement is crushing and deep-rooted," Joseph told his friend David Geisinger, a fond admirer of Harriet's. "Every day it seems more intense, but I know the hand that inflicts it does not willingly afflict or grieve the children of men. . . . [You and I] shall meet her there, in that unknown place of departed spirits, I trust."[9] Then, on 8 September 1866, Joseph Smith lost his other (and older) son, Commander Albert N. Smith, a man in his early forties, who was serving as Chief of the Navy's Bureau of Equipment and Recruiting. Thereafter, Joseph and Harriet's daughter, Anna, was the only member of the immediate family still alive.

History does not know who chose the image for the memorial window to Admiral Joseph Smith at St. John's. Possibly it was Anna. This depicts the gospel story in Matthew 14:28–31: on a stormy night the apostles are out in a boat on the Sea of Galilee when they see Jesus walking on the water toward them. Peter leaps from the boat and starts walking across the water toward Jesus, then—realizing what he is doing—panics and begins to sink. The window captures the moment when Jesus reaches out and saves Peter—a rich visual text from which to speculate about the inner Joseph Smith.

Smith's rather gruff appearance and his no-nonsense official persona concealed a more warm and caring human being—a side of his personality revealed in the nearly one hundred surviving private letters he wrote his friend Andrew Hull Foote between 1847 and 1860. "I am a friend to old sailors," he once said in relation to his oversight of the Naval Asylum. *Ungentle Goodnights* will support that self-assessment with many a story of Smith's repeated forgiveness of beneficiary misbehavior. He was especially indulgent to former lower-deck shipmates. Any sailor-beneficiary who had been at sea with him—even those on the receiving end of his tough shipboard school of discipline—could almost always play the old-shipmate card successfully with Joseph Smith.

KEEPING THINGS SHIPSHAPE

The nineteenth-century United States Navy issued a variety of printed regulations stating its expectations of, and defining unacceptable conduct by, officers, sailors, and Marines. Officers commanding individual ships supplemented these printed instructions by preparing their own—and occasionally idiosyncratic—internal rules and regulations for the vessels under their command. These practices transferred naturally and easily to the United States Naval

Asylum. When the Bureau of Yards and Docks assumed responsibility for the Asylum in 1849, Commodore Joseph Smith immediately issued a set of printed general regulations—a handsome sheet intended to be posted around the Asylum—that he reissued in 1851 with substantial revisions. The successive governors of the Asylum posted their own sets of internal regulations designed to supplement with housekeeping details the more general regulations established by Commodore Smith. Four sets of these internal rules survive—those issued by Governors William W. McKean in 1843 (and still in force when Smith drafted the 1849 version of his "Regulations for the U.S. Naval Asylum"), David Geisinger (1851), George W. Storer (1854), and J. R. M. Mullany (1878). Studied together, these general printed regulations and manuscript internal rules make it possible to reconstruct many of the routines of daily life on Gray's Ferry Road.

Strangely enough, the regulations give no indication of when or how the beneficiaries were awakened in the morning, although one of the designated beneficiary-postmen had to be up and on his way to the post office at 5:30 a.m. to post outgoing letters and collect incoming mail. The other beneficiaries cannot have been far behind him, because they had to be dressed and have their rooms swept before the bell rang for breakfast at 7 a.m. (1 April through 30 September, defined as "summer" in the Asylum's rules) or 8 (1 October through 31 March); the 8 a.m. "winter" breakfast hour was later changed to 7:30. Beneficiaries were expected to wear jackets at all meals, be otherwise properly dressed, sober, and orderly. They ate under the watchful eye of the master-at-arms, who was in the dining hall at all meals "to preserve order"; that responsibility included a prohibition on loud talking, improper language, and rude conduct to the mess hall waitresses. Forty-five minutes were allowed for the morning meal, after which the tables were cleared. Or not quite, because watchmen and gatekeepers and anyone else who had been on duty during breakfast now came in to eat once they had been relieved by their opposite-number breakfasters.

Meanwhile, the gates had been opened at sunrise and beneficiary–petty officers had hoisted the colors on the tall flagpole in front to the building. If they wished, any beneficiaries who were not confined to the grounds for misconduct or were patients in the hospital were free to leave the premises for the day—always exiting and returning through the northeast gate and strictly charged to be back through the gate by sunset unless they had permission to be out later. Those who chose to remain at the Asylum might work at their paid jobs—kitchen and laundry assistants, captains of the heads, and several others. (These jobs will be one of the subjects of chapter 8.) Men without paid employment might head to the little shop near the west gate, where those skilled in the craft built beautiful ship models for sale or for display in the Asylum's chapel. Still others would settle down in the designated smoking rooms to read the day's newspapers, play board and card games, chat, or simply snooze a bit in the air filled with the pleasant smell of good tobacco.

His breakfast duties over, the master-at-arms took a tour of the building to make certain that he could, by 10 a.m., report to the executive officer that all was in order for the day's inspection. That inspection was typically a walk-through of the building's shared spaces by the governor and the executive officer, during which one can imagine the governor saying things like "That door wants painting, Mr. Foote." The executive officer (later the master-at-arms) was also charged to inspect regularly, at a different time of day, the individual rooms of the beneficiaries to make sure that they were clean, tidy, and the beds made.

Dinner, the principal meal of the day, was served at noon, with those beneficiaries on watch and gate duty eating, as at breakfast, when they had been relieved. Beneficiaries' afternoons were occupied with the same activities as the morning, with a beneficiary-postman making the second mail run of the day at 2:30 p.m. Supper was served at 6 p.m.—or 5 p.m., October through March—with this "winter" supper hour modified in later years to 5:30.

At sunset the colors were lowered and one of the beneficiary–petty officers made a round of the grounds, verifying that only persons attached to the Asylum were within the walls, sending any beneficiaries he found on the grounds into the building, and locking up the institution's outbuildings, such as the stable. Within the building, lights were required to be out and all fires, except those in the furnaces, thoroughly extinguished by 10 p.m. during the warmer months or 11 during late fall, winter, and early spring. Come 11 p.m. in summer and 10:30 in winter (later changed to 10:30 and 10 respectively, then back again to 11 and 10:30) gates to the grounds were secured and all doors to the Asylum building, except the main entrance, were locked. The gatekeepers—who slept in the lodges by the gates—settled down for the night. A night-time beneficiary-watchman, stationed just inside the main entrance of the Asylum building, made note of any beneficiaries who came in after gate-close and lock-up times or who were intoxicated—the list to be turned over to the executive officer next morning. Every two hours the watchman toured the building to make sure that no lights were on in any beneficiary's room and that all was quiet; he had strict instructions to report to an officer immediately any noise he heard. Toward morning the watchman turned out the postman for his 5:30 trip with the mail and another day began at the United States Naval Asylum.

As sources for history, rules and regulations have their limits. They promulgate a framework of how things *ought* to be. In real life those governed by rules and regulations often ignore them, sometimes violate them, and not infrequently try to figure out ways around them. When officers attached to the Asylum are admonished to prevent "all immoral practices" among the beneficiaries; when drunkenness, fighting, abusive, or profane language are enumerated as types of beneficiary misconduct deserving punishment; when beneficiaries are warned to stay out of the kitchen and to cease fraternizing with the women who work there because it interferes with their duties, then one knows that there was no shortage of real life at the United States Naval Asylum. Of that real life there are abundant records.

FIVE

A Curious Character

"Time prevents me from entering into [an] anecdotal history," Dr. Edward Shippen, one of the earliest historians of the Naval Asylum, remarked in a lecture. Then he added: "but I may say that many curious characters have been inmates of the institution." History does not know which particular beneficiaries Dr. Shippen had in mind when he spoke those words, but Davidge Griffith Ridgely would certainly have qualified.

Ridgely—a man about whose life more is known than the typical beneficiary—was born in Anne Arundel County, Maryland, on 17 February 1794, the tenth and last child of his parents. Davidge's distinctive first name derived from his mother's side of the family. She was the daughter of Charles Griffith and Anne Davidge. His father, Henry, was a blacksmith. Of him Davidge probably had only vague memories, if any, because Henry died in 1799, when his son was five. He might have remembered a bit more of his childhood home, which his father tried (unsuccessfully) to sell in 1797, advertising it in Annapolis' *Maryland Gazette*:

> I OFFER for SALE my PLANTATION near this city,
> it contains two hundred and thirty-seven acres, about
> one half thereof in wood; it borders on the Severn river,
> and is situate between two and three miles from this city.
> There are several very beautiful situations and prospects,
> commanding a view of the river and bay. The improve-
> ments are, an overseer's house, a kitchen, and a new
> framed barn. It has also several springs of excellent water.
> Possession may be had immediately.

There appears to have been a full measure of real estate hype in the advertisement, because while Henry's estate was being settled in 1800 the property received a less euphoric description: There were 221 total acres—115 in woods, 85 acres of land under cultivation, with fences in "tolerable repair," and another 31 acres of cut-down woods not yet under cultivation; a primary dwelling house, 36 feet long by 16 feet wide, part frame and part log, but "out of repair"; a frame barn, measuring 16 feet by 20 feet, "out of repair"; a corn house, 12 feet by 15 feet, in "tolerable repair"; a meat house, 8 feet by 10 feet, described as "new"; a blacksmith's shop, 16 feet by 18 feet, also in poor condition; a log kitchen, 12 feet by 16 feet, "much out of repair"; one log dwelling house, 16 feet by 20 feet, "in tolerable repair"; as well as a garden, a young—but bearing—apple orchard of 120 trees, 5 horses, 12 head of cattle, 17 pigs, 5 sheep, and sundry farming equipment. It would appear that Henry Ridgely had gotten himself into deeper financial waters than he could manage, but it may also be that declining health kept him from improving the property as he had once hoped.

Henry died without a will, which may indicate a sudden death. The settlement of his estate, solvent but encumbered with significant debt, dragged on into 1805. How Rachel Ridgely supported herself and her eight minor children after Henry's death is not evident from the surviving estate records.[1] However, she lived in an extended network of kin, and it is clear that young Davidge received a substantial education. This *may* have included attendance at St. John's College in Annapolis. Unfortunately, that cannot be established, because six leaves that included the years of his possible attendance have been cut from the college's Matriculation Book and there is no other record of students from this period.[2] Ridgely's naval superiors probably had mixed feelings about his literacy achievements, because—as will be seen—he was able to bombard those in authority with long, frequent, and correctly spelled letters of complaint that displayed a sophisticated vocabulary. Even if he was prone to run-on sentences, and although his meaning was not always clear, Davidge Ridgely was markedly more literate than the majority of his fellow beneficiaries.

By the War of 1812 years, Ridgely had relocated to the city of Baltimore, where he served as a private in the Fifty-first regiment of Maryland militia—service with which he was credited when he applied for admission to the Naval Asylum.[3] The ten years of Davidge

Ridgely's life following this War of 1812 service are blank pages in his story. In 1825 Ridgely reappears in the historical record when he enlisted as a new recruit in the ship-of-the-line *North Carolina*, bearing the pennant of Commodore John Rodgers during the latter's command of the United States Mediterranean Squadron in 1825–27. The only evidence found for Ridgely's presence in *North Carolina* is his own statement; he apparently served under an assumed name that cannot be decoded in either the ship's muster rolls or its punishment book. One can only wonder why Ridgely chose to enlist under an assumed name. From what was he hiding? Perhaps from himself and a failure in some earlier career attempt? Thinly disguised identity was a practice that he continued for his subsequent enlistments, which can be traced in the rolls—ship-of-the-line *Delaware*, as an ordinary seaman named David Ridgway between December 1827 and February 1830; frigate *Potomac*, as an ordinary seaman of the same name between May 1831 and January 1832, but reduced on the latter date to landsman for the balance of the cruise and discharged as such in January 1833; frigate *Brandywine*, as ordinary seaman David Ridgely, from October 1834 until May 1837.

Davidge Ridgely's final service that can be documented was as an ordinary seaman in the ship-of-the-line *Ohio*, for which he enlisted at Philadelphia in August 1838 as David Ridgeway and from which he was invalided home from the Mediterranean in the storeship *Dromo* in April 1840. What is notable about this fifteen-year service record is that Ridgely never advanced beyond the rate of ordinary seaman and was once reduced from that rate to landsman; lower than that he could not go. A typical sailor with this much service would have entered as a landsman and been promoted to ordinary seaman, seaman, and perhaps petty officer, as he gained experience and skills. Not Davidge Ridgely. An explanation can be found in the evaluation written by Surgeon of the Fleet Thomas Williamson when he invalided Ridgely home from *Ohio*: "Has been under treatment for severe stricture of the urethra, disease of prostate gland, and erysipelas of the face—is unfit for service and worthless on board ship—ought to be discharged."[4] Sick man or not, less than a month before Dr. Williamson wrote his evaluation Ridgely had been punished with twelve lashes for insolence.[5] It was far from the last time he would be guilty of similar conduct.

Dr. Williamson's negative—and apparently well-justified—evaluation notwithstanding, Davidge Ridgely was somehow able to muster the support and documentation necessary to secure admission to the Naval Asylum not long after his 1840 discharge from the service as an invalid. (Although Ridgely's appointment as a beneficiary at the Asylum ranked him as *seaman*, there is no evidence in any surviving muster roll that he ever achieved that rating.) It was the first of three admissions or readmissions to the institution. None of his stays there was a happy experience, primarily because by this stage of his life Ridgely was a troubled person.

Of Ridgely's three residencies at the Naval Asylum, the first, about which the least is known, lasted from 1 September 1841 to 20 March 1843. He seems to have been temporarily expelled at an uncertain date and readmitted on 11 October 1842. Six months later even Andrew Hull Foote, temperance advocate and committed reformer, had reached the limit of his tolerance. Ridgely, he reported, had been "drunken and riotous" for several weeks. On 4 March Governor William W. McKean parked Ridgely in the cells for a few days to dry out, then ordered him confined to the Asylum grounds with the stipulation that, if Ridgely again left the Asylum, he would not be permitted to return until his conduct had been referred to the Secretary of the Navy for a possible dismissal order. Sure enough, on 13 March 1843, while McKean was away and Foote in command, Ridgely somehow managed to get off the grounds and then sneak back. Confronted by the duty officer and told that he must leave *immediately*, Ridgely threatened to strike and stab him. Luckily for Ridgely, it was all threat and bluff; no actual violence against the duty officer occurred. Ridgely was secured, escorted to the northeast gate, and expelled from the grounds. Three days later he reappeared at the gate in what was described in the Asylum's daily log as "a distressed condition," and begged to be readmitted. Indulgence of a sort was granted: Ridgely was lodged in one of the cells pending the Secretary of the Navy Abel P. Upshur's decision on permanent dismissal. That came through on 20 March 1843, and Davidge Ridgely's first stay at the Naval Asylum was over.

At the end of February 1845 Davidge Ridgely came back for his second period at the Asylum. It was, if anything, more unhappy and restless than his first stay. A theme of alleged persecution begins to appear in his increasingly frequent letters of complaint. Keeping Ridgely at the Asylum was no easy task for the authorities. He left the grounds without permission on 2 July 1845, but was back by 11 July. Then, on the night of 2–3 August he disappeared again, not to return until 12 September. In the new year, on 8 February, he vanished once more, taking with him all his clothing—an indication that he probably did not intend to come back. But return he did on 12 March. During the months between May 1845 and 3 April 1846 Ridgely was punished at least twelve times, typically by being confined in the cells for two or three days. His final confinement was for five days. On his release, Ridgely more or less immediately decamped for Washington, where he appealed to Maryland's successive Whig senators, William D. Merrick and Reverdy Johnson, to help him get a pension so that he would not have to live at the Naval Asylum. He would almost certainly have known these men personally; both were his approximate age peers and natives of Annapolis. Such powerful personal connections notwithstanding, Ridgely's pension application was turned down.

Davidge Ridgely's whereabouts for the next few months are unknown, but by November 1846 he was back at the Asylum and confined in the cells for a week under a charge of intemperance, followed by another three-day confinement in December. Perhaps not too long thereafter Ridgely left for Baltimore. From that city, in March 1847, he again appealed for a pension, alleging that he was ill and without money and that he had been compelled to leave the Asylum because Governor Charles W. Morgan was sick and heard reports of Ridgely's behavior filtered through "a few Irish hirelings, who misrepresent me on all occasions [and] have much abused me by false reports" to Commodore Morgan. Exactly who the "Irish hirelings" might be is not entirely clear, but Ridgely almost certainly refers to the Asylum's then master-at-arms, John Fitzmorris, and some of the institution's civilian laborers who assisted Fitzmorris in maintaining order among the more obstreperous beneficiaries. In the event, Governor Morgan was not too sick to tell Ridgely that, if he left the Asylum again, he could not return.

By 2 July 1847 there was a newly appointed governor at the Asylum, Commodore Jacob Jones, and Davidge Ridgely had been back long enough to go on a major drunk that landed him in the cells—this time for a week. Nothing daunted by his confinement, Ridgely was drunk again on 28 July and confined to the cells for another week. For the next few months Ridgely's conduct record is blank—apparently a prolonged period of more-or-less acceptable behavior. On 4 May 1848 Commodore Jones granted him an indefinite leave of absence to visit family members in Maryland and his older brother, William, in Wabash County, Illinois. If Ridgely made it as far as Illinois, it may have been a quick trip; he was back from his leave on 22 July.

One instance of drunkenness and disorderly conduct on 9 October 1848 that landed Ridgely in the cells for two days aside, things ran along smoothly—facilitated perhaps by leave covering most of May 1849 for another visit to Ridgely's family in Maryland—until the summer of that year, when a series of alcohol-induced confinements led to a culminating showdown with authority. The Asylum had just been transferred to the jurisdiction of the Bureau of Yards and Docks and Commodore Joseph Smith had lost no time in issuing his new set of regulations for the institution. The document included this statement: "In consideration of the liberal provision which has been made for [beneficiaries at the Naval Asylum], they will be required, at the discretion of the Governor or Commanding Officer, to perform such duty [for the benefit] of the Institution as their age, physical abilities, and condition will allow." This new regulation did not suit Ridgely and a few of his fellow beneficiaries; they refused to cooperate when ordered to make woven mats for the building's hallways.

Joseph Smith was *not* pleased. From his lifelong tough-commander perspective, Ridgely and his fellow refusers "have manifested a spirit of insubordination which must at once be put down." Smith instructed Jones to stop the men's tobacco ration and their pocket money and to curtail their meals of "the *luxuries* of the table"—in Ridgely's case butter and coffee at breakfast. Any good sea lawyer among the Asylum's beneficiaries could have made a case (1) that because the beneficiaries were no longer legally members of the Navy, they could not be ordered to perform tasks or be insubordinate; (2) that it was not equitable to require that the able-bodied should perform free labor when their disabled fellows did not; and (3) that some beneficiaries were paid to perform tasks from gatekeepers to captains of the heads, so why should others be compelled to do unpaid work? Ridgely's fellow strikers failed to stand their ground, and quickly backed down in the face of Smith's sanctions. Not Davidge Ridgely. He asked Commodore Jones for a formal discharge from the Asylum, a request with which Jones happily complied on 11 October 1849.

Now began Davidge Ridgely's sporadic and long-running relationship with another Philadelphia institution. Either immediately or within a few days he crossed the Schuylkill to Blockley alms house, where he asserted with a straight face that he was a native-born Philadelphian and a resident of the city. Released on 30 November 1849, Ridgely came back to Blockley's medical ward on 3 April 1850 with a case of intermittent fever that kept him there until he was discharged as cured on 1 May. His absence from Blockley was brief. On 6 May he was admitted to the alms house section, discharged on 22 May, readmitted on 27 July, again discharged on 21 August, only to return to the medical ward on 5 April 1851 with an attack of rheumatism.

It was from Blockley that Davidge Ridgely began a vigorous campaign aimed at securing his third admission to the Naval Asylum. How and where Ridgely lived in the intervals between his stays at Blockley is unknown, but during these periods he made frequent appearances at the Asylum gates begging Commander Henry A. Adams, the executive officer, for readmission. Adams, who was not keen on seeing Ridgely readmitted, simply told him he would have to apply to Commodore Smith at the Bureau of Yards and Docks—with Adams' lack of enthusiasm evident in his declining to write in support of Ridgely's application. From Blockley in late April 1850 Ridgely appealed to Smith, claiming that he had been unfairly expelled from the Asylum because he was physically unable to perform the work required of him—a charge vigorously denied by the Asylum's resident surgeon. Now, for the first time the theme of religious persecution appears in his letters. He hopes, without further explanation, that Smith will readmit him "without curtailing my religious feeling more than other American citizens placed in similar situations."

Before acting on the application, Smith checked with Governor Jacob Jones, who stated his version of Ridgely's departure from the Asylum and added that "his character was drunken and troublesome." Application rejected. Never one to be accused of lack of persistence, Ridgely tried writing directly to Secretary of the Navy William A. Graham, asserting that he had been forced to leave "in consequence of being subject to the universal Catholic church government" and asking to be "reinstated in my home without being subject to the discipline of the above church." The Catholic business may have been another slam at the "Irish hirelings," who would have been Roman Catholics; however, it appears more likely that Ridgely conflated the typical Episcopal Sunday service at the Asylum with Roman Catholicism. He did not reveal what his own religious preference may have been, if any. Graham passed the letter on to Joseph Smith without comment, and Smith filed it.

Clearly the written word was failing him, so—soon after his discharge from the medical ward at Blockley at the end of April— Ridgely made his way to Washington to push his case in person. Whether he enlisted the clout of political acquaintants from Annapolis days or played the old-shipmate card with Commodore Smith—Ridgely had been an ordinary seaman in *Ohio* when Smith was her captain, and they had both been invalided home in the storeship *Dromo*—is unknown, but the visit got results: On 22 May Smith handed Ridgely a letter to Commander Adams granting him readmission to the Asylum on the grounds of "his dependent condition and inability to support himself by manual labor." What exactly Smith meant by *dependent condition* is not clear, but he may have perceived that Ridgely was slipping from eccentricity into real mental illness that would—the Navy's care aside—condemn him to a life of crazy-talking homelessness.

On 26 May 1851 Davidge Ridgely began his third, best-documented, and final stay at the United States Naval Asylum. Within eight days he was already at odds with Governor David Geisinger, who complained to Joseph Smith that Ridgely "is making trouble by refusing under frivolous pretenses to comply with that regulation which requires the [beneficiaries] to assist in such light work about the house and grounds as they are able to perform." Geisinger appealed to Smith for a final solution to the Ridgely problem: "From his drunken habits and perverse disposition he appears to be unworthy to remain in the Asylum."

But Smith still wanted to help, not dismiss, the troubled Ridgely. "It is hoped," he replied to Geisinger, "that duties of the lightest possible kind—duties merely nominal and such as shall afford a reasonable occupation of his time—may be assigned him. By pursuing a kind and somewhat indulgent course of treatment and discipline towards this man he may be entirely reformed and thus secure to him in his infirm and declining years a comfortable home for the remnant of his days." Then, in a none-too-subtle reminder of who was in charge here, Commodore Smith concluded: "Under these circumstances I can but hope that the officers will give their aid in carrying out the views above expressed."

Under this directive, relations between Davidge Ridgely and the officers of the Naval Asylum generally ran along smoothly for

about a year. The institution's log records only three instances of
Ridgely being punished for the usual offenses—drunk and noisy
and absent without leave—before the first day of June 1852. Then
things unraveled once again. An intoxicated Davidge Ridgely came
in through the gate, encountered a civilian on the Asylum grounds,
kicked and verbally abused him—all without any provocation. This
event set off a torrent of correspondence. Ridgely complained to
the Navy Department that he was being persecuted under a system of Asylum government "that prohibits the use of thought and
action in many cases that I consider essential to the welfare of
every citizen of the United States." The Asylum's executive officer
defended his very different perspective on this troubled man.

> BENEFICIARY DAVIDGE RIDGELY: Some four or five
> months since the supper bell rang. When I took my seat
> at the table and was in the act of putting some food in
> my plate when a man by the name of [Thomas] Harris,
> who sat on the opposite side of the table, reached over
> the table and seized hold of my plate, when a struggle
> ensued between us, upon which I was seized by several
> of the [men] of the household, choked until senseless,
> taken to the cells and there kept for several days.
>
> EXECUTIVE OFFICER ISAAC STERRETT: The state-
> ment made by Ridgely in regard to a struggle between
> himself and Harris at the supper table is not correct.
> During more than four years that Harris has been an
> inmate of the Asylum he has never been subjected to
> the slightest punishment or restriction, having always
> been strictly temperate and orderly. On the 3rd of
> March last Ridgely went to the supper table *drunk* and,
> failing to reach the butter, he became furious and com-
> menced breaking the dishes and probably would have
> destroyed all within his reach had he not been removed
> from the table and room, which was done by the
> master-at-arms, assisted by one of the laborers. He was
> led out by the collar and not choked until senseless, as
> he represents. He was, for this offense, confined
> twenty-four hours in the cells, restricted to the
> grounds, and pocket money stopped for one month.
> When released from the cells he declared he knew
> nothing of what had occurred at the supper table.

RIDGELY: I am yet under the necessity of soliciting your further indulgence ... to allow me the privilege of church doctrine similar to that adopted by the Senate and House of Representatives [of] the United States or otherwise allow me to choose my church doctrine and thereby prevent many unwarrantable accusations that have heretofore, and may hereafter, be brought against me.

STERRETT: No beneficiary who has conscientious scruples against the forms of worship at the Asylum has ever been coerced to attend such worship. All beneficiaries wishing to attend church outside the Asylum grounds have, without exception, been allowed to do so, unless restricted for misconduct. Above thirty avail themselves of this privilege every Sunday. Davidge G. Ridgely has never, to my knowledge, attended divine service at the Asylum. He was allowed to suit himself in the choice of a church outside the grounds until his conduct rendered it necessary to prohibit his so doing. Since that time he has only been coerced to be present in the chapel *during* [Sunday] *muster*, after which he was at liberty to go wherever he pleased within the limits of the Asylum.

All this came to its denouement in May and June 1853, initiated by what Lieutenant Louis Sartori described as an insolent and disrespectful face-off over the clothing allowance credits available to Ridgely when he attempted to get replacement garments for similar articles that he said he had lost. According to Ridgely's story, he was heading for Philadelphia's waterfront on a month's leave of absence, with his clothing in a bag, when he ran into a one-eyed former Marine named James Jester, a man who shared Ridgely's fondness for ardent spirits, noisy behavior, and unauthorized absences. He had been terminally dismissed from the Asylum a few days earlier. Jester told Ridgely that he had had eaten nothing since the previous morning. Together they went to what Ridgely described as John Radford's "eating house" (at 11th and South Streets) but which the Philadelphia city directory of the time calls a tavern. There Ridgely purchased dinner for the two of them. He then deposited the bag of possessions that he was carrying with Radford, perhaps as security for a loan of cash. Radford assured Ridgely that the bag would be kept until he returned for it. How

Ridgely spent the next seven days he conveniently omitted from his narrative. When he came back to Radford's a week later to claim the bag, he learned that Jester had managed to finagle it from Radford, egged on—according to Ridgely—by Ridgely-disliking Asylum beneficiaries who asserted that they could, in some mysterious manner, get Jester readmitted through this theft. The foul deed, again according to Ridgely, left him without his clothes and unable to continue on his leave. Enlisting the aid of a police officer, and armed with a warrant for Jester's arrest, Ridgely and the policeman spent the morning trying to find Jester, but without success—most likely because Jester had already absconded from Philadelphia. When Ridgely returned to the Asylum later that day asking to be readmitted, Commander Sterrett and Commodore Geisinger declined to accept Ridgely's tale, in spite of a Ridgely-flourished warrant for Jester's arrest. They preferred to assume that Ridgely had sold or pawned his government-supplied clothing to purchase alcohol.

To dramatize his anger at Lieutenant Sartori, who told Ridgely that he was not yet eligible for another clothing issue, the latter refused to look at the lieutenant or speak to him as they passed in the hallways or on the grounds. When Sartori asked Ridgely to offer the customary salute as they encountered each other, Ridgely shouted in a loud and belligerent manner, "You will never be saluted by me!" All this, and much more, was reported to Commodore Geisinger by Sartori, with the lieutenant observing that Ridgely was the only beneficiary who had ever been disrespectful to him and that, "as far as I can learn not one of the beneficiaries will associate with him in any manner whatever."

After two years of trying to cooperate with Joseph Smith's prescription for redeeming Ridgely, Commodore Geisinger's patience was at its end. He had been treating Ridgely with leniency, "knowing his inability to take care of himself on account of his unfortunate temperament and habits (never being able to go outside of the grounds without getting drunk) and believing him to be partially deranged." Geisinger's verdict of partial insanity was seconded by Surgeon James McClelland, who said that Ridgely was "hardly responsible for his actions." Geisinger raised the possibility of transferring Ridgely to the Norfolk Naval Hospital, which had the Navy's facilities for caring for the insane and to which other mentally ill beneficiaries had been sent. Commodore Smith and Secretary of the Navy James C. Dobbin rejected this option, perhaps influenced by Geisinger's prediction that Ridgely would soon find his way to the Philadelphia alms house, "where he has been before and which is a much more suitable place for him than the Asylum." On 16 June 1853 Secretary Dobbin ordered Davidge Ridgely's final dismissal from the United States Naval Asylum.

Fulfilling Geisinger's prediction, on 6 August 1853 Ridgely showed up at Blockley and was admitted to the alms house section for nineteen days. Around this time he made his way back to the Asylum to plead with Commodore Geisinger to readmit him. Nothing doing, said Geisinger: Ridgely would have to apply to Commodore Smith at the Bureau of Yards and Docks. This Ridgely did in early October, writing from the Baltimore poorhouse. By now even Joseph Smith's fabled patience with old sailors was exhausted. Ridgely's request was ignored and filed away. Some time thereafter Ridgely wandered back to Philadelphia where, on 23 March 1854, he was admitted to Blockley's medical ward suffering from the effects of a "debauch." After drying out for five days in the medical ward, Ridgely was moved to the alms house section and from there discharged to the streets on 19 April.

Between 23 March 1854 and 14 February 1861 Blockley was Davidge Ridgely's primary residence, as far as any surviving record shows. He was admitted to Blockley 13 times during that period; the shortest stay was 8 days and his two longest 197 and 255 days. Of the 2,521 days between 23 March 1854 and 14 February 1861 Ridgely spent 965 of them—38 percent of that period—within Blockley's walls. Typically he lived in the alms house section, but on three occasions he was admitted for medical treatment—once for the results of a debauch, another time for dysentery, and still another for a fracture, presumably the result of a fall while drunk. Beginning with his admission on 17 July 1854, Ridgely ceased to claim that he was a native and resident of Philadelphia, but asserted that he had been born in, and was a resident of, Wales. Because there is no question that he was born in Anne Arundel County, Maryland, the reason for this switch is a Davidge Ridgely mystery. Perhaps he feared that, should the Philadelphia welfare authorities discover he was really a Marylander, they would ship him back to his home state. How did Ridgely survive during the 1,556 days he was not at Blockley? Another mystery. Perhaps he lived rough on the Philadelphia waterfront or along the Schuylkill. Possibly he worked odd jobs to pick up money for food and alcohol. All that is known for certain is that he left Blockley for the last time on 14 February 1861 and never returned.

If that had been the last record of Davidge Ridgely, one might imagine him drunk and dying, possibly unidentified, on the Philadelphia waterfront or somewhere on the road to Maryland during the late winter of 1861. But, no, not so. On 20 August 1862 the Baltimore *Sun* reported that "Yesterday afternoon an aged man named Davidge G. Ridgely was brought to the city from Williamsport [Maryland], on the Potomac, on the charge of refusing to take the oath" of allegiance to the Union that was being administered by the authorities during what was essentially a military occupation of the Confederacy-leaning Maryland. After a brief incarceration at Fort McHenry, Ridgely was transferred with other civilian detainees to Fort Delaware (in the state of the same name) on 25 August. And there, at Fort Delaware, the trail of Davidge Ridgely's life turns cold. Was he really a pro-secession Marylander? Or was this just stubborn, contrarian Davidge Ridgely refusing to take the oath because his years of service in the Navy proved his loyalty? Those questions are never likely to be answered. Records of prisoners held at Fort Delaware are spotty during the earlier years of its use as a prison. Perhaps Ridgely died there.[6] More likely he was soon released because of his age—at sixty-eight, Davidge Ridgely was not much of a threat to the Union, if still capable of being a thorn in the flesh to the Fort Delaware authorities—and disappears from history's record.

With the story of Davidge Ridgely, *Ungentle Goodnights* comes up against a wall rarely penetrated in the writing of nineteenth-century naval enlisted history. Ridgely's life is one of the most extensively documented, both in his own words and those of others, of any Naval Asylum beneficiary. But the historian cannot get inside Ridgely's head, cannot see his life through his eyes. One cannot know the unrecorded life experiences that could explain why Davidge Ridgely behaved as he did. Even looked at from the outside, unanswered questions remain: Was Ridgely a sad and unfortunate man unfairly picked on by cruel fellow beneficiaries? Or was he an assertive and annoying individual, somewhat deranged but of self-serving confidence, who quickly wore out his welcome with those around him? Enlisted history must be satisfied with what it can learn from the superficial half of Davidge Ridgely's life story.

SIX

Deserving Old Men, Once Young

D r. Shippen hurried on, in his lecture about the Naval Asylum, to clarify his "curious characters" comment by adding that "hundreds of old men, who have deserved well of their country, have here passed their declining years in tranquility and comfort." Whether these two—the curious characters and the deserving old men—were mutually exclusive categories remains to be decided by readers of *Ungentle Goodnights*. But a means exists that can help to draw a collective portrait of the institution's now elderly and disabled residents, who had once been young, active, able-bodied men.

That is an unpublished manuscript volume with the title "Biography of Beneficiaries United States Naval Asylum Philadelphia." The book itself is a minor mystery. Anything that can be learned about its creation must be inferred from evidence within the volume. "Biography of Beneficiaries" was discovered among the papers of George W. Storer, governor of the Naval Asylum from 6 July 1854 to 1 September 1857. The volume is entirely written in one unidentified hand. Within its covers are the life stories—some all too brief, others extended autobiographical statements—of 172 of the 432 men who entered the Asylum as beneficiaries before September 1857. The project may or may not have been Storer's idea, but it must have been created with his support and encouragement. Biographies of beneficiaries who were dead by the time the volume was compiled were collected from a now-missing volume, maintained under the governorship of James Biddle, that recorded copies of applications for admission. Living beneficiaries who appear in "Biography of Beneficiaries" may, in some cases, have written out the stories of their lives themselves, but it is more likely that they narrated them orally to junior officers attached to the Asylum, who wrote them down. The sketches, which are typically written in the third person, occasionally lapse into the telltale first person: "I then joined . . ." Of the junior officers who may have participated in the project, only Lieutenant (later Commander) Henry K. Thatcher, who was attached to the Asylum from 23 September 1854 until 3 March 1857, can be positively identified; one of the sketches notes that it was dictated to him. All of the biographies follow a uniform format, leading this historian to surmise that the rough notes of the interviews were rewritten by a single person. As for when the life stories of the then-living beneficiaries were taken down, only two of the sketches are dated—one in January and the other in June of 1855—although new biographies continued to be added until within a few days of the termination of Storer's governorship.

No claim is here made that the 40 percent of the pre-September 1857 beneficiaries whose life stories are recorded in "Biography of Beneficiaries" is a valid random sample of the whole, but the volume preserves vital data about the lives of nineteenth-century sailors and Marines that would otherwise be unknown. Imperfect or not, it is the best source available. With some exceptions, the Navy's official records, whether applications for admission to the Asylum or applications for pensions, record only the man's service career. The "Biography of Beneficiaries" sketches begin with birth and typically record pre-service lives at sea or ashore. Lacking "Biography of Beneficiaries," only a tiny portion of this information would be known; no useful generalizations about pre-service lives could be drawn. Life stories recorded in the volume focus the greater part of their narratives on active-duty careers in the Marine Corps and the Navy; these autobiographies are drawn upon and quoted as sources throughout *Ungentle Goodnights*. The present chapter will focus on what can be known collectively about the pre-enlistment lives of men who entered the U.S. Navy and Marine Corps. It will also follow some representative men through their subsequent service careers and their residences at the Naval Asylum. This will involve, at places, a moderately strong dose of numbers, because the statistics are essential to drawing an accurate profile of the Asylum's beneficiaries. However, it should not be assumed that the numbers offered here are chiseled in stone. They are, of necessity, a bit soft and more indicative than authoritative; the sketches vary in length, in quality, and in the sources on which they were based—including, in some instances, the testimonies of old men with admittedly failing memories.

Of the 172 men whose lives are recorded in the "Biography of Beneficiaries" volume, 128 had served in the Navy and 52 in the Marine Corps. But wait: adding 128 and 52 gives a total of 180—not 172. That is because eight of the men had experience in both services. This may come as a surprise, given the alleged adversarial relationship between the two branches—a hoary tradition derived from the Marines' supposed role in maintaining order on shipboard. That perception may stem from the situation in the British navy, where many sailors had been forcibly pressed into service and the institution was plagued by occasional mutinies, large and small. In the U.S. Navy, however, all sailors served voluntarily, and there was less need for the Marines to exercise a controlling role vis-à-vis the sailors, although the latter certainly respected the Marines' traditional duties as sentries on board ship and at navy yards. Thus far speculation. What can be said with certainty is this: there is no evidence that naval beneficiaries saw themselves as in any way distinct from Marine beneficiaries at the Asylum. They lived together; they ate together; they slipped away to drink together; and they conspired together to circumvent the officers when desirable. But, because sailors and Marines had followed different career paths to reach the Asylum, each group will here be analyzed separately, when appropriate. The eight men who had been in both services will be counted twice—once with each group.

There is one topic on which the "Biography of Beneficiaries" volume is not much help. That is in establishing an accurate age profile of the beneficiaries. Beneficiary age is marshy historical ground. There is the underlying problem mentioned elsewhere. Most sailors (and, to a lesser extent, Marines) consistently reported widely varying ages to recording officials. It was a convenient and self-serving practice. A sailor in his forties or fifties would claim to be younger than he actually was to insure being accepted at the recruiting rendezvous. When that same sailor wanted to be admitted to the Naval Asylum or gain a pension, it might be to his advantage, would it not, to claim to be a few years older than he thought he was? *He thought he was* are key qualifying words here, because, after years of reporting convenient ages, the sailor may not have known his real age. Then, too, this was an era when knowing and reporting one's date of birth accurately was less of an expectation than it would become in another century. "I was born in the north of Ireland," Marine John Carr told the officer who took down his life story, "but I do not know in what year." When a beneficiary told his interviewer "I am fifty years of age," that was not much more helpful, because only two of the 172 biographies are dated as to the year when they were recorded.

Thirty-nine of the 172 beneficiaries did report either a date or a year of birth. How reliable are these? The case of Signal Quartermaster Francis R. Swain makes the historian cautious. Swain was well-educated and had made numerous merchant voyages in the capacity of chief mate. He assured Lieutenant Thatcher, who took down his story, that he had been born in Newburyport in 1802. Swain got the town right, but Newburyport's demographic records reveal that he was actually born on 7 June 1806. Cautions noted, the recorded birth years are sufficiently accurate to permit a speculation. Twenty-nine of the 39 beneficiaries reported being born between 1784 and 1801. This means that they would have spent their formative childhood and early adult years in a time in which world-wide conflict—the quarter-century of the wars of the French Revolution and the Napoleonic era—was the norm. Those wars affected each of them in different ways and degrees, but they surely shaped the world view of men who grew up during them. If this proportion is valid for the larger group of pre-1866 beneficiaries at the Naval Asylum, they would have shared certain—if perhaps unconscious—attitudes and values just as surely as did Americans who were young in the 1940s and the 1950s. One may not wish to push this speculation too far or too hard, but it is worth bearing in mind when exploring the lives and the mindsets of the Asylum's beneficiaries.

By moving on to birthplaces of the 172 men sketched in "Biography of Beneficiaries," the historian can escape the quicksands of speculation for the safety of firmer statistical ground. Whatever lies they may have told recruiters about asserted birth in the United States, by the time they reached the Asylum, the foreign-born Marines and sailors had typically served the government for two or more decades. They were old and often were disabled; and they knew that there was absolutely no likelihood that they would be expelled from the Asylum because they had lied to the recruiters and said they were American-born. When questioned for "Biography of Beneficiaries" they told the truth. As the historian analyzes this place-of-birth data some strong patterns leap out from the tally sheet.

Looking first at the Navy men, one discovers that foreign-born sailors were one-third (35.2 percent) of the sailor-beneficiaries whose lives are recorded in "Biography of Beneficiaries"; two-thirds (64.8 percent) of them had been born within the United States. Among the eighty-three native-born sailors, two-thirds of them (65.1 percent) came from just four states—New York, New Jersey, Pennsylvania, and Maryland—plus the District of Columbia. New England, traditionally seen as a strong seafaring region, was the place of birth of one-quarter (24.1 percent) of the sailor-beneficiaries, while the southern states from Virginia to Louisiana were the origin of fewer than one sailor-beneficiary in ten (8.4 percent). (The remaining men needed to make these numbers add to 100 percent were an American citizen born at sea in a merchant vessel and a sailor who said he was born on the River Raisin in Michigan.) One caveat needs to be noted immediately: twenty-four of the eighty-three sailors (28.9 percent) reported birth in the city of Philadelphia or the state of Pennsylvania. This raises the possibility, for which there is scattered supporting evidence, that elderly Pennsylvania-born sailors sought out the Naval Asylum in order to be close to kin. Even allowing for that, these numbers confirm what has already been discovered with respect to the pre-1816 officer corps, the personnel of the Navy were overwhelmingly and disproportionately drawn from the five Middle Atlantic states—New York, New Jersey, Pennsylvania, Delaware, and Maryland.[1]

Geographical origins of forty-five foreign-born sailors are also heavily biased. Among them, twenty-nine (two-thirds or 64.4 percent) came from the British Isles: Ireland (sixteen), England (ten) and Scotland (three). A little over a quarter of the sailors of foreign origin (twelve or 26.7 percent) were born in countries or regions bordering on the North Sea or the Baltic—Holland, Belgium, Norway, Denmark, Sweden, Germany, and Poland. Men from France, Italy, and Nova Scotia account for the tiny balance (four men or 8.9 percent) to make up the whole forty-five foreign-born. When pre–Civil War naval officers speak disparagingly about "foreigners" in the Navy, it probably conjures up, in the minds of those uninformed about the reality, images of ships manned with Africans, Chinese, or Pacific Islanders. In fact, the "foreigners" were ethnically indistinguishable in their origins from the so-called native-born Caucasian American population.

. . . AND A FEW MARINES

The profile of the origins of the fifty-two Marine-beneficiaries is strikingly similar to the Navy men—with one soon-to-be-noted exception. Two-thirds (65.4 percent) of the Marines in the "Biography of Beneficiaries" volume reported birth in the United States; one-third (34.6 percent) in foreign lands. Among the thirty-four U.S.-born Marines, their geographical origins closely parallel those of the sailors: Slightly more than two-thirds (70.6 percent) reported birthplaces in the Middle Atlantic region from New York to the District of Columbia; one man in five (20.6 percent) was from New England; and a mere two men reported birth in the South— one from Georgia and another from Louisiana. The same red flag about regional family ties and residence at the Naval Asylum that was hoisted with respect to the sailors applies also to the Marines: eight of the thirty-four said they had been born in Pennsylvania. It is when one turns to the countries of origin of the eighteen foreign-born Marines that a marked difference appears between the sailor-beneficiaries and their Marine counterparts. Twelve— two-thirds of them—were from Ireland; the remaining six from a scattershot of places with no particular pattern to be discerned: England, one; Poland, two; Switzerland, one; Trieste, one; and Madeira, one. But, of course, they are all Europeans, even the man from Madeira.

There is one other facet to be explored about the fifty-two Marines, although in this case the data do not come exclusively from the "Biography of Beneficiaries." The Marine Corps was interested in knowing the trade or occupation in which its recruits had been trained as apprentices or had followed as adults, and it recorded this information on forty-seven of the fifty-two men. For many of the men, there is no discernable pattern in the occupations for which they had been trained or in which they had worked before joining the Corps. Thirty-six listed skills or experience ranging from baker to tobacconist, with barber, cabinetmaker, carpenter, clerk, coach maker, cooper, cotton spinner, painter, shoemaker, and others in between. The record is silent as to why they rejected these occupations and chose to seek a different life in the Marine Corps. Dislike of the work? Failure at the trade? Boredom? There must be many different life stories, now lost to history, behind the one-word occupational labels. George Rogers, from Cumberland County, Maine, who enlisted when he was thirty years old, told the person who interviewed him for "Biography of Beneficiaries": "The first of my manhood was spent in attending horses, driving stages, etc." In the Marine recruiting record this work experience is reduced to a single word: "Laborer."

Two former occupations were reported by larger numbers of Marines. The five men clumped in each category stand out from the otherwise scattershot list of single occupations. Those two occupations are *farmer* and *leather tanner*. More future Marines had fled these jobs than any others, and the reasons are not hard to surmise. Stories of young men who escaped the boring drudgery of the farm for lives that promised bigger rewards or greater adventure are a hardy perennial of United States history. This abandoned occupation should cause no surprise. As for young men apprenticed to the trade of leather tanner—hard physical work carried on while breathing the noxious odors of human urine, animal dung, and decaying flesh—it is hardly surprising that the Marine Corps offered a tempting escape.

But by far the largest group of enlistees in the Marine Corps— a group that includes some of the men trained or apprenticed to the trades or occupations cited above—were the eighteen men who reported previous military service. Ten of the eighteen were foreign-born; eight were natives of the United States. Three of the ten came to the United States and enlisted directly in the Marine Corps. Valentine Wilhelm was born in Switzerland, probably in the mid to late 1770s. After three years' service as a Swiss soldier, Wilhelm enlisted in the British army, serving for thirteen years in that force. With the end of the Napoleonic Wars and the consequent reduction in the need for professional soldiers in Europe, Wilhelm—now a man approaching forty years of age and a lifelong bachelor with no ties to his homeland—made his way to the United States. He enlisted in the Marine Corps at Sackets Harbor on 12 March 1817 and thereby began a career of eighteen years in the U.S. service. Wilhelm shaved a few years off his age for the recruiter, told him honestly that his only trade or occupation was that of soldier, and falsely asserted that he had been born in Bedford, Pennsylvania—perhaps because he had relatives already settled in that area, where the Wilhelm name can be found in the federal censuses. Valentine Wilhelm spent most of his United States career in Marine detachments at various navy yards, but he also did two tours of duty at sea, one in the frigate *Brandywine* and the other in the schooner *Shark*. In August 1835, at the expiration of his fourth enlistment, Marine Corps Commandant Archibald Henderson found Wilhelm "too old and infirm to do military duty"—his right foot had been frozen while he was on post at the New York (Brooklyn) Navy Yard, causing three of his toes to be amputated—and secured him a place at the Naval Asylum. He died there five years later.

The more common pattern for the immigrants—men both with and without European military experience—was to come to the United States, enlist in the Army, serve in that force for a number of years, then transfer to the Marine Corps. There were ten such individuals. Each had his own unique history, as did Hugh Semple, who was born in County Tyrone, Ireland, in the mid-1780s and who emigrated to the United States in 1805, when he must have been about twenty years old. What happened next in Semple's life is unknown, though there is evidence that he may have lived in Newburg, New York. Somewhere along the way he learned music; almost the whole of his military career was as a drummer. Hugh Semple liked to keep precise and accurate records of his life. He knew the exact day of his arrival in the United States—14 November—and that on 23 May 1819 he enlisted in the U.S. Army for five years as drummer, serving most of his time at posts on the western frontier. Following Semple's Army discharge—the one life-date he failed to record—there is an eleven-year gap until he enlisted in the Navy on 10 June 1834 as drummer for the frigate *Hudson*, receiving ship at the New York (Brooklyn) Navy Yard. Semple's service in *Hudson* was relatively brief: he was discharged on 14 November 1835, but that early release may have been to allow him to enlist in the Marine Corps on the twentieth of the same month. He served in the Corps continuously until 18 December 1848, when he was discharged as "worthless," not much of a commendation for a man who had devoted eighteen years of his life to the service of his adopted country. Like many a discharged veteran of later days, Hugh Semple fell upon hard times. May 1849 found him in the Kings County alms house at Flatbush, Long Island. The county superintendent of the poor, J. C. Rhodes, eager to have one less pauper to support on his budget, appealed to Secretary of the Navy William Ballard Preston to learn if Semple was entitled to admission to the Naval Asylum. He was, no doubt to the relief of Superintendent Rhodes. On his admission to the Asylum, 4 July 1849, Hugh Semple was immediately dispatched to the medical wing with chronic dysentery that required eighty-five days of hospitalization to get under control. He lived at the Asylum for ten and a half years, drinking to excess fairly regularly and occasionally having to dry out for several days in the hospital. Death came for him on 20 December 1859.

Among the eight Marines born in the United States who entered the Corps after earlier Army service, Charles Richard Thompson left the most detailed life record, although one not without its ambiguities. Thompson usually stated that he had been born in Charlotte, Vermont, but he sometimes asserted Essex, New York—directly west of Charlotte, but on the other side of Lake Champlain—as his place of birth. Perhaps his family moved back and forth across the lake, and he was not really sure on which side he had come into the world. (Although there are several Thompsons listed in the federal censuses of the period, none of them was of sufficiently prominent status to merit mention in the voluminous nineteenth-century history of Essex County, New York, with its laudatory life-sketches of local worthies, so one cannot be certain of the young boy's parents.) Thompson was equally ambiguous about his age. In each of his first four Marine Corps enlistments he said he had been born in 1801; but, as the years went forward from there, his asserted birth date receded farther and farther into the 1790s until, just three days before his death, he claimed to have been born around 1792.

When Thompson sat down with the compilers of the "Biography of Beneficiaries" volume to tell his life story, he began it in August 1814, when he joined the privateer schooner *Amelia*, Captain Alexander Adams, armed with six guns, at New York. According to Thompson, *Amelia* fell in with an unescorted group of British merchantmen from Cork, Ireland, capturing five prizes, of which two were burned. *Amelia* then steered toward the Hebrides, encountered a letter-of-marque from Greenock, Scotland, and captured her after an action of fifty-four minutes. Thompson was assigned as one of the prize crew, which had the good fortune to get its prize safely into New York. It was a fine old war story, but Thompson was telling it forty years after the fact. How accurate was his memory? The reality is that Thompson probably still had his journal or diary

of the voyage and was working from that; all the details he provided are confirmed by a contemporary newspaper account derived
from *Amelia*'s log.[2] According to the newspaper story, *Amelia* had
sailed from New York on 1 August 1814, cleared Sandy Hook on
8 August, took her five prizes between 26 and 31 August, and on
4 September captured, "after a long chase and action of 40 minutes,"
the British ship *Neptune*, bound from Greenock to Newfound-
land. *Neptune* was armed with eight guns, two more than *Amelia*
carried, but was too shorthanded in crew to use her superior fire-
power to advantage.

After war's end in 1815 Thompson continued to follow the sea
for a while, making a voyage to Nantes in a merchant ship commanded by Lieutenant John D. Sloat, then on leave from his career
as an officer in the U.S. Navy. Here follows a gap in Thompson's
life story until 23 November 1822, when he enlisted in the U.S.
Army as a private—described by the recruiter as sixty-seven inches
tall, with brown hair, blue eyes, and light complexion. Thompson
stated his previous occupation to have been that of farmer. This last
bit of data suggests that he may have returned to the Lake Champlain region after his sea voyages, tried to settle down in rural life,
then abandoned it for a military one. Thompson served two five-year
enlistments, separated by a break of eleven months when he apparently visited the home country again. During the first enlistment he
served in the Second Regiment of Artillery, then in the Fourth Regiment of Artillery following his reenlistment. Save for brief inland
duty during the Black Hawk War of 1832, Thompson was stationed
in forts on the eastern seaboard throughout both enlistments. At the
expiration of his second enlistment, 14 October 1833, Thompson—
now described as a man with gray eyes, black hair, and dark complexion—made his way to Philadelphia and enlisted, one week to the
day after his Army discharge, in the Marine Corps. He served in the
Corps continuously until 5 December 1855, rising to the rank of
sergeant, a clear indication of superior abilities. At the Naval Asylum,
which he entered the day after his final discharge from the USMC,
Charles Thompson was regarded as a model beneficiary, assigned
to the responsible role of watchman, and with only one instance of
off-grounds intoxication noted in the institution's log. An apparently
healthy, if aging, man, Thompson was hospitalized only once during his years at the Asylum. On 22 September 1863 he was admitted with what was diagnosed as chronic diarrhea. Three days later
he was dead.

IT'S A SAILOR'S LIFE FOR ME

Charles Thompson's amphibious career brings analysis of the narratives in "Biography of Beneficiaries United States Naval Asylum Philadelphia" back to the 128 men who had served as naval ratings and the paths they followed to reach the U.S. Navy. Here the big story is the role of the merchant service as the spawning ground from which the Navy recruited its sailors. At least 84 of the 128 reported service in merchant ships before their first enlistment in the Navy. The 84 include a few men who did not formally report merchant service to the compilers of "Biography of Beneficiaries," but whose first enlistment in the Navy was at the rate of *seaman*, absolute evidence of significant working experience at sea. However, it should not be assumed that the other 44 beneficiaries had no merchant service experience before joining the Navy. The compilers of "Biography of Beneficiaries" clearly sought information about their subjects' merchant service, but they did not always get it. In the case of deceased beneficiaries whom they could not interview, the compilers had to depend on old paper records that did not typically report merchant service. Some living sailors were, for whatever reasons, not forthcoming about their merchant service, even though such service can be inferred (as mentioned above) from the ratings at which they joined the Navy. Neither is it always possible to tell among the sailors who reported foreign birth, whether the merchant service they asserted occurred in the country of birth, in the United States merchant marine, or in both. Only in the cases of two beneficiaries, one of whom entered the Navy as a *landsman* and the other as a *boy*, can it be said with some assurance that they had no significant merchant service at sea before enlisting in the Navy. In the end, all that *Ungentle Goodnights* can assert with certainty is that, among the 128 naval-service beneficiaries, some unknown number greater than 83 had merchant service experience before turning to the Navy as a career.

Behind the simple statement, "I was in the merchant service about fifteen years," which was all the "Biography of Beneficiaries" compilers got out of Thomas J. Collins and many narratives of similar brevity, there must have been now-lost stories unique to each beneficiary. Fortunately for history, a few veterans were more loquacious. One of them was Charles Lindsay—or Charles Lindsey (there is good authority for either spelling of his family name). He was born in Philadelphia in 1799, according to the oral statement he made to the compilers of the "Biography of Beneficiaries" volume, but—in typical sailor fashion—at other times in his life he asserted ages that would have placed his birth somewhere between 1802 and 1805. "As soon as I found I could do something towards my own support," presumably in his early teenage years, "I got employment in an oyster boat and remained there until 1819." Well, with one interruption, that is. Around 1814, with the War of 1812 in progress, Lindsay decided to run off from the oyster boat to which he was apprenticed, and enlisted for the frigate *Guerriere*, recently launched and fitting for sea at Philadelphia. The owner of the oyster boat quickly discovered Lindsay's whereabouts, and reclaimed his absconding apprentice, thus prematurely ending Lindsay's first attempt at a naval career. Lindsay's story cannot be verified from *Guerriere*'s rolls, presumably because he took the precaution of enlisting under a false name in the vain hope of escaping detection, but there is no reason to doubt the story's essential truthfulness.

When his oyster-boat apprenticeship ended at age twenty, Lindsay resumed his search for a blue-water career, entering on board a whaler hailing from Newport, Rhode Island. He sailed in various merchant vessels until 1831, when a fortuitous opportunity to rejoin the Navy offered itself. Lindsay was, for unknown reasons, on the beach at Gibraltar when he seized the opportunity to return to the United States by enlisting on 11 March as an ordinary seaman in the sloop-of-war *Fairfield*, Commander Foxhall A. Parker. That first naval experience was brief. Lindsay was discharged at Norfolk on 21 May 1831 when *Fairfield* paid off at the end of the cruise. But Lindsay must have found that the Navy suited him well. Thereafter—except for shore leaves between voyages and one longer period "in consequence of family troubles," Lindsay's naval service was continuous until the mid-1850s. The "family troubles" may have been the illness and death of Lindsay's wife, although all that is currently known about his marriage is that he was a widower in later life. It was a typical lower-deck career—three-year cruises to the Brazil station (three times), to the Mediterranean (twice), and to the Pacific Ocean (twice), including participation in Commodore Matthew C. Perry's 1853–54 expedition to Japan. For Lindsay his naval career's highlight, when he came to recount its history, was the 1846–48 war with Mexico, with exciting detached service from the brig *Porpoise* up Mexico's coastal rivers in ships' boats.

A "severe hurt," not otherwise explained in the discovered records of his life, ended Charles Lindsay's naval service in 1855; he was admitted to the Naval Asylum on 22 September of that year.

The Asylum's monthly record of beneficiary behavior uniformly rated him as "very good" or "good" during his first two decades of residence. Consequently, it is no surprise that he was employed as outdoor watchman and gatekeeper for many years. Eventually, however, the Asylum's alcohol-laden underlife began to pull him into its orbit. In November 1869 Lindsay was hospitalized for three days with what was diagnosed as delirium tremens, although his behavior continued to be rated as "very good." May 1874 saw him disrated as gatekeeper for drunkenness; and a fall on the ice on 27 December 1880 "after a debauch" brought Lindsay to the hospital with a contused wound of the scalp about an inch and a half long that kept the elderly man under treatment there for a week.

The last day of Lindsay's life is the best recorded of them all. About 4 in the afternoon on 8 January 1887 the eighty-four-year-old beneficiary (as he then reported his age to be) was apparently crossing Gray's Ferry Road in a state of intoxication when he was knocked down and run over by an ice wagon, the driver of which made his escape without identifying himself or accepting any responsibility. Lindsay was carried on a stretcher into the naval hospital. There he was given, recorded Assistant Surgeon Charles P. Henry, "as thorough an examination as the stress of circumstances permitted. He was extremely restless and intractable, rolling and striking out with his injured arms and muttering oaths and complaints." That challenging examination revealed that Lindsay had sustained comminuted fractures—in which the bone is splintered or crushed into many pieces—of the left humerus and the right radius, a fracture of the nasal bone, and a deep surface wound to the nose about one and a half inches in length. The soft tissues of the orbital region of Lindsay's skull showed signs of contusion. No other evidence of injuries was discovered, reported Dr. Henry, "at this unavoidably hasty and imperfect examination. So extreme was his restlessness and so great the displacement of the humeral fragments that the serious accident of conversion to compound fracture was imminent." Lindsay was sedated with a quarter gram of morphine, administered by hypodermic, and the fractured arms were then placed in splints. "Copious draughts of strong coffee sobered up the patient a little, but he would permit no examination of the arms." Further sedation was urgent to permit the better splinting and bandaging of Lindsay's arms, so he was given hyoscine. This put him to sleep and the splints and bandages were reworked and improved. At 10:30 that night he was observed to be sleeping quietly.

The next morning, 9 January, Lindsay was able to eat a small amount of breakfast at 7 a.m., but an hour later he was observed to be "drowsy and stupid, but can be made to answer questions, although incoherently." His pulse was taken: "112, full and regular," and the fractured arms showed no signs of swelling. Nevertheless, Lindsay appeared to be sinking toward death all through the morning and early afternoon; he died at 3:05 p.m. No autopsy was carried out, and no specific cause of death was determined. Perhaps he had undetected internal injuries or brain damage—the newspaper report of the accident said that his skull had been fractured—and Assistant Surgeon Henry's report to his superior seems somewhat defensive and self-justifying in tone. He may have thought to himself that Lindsay was an old man in his eighties given to alcohol abuse; that death would come soon, one way or another; and that further documentation was unnecessary.

In spite of the pervasive career pattern of merchant service first, then Navy among these eighty-four beneficiaries, there were exceptions and other paths. Nine beneficiaries (who are not counted among the eighty-four) told the compilers of "Biography of Beneficiaries" that their first experience at sea was a cruise in a naval ship. Eight others (included in the eighty-four) told of making merchant voyages between naval enlistments, before deciding to complete their sea careers in the Navy. This number probably under-reports the lived reality.

Six of the eighty-four beneficiaries who reported merchant service before joining the Navy also mentioned privateer or letter-of-marque service during the War of 1812. How financially rewarding they found their ventures in for-profit warfare they did not say. Eight men among the eighty-four beneficiaries who reported merchant service before enlisting in the U.S. Navy told of being pressed into Britain's Royal Navy. Four of them were foreign-born and had experienced impressment while sailing in British merchant vessels. The other four were U.S. citizens who were taken from American merchantmen.

Robert Morris, one of the relatively few beneficiaries from the southern states, experienced both impressment into the Royal Navy and the rewards and frustrations of privateering life. For much of what follows, the historian has only Morris' autobiographical narrative, as recorded in the "Biography of Beneficiaries" volume, as a source; but when Morris' memories can be checked against other records, his recollections appear to be sufficiently accurate. He was born in 1790 in Wilmington, North Carolina. As a young boy Robert worked on a farm herding cattle until 1802, when—no surprise, given the boring nature of that work—he ran away and shipped on board a vessel bound for Liverpool. Soon after his arrival in England, young Robert apprenticed himself to a collier for five years. In 1807, just as his apprenticeship was about to expire, he was pressed on board the Royal Navy's bomb ship *Fury* to participate in Admiral James Gambier's August–September attack on Copenhagen. On the fleet's return to England, Morris deserted from *Fury* and entered for the transport *Mariner*, which carried troops from Halifax to Martinique and prisoners-of-war from Martinique to England. Discharged at the end of *Mariner's* passage, Morris shipped in a merchantman named *Wanderer*, but was soon pressed by His Majesty's brig *Zephyr*. Once again displaying his desertion skills, Morris escaped from *Zephyr* in the Downs after ten weeks on board and made his way to London where he shipped for a voyage to Australia and back. This was followed by a voyage to China. On returning from China, Morris—according to his own account—served in transports and storeships supporting British forces during the Peninsular War in Spain. He next turns up in Halifax in 1814, though without explaining how he got there. At Halifax he was once again pressed by an unnamed Royal Navy sloop-of-war. Slippery as ever, Morris swam ashore on his third night of impressment, and shipped on board the schooner *Henry* bound for Martinique with a cargo of fish.

By now the War of 1812 was in its third year. On *Henry's* third day out from Halifax (27 July 1814) she was captured by the United States privateer *Saratoga*, Thomas Aderton commanding. Morris revealed himself to Captain Aderton as an American citizen and was signed onto *Saratoga's* crew. On 13 September, when southeast of Madeira, *Saratoga* fell in with the letters-of-marque *Swiftsure* and *James*, engaged, reduced them to "complete wrecks," and captured both. Unfortunately for *Saratoga's* profitability, both prizes were recaptured before they could reach a U.S. port. Continuing her voyage, *Saratoga* captured (1 October) the ship *Ann Dorothy* from Buenos Aires loaded with hides and tallow, the ship *Enterprise* (5 October) from Africa carrying hides and ivory, and the schooner *Mary* (30 October) with a cargo of fish. En route to the United States *Ann Dorothy* was recaptured by the British frigate *Maidstone*, but was subsequently recaptured by the American privateer *David Porter* and brought safely into port; the other two prizes

made it in without incident. *Saratoga* put into Wilmington, North
Carolina, in early November and paid off her crew.[3] More by accident than design, Robert Morris was back at the hometown he had
left twelve years earlier. Whether there were any family members
there to greet the long-absent sailor he does not tell.

Morris worked "along shore," he said, until the Treaty of Ghent
ended the War of 1812, when he returned to the merchant service.
May 1815 found him in New Orleans, where on the twenty-third
of that month he took out a U.S. Seaman's Protection Certificate,
which described him as twenty-four years old, five feet, five inches
tall, with black hair, hazel eyes, and a brown complexion. His most
distinguishing feature, according to the document, was the two middle toes of his right foot, which were joined together. Morris continued in the merchant service until June 1817, when he enlisted in
the Navy for the first time and was drafted to *Franklin*, Commodore Charles Stewart, for a cruise to the Mediterranean. Discharged from *Franklin* on 2 May 1820, Morris—for whatever
reason—had it with the Navy for the moment and went back to
merchant voyaging for the next sixteen years. Apparently none of
this merchant service was sufficiently eventful to merit mention in
his autobiographical statement.

Morris returned to the Navy in 1836 and thereafter served
continuously until November 1851, usually as a quarter-gunner or
gunner's mate. He said that during his last full enlistment, in the
sidewheel steamer *Mississippi*, a block fell from aloft, struck his
shoulder and rendered his arm completely useless. *Mississippi*'s commanding officer, Captain John C. Long, later questioned the falling-
block story, saying that the block merely grazed Morris' arm, but
attributed the problem to an unusually severe case of rheumatism:
"Most seamen advanced in life are more or less affected with this
complaint, which incapacitates them for service." Long recommended Morris for admission to the Naval Asylum, reporting that
in *Mississippi* "he was a very trusty, good man. . . . He set a good
example to the crew by being sober not only on board ship but when
on liberty on shore and always returned promptly at the expiration
of his liberty." Because Morris' naval service did not add up to twenty
years, Commodore Joseph Smith initially balked at admitting him
to the Asylum, but Captain Long came eloquently to Morris' support, and he was eventually admitted on 10 January 1852.

Given Morris' reputation for reliability and sobriety, he was
assigned to the responsible posts of petty officer and gatekeeper at

the Asylum. Unfortunately, his preference for sobriety was beginning to fail him; he was disrated from both jobs for incidents of
drunkenness and insolence. Alcohol abuse did not become a truly
serious problem with Morris for his first few years at the Asylum,
but between 27 September 1858 and 1 October 1861 twenty-three
alcohol-related offenses were recorded against him in the Asylum's
log. His behavior rating in the monthly muster rolls spiraled downward from "very good" (1853), through "once drunk" (1855), "fair"
(1857), "occasionally intemperate" (1859) to "very intemperate"
(1861 to 1865). One cannot know for certain what caused this
progressive descent into confirmed alcoholism, but it is not hard
to imagine that a man whose pre-Asylum life had been filled with
so much activity and adventure must have found the relative idle-
ness of old age a heavy psychological burden, relieved only by drink.
One serious siege of diarrhea that required thirty-seven days of
hospitalization in 1854 aside, Morris' general health apparently
remained good in spite of his heavy drinking until 5 May 1865
when he was admitted to the hospital with an acute case of what
was diagnosed as peritonitis and died the following day.

Perhaps most unexpected among the paths that led to naval
careers were those of the six men who reported service in the U.S.
Army but no sea experience before enlisting in the Navy. Among
these crossovers was Thomas Scantling, born in Pennsylvania around
1785. Thereafter Scantling's life is a blank page until 1 November
1808 when, at approximately twenty-three years of age, he enlisted
in the U.S. Army. It is possible that his Army career was preceded
by some employment at sea, but no evidence of this has been found.
Scantling's Army service got off to an unpromising start when he
was court-martialed on 19 April 1810 for disobedience of orders
and sentenced to receive fifty lashes by way of punishment. According to anti-flogging advocates, this experience should have damaged Scantling's morale, affected his personality negatively, and
made him a poor soldier; but the actual record is one more piece
of evidence that is slowly calling into question this argument for
abolishing corporal punishment. Thereafter Thomas Scantling was
successively promoted to the more responsible ranks of corporal and
sergeant, reenlisted for the duration of the war on the expiration
of his first five-year tour, and fought at the battle of New Orleans
under Andrew Jackson. At the end of the War of 1812 Scantling
was discharged from the Army, 8 April 1815, and disappears from
the historical record until August 1817 when he enlisted for the

ship-of-the-line *Franklin*, Commodore Charles Stewart, in which he made successive cruises to the Mediterranean and the Pacific in the capacity of ordinary seaman. Service in *Franklin* ended in September 1824, after which Scantling enjoyed a period of freedom ashore on his accumulated pay before rejoining the Navy in 1825. Following a period of shore duty at the New York (Brooklyn) Navy Yard, Scantling was detailed on 13 May 1827 to the frigate *Java*, Commodore William M. Crane, bound for the Mediterranean. There he was transferred to the frigate *Constitution* on 16 March 1828, served in her and in the frigates *Constellation* and *United States*, before ending his active naval service with his discharge on 29 December 1834. In those four ships Scantling was still rated no higher than ordinary seaman, a clear indication that he never became a proficient sailor. Scantling asserted that toward the end his service in *United States* he caught a severe cold that resulted in the loss of vision in one eye. His subsequent attempts to reenlist in the Navy were rejected on the grounds that he was unfit for service.

In May 1835 Commodore James Barron, commandant of the Philadelphia Navy Yard, reported to the Navy Department that Scantling "is now reduced to the lowest ebb of poverty and wretchedness—is laying sick in a poor boarding house in this city, the proprietor of which cannot afford to keep him, and of course has become an object of some interest to the community at large, and particularly to the naval officers, who all—with his poor relations— are anxious to see him provided for in the [Philadelphia] Naval Hospital and, if he recovers and requires it, to see him placed in the Naval Asylum." Sharp advocate that he was, Commodore Barron did not fail to mention prominently Scantling's Army service at the battle of New Orleans and "in various other campaigns" under sitting President Andrew Jackson. Scantling's fifteen years in the Navy failed to meet the twenty-year requirement for admission to the Naval Asylum, but his Army service—especially at the now-legendary victory at New Orleans—was apparently taken into consideration; he was admitted to the Naval Asylum on 5 August 1835.

Within sixteen months Scantling had earned the disapproval of then-superintendent Lieutenant James B. Cooper—no difficult task it will be recalled—and was dismissed on 26 November 1836, on the grounds of repeatedly being riotous, drunken, and abusive. It is unknown where Scantling lived or how he supported himself after his expulsion, but about a year later, in October 1837, he traveled to Washington and appealed in person to Secretary of the Navy Mahlon Dickerson for readmission. No luck there; his request was turned down once Dickerson had reviewed the record of Scantling's dismissal. Nothing daunted, in January 1838, Scantling petitioned Congress either to grant him a pension or restore him to the Naval Asylum. The House Committee on Naval Affairs declined to act on Scantling's petition.[4] At this point there is a gap in the paper trail, possibly indicating an oral intervention with the Navy Office by some influential person. However that may have been, Thomas Scantling was readmitted to the Naval Asylum under the more benevolent administration of Commodore James Biddle on 26 December 1838, and died there six months later on 8 July 1839.

Governor Storer's "Biography of Beneficiaries United States Naval Asylum Philadelphia" project does not offer reliable or comprehensive answers to a number of questions that historians would wish to ask. Who were the parents of these 172 beneficiaries? How many of the beneficiaries were or had been married? Why did they choose to go to sea? Why did they join the Navy or the Marine Corps? Why did they prefer the Navy to the merchant service or the Marine Corps to the Army? However imperfect they may be, the life stories recorded in "Biography of Beneficiaries" offer the best available profiles of the many individuals who provided the essential manpower for the pre–Civil War nation's Marine Corps and Navy.

SEVEN

THE FEW, THE FORTUNATE

S cots. Irishmen. Frenchmen. Germans. Poles. Danes. Norwegians. Swedes. These lower-deck sailors might be denigrated by officers of the U.S. Navy as allegedly undesirable "foreigners," but after years of service in the merchant marine and the Navy of the United States, only their accents and their commands of colloquial English would distinguish them from their U.S.-born peers at the Naval Asylum. What they shared was far more of a bond than any differences among them: they were all white men of northern European origins.

But what of men of darker skin pigmentation? Were elderly or disabled sailors of color able to find refuge at the Asylum? Yes, but only a handful. Among the five hundred forty-one men admitted to the Asylum between 1831 and the end of 1865, a mere nine can be identified as persons of color. It is possible that the small number of beneficiaries about whom only the sketchiest life details survive may include some men of color, but these nine are all who have been positively identified as such.

Nine men amount to 1.7 percent of all the beneficiaries—hardly an accurate sample of the demographic realities of the active-duty Navy in the first sixty years of the nineteenth century. During the War of 1812, sailors of color—almost exclusively men of African or mixed-ethnicity descent—amounted to between 9 percent and 10 percent of the Navy's enlisted force, and that percentage may have risen as high as 20 percent on the Great Lakes. Between June 1837 and April 1839, approximately 9 percent of the sailors enlisting at Boston's recruiting rendezvous were men of color. However, by 1843–44 sailors of color passing through the receiving ship *Ohio* at that same port had dropped to between 6 percent and 7 percent of all lower-deck men, and by the summer of 1858 the number of new recruits and reenlistees who were men of color had dropped still further to 5 percent of the total enlistees. These declining numbers reflect the Navy's goal of keeping the proportion of sailors of color in the enlisted force at not more than 5 percent of the Caucasian enlistees as inter-racial tensions mounted in the run-up to the Civil War. However explicitly racist it may have been, achievement of this quota was certainly facilitated by the mounting numbers of white northern Europeans emigrating to the United States between the War of 1812 and the Civil War and their availability as potential recruits for naval service. (For precise numbers and the sources on which these estimates are based see Appendix: Sailors of Color in the Pre–Civil War U.S. Navy.)

No formal policy barring sailors of color from the Naval Asylum has been discovered, nor is there surviving evidence of applicants being turned down because of ethnicity. That said, there was clearly a disinclination for sailors of color to apply for residence at the Asylum, probably from a perception that it was white men's turf where they would not be all that welcome. In the 1870s it was the practice for beneficiaries of color to mess at a separate table, but there is no evidence one way or the other whether this segregation was policy in earlier years. It is almost certainly no coincidence that at least five of the nine beneficiaries of color had served at least part of their naval careers in such capacities as wardroom steward or wardroom cook, captain's cook, or commodore's cook, and one as ship's cook. Such ratings would have brought men of color into familiar daily contact with high-ranking officers who would have known about the Naval Asylum and been in a position to encourage and facilitate applications for admission.

Who were the members of this small and select cadre who made it through the gate on Gray's Ferry Road with permits of admission? As *Ungentle Goodnights* assembles the Asylum's beneficiaries for muster, let two of the nine men of color step forward from the ranks and tell their stories.

JUST ANOTHER SAILOR

"I am so old I have lost the run of the time I was born," Samuel Howard told one of the Asylum's junior officers who took down his autobiographical statement in the mid-1850s. But he did know where he began life—Trap-town, Kent County, Maryland, presumably the small settlement called Trap or Trappe on nineteenth-century maps of the county and long since vanished. Naval Asylum authorities estimated Sam Howard, as he was often known, to have been born anywhere from 1779 to 1787. Unlike many of the other beneficiaries interviewed, Howard offered no story of his life before he joined the Navy at New York in 1812. By then he would have been a man in his late twenties or early thirties with significant seafaring experience. This silence raises at least the suspicion that he may have been a runaway slave and might have changed his name from that by which he was called as a child.

The U.S. Navy that Sam Howard entered in 1812 was a less-segregated force than it would become by the time he died. One sailor in ten was a black man. All enlisted and petty officer ratings were open to sailors of color, although warrants as boatswains or carpenters or sailmakers, let alone commissions as officers, were an absolute impossibility. From New York, Howard—rated as seaman—was sent to Lake Ontario and assigned to the schooner *Pert*. Even as an old man, he recalled the War of 1812 years as ones filled with the most memorable events of his life—the loss of *Pert*'s commanding officer, Sailing Master Robert Arundel, severely wounded by the explosion of a gun, then knocked overboard and drowned in action with the British on 10 November 1812; the captures of York and Fort George; and the seizure of nine Canadian merchantmen as prizes. By July 1814 Howard had been transferred to the frigate *Superior*, but—for some now unknown reason—was only rated as ordinary seaman in the larger ship. Although the wounds to his body cannot be positively traced to battle injuries on the Lakes during the War of 1812, his 1850s interviewer noted that Howard "bears the mark of a bullet, one in his head, one in the right arm, and one on the left side"; an earlier medical record mentions a "wound of arm and loss of eye." In addition to his pay, Howard's War of 1812 service earned him thirteen dollars in prize money.

At war's end Howard was dispatched with a draft of men from *Superior* to bring the frigate *United States* from New London, Connecticut, where she had been blockaded, to Boston; then it was on to Portsmouth, New Hampshire, to sail the frigate *Congress* to Boston. Still rated ordinary seaman, Sam Howard remained in *Congress* when she joined the Mediterranean Squadron later in 1815. He was transferred to *Macedonian*, another ship of the

Mediterranean Squadron, on the first day of January 1816, and discharged from her in mid-July of the same year. Because of the confusing and contradictory records of Samuel Howard's service, it is not possible to follow all the details of his naval career, but April 1821 through July 1828 found him, now restored to seaman's rating, cruising the Mediterranean in *Constitution* under Jacob Jones, Thomas Macdonough, and Daniel Todd Patterson. His last before-the-mast service was in the sloop-of-war *St. Louis*, which he entered in September 1832, once again down-rated to ordinary seaman. In December of that same year, though, Howard was promoted as *St. Louis'* ship's cook, a petty officer billet; it was as cook in various naval vessels that he spent the balance of his naval career. Was he being segregated into a food-service capacity just because he was black? Almost certainly not. By 1832 Howard was a man probably in his fifties and, one can assume, no longer physically fit for the more demanding duties of ordinary seaman or seaman. Equally important, he was a skilled cook and sought out by commanding officers for that reason. Credited by the Navy Department with thirty-five years of service at the end of his final enlistment, Samuel Howard was admitted to the Naval Asylum on 16 May 1845.

If Howard had been well-integrated with his white peers as sailor and ship's cook, at the Naval Asylum his behavior fitted in just as comfortably. He had the same well-established fondness for alcoholic refreshment and delight in contrary-to-the-rules behavior as many of his Caucasian fellow-beneficiaries—traits that led the Asylum's leadership to evaluate his character successively as "bad, but better of late," "intemperate," and "fair." In the ten and a half years between May 1846 and November 1856, the Asylum's log records Howard as being punished on twenty-one occasions, with at least eighteen or nineteen of the offenses alcohol-related: "Drunk and lying out; had to be brought in." "Breaking out through the fence and smuggling in liquor." "Brought in dead drunk." Selling two blue shirts, four pair of cotton socks, and two cotton handkerchiefs—presumably to raise money to purchase alcohol. This may also have been the purpose of "stealing beef and bread from [the] dining room."

Worn out by a life of hard work at sea and hard living ashore, Samuel Howard slowly faded away in the spring and summer of 1858, dying on 27 August with the cause of death given only as "debility." He must have been near or past eighty years of age. The notice of his death in the Asylum's log was as color-blind as his naval record had been: "At 8:15 p.m. Samuel Howard, Beneficiary, departed this life."

THE SAILOR WHO WAS IN LOVE WITH THE SEA

James Forten Dunbar is the Naval Asylum's beneficiary-of-color about whom the most is known. Indeed, he has become a minor celebrity among nineteenth-century African American seafarers. Dunbar was one of the featured mariners in Philadelphia's Independence Seaport Museum's 2009 exhibit and catalog, *Skin & Bones: Tattoos in the Life of the American Sailor*. He was also the subject of a paper at a scholarly conference—a presentation, subsequently published, that uncovered much about the earlier half of Dunbar's life, but substantially missed the second—the Navy—part of his story.[1]

James F. Dunbar, as he usually identified himself, was born in Philadelphia on 1 July 1799, the fourth child to survive to adulthood of William Dunbar, a merchant mariner, and Abigail Forten. William died in 1805 at the seamen's hospital in New York. Fortunately for his family, Abigail's brother, James Forten, was a prosperous Philadelphia sailmaker who was able to provide well for his relatives. In July 1810 James Dunbar, then eleven years old, took out a seaman's protection certificate, in which he was described as a free mulatto, fifty-five inches tall, with black hair and yellow complexion, and having distinctive scars from a dog's bite to his right arm, from smallpox vaccination on his left arm, and from an unrecorded cause on his left thumb. Presumably young James was about to make a voyage as a boy in a coasting vessel, but of this early initiation to his lifelong career as a mariner there is no surviving record; coasting vessels were not required to deposit crew lists with the collector of customs, as did those bound on foreign voyages. During his teenage and young adult years—in addition to unrecorded coasting voyages in which he honed his skills as a sailor—James Dunbar must have spent time apprenticed in his uncle's business, as several of his later naval enlistments were in the capacity of sailmaker's mate or as a member of the sailmaker's crew. He may even have been skilled enough in his trade—assuming he was literate, which is doubtful—to be rated as sailmaker, save for one insurmountable obstacle: as a black man he was automatically barred from that warrant officer's appointment in the Navy.

In April 1819 James Dunbar began a decade of mostly long-voyage service in the merchant marine when he signed on the ship *William Savery* for a seventeen-month voyage to Canton via Liverpool and perhaps other ports as well. After a winter at home in Philadelphia, in April 1821 he again sailed for China, with an intermediate stop at Savannah, Georgia, this time in the ship *Thomas Scattergood*, with the rating of seaman. *Scattergood* returned to Philadelphia in late April 1822; on the thirtieth of that same month James Dunbar married Mary Welsh, with whom he eventually had two children, Abby and James. The short interval between *Scattergood*'s arrival and the marriage suggests that James had already established a relationship with Mary, possibly in the interval between the two China voyages, and that the couple waited until James' substantial earnings from *Scattergood*'s voyage enabled them to marry. That is speculation. What is known is that James' seafaring was, immediately following his marriage, confined to two short voyages (again rated seaman) to Havana in the summer of 1823 in the schooner *George Hand, Jr.* and in the brig *Rachael & Sally*, the latter a Charleston, South Carolina, vessel sailing from Philadelphia. Thereafter, James Dunbar disappears from the crew lists until April 1825. Perhaps he was working in a Philadelphia sail loft. Was he was bored with shoreside life—a recurring strand in his life story—or did he feel the need for better money with the birth of his daughter, Abby, in that year? Whatever the reason, James Dunbar sailed for China in April 1825 in the ship *Dorothea*, returning eleven months later. After a year at home, Dunbar was off on yet another merchant-service voyage to China (April 1827) in the Baltimore-based ship *Woodrop Sims*.

Following *Woodrop Sims*' return to Philadelphia at the end of April 1828, there is another gap in Dunbar's seafaring record.[2] At least part of the immediately following years may have been spent in merchant voyaging, as October 1832 found him on the beach at Valparaiso, Chile, when he was offered the opportunity for a career change by signing on the U.S. frigate *Potomac* as a seaman. Thirteen months later Dunbar was discharged and paid off on 20 November 1833, not at the end of *Potomac*'s cruise, but at Callao, while she was still on the west coast of South America. Why? The surviving paper record offers no answer. Perhaps he was seconded to an American merchantman in need of an experienced seaman to get across the Pacific to China and home to the United States.

That can only be speculation, but after his thirteen months in *Potomac* it was a naval sailor's life for James F. Dunbar. On 20 March 1835 he joined the sloop-of-war *Peacock*, Captain Edmund P. Kennedy, as a seaman, sailing from New York in April 1835 and returning to Norfolk in November 1837. This was the first of three around-the-world cruises in Dunbar's naval career, but it is possible that he had already circumnavigated the globe in his China-trade days. Among other missions, *Peacock* delivered ratified copies of previously negotiated treaties with the Sultanate of Muscat and Oman, and the Kingdom of Siam. In her approach to Muscat the sloop ran aground on a reef, and was only kedged off after she had thrown cannon and roundshot overboard. Return to the United States was via the Hawaiian Islands, Peru, and Brazil. His accumulated pay in his pocket, Dunbar was discharged from *Peacock* on 16 December 1837.

Three months ashore, and Dunbar again was ready for the sea and another circumnavigation, this time as a seaman in the sloop-of-war *John Adams*, Commander Thomas W. Wyman, which he joined on 19 March 1838. *John Adams* departed Hampton Roads in May and returned to Boston in June 1840. Her cruise included a bombardment of Kuala Batu, Sumatra, by the U.S. squadron commanded by Commodore George C. Read, which may have been Dunbar's first experience of naval combat. Dunbar's third and final circumnavigation as a naval sailor was in the frigate *Constellation* under Captain Lawrence Kearny. Highlights of this cruise included a year-long stay in Chinese waters, protecting and promoting American trade interests, followed by a return voyage that touched at Australia, New Zealand, and the Hawaiian Islands. At Honolulu Kearny had to deal with a tense international situation. An over-eager Royal Navy captain, Lord George Paulet, had made an unauthorized annexation of the Hawaiian Islands. Paulet's action was soon disavowed by his admiral, but until the situation was defused by the admiral's action the prevailing mood at Honolulu was touchy, requiring both tact and firmness on Kearny's part.[3]

Dunbar's personal record in *Constellation* is ambiguous. He served as officers' cook from 28 October 1840 until 13 February 1841, when he was disrated to seaman for two years. He was then rated commodore's steward on 11 February 1843, but held that responsibility for only a month and a half. He was again disrated to seaman on 1 April 1843 and remained in that rate until his discharge from *Constellation* on 31 December 1843 at the end of her cruise. Do these two disratings reflect shortcomings on Dunbar's part? On the basis of the surviving record it is impossible to know, but there is certainly a question here.

Although several holes in the story of James Dunbar's life have already been mentioned, in the 1840s and early 1850s it becomes even more difficult to reconstruct his activities with accuracy. This is one more example of the problems of trying to build a life story from records created by an elderly man, more especially when those self-created career narratives are sometimes in conflict with each other and with the Navy's official records as well. After Dunbar's return from *Constellation* family responsibilities may have kept him shoreside for a time. On 15 November 1844 his daughter Abby, then a young woman of nineteen, died of "consumption of the lungs." Son James would die on 26 May 1848, aged eighteen, with "bloody-flux by the lungs." His wife, Mary Welsh Dunbar, simply disappears from the historical record, without any indication of when, where, or how.

In later life Dunbar asserted that in his naval cruises before *Constellation* he was rated sailmaker's mate. In fact, the relevant rolls record him as *seaman*, although it is probable that he worked as a skilled member of the sailmaker's gang. *Constellation's* cruise marks a shift in his seafaring life. Beginning with his three and a half months as officers' cook in that frigate, it was chiefly in various food-service ratings that Dunbar worked for much of the remainder of his naval life. Was this change of course a reflection of the increasingly restricted role of African Americans in the U.S. Navy of the 1840s and 1850s? There is no sure answer to that question, but at this point in Dunbar's naval service there are suggestive parallels to the life of Samuel Howard. James Dunbar was now a man in his mid-forties; he may have found food service less physically demanding. Or he may just have been a good cook. His services in that capacity were henceforward always in demand by captains and wardroom officers.

Dunbar served as wardroom steward in the screw steamer *Princeton*, Captain Robert F. Stockton, for five weeks in 1844. Thereafter he can be traced as officers' steward and officers' cook in the bomb brig *Stromboli* during the war between the United States and Mexico; as cook to Captain John Gwinn (and presumably to his successor,

Captain Thomas Conover, following Gwinn's death on 4 September 1849) during the frigate *Constitution*'s last Mediterranean cruise, December 1848 to January 1851; and as officers' cook in the second *Princeton*, a screw steamer, beginning in February 1854 before transferring to the frigate *Potomac* with the same rating in July 1855.

Dunbar was discharged from *Potomac* in November of that year. Presumably this was a medical discharge stemming from an injury to Dunbar's perineum when he was thrown against *Princeton*'s side during a heavy gale. Now, if not earlier, began a long conflict between Dunbar's declining health and his keen desire to remain on active duty at sea. In May 1856 he was back afloat as captain's cook in the newly recommissioned sidewheel steamer *Susquehanna*, but was confined to the sick-list on 8 June, unable to urinate and with his joints swollen and extremely painful from rheumatism. Dunbar attributed the former disability to his injury in *Potomac*. Both conditions responded well to medical treatment, but Dunbar was transferred to the sidewheel steamer *Fulton* on 23 June and thence to the Norfolk Naval Hospital on 28 June with the diagnosis of spasmodic stricture. From that hospital Dunbar wrote—or, more accurately, had someone write for him—to Secretary of the Navy James Dobbin on 25 August. He gave a detailed, if not entirely accurate, summary of his career and asked to be admitted to the Naval Asylum for "the remainder of my life . . . as now my health is too feeble for further sea service." After some correspondence back and forth to clarify details of his service record and the extent of his disability, Dunbar was admitted to the Asylum on 3 October 1856.

Scarcely had Dunbar arrived at the Naval Asylum when he experienced a seemingly miraculous recovery from being too feeble for sea service. After fifteen days at the institution Dunbar walked away and reenlisted at the recruiting rendezvous in Boston on 20 October 1856, more or less accurately reporting his age as fifty-six. He was then detailed as sailmaker's mate to the sloop *Cyane*, Commander Robert G. Robb. In *Cyane* Dunbar served successfully until 3 February 1858, when he was honorably discharged and immediately reenlisted in the Navy. Almost certainly Dunbar, who seems to have loved roaming the globe, had found sitting around the Asylum a life not to his liking, and had made an unauthorized exit back to the familiar world of the U.S. Navy.

Dunbar's service in *Cyane* was followed by a posting to the steam frigate *Colorado* as officers' cook, a tour of duty that was cut short by a recurrence of his urinary problems—stricture of the urethra and cataract of the bladder, compounded by a severe attack of hemorrhoids. These failed to respond to more than two months of shipboard treatment; Dunbar was transferred in August 1858 to the Boston (Chelsea) Naval Hospital as "unfit for the service."

By 10 January 1859 Dunbar had recovered sufficiently to reenlist and was soon thereafter posted to the steam frigate *Niagara* in the capacity of officers' cook for a special mission that transported two hundred Africans, liberated from the captured slaver *Echo*, from Charleston, South Carolina, to Liberia. That mission accomplished, Dunbar was transferred to the screw sloop *Brooklyn*, in which he served as cabin cook from late January 1859 until mid-November of the following year. Service in *Brooklyn* must have been hard on Dunbar's health. Once again a sick man, he was relieved of his cabin cook duties on 11 November 1860 and re-rated as landsman until he could be discharged, on 10 December, to the Norfolk Naval Hospital with chronic rheumatism. From the hospital Dunbar appealed to Commodore Joseph Smith for readmission to the Naval Asylum. Smith grumbled: Dunbar had forfeited any claim to residence at the Asylum when he left without permission in 1856. Then, the regulations reasserted, Smith relented. Dunbar could be readmitted on probation if he promised never again to break the rules. Dunbar promised and was readmitted on 28 January 1861.

This second residence was even shorter than the first one. By 29 January James Dunbar was absent without leave, returned late on 4 February, was granted a three-month official leave of absence—and disappeared again. The Civil War was beginning, and Dunbar just could not sit on the sidelines. On 26 April 1861 he enlisted at the naval rendezvous in Philadelphia, reduced his age slightly by claiming to be fifty-eight, and was assigned to the screw steamer *Union*, a civilian-owned vessel just acquired by the Navy. Her skipper was John R. Goldsborough, last met in *Ungentle Goodnights* as a newly fledged lieutenant concerned about the declining mental and physical health of Commodore John Rodgers, but by now risen to the rank of commander. It is possible that Goldsborough, who may have known about Dunbar's culinary skills, encouraged him to enlist, as Dunbar was quickly rated as officers' cook. *Union*, assigned to the Atlantic Blockading Squadron, seized two Confederate merchantmen and destroyed a prize captured by the Confederate

privateer *York*, which marauder she soon thereafter forced aground.
James Dunbar's Civil War was off to a running start, and he could
anticipate some prize money in his pocket, but by November he
had been declared unfit for duty. One more time he appealed to
Joseph Smith for readmission to the Asylum. Smith, characteristically firm but forgiving, warned Dunbar to mend his ways, but
overlooked his faults this time and granted another readmission,
effective 26 November 1861.

Did James Dunbar appreciate Smith's kindness and mend his
ways? That was just too much to ask, especially in the middle of a
war. Dunbar stuck it out at the Asylum through December 1861
and January 1862, but on 6 February he vanished from the grounds
and on 14 February enlisted at the New York recruiting rendezvous, this time correctly reporting his age as sixty-two. His new
assignment was as captain's cook in the transport *Massachusetts*.
By the time *Massachusetts* was put out of service Dunbar was once
again ill; he was transferred to the receiving ship *North Carolina*,
apparently recovered, and was assigned to the screw sloop-of-war
Lackawanna with the rate of seaman. From *Lackawanna* Dunbar
was, on 29 January 1863, once again sent to the hospital at Norfolk, suffering from the effects of old age, an inability to hold his
urine, and an injury sustained in a fall in *Lackawanna*. Almost immediately on his admission to the hospital—and presumably in an
effort to do an end run around Joseph Smith—Dunbar appealed
directly to Secretary of the Navy Gideon Welles for a permit to
the Naval Asylum. The letter gave a detailed account of Dunbar's
naval service, but conveniently omitted any reference to his three
previous admissions to the Asylum. That tactic failed. Welles simply passed the letter to Smith, who—perhaps so encouraged by
Welles—suppressed the reservations he must have felt and issued
Dunbar, who was still hospitalized at Norfolk, yet another permit
of admission on 14 May 1863.

In early June Dunbar duly appeared at the Naval Asylum,
deposited his permit at the Asylum's office, walked off the grounds,
and headed for Philadelphia's naval recruiting rendezvous. There
Dunbar was quickly rejected as a recruit because he was identified
as an Asylum beneficiary and thus not eligible for enlistment. James
Forten Dunbar was a man who did not become discouraged easily.
On 12 June he showed up at New York's recruiting station, was
allowed to enlist, but was subsequently rejected for unknown reasons
when he reported to the receiving ship on 15 June. Undaunted, off

to Boston went Dunbar, where on 9 July he finally met with success. The recruiting officer recorded him as a mulatto, sixty-five and a quarter inches tall, sixty-five years old (he was actually sixty-four), with thirty-seven years of previous naval service, a tattoo of a ship on his right arm, one of a mermaid on his right forearm, another of a man and a woman on his left arm, and a family group on his left forearm. James Dunbar carried the history of his life on his body.

Always a desirable recruit because of his skills with food, Dunbar was assigned as officers' steward to the sidewheel steamer *Daffodil*, operating as a tug in the coastal waters of Georgia and South Carolina. Yet one more time sea-loving James Dunbar discovered to his chagrin that he was not physically fit for active duty and was discharged, by way of the screw steamer *Home*, to the receiving ship *Princeton* at Philadelphia's navy yard. Mid-May 1864, less than a year after his Boston reenlistment, James Dunbar was ready to pitch it in again. From *Princeton* he wrote to Joseph Smith, claiming to be seventy-one (he was actually sixty-four going on sixty-five) and asserting that, because of age, he was no longer able to perform his duties shipboard. Admiral Smith was not sympathetic. "Dunbar's conduct," he told the officer who forwarded the application, "whilst an inmate of the Asylum before was so palpably in violation of the regulations of the institution as to forfeit all claim on his part for readmission."

With that option closed, the ever-persistent Dunbar made his way to Baltimore where, on 14 September 1864, he was able to enlist as a seaman for the screw steamer *Tuscarora*. In her, Dunbar participated in some of the most memorable events of his Civil War career when *Tuscarora* took part in Admiral David Dixon Porter's December 1864 and January 1865 attacks on Fort Fisher at the mouth of the Cape Fear River, the Confederacy's last significant open route to the sea. Dunbar later said that he was wounded in one of these attacks, but he is not listed among *Tuscarora*'s casualties in the official reports.[4] Like many another veteran before and since, Dunbar may have been trying to make his service story a bit better than it really was. This is not the only evidence of such a habit on Dunbar's part, as he often claimed to have served in rates higher than are supported by the relevant ships' muster and pay rolls.

Not too long after the second Fort Fisher battle Dunbar's age and health caught up with him yet again. On 9 March 1865 *Tuscarora*'s surgeon, John Y. Taylor, sent him off to the Philadelphia Naval Hospital, where he was admitted on 27 March. Surgeon

Taylor described Dunbar as "affected with rheumatism, stricture of the urethra, and occasional incontinence of urine. On account of age and infirmity, I regard him as unfit for duty in the naval service." From the Philadelphia hospital, on 4 April, Dunbar made one more appeal to Admiral Smith for admission to the Naval Asylum, claiming that he was "entirely used up." Again he said nothing about his earlier periods at the Asylum, apparently hoping to fool the admiral. He almost did. "The fact escaped me that he had been an *old offender*," wrote Smith, catching his near-mistake at the last minute. "Indeed [he bears] the worst record of any man in the institution, having been expelled, deserted, broken leave, and shipped no less than four times after that many readmissions." Application denied!

On 20 April 1865 Dunbar was discharged from the Philadelphia Naval Hospital and transferred to the naval hospital at New York. No patient register for this hospital for these years seems to have survived in the archives, but it would appear that after a time under medical care there, Dunbar was transferred to the receiving ship *North Carolina*, also at New York, to serve out his time until 6 July 1867. Then he was discharged from the Navy for the last time. Immediately thereafter Dunbar made one final attempt to return to the Naval Asylum, with Admiral Charles H. Bell, commandant of the New York (Brooklyn) Navy Yard, advocating on Dunbar's behalf. Bell wrote the Asylum's governor, Hiram Paulding, describing Dunbar's service in the South Atlantic Squadron's blockade of the Confederacy's eastern coast and in the assaults on Fort Fisher. Paulding passed Bell's letter along to the Bureau of Yards and Docks, noted only one of Dunbar's four expulsions from the Asylum, cited his war service, reported that Dunbar was now disabled, and recommended his readmission. Perhaps luckily for Dunbar, Joseph Smith was away from the office when Bell's and Paulding's letters arrived. The task of answering fell to Admiral Melancton Smith, Chief of the Bureau of Equipment and Recruiting, who was standing in for Joseph Smith. Melancton Smith reviewed Dunbar's troubled history at the Asylum, then kicked the readmit-or-not-readmit choice back to Paulding's discretion. Paulding's decision was favorable. As of 3 August 1867, Dunbar was admitted as a beneficiary for the last time.

Almost immediately Admiral Paulding had a job for him. Serious trouble loomed that no commanding officer wanted—bad food and unhappy former sailors and Marines at the Naval Asylum. "The most respectable beneficiaries of this institution complain that the cooking of their ration is so badly done that, much of the time, from this cause, their food is not palatable," Paulding reported to Joseph Smith. The governor and the executive officer, Captain Dominick Lynch, checked out the food and discovered that, yes, it was badly cooked. Paulding had a solution: "The beneficiaries say they would like to have a ship's cook, a man that has been accustomed to prepare their food, and I feel well assured that such a change would greatly contribute to the health and comfort of our fine old fellows. We have a beneficiary, an intelligent colored man by the name of Dunbar, who has been a ship's cook in the Navy for most of the active period of his life, who would accept the situation. He is lame from a wound received at Fort Fisher, but seems otherwise in good physical health. He is popular with the men and I think would fill the place in a satisfactory manner." Dunbar would be allowed to hire his own assistants, who would presumably be men. That would definitely be a step in the right direction, Paulding asserted with misogyny reminiscent of Governor Charles W. Morgan, as "it would be beneficial to dispense with female help whenever it can be done conveniently."

Admiral Smith replied in his grumble-first-but-then-agree mode: "The beneficiaries are supposed [to be], and [are] so certified, as unable to perform manual labor, and therefore the inconsistency of employing them on full pay. I doubt very much the advantage of employing a beneficiary as head cook. I think women do much better in a house on shore [than] men, if the right kind can be had." With that opinion on record, Smith then told Paulding that he could try the experiment of using James Dunbar as head cook for three months. Paulding mulled over this contradictory directive and decided to respect Smith's opinions. James Dunbar did not get the job. The incident is important, though, because it shows the respect and friendship with which his fellow beneficiaries regarded this black sailor.

Two years later James Dunbar found himself a news item in Philadelphia's papers, though not in the best of circumstances. During the afternoon of Thursday, 2 September 1869, Policeman Michael McLaughlin was walking his beat along Bedford Street near Eighth when he came upon Dunbar lying on the sidewalk with his throat cut. The wound was serious, but not quite so dangerous as to threaten Dunbar's life. He was able to tell McLaughlin that he had gone to a nearby "house"—quickly identified as a brothel located on a short alley called Brown's Court leading north from the 700 block of St. Mary Street—allegedly to rest and had stretched out on one of the beds. After a while Ellen (or Ella) Smith, one of the prostitutes who worked there, woke Dunbar up and told him that if he was going to lie there any longer, or even stay in the house, he needed to pay up. (Clearly, Dunbar was monopolizing Smith's working space. His state of sobriety is not on record.) Dunbar said he refused to pay and drew his knife to frighten Smith off. Beyond that, he told McLaughlin, he could remember nothing, but he now realized that he no longer had in his possession the $152 he carried earlier that day. McLaughlin got Dunbar to the nearby Pennsylvania Hospital, from which he was transferred to the hospital at the Naval Asylum the next day.

Meanwhile, later on 2 September, the police descended on the brothel and arrested Ellen Smith and Annie Williams, both white and members of the world's oldest profession, as well as one Thomas Price, an African American whose role at the establishment is unclear. From the speed with which they were identified and picked up, all three must have been well known to the police already. Ellen Smith told the officers that when Dunbar drew his knife she had yelled *Murder!*, which brought Price to her aid. Price "escorted" Dunbar downstairs and out into the street. That, said Ellen Smith, was the last she had seen of James Dunbar.

Dunbar's wound may not have been mortal, but it was serious enough to keep him confined to the Philadelphia Naval Hospital for thirty-five days, during most of which he was in no condition to testify in court. Price, Smith, and Williams remained under arrest, although apparently free on bail. By 30 September Dunbar was sufficiently fit to go to alderman's court, where he now told an entirely different story. Omitting any mention of the brothel or his presence therein, he testified "that he left the Naval Asylum, of which he is an inmate, having been forty-two years in the Navy, and, meeting several young fellows, he was drugged, robbed, and had his throat cut. He could not tell who had done it, but he was satisfied that the persons under arrest had no hand in it, as he knew them and had always been treated well by them." The case now had nowhere to go, and the alderman discharged Price, Smith, and Williams.[5] Where is the truth in these seemingly conflicting stories? It was typical and well-recorded behavior for members of the Philadelphia social stratum to which James Dunbar, Ellen Smith, Thomas Price, and Annie Williams belonged to close ranks to frustrate prosecution and would-be regulation in the face of a judicial system controlled by the city's middle and upper classes.[6] Or was he really attacked by the young men after Price had put him out on the street? History can never know for certain what happened.

In mid-April 1870, when he was seventy years old, James F. Dunbar had one last fling of beneficiary misbehavior. He went absent without leave for thirteen days, during which disappearance he sold a coat belonging to another beneficiary. The punishment awarded reflected the seriousness of the coat theft rather than the absence without leave: no pocket money for six months, no tobacco for six months, no leaving the grounds until 24 October. Whether Dunbar chose to walk out through the northeast gate on a freedom-inspired spree on 24 October or the days thereafter is not on record, but on 5 November he was admitted to the Philadelphia Naval Hospital for what would prove to be his final illness.

True to the pattern of his life, James Forten Dunbar did not go easily. He came to the hospital with acute diarrhea—frequent bowel movements, composed of blood and slime, accompanied by intense pain. By the next day treatment had reduced the number of discharges, Dunbar's pain was greatly relieved, and the blood had disappeared from his stool. His appetite was good. It looked as though he might be on the mend. Then, on 9 November, the medical staff noticed for the first time that Dunbar's mind was "becoming very weak." As to whether there had been any evidence of mental decline before his hospital admission, there is only silence. Three days later a similar note was made in his hospital record, but come 14 November there was a hint of optimism—"Appears very much brighter this morning"—and his bowels seemed to be returning to normal functioning. The optimism was premature. Next day Dunbar's mind was again described as "weak" and appeared to be wandering at times—perhaps to his lost family or his adventures at sea. One day later (16 November) his thoughts were still wandering, and now he was refusing to take his medicine. That night, at 1 a.m., he awoke from a sound sleep, delirious and noisy. A dose of chloral hydrate calmed Dunbar down; by daylight he seemed better, but his mind was still wandering. "He has almost constantly a low muttering delirium. It is with great difficulty that he can be persuaded to take any nourishment," the hospital record noted on 19 November. By the twentieth the old sailor was very restless and nervous. The remedy: another dose of chloral hydrate, after which Dunbar fell asleep for several hours. On 22 November there was a positive note—"He is rather more rational this morning"—which was reversed the next day: "He is wandering in his mind." By 24 November the doctors were certain they were going to lose James Dunbar, but he hung on fighting: "Condition of mind unchanged," the daily medical record noted. "He is more comfortable through the day than at night, when he becomes very nervous, muttering constantly, and attempting to leave his bed." More chloral hydrate: it "causes him to sleep quietly for several hours, and on being aroused he appears more rational." 25 November: "Gradually becoming weaker and less rational." 26 November: "Patient is unconscious and in a dying condition." Medication stopped. At 4:15, in the gathering darkness of that late fall afternoon, James Forten Dunbar departed on a final voyage to an unknown destination.

EIGHT

SHIPMATES

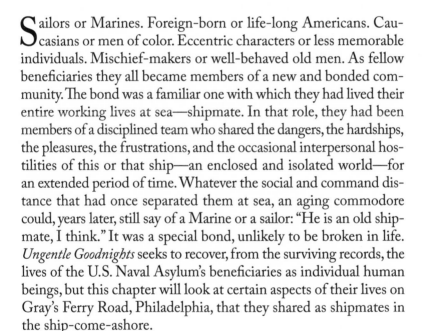

Sailors or Marines. Foreign-born or life-long Americans. Caucasians or men of color. Eccentric characters or less memorable individuals. Mischief-makers or well-behaved old men. As fellow beneficiaries they all became members of a new and bonded community. The bond was a familiar one with which they had lived their entire working lives at sea—shipmate. In that role, they had been members of a disciplined team who shared the dangers, the hardships, the pleasures, the frustrations, and the occasional interpersonal hostilities of this or that ship—an enclosed and isolated world—for an extended period of time. Whatever the social and command distance that had once separated them at sea, an aging commodore could, years later, still say of a Marine or a sailor: "He is an old shipmate, I think." It was a special bond, unlikely to be broken in life. *Ungentle Goodnights* seeks to recover, from the surviving records, the lives of the U.S. Naval Asylum's beneficiaries as individual human beings, but this chapter will look at certain aspects of their lives on Gray's Ferry Road, Philadelphia, that they shared as shipmates in the ship-come-ashore.

WHO'S WORKING?

Beneficiary life at the Naval Asylum was supported by a corps of civilian employees who performed the basic tasks necessary to keep the place functioning. The number of these workers gradually increased over the years, and there was some fluctuation among roles. *Ungentle Goodnights* will not track these changes. The civilian staff, as it was organized in 1849 when the Bureau of Yards and Docks was assigned responsibility for the Asylum, will be taken as typical of that which the beneficiaries knew.

Ultimately all of the Asylum's civilian employees were the responsibility of the executive officer, under the general direction of the governor. However, a major segment of those employees were the housekeeping staff, which was directed by the *matron*. She—if a sufficiently formidable person—was something of a power on her own. In 1849 that position was filled by Mrs. Sarah A. Gould, her broad responsibilities well described by Governor Jacob Jones: "She receives and is accountable for the provisions, etc., allotted for [the beneficiaries'] use, superintends the cooking and arrangement of table and serving the meals, and by her presence during meal hours contributes greatly to good order and quiet at table. [She] has charge of the laundresses, receiving, assorting, and serving out the clothes." Under Mrs. Gould were a head cook; four assistants to the cook, who were also responsible for serving the beneficiaries in the dining room; and three laundresses. The latter not only washed and ironed the table linen and bedclothes, but also did the laundry for all the beneficiaries. It was a huge job for just three women. They needed help and—as will shortly be told— they got it.

Mrs. Gould's little empire aside, the remainder of the civilian staff was directly under the executive officer. Foremost among them was the master-at-arms, the institution's chief security officer. Any sailor or Marine beneficiary would have been familiar with the master-at-arms' shipboard role as, in effect, the vessel's chief of police, a role now translated Asylum-side. In June 1852 a ship's corporal—another familiar onboard figure—was authorized to assist the master-at-arms. When it came to the maintenance of the Asylum physical facilities, the key man was the carpenter's mate. Governor William W. McKean described an incumbent he considered the ideal person for the job: "He is not only a good carpenter but has a general knowledge of mechanics. Since I have been attached to the Asylum he has rendered services to the government which could not have been obtained for the amount of his wages by assisting to repair injuries done by [a recent] storm, making coffins, putting in window glass, repairing skylights, etc." Even as McKean was writing, the carpenter's mate, Charles A. Holst, was "fitting a strip on each of the [beneficiaries'] rooms to hang their pictures and clothes, the walls having been much defaced by driving nails in them." Also reporting to the executive officer was the class of civilian employees called *laborers*. Three of them were a mixed crew of two women and one man who were employed under the job title of *scrubbers*; they had responsibility for washing down the several floors of the entire building once a week. The remaining three laborers—all of them male—had a full plate of duties. "These men," reported Executive Officer Henry A. Adams, "perform all the outdoor work, keep the roads, walks, and lawns in order, trim and prune shrubbery, attend to the horse and stables, keep the cellars clean and wash out the sewers, dig graves, bring coal from the cellars to the [beneficiaries'] sitting rooms, attend the fires in the furnaces by day and night, and perform various other duties, the necessity for which is constantly recurring." A final civilian under the executive officer's supervision was the barber, a mulatto man named Henry Marcus, who shaved each beneficiary three times a week and cut his hair as necessary.

Beyond its small corps of civilian employees, the Naval Asylum depended on beneficiaries of sound health to perform a variety of tasks essential to keep the place functioning. They received extra compensation for such work. In this the Asylum was again turning to the organizational model with which its officers and residents were familiar—the warship, where the hands-on work of the vessel was directed and executed by its petty officers, a corps of senior ratings. The number of beneficiaries so employed at the Asylum and the precise details of each job varied over the years, but the structure as it existed in June 1853 can be taken as typical.

Three beneficiaries, designated *petty officers* and paid three dollars per month, had a long roster of responsibilities to keep them busy. As described by Governor David Geisinger, it was the petty officers' duty "to take care of the colors, to inspect provisions received for daily use, to patrol the grounds by day and prevent trespasses by visitors or others, to receive the daily allowance of sugar, tea, and coffee and see that none of it is abstracted by the [paid] servants, to preserve order at the table and assist the master-at-arms when called on, to report the stable carefully locked up and no strangers or [beneficiaries] about the grounds at sunset, and perform other similar offices which can only be entrusted to the best and steadiest men."

Equally—or perhaps even more—demanding were the jobs of the six *gatekeepers*, the high level of responsibility reflected in the monthly pay that the more senior of them received. As already noted, the northeast gate on Gray's Ferry Road was the primary entrance to the Asylum grounds. Here the senior gatekeeper was paid five dollars per month and his assistant four dollars. The southwest gate, also on Gray's Ferry Road, had less traffic. Here the two gatekeepers were paid respectively three dollars and two dollars per month. At the Asylum's back door—the gate on Sutherland Avenue, known officially as the northwest gate—the two men assigned there each received two dollars. Keeping all six of these jobs filled well was a major headache for the governors and executive officers. "The gatekeepers must be sober, trusty, and vigilant men," Governor Geisinger told Commodore Joseph Smith in July 1851. "Very few among the beneficiaries can fill the situation properly." Governor William W. McKean elaborated on the problem nearly a decade later: "I find great difficulty in selecting from among the beneficiaries suitable men to fill the situation of gatekeepers at the northeast gate, which is the thoroughfare to the institution. The best men are unwilling to take the situation, as they are required to report all beneficiaries who may return intoxicated or who may be detected in smuggling liquor, and the drinking men of course cannot be depended on. The only men I have heretofore been able to place any confidence in have recently been several times intoxicated, and on Friday night last the man upon whom I have *mainly* depended . . . was found drunk in his bed at the [gatekeepers'] lodge at 9 o'clock in the evening. He is now in the hospital, and I am really without proper persons to fill the position."

Four *watchmen* each earned three dollars a month and apparently alternated day-on, day-off. During the day one of them sat just inside the main entrance to the Asylum building to direct any outside visitors to their destinations—perhaps to the office of the governor or that of the executive officer. Come evening, explained Governor Geisinger, the responsibilities expanded. The on-duty watchman was required "to inspect the house thoroughly every two hours during the night to see that the fires are all safe, that there are no improper lights burning, and no noise or disorder in any of the rooms." Help for the overworked women in the laundry came from two beneficiaries called *washmen*; their monthly wage was three dollars each. "They must be strong and willing," continued Geisinger. "They make the fires, assist the women in lifting the heavy boilers, help to hang out and bring in the clothes, carry out the water from the washroom in buckets, and perform other services." It was a tough job—"very few of the men are able to do this work"—but it did have a fringe benefit not mentioned by Governor Geisinger: the washmen got to hang out with some of the few women in this over-whelmingly male institution. Rather lighter in its physical demands was the job of *assistant to the purser's steward* (at three dollars per month). It demanded a beneficiary who was methodical and liter-ate, as he had to help the steward receive and track all the stores needed to keep the institution functioning.

Two *messengers* or *postmen*, each paid three dollars a month, had an official excuse to go into town. The Philadelphia post office was more than two miles from the Asylum and the messengers, who alternated week-on, week-off, traveled there on foot twice a day to post outgoing letters and pick up the incoming mail. They did other as-long-as-you-are-going errands and collected the Philadelphia newspapers to which the Asylum subscribed. Messenger was another headache job for the governor or executive officer to keep filled. Two round trips to the post office meant about ten miles of walking each day. "I am informed and believe," complained Executive Officer Peter Turner, "that to men of the age and physical ability of the benefi-ciaries this distance in the warm weather and on rainy or other-wise inclement days it is far too great for their endurance. . . . The present postmen, who are well suited for the place, find it too much for them and are about giving it up, and I fear great difficulty will be experienced in procuring suitable ones in their places." Joseph Smith proved atypically unsympathetic to the elderly beneficia-ries: he insisted that he did not have the discretion to provide car-fare so that the postmen could take advantage of the street railways to perform their duties.

Then there was a final category of in-house employment for beneficiaries: five *water-closet tenders*. This job's duties were just what the name said—to keep the toilets clean and in order—added to which the job-holders were expected to sweep up the building and have things shipshape. Two of the five were compensated at two dollars per month; three at one dollar. No special skills or extra-ordinary trustworthiness needed here; keeping the toilets clean was often the job assigned to beneficiaries who were behavior problems.

DOUBLE-DIPPING

Commodore Joseph Smith thought the law establishing the Naval Asylum was unambiguous. Its intent was to provide a comfortable home for disabled and decrepit sailors and Marines "when they are no longer capable of supporting themselves" by their own physical labor. Less than a month after responsibility for the Asylum was transferred to him in 1849 he learned of practices there that seemed to evade the law. Before Commodore Smith assumed oversight of the institution, beneficiaries were admitted either on the basis of proven long service or because they were commuting a pension, but no assessment by a naval surgeon of a man's physical abilities or limitations was required as part of the admission process. The governors had permitted a small number—the exact count is unknown—of the beneficiaries to live off the Asylum campus with their families and work at full-time jobs to earn income. Typically such men were expected to show up for Sunday morning muster; once a month they collected their beneficiary's allotment of clothing and tobacco and the one dollar in pocket money. That was the last anyone at the Asylum saw of them until the next Sunday or the next issue day.

Smith was determined to run a tighter ship. With the approval of Secretary of the Navy William Ballard Preston, the commodore put an immediate stop to the practice of off-grounds living and off-grounds work. If a man could earn a living at a full-time job, he had no business being a Naval Asylum beneficiary. This brought from the affected beneficiaries letters of protest, appeals to a sympathetic congressman, and charges of being unfairly deprived of their rights, but Smith stuck to his decision and repeated it many times in the future.

That now-forbidden practice of living off-grounds and working a full-time job aside, there was nothing to prevent a beneficiary from taking a part-time day job compatible with his physical limitations. Unless a man was on the gate list—restricted to the grounds for behavior problems—he was free to walk out after breakfast. If he was careful to be back (sober) by sunset, no one necessarily knew where he was and what he was doing in the interim—unless he attracted the attention of the city police. Fellow-beneficiaries and the Asylum's executive officer were typically aware of such daytime employment, but there was no administrative reason to make a record of it. *Ungentle Goodnights* might never have discovered the practice but for the poor judgment of a beneficiary named William Turner.

Turner was born in Port Tobacco, Maryland, probably in 1807 or 1808, but possibly as late as 1810. He first entered the Navy in the late 1820s. Clearly a competent seaman, Turner had risen to the rank of boatswain's mate in the receiving ship *Allegheny* at Baltimore by the autumn of 1857. One day, while a gang under his supervision was raising the water tanks from *Allegheny*'s hold in order to clean underneath them, one of the tanks accidentally fell on Turner's left foot, crushing it. This, and subsequent complications of the injury, entitled Turner to a pension, granted in August 1860. He commuted the pension for admission to the Naval Asylum in February 1861. One of those handy individuals who can do many different tasks successfully, William Turner—with the full knowledge of executive officer, Commander Peter Turner—held a variety of part-time day jobs while a beneficiary. He hung wallpaper in some houses under construction; he served as sexton at a nearby church. By 1864 the crushed foot did not seem to be limiting his activity. "In all appearances it now does him no injury," commented Governor Frederick Engle, "for he is a remarkable fast walker of 50 years of age."

Sometime early in 1864 Turner, who was still living at the Asylum as a beneficiary, unwisely decided to press his luck and took a full-time day job at the Navy Yard, for which he was paid two dollars a day—a clear violation of the rules. Somehow Governor Engle got wind of what was going on. In March he asked Commodore Cornelius K. Stribling, the yard's commandant, if Turner was indeed working at the yard, only to be assured that there was no such name on the rolls. Stribling's denial notwithstanding, Engle continued to be suspicious; in October he consulted now-Admiral Joseph Smith for advice. A sharp-eyed clerk in the Bureau of Yards and Docks looked over the Philadelphia yard's pay rolls and—sure enough—there was William Turner at two dollars per day in the June, July, August, and September returns. Out of the Asylum he went. (Turner was eventually readmitted to the Asylum in 1868, compiled a notable record of alcohol-fueled misbehavior, reformed, dried out, and died there on the last day of January 1894.)

William Turner was far from alone among the beneficiaries. Others, too, had a powerful motive to pursue extra income through off-grounds day jobs: the financial pressures created by the existence of family members—wives, children, siblings—who were wholly or partly dependent on the money the beneficiary could earn.

MURKY WATERS

For the historian of the nineteenth-century United States Navy no subject is more elusive than the married lives—if any—of its Marines and sailors. The life records of the Naval Asylum's beneficiaries offer but small help to bring this subject into sharper focus.

Only during the governorship of Commodore James Biddle (August 1838–April 1842) was systematic information collected on the family status—single, married, separated, widower, living or dead children—of men applying for admission to the Asylum. That period aside, the historian can only discover information about the marital status of the beneficiaries from references that pop up erratically in a variety of sources, none of them comprehensive—pension applications, mentions in the governors' correspondence, Philadelphia city death certificates, and receipts for beneficiary estates. Given the fragmentary nature of these records, no reliable statistical profile can be compiled concerning the married or bachelor lives of the five hundred forty-one men who were admitted to the Naval Asylum before 1866.

At the richer end of the trail of tidbits with which history must work in reconstructing sailor or Marine marriages is John Strain, a beneficiary who could trace his naval service back to the battle of Lake Champlain in 1814. Strain was a problem resident at the Naval Asylum who was expelled four times. His appeals for reinstatement—Strain was a master at the prose of self-pity—generated a more-voluminous-than-usual documentary record of his life; from that record and a handful of other sources, these clues to his marriage and family life can be extracted: In February 1852 he writes from Pineville, Gloucester County, New Jersey, that he has an affectionate wife and two children. Five years and three months later Strain again writes from Pineville that he has lost the last relation that he had in the world—presumably his wife—and that he is now left to cope alone. Twelve days later he reports that because he had a sickly wife (now apparently dead) and a crippled daughter—is she alive? what happened to the other child?—he has not been able to save for his old age. (Strain was in his mid-fifties.)

At this point occur two of Strain's four residencies at the Naval Asylum—August 1857 to August 1860 and December 1860 to March 1862—both terminating in dismissals for gross misconduct and during which there is no mention of any living family. During the second of these residencies the story of John Strain's sexual and marital life fills out a bit, though frustrating holes abound. Late in March 1861 Strain has sex with an Irish immigrant named Ellen Ray. How long Ellen had been in Philadelphia, how she and John met, and how long they had been having sex together are unknown. In early April, just before the outbreak of the Civil War hostilities, Ellen—unaware that she is pregnant—travels on to New Orleans. There, on 25 December 1861, their son, John Francis Strain, is born. With New Orleans a Confederate city until the end of April 1862, at what point John becomes aware that he was again a father is unknown. What can be said is that, following the capture of New Orleans by the forces under David G. Farragut, John does not hurry south to Ellen. He is dismissed from the Asylum on 15 March 1862, is in Pineville in April 1862, on Staten Island in March 1863, and in Philadelphia in January 1864. From all of these places he dispatches (unsuccessful) appeals for readmission to the Asylum. After January 1864 John works his way south and west through employment at different navy yards until he reaches New Orleans; he and Ellen are married on 2 December 1864. Here is one more puzzle in the John Strain story: John Francis Strain's birth in December 1861 is the only record of his life. What has become of him?

However that may be, a reunited John and Ellen quickly make up for time lost in separation. Twin daughters, Elizabeth and Mary Ellen, are born on 13 August 1865.[1] By December 1865 John is back in Philadelphia, from where he again writes Admiral Joseph Smith, mentioning—with a flourish of virility—that he, at the age of sixty-three years and fourteen days, has become the father of twins. Work has dried up in New Orleans. He has come north in search of a job to support his family, but has been compelled to leave Elizabeth and Mary Ellen in New Orleans because they are too young to travel. What has become of Ellen (Ray) Strain? She has disappeared from the record of John's life, never to reappear. By the time he writes Joseph Smith his December 1865 letter, John Strain has found work as a member of the caretaker crew for the Civil War ironclads mothballed at Philadelphia's League Island Navy Yard, a job he continues to hold until he is admitted as a resident at Sailors' Snug Harbor on Staten Island in May 1867. The record of that admission states that Elizabeth and Mary Ellen are residents of the seamen's children's home on Staten Island, lists his wife as Ellen Strain, but offers no other clue about Ellen. Is she alive? If yes, where is she? With that entry the bits-and-pieces story of John Strain's married life comes to an end. Strain descendants add the knowledge that the twins lived into adulthood, married, and had children themselves. The old sailor dies at Snug Harbor on 25 April 1876 after what appears to have been an uneventful residence of almost nineteen years.

For those beneficiaries who were either lifelong bachelors or whose wives were dead little speculation is required to see why they would choose to become Asylum beneficiaries. Even if they had married adult children and might try finding an old-age home with them, more often than not Grandpa was soon seeking admission or readmission to the Asylum. John Wolfenden, a beneficiary in his eighties whose naval service stretched back to the Quasi-War with France, left the Asylum in August 1847 to live with his son in North Carolina. Three years later, come July 1850, Wolfenden was appealing to Joseph Smith for permission to return on the grounds that the North Carolina climate did not agree with his health, but added: "I have concluded there is no home like the Asylum."

The puzzling question for the Asylum's historian is this: Why would a man whose wife was alive and who may have had children or other relatives living at home choose to become a resident of the Asylum? This occurred a surprising number of times. Six reasons suggest themselves, though some of the reasons can only be informed speculation, with no documentary evidence to support the speculation:

First, as with William Turner before he pushed his luck too hard, there was the opportunity for small part-time jobs in the neighborhood. Beneficiary William H. Robinson spoke to this—and to the stresses of domestic economy for a married beneficiary—when in mid-1853 he asked Governor David Geisinger whether, instead of eating in the dining room, he might be allowed to draw in cash the money the Asylum was spending for his meals. "I have a wife and one child looking to me for support. I have only $1.00 pocket money"—more on this shortly—"and I use all my exertions to get all the small jobs I can and use the most strict economy, and I can scarcely make out to support my small family." The answer: no, that was not permitted under the regulations. Keeping his family afloat financially can only have become more difficult for Robinson and his wife; by 1857 they had another child to feed.

Second, each beneficiary received one dollar per month in pocket money and a monthly issue of two pounds of tobacco. He was also allowed to draw up to three dollars per month (or thirty-six dollars per year) in clothing supplied by the purser.[2] If a beneficiary could forego the use of tobacco himself, he could probably sell all or part of his monthly allowance for needed cash. Selling the clothing issued by the purser was strictly forbidden by the Asylum's internal regulations and severely punished if detected, but it was a difficult rule to enforce. Violations were typically recorded at the Asylum when clothing was sold off-grounds to raise cash for alcohol; but the proceeds of contrary-to-regulations sales could just as easily have been diverted to family support.

Third, there was the possibility of earning money from the in-house jobs for beneficiaries described earlier in this chapter. In the year before his appeal to Governor Geisinger describing the difficulty of supporting his family, William H. Robinson worked for two months as the northeast gatekeeper, a job in which he earned four dollars per month. Robinson was not a particularly well-behaved beneficiary, so it comes as no surprise that he was disrated from this responsible work at the end of the second month. He sat out a month of unemployment, after which he was appointed one of the washmen, assisting with the laundry at three dollars a month from November 1852 through March 1853. Whether this job ended because of performance problems or because the Asylum administration cycled the job among several beneficiaries who wanted in-house work is unknown. Contrary to the Robinson experience, the surviving records offer just enough fragmentary evidence to tempt the speculation that those beneficiaries who were successful in performing the more responsible of the in-house jobs—watchman, gatekeeper, petty officer, messenger—were married men with families. However, because there is no complete roster that records the marital status of beneficiaries and because the muster rolls that show in-house employment cover only the period October 1851 through October 1862, there is no reliable way to check out this speculation.

Fourth, meals served at the Asylum were generous—even hearty. For the married beneficiary eating at the institution, that made one less mouth to feed at home. Moreover, although it must be stressed that there is absolutely no documentary evidence to support the speculation, it is hard to believe that some of the leftovers from the Asylum kitchen did not make their way to nearby beneficiary families.

Fifth, wives of beneficiaries may have—almost certainly must have—held jobs, perhaps as domestic servants in the middle-class homes around Rittenhouse Square or as barmaids in the many neighborhood taverns. There are no records known to *Ungentle Goodnights* that would track such employment, but it is impossible to believe that it did not occur.

Sixth and finally, not only did beneficiaries have the benefit of three ample meals a day at the Asylum, they also benefited from free medical care for themselves. On Sunday, 27 February 1870, married beneficiary Matthew Cain—a man with thirty-four years of combined service, first in the Army and later in the Marine Corps, and one who was highly respected and trusted in the roles of watchman and gatekeeper at the Asylum—walked the half-mile or so to the home where his family lived. He experienced a heart attack immediately on his arrival. A message to the Philadelphia Naval Hospital at the Asylum quickly brought Surgeon Archibald C. Rhoades to the Cain residence, where the surgeon decided that Cain was too ill to be moved. The old Marine continued to be treated at home until the following Saturday, 5 March, when the doctor decided that Cain's recovery was proceeding well enough to permit him to be moved to the hospital on a stretcher. He continued to improve. Recovery was anticipated, but there was no happy ending to this story. Matthew Cain experienced a second heart attack on 16 March and a third on 17 March, from which he died at 6:40 that evening.

MARGARET TELLS HER STORY

To almost any generalization there is an exception. This holds true for the sparse historical record of beneficiary marriages. The exception is a woman named Margaret Jones Flanagan, who told the story of her life in compelling detail. No claim is made here that her story is typical of any other of the unknown number of beneficiary marriages. It is Margaret's story. But, because it is the only wife's account of her life to survive, it deserves to be recorded in *Ungentle Goodnights*. Margaret Flanagan could neither read nor write, but she was described as "a very bright and intelligent old lady" when she dictated her life story. She was eloquent as well.

Margaret was born in Camden County, North Carolina, to Benjamin and Cora Jones. When she told her life story she showed the person who was writing it down the family Bible in which her date of birth was recorded; this date failed to make it into her autobiographical statement, but it was probably in the year 1814. Beyond the details of her birth, the first event of her early life that

Margaret reported was her April 1847 marriage, near Elizabeth City, North Carolina, to a man named William Mashlin. "I was acquainted with him about two years before my marriage to him. He was a shoemaker by trade and an Englishman by birth. So he told me." That suggestion of skepticism about her husband's story was intentional: "At my marriage to him he claimed to be in his forty-first year, but I think he was older." (William Mashlin, it might be noted, was not the first or the last man to lie about his age to catch the woman he desired.) "He was," she continued, "at that time in fair general health. If he had any relatives anywhere in the country, I never knew them. He never spoke of any relatives. He had a scar on his forehead, which he said was received by being shot when crossing over to this country from Canada. He said he was in the British army and deserted." Again, it is hard to ignore the undercurrent of skepticism as Margaret tells her story.

Following their marriage, Mr. and Mrs. Mashlin moved to Norfolk, Virginia, where they lived from November 1847 to May 1848. From there they migrated to Richmond, where they remained until the end of July, when Mashlin proposed that they travel farther west. By now the bloom was off the marriage: "I was sick abed and refused to go with him. He had no money, and I had to support him. [Although] he was not a drinking man, he mistreated me very much. He beat me once and otherwise mistreated me." William and Margaret parted ways—permanently. "He said he was going to Pittsburgh, Pennsylvania. I never saw him since. He never wrote to me. I never saw any person who saw him. . . . I never made any inquiry after him. To tell you the truth, I was glad to be rid of him," said Margaret—neither the first nor the last woman to utter that sentiment.

Margaret returned to Norfolk and opened a boarding house. Then, in 1852, one of her boarders, a man named James Benson, read her a news item from one of the Norfolk papers. It reported an accident in a coal mine in which seven or eight men had been killed. Among the dead was William Mashlin. Margaret was legally a free woman.

Enter Margaret's life a Marine sergeant, five feet, seven inches tall, with black hair and hazel eyes, named Stacy Flanagan, a veteran of the war with Mexico and now attached to the receiving ship *Pennsylvania* at Norfolk. Stacy, his wife Susan, and their son lived next door to Margaret's boarding house. In August 1855 Susan and the couple's son died when yellow fever swept Norfolk. Their loss was a traumatic blow to Stacy, but soon enough he and Margaret—both in their mid-forties at the time—decided to move on with their lives and were married on 31 January 1856.

Five years later—even though the Civil War was just beginning—Stacy Flanagan decided it was time to end his Marine Corps career. He had served twenty-six years and six months and was now—he said—in his late fifties; a hernia incurred during the war with Mexico was a continuing problem; and he just did not have the stamina for wartime active duty. With his excellent service record, admission to the Naval Asylum (16 May 1861) was a foregone conclusion. There, a single incident of alcohol abuse aside, Flanagan quickly became one of the more reliable beneficiaries, holding the responsible jobs of watchman and gatekeeper.

Margaret seems to have stayed on in Norfolk, even while the city was controlled by Confederate forces, but eventually moved to Philadelphia to be with her husband. She rented a room at 2216 Pemberton Street, close to the Naval Asylum. "We were never separated," she recalled in old age. "He used to come from the Asylum and stay with me whenever he pleased. He used to come to see me every day." Perhaps in part because of happy married life, Stacy Flanagan lived as a beneficiary for many years, finally dying of heart disease on 24 November 1892. "I was present at his death," Margaret noted simply as she brought her autobiographical statement to a close.

Now Margaret was a widow, coping alone in Philadelphia. A year and a half after Stacy's death two of her friends reported that she "is in destitute circumstances, wholly dependent upon charity for subsistence. She is a confirmed invalid, suffering from . . . the result of age and is liable to die at any time. She is nearly eighty years of age and unable to do any kind of work." Because Stacy and Margaret had married while he was still an active-duty Marine with Mexican War service, Margaret was eligible for a widow's pension of eight dollars per month, retroactive to the day after Stacy's death. This supported her for the next eight and a half years until her own death on 16 December 1902.

SHUTTING THE DEVIL'S WORKSHOP

Naval Asylum beneficiaries, wrote Walter Colton, the institution's second chaplain, "Are fond of reading." Even to the seasoned historian of the United States Navy this statement comes as something of a surprise. Left to guess on the basis of evidence encountered in the archives—letters written for them, documents signed with an X—one might have supposed that an unknown fraction of the Asylum's first five hundred forty-one beneficiaries were not able to read and that a smaller number were able to write. Clearly, Chaplain Colton thought otherwise, and he was on the ground. The extent of literacy among before-the-mast mariners has been variously assessed by historians.[3] Those conflicting opinions will not be resolved by *Ungentle Goodnights*. No document, no evidence exists in the Asylum's surviving archives that would offer a statistically sound answer to questions such as what proportion of the Asylum beneficiaries could read and what number could write more than their names?

Ungentle Goodnights will take Chaplain Colton at his word: lots of beneficiaries liked to read. And that was a good thing, the chaplain continued, perhaps too optimistically: "If their minds can be kept interested and employed, they will not feel that restlessness and impatience of restraint which lead to violations of decorum and disorder. The adage is as true now as when [George] Whitefield uttered it—'the brain of the idle man is the Devil's workshop.'" As to what the beneficiaries liked best to read there is no dispute. It was newspapers and magazines—as many as they could get their hands on. In February 1844, even before Chaplain Colton's appeal, Secretary of the Navy David Henshaw had authorized the expenditure of fifty dollars per year for newspapers and magazines. This earlier authorization was apparently lost sight of in the transition between Governor William W. McKean and Governor Charles W. Morgan, resulting in Colton's unnecessary May 1845 request for what had already been authorized. Colton's appeal eventually reached the desk of Secretary of the Navy George Bancroft. Bancroft liked the idea but thriftily cut the authorized expense to thirty-five dollars per year, which Governor Morgan thought adequate. In the 1840s the newspapers received by subscription were all ones published in Philadelphia. When Commodore Joseph Smith assumed oversight of the Asylum in July 1849 he questioned the desirability of limiting the subscriptions to Philadelphia papers and suggested more variety from other parts of the country—though, of course, only under the condition of keeping expenses in line by dropping a Philadelphia paper in favor of one from, say, Norfolk. Wherever they might be published, by the 1850s government-provided newspaper subscriptions for the Asylum's smoking rooms had become an unchallenged tradition.

Harper's Weekly featured the Naval Asylum's reading room in its 23 February 1878 issue. Beneficiaries play games, smoke, read newspapers, or doze quietly in their chairs. Thirty-four of the men whose life stories are the basis of this book were still alive and in residence at the Asylum when the photograph was taken from which this image is redrawn. Sadly, there is no record of the names of the men pictured. THE NEWBERRY LIBRARY

Beyond newspapers and magazines the Asylum also offered its residents a library of books, though not much is known about what was on the library's shelves before the late 1860s. In January 1843 Executive Officer Andrew H. Foote reported that he was trying to organize a library for the beneficiaries, and asked that any unwanted books in storage at the various navy yards be sent to the Asylum. Whatever may have been the success of this appeal, in October 1854 Governor George W. Storer told Joseph Smith that he found "the library very deficient, most of the books being in a dilapidated state, and many but odd volumes [of multi-volume sets, and] but few that could be of any interest to the beneficiaries." Storer purchased some new books for the library, but eight years later Governor Frederick Engle reported that "the beneficiaries have read all the few books in the library and hence have lost the only proper source of amusement and instruction they have. No books have been purchased for the last three or four years and [an appeal for funds to buy new books now is made] at the urgent desire of many of the best men in the house." Not until 1867, with his heavy Civil War responsibilities finally behind him, did Joseph Smith give serious attention to the Asylum library. In October of that year he asked that a catalog of all the books and periodicals in the library be created and additions to the collection noted as received. This resulted in the first surviving list of the library's contents, dated March 1868, that was soon followed by a recommendation that a beneficiary, "if there be one fit and trustworthy," be appointed as librarian. Thereafter Admiral Smith personally reviewed all requisitions for the purchase of books for the library, disapproving some titles, adding others he thought desirable, and questioning any proposed additions "I should think could not interest the old salts much."

That March 1868 catalog reveals a library of more than six hundred titles. The quality of the collection is surprisingly good. It testifies to the sophisticated reading tastes of the Asylum's beneficiaries and comes down on the side of those historians who argue for a high degree of before-the-mast literacy and book-reading. (Two caveats to that: there are no records of which beneficiaries were reading which books; additionally, one does not know to what extent the library's borrowing clientele may have come from the officers attached to the Asylum and their families.) Prominent on the shelves were long runs of the work of the nineteenth century's most popular novelists: James Fenimore Cooper, Charles Dickens,

George Eliot, Frederick Marryat, William Makepeace Thackery, and Sir Walter Scott. Then-contemporary novelists, whose reputations stand tall in the twenty-first century, were there as well: Nathaniel Hawthorne represented by *The Scarlet Letter* and *The House of Seven Gables*; Herman Melville by *Typee* and *Moby Dick*, and even *White-Jacket*, with its critical portrayal of enlisted life in the U.S. Navy. Add to which there was a good supply of popular fiction of the day, books that are now forgotten or of interest only to specialist scholars—Henry Morford's *The Days of Shoddy: A Novel of the Great Rebellion in 1861* (1863) or John W. De Forest's *Miss Ravenel's Conversion from Secession to Loyalty* (1867).

Biography appears to have been popular, with lives available ranging from those of George Washington and John Paul Jones, through Napoleon Bonaparte, Aaron Burr, Andrew Jackson, and Zachary Taylor, to contemporaries General George B. McClellan and sitting President Andrew Johnson. History stood on the shelves in classic works, whether Edward Gibbon's *The History of the Decline and Fall of the Roman Empire* or William Hickling Prescott's *History of the Conquest of Mexico*. Of more contemporary interest were a substantial number of titles that chronicled the recent national trauma of the Civil War, both graphic personal narratives—*The Iron Furnace; or, Slavery and Secession*, by the Rev. John H. Aughey, a "refugee" from Mississippi—and authoritative documents: *General Sherman's Official Account of His Great March through Georgia and the Carolinas, from His Departure from Chattanooga to the Surrender of General Joseph E. Johnston and the Confederate Forces under His Command*. Travel and the exotic were popular with nineteenth-century readers. The Asylum's beneficiaries were no exception. One beneficiary might pick up William C. Prime's *Tent Life in the Holy Land*, another *A Popular Account of the Thugs and Dacoits: The Hereditary Garotters and Gang-robbers of India*, by James Hutton. Closer to home was a book by one of the Asylum's own—Chaplain Walter Colton's narrative of his part in the war with Mexico, *Three Years in California*, published in 1850.

No library of the time was complete without an ample selection of religious works. The spectrum in the Asylum's library was broad. It ran from books of straightforward faith—William Berrian's *Sailors' and Soldiers' Manual of Devotion* and John Whitecross' *Anecdotes Illustrative of Select Passages in Each Chapter of the New Testament*—through historical and theological analysis represented by

Horatius Bonar's *Man, His Religion and His World*, to touch the frontier of doubt in David Nelson's *The Cause and Cure of Infidelity, Including a Notice of the Author's Unbelief and the Means of His Rescue*. If the latter work failed to relieve anxiety about life after death, a questioning beneficiary could take a different tack through Robert Dale Owen's advocacy of spiritualism and apparitions from beyond the grave: *Footfalls on the Boundary of Another World*.

Surprisingly perhaps, the Asylum's library contained relatively little by way of naval history. Perhaps the old sailors and Marines had lived enough of their service's history and wanted to read about anything else. What little there was included the two volumes of James Fenimore Cooper's *Lives of Distinguished American Naval Officers*, a classic much treasured by twenty-first century collectors and naval historians, and Abel Bowen's celebration of the War of 1812, *The Naval Monument, Containing Official and Other Accounts of All the Battles Fought between the Navies of the United States and Great Britain during the Late War, and an Account of the War with Algiers*. Of the numerous ex-sailor autobiographies published before the Civil War only Henry James Mercier's *Life in a Man-of-War; or, Scenes in "Old Ironsides" during Her Cruise in the Pacific* made it to the shelves of the Asylum's library. If the ghost of two-time Asylum Executive Officer Andrew Hull Foote, who died an admiral in 1863, ever revisited the home on Gray's Ferry Road, he must have been pleased to see that the library still held a copy of his 1854 book *Africa and the American Flag*. This, Foote's most significant literary work, combines a description of West Africa, the founding and history of Liberia, and a narrative of Foote's command of the brig *Perry*, 1849–51, the latter as part of the joint British and American effort to suppress the illegal slave trade. Fittingly enough, *Africa and the American Flag* is dedicated to Foote's friend Commodore Joseph Smith.

The beneficiary chosen as librarian to preside over this collection was a man named Angus Wheeler. He is "a large, fleshy, florid man—eyes ferrety and wandering," wrote Assistant Surgeon John L. Neilson as he checked Wheeler into the hospital on 12 January 1872 with a diagnosis of incipient delirium tremens. Wheeler had been drinking steadily for seven or eight days; two days before his admission he began to experience stomach pains, nausea, and vomiting. It had been at least forty-eight hours since he had last been able to sleep. Wheeler needed to dry out, and the hospital was the best place. What Dr. Neilson, habitually censorious and

condescending toward his alcoholic patients, may not have known
was that he was admitting one of the Asylum's better-educated
beneficiaries and one of the few who was a veteran of all three of
the young country's armed forces: Army, Marine Corps, and Navy.

Something of a physical wreck now, if still intellectually capable, Angus Wheeler had once been a promising young man. He
was born in Harford County, Maryland, almost certainly in 1800.
The family was probably Roman Catholic. Upon his father's death
in 1809 nine-year-old Angus came under the care of the Rev.
Francis Beeston, Rector of the Catholic cathedral at Baltimore.
Father Beeston enrolled Angus in Georgetown College, where he
remained as a student from May 1809 until November 1815. Not
yet a degree-granting institution, Georgetown's curriculum resem-
bled that of an academy or preparatory school more than the twenty-
first-century university. Angus was a strong student academically,
winning honors in Christian Doctrine during one year of his enroll-
ment and in Latin and Greek another year. After he left Georgetown, aged fifteen, Angus Wheeler disappears from the historical
record for eight years. A not-particularly-reliable family tradition
holds that he studied to be a physician.[4]

That may be, but the next definite record of Angus Wheeler's
life comes in November 1823, when he enlisted in the Marine
Corps, quickly advanced to sergeant—a promotion that suggests
some previous, but unrecorded, military experience—and was
detailed to the frigate *United States*, Commodore Isaac Hull, for her
1824–27 cruise to the Pacific coast of South America. Hull almost
immediately gave Wheeler an additional assignment as the frigate's master-at-arms, a posting that he filled for the entire cruise.
When *United States'* crew was discharged at Norfolk in April 1827
Wheeler rounded out his five-year Marine Corps enlistment in
the Corps' barracks at the New York (Brooklyn) Navy Yard.

Now Wheeler made one of his several career swerves, signing
on—or possibly being recruited—as purser's steward in the sloop-
of-war *Natchez*, 1829–31, a petty-officer rating for which his education made him strongly qualified. Wheeler made two cruises in
Caribbean waters in *Natchez*, after which he returned to the Marine
Corps for a short enlistment, October 1831–June 1832, as sergeant
with the detachment at the Boston (Charlestown) Navy Yard. One
suspects that he was released from this enlistment early because
he was needed as purser's steward in the sloop-of-war *Fairfield*,

Commander Elie A. F. Lavallette. In her, Wheeler made a May 1833–December 1835 cruise to the Pacific Ocean—the second of his three recorded voyages to that remote part of the world.[5] *Fairfield* service was followed by another career swerve: Angus Wheeler joined the Army as a private in Company F, Second Dragoons. His Army service, April 1839–April 1844, included, Wheeler later said, "about" three years of campaigning in Florida during the Second Seminole War.

Following his Army discharge there is a small hole in the record of Wheeler's life before his final career swerve—this time back to the Navy. He joined the frigate *United States*, Captain Jesse Wilkinson, in 1846 for a two-year cruise up the Mediterranean. The badly damaged condition of *United States'* surviving rolls makes it impossible to recover Wheeler's rating or his dates of enlistment and discharge; considering his earlier and succeeding service it is probable that he was once more posted as purser's steward. Discharge from *United States* is followed by a larger hole in Angus Wheeler's life story until he joins the sloop-of-war *Vincennes*, 2 March 1853, as purser's steward for his third recorded voyage to the Pacific and his first to sub-Arctic and Arctic waters as a participant in the United States Surveying Expedition to the North Pacific Ocean, 1853–56.

The North Pacific Exploring Expedition was Angus Wheeler's last service at sea. Discharge from *Vincennes* on 25 January 1856 was soon followed by a May admission to the Naval Asylum. As with many of his fellow-beneficiaries met in *Ungentle Goodnights*, Angus Wheeler indulged in periodic spells of alcoholism, some of them marked by verbal abuse and physical violence toward his peers. Probably because of his unique role as librarian—was there another beneficiary who could have done the job as well?—and also because of his clerical ability to assist the governor's office with the occasional paperwork overload, the Asylum authorities cut him an ample measure of slack in their periodic evaluations of his conduct: "Occasionally intemperate." "Slightly intemperate." "Intemperate at times." Such evaluations appear lenient indeed when read alongside Wheeler's record of alcohol-fueled misconduct and violence recorded in the Asylum's log. Angus Wheeler's final hospital admission for alcohol abuse occurred on 24 April 1874. He died ninety days later on 23 July. The official cause on Wheeler's death certificate is dropsy and cirrhosis of the liver, but the autopsy conducted eight hours after his death revealed the full extent of alcohol-related damage to his body: a cirrhotic and enlarged liver, an enlarged spleen, one kidney marked by fatty degeneration, and a distended gallbladder with three gallstones.

LIFE'S BUSINESS IS OVER

Concern for the spiritual welfare of its enlisted force, if it existed at all, was a low priority for the United States Navy of 1794–1815. With some exceptions, naval chaplains were not clergy, but well-educated men, more valued as schoolmasters to a frigate's midshipmen or as secretaries to relieve a commodore's paperwork burden than for any religious role they might fill. These priorities reflected the attitudes of the larger community that the Navy served. Broadly speaking, the early republic was a secular society, one more absorbed with the political, diplomatic, and military demands of establishing a new nation and insuring its respect abroad than with less-immediate spiritual matters. God was acknowledged and invoked. Churches existed and were attended. But, for the typical citizen, God—or, if one preferred, the Supreme Being—was conveniently remote and not overly concerned with individual humans, their behaviors and needs. So, too, the U.S. Navy was primarily focused on getting itself organized, being taken seriously as an arm of the federal government, and fighting three maritime wars. Recruiting, training, clothing, feeding, and retaining an enlisted force were the front-and-center concerns. All this began to change after 1815, as a strong revival of personal religious involvement and enthusiasm took hold in the new nation. The nation's Navy was not immune to this sea-change in the prevailing ethos. Beginning in 1816, and with increasing consistency thereafter, the Navy sought Protestant clergy for its chaplains; they, in turn, gave a new emphasis to the shipboard religious services and began voicing concern for the moral welfare of sailors.[6]

Eventually, if slowly, this newfound interest in the spiritual well-being of the lower deck reached the United States Naval Asylum and beneficiaries. The first resident chaplain, John Walter Grier, was not appointed until April 1842, when the Asylum had been in operation for over a decade. As to whether, before Grier's appointment, there had been occasional services at the Asylum by clergy from the Philadelphia area, or whether—as would have been the custom on shipboard—the governor or the executive officer led a Sunday service the record is completely silent. During the years that are the subject of *Ungentle Goodnights* sixteen clergymen served as chaplains at the Naval Asylum: six of them Episcopalians, five Presbyterians (including the Reverend Grier), three Methodists, one Baptist, and one Congregationalist. At least in the nineteenth century, and contrary to the oft-repeated assertion, the Episcopal faith was clearly not the unofficial religion of the Navy; many denominations were equally honored and served.

By 1846 Sunday's pattern had settled down to this: 10 a.m., general muster of the beneficiaries, followed by service in the chapel; 1 p.m., service in the hospital; 7 p.m., evening service in the chapel. The morning service was enhanced by a professional organist and two female vocalists. It took a while to persuade the Secretary of the Navy that it was important to fund stipendiary music at the Asylum, but the chaplains and the governors were unanimous in support of vocal music's necessity. "Sailors are extremely partial to this portion of public worship," said Walter Colton, the Asylum's second chaplain, "and without it, it is impossible for me to give that interest to these services which they ought to possess and which the contentment and moral benefit of the [beneficiaries] require." Governor Charles W. Morgan was even more to the point. Without music the chapel service was "exceedingly monotonous." Persistence eventually won the day; the secretary agreed to the expenditure. Once approved, the organist and two soloists at Sunday worship became an Asylum tradition that continued well into the 1880s—and perhaps beyond.

More variety and interest: the beneficiaries did not have to listen to the same preacher every Sunday. Through the years a long list of guest clergy—many from Philadelphia, others from farther away but passing through the city—officiated at the chapel. The Asylum's log records at least one occasion when Governor William W. McKean led the evening service. On 23 April 1854 the Asylum's executive officer, Andrew Hull Foote, preached the sermon, an opportunity the zealously religious Foote must have relished. Whether the elderly beneficiaries, deaf or not, could hear the sermons was another matter. The rotunda was the Asylum's only space large enough for church service, but it had infamous acoustical problems: echoes bounced around, and the speaker's voice—unless it was truly stentorian—disappeared upward into the dome. Successive governors proposed and tried various solutions to remediate the problem, but it was never really solved in an era lacking electronic magnification for the human voice.

What of the Asylum's Roman Catholics—most of them Irish—amid all this nineteenth-century American Protestantism? Before June 1847, when Lieutenant Alonzo B. Davis became executive officer, Roman Catholics were not permitted to leave the grounds to attend Sunday Mass—presumably at St. Patrick's, the nearest Catholic church, located on Twentieth Street between Locust and Spruce. Davis immediately reversed this restriction. Thereafter, in a policy more than once emphatically reaffirmed by the Navy Department, Roman Catholic beneficiaries were required to attend Sunday muster, but could fall out before the Protestant service began and (assuming they were not confined to the grounds for some infraction) head off to St. Patrick's. Or did they? In 1858 Governor William W. McKean told Commodore Joseph Smith that he had reason to believe that some beneficiaries were only claiming to be Roman Catholics so that they could be excused from the Asylum's Sunday service and get off the grounds but never darkened the door at St. Patrick's or any other church. Other than avoiding church at the Asylum, what the motivation for this deception might have been is unknown. Certainly not a thirst for alcohol, as Philadelphia's blue laws kept taverns well locked up on Sundays. Smith proposed that McKean check with the pastor at St. Patrick's to see which beneficiaries actually attended Sunday Mass; whether the governor followed up on this suggestion is not on record.

Religious faith or its absence is intensely personal, the truth of the matter typically known only to the individual. In the case of the Naval Asylum's beneficiaries not one of the five hundred forty-one men who are the subject of *Ungentle Goodnights* left behind a single word on that subject. When writing about religion at the nineteenth-century Asylum the historian can only speak of its external manifestations. The closest one can come to beneficiary beliefs—or perhaps fears—are the final days of Richard Merchant. A man in his early fifties, Merchant was born in Baltimore, learned the printer's trade, and did one three-year enlistment in the Army before moving to the Marine Corps. In the latter force Merchant served five consecutive enlistments until ill health forced his discharge in October 1845 and his immediate admission to the Naval Asylum and its hospital. The Asylum's log for 22 December 1845 records that the recently assigned chaplain,

Theodore B. Bartow, an Episcopalian, baptized Merchant, "now sick in the hospital." Two weeks later, Merchant—by now close to death—received Communion from Chaplain Bartow and succumbed three days later, one hopes at peace with himself and his God. On 12 April 1846 Bartow administered Communion to three more unidentified hospital patients, presumably men in imminent danger of death. In June the chaplain requested Governor Charles W. Morgan's permission to purchase vessels—a flagon, a plate, and a chalice—appropriate for the administration of Communion, noting in justification: "There are several communicants in this house of the Episcopal, Methodist, Lutheran and Presbyterian denominations to whom I am frequently called to administer the Holy Communion. To use the common vessels from our [dining] tables, as we are now obliged to do, seems irreverent." Bartow's request was passed up the line to Secretary of the Navy George Bancroft and speedily approved.

That is pretty much the sum total of what is known about individual religious faith among the five hundred forty-one men who entered the Naval Asylum before 1866. By its nature the real work of the institution's chaplains left few footprints in the surviving record: "The business of life is over with most of the beneficiaries, and their advanced age makes it certain they will soon enter upon another state of existence," Governor William W. McKean reminded Commodore Joseph Smith when advocating the importance of having the chaplain reside on the Asylum's grounds. "With this view of the case, nothing can be of so much real importance to them as the instructions of a conscientious chaplain. The mere preaching a sermon on the Sabbath is a small matter in comparison to the good that could be done by constant intercourse with them."

McKean's is the best and most detailed statement that an Asylum governor made about a chaplain's central, but largely unrecorded, role in the life of the institution. As to how well the men who successively filled that office met the ideal there survives only one scrap of evidence. When Beneficiary John Hanford, a notorious alcoholic, orally harassed and physically threatened Chaplain Henry Wood in October 1865, the whole ugly business had to be reported up the line to Joseph Smith. Governor Frederick Engle came vigorously to Wood's defense. "I was much surprised [at Hanford's behavior] for I thought Mr. Wood had the love and esteem of everyone," wrote Engle. "Certainly he deserves it. His whole time is in the service of the hospital patients, frequently placing him at considerable expense in searching up their relatives, attending to the wants of the dying, and in carrying out their wishes after death." If Governor Engle's was a fair assessment, the Reverend Henry Wood was a worthy spiritual ancestor of the heroic Navy chaplains of World War II.

NINE

WHAT SHALL WE DO WITH THE DRUNKEN SAILOR?

Violence was always lurking below the orderly surface of life at the United States Naval Asylum. Alcohol was the agent that propelled violence to the surface.

At supper in the late afternoon of 7 May 1845, an intoxicated beneficiary, Michael Johnson, saw Philip Graba, a fellow beneficiary for whom he had an intense dislike, enter the dining room and approach the opposite side of the table to that on which Johnson was sitting. Johnson rose and came around the table, armed with a large stick and the intention of beating Graba. Master-at-Arms John Fitzmorris, whose responsibility it was to maintain order in the dining room, intervened to prevent a fight, whereupon Michael Johnson struck Fitzmorris instead. Fitzmorris managed to force Johnson to the floor—no easy task, as a fellow beneficiary later described five-foot-three Johnson as "a middling small man, but powerful strong for his size." The master-at-arms then sent for Asa Curtis, the gunner assigned to the Asylum staff, to help him control Johnson. Curtis in turn called in Lieutenant Robert E. Johnson, the executive officer, who told Fitzmorris and Curtis to take Michael Johnson up to the cells and confine him. The two of them had gotten the struggling Johnson as far as the landing between the basement and the first floor when Johnson announced that he was not going to be confined; he was going to see the governor, Commodore Charles W. Morgan, to complain about the manner in which he was being treated. This brought on a three-way struggle that resulted in Michael Johnson, John Fitzmorris, and Asa Curtis all falling to the floor, with Johnson sustaining a nasty wound when his head hit the bannister or the stair edge in the fall.

Beneficiary Johnson now grabbed Fitzmorris by the neckerchief, at which point Executive Officer Johnson intervened and allegedly told Fitzmorris, "Choke the damned son of a bitch—Choke him!" while (also allegedly) stamping his foot on Michael Johnson's chest and neck. By this time someone had retrieved the leg and hand restraints, which were used on strongly agitated or violent beneficiaries. Fitzmorris and Curtis got these on Michael Johnson and—with the devices in place—finally propelled him into a cell, where Assistant Surgeon Richard T. Maxwell treated him for his injuries. A subsequent court-martial censured Robert Johnson for his brutality to Michael Johnson and one other beneficiary, sentencing him to a six-month suspension from duty and a public reprimand from the Secretary of the Navy.[1]

The title of the worst beneficiary at the Naval Asylum was a hotly contested one, but Michael Johnson was a strong contender for the dishonor. Several of the witnesses at Lieutenant Robert Johnson's court-martial were asked to give their impressions of beneficiary Johnson:

> BENEFICIARY HUGH SCOTT: He was bad, both on board ship and ashore.
>
> GUNNER ASA CURTIS: A man I considered a very dangerous man. . . . He was very troublesome whilst drunk and an ugly man at any time. A bad man I should call him.
>
> BENEFICIARY JOHN WARD: He is a very drunken character—very ill-disposed, violent, and passionate. He is not an agreeable man whilst sober amongst agreeable people.
>
> MASTER-AT-ARMS JOHN FITZMORRIS: I believe him to be about as bad a man as I ever came across. He was [at the time of the dining hall incident] about three parts drunk—his worst time. He has never acted improperly to me when sober; he is dangerous when drunk. . . . I took some very large sticks at one time from him. One of them had a spike in the top of it about an inch or an inch and a half long.

Who was Michael Johnson, this man so powerful and so feared? Fortunately for history, he left a not-always-accurate manuscript autobiographical statement that, together with records created about him at the Naval Asylum and elsewhere, enables the reconstruction of his life in some detail.

Unusually for a sailor, Johnson asserted that he knew the exact date of his birth—4 January 1781. It had been, he said, at Salem, Massachusetts, where his family was positioned so low on the socioeconomic hierarchy that his birth escapes notice in the published six-volume register of Salem nativities, marriages, and deaths before the year 1850. Young Michael presumably first went to sea in the merchant service around April 1805, when he swore out a seaman's protection certificate at the Salem customs house. In this document he said he was sixteen—the typical age for entering the adult working world—which makes the asserted January 1781 birth date one among several pieces of misleading or fallacious data in his autobiographical record.

Johnson's earliest recorded naval service was in the brig *Hornet*, Master Commandant James Lawrence, for a voyage to France. He signed on 1 September 1811, rated as seaman, evidence that the previous six years afloat had made him a fully skilled mariner. One day, while *Hornet* lay at Cherbourg, Johnson was sent ashore in command of one of the brig's cutters. The wind rose to gale force. Johnson and his cutter were unable to return to *Hornet*, taking shelter alongside a French lugger in the port. In coming alongside under the rough conditions, Johnson's arm was caught between the cutter and the lugger, breaking the arm and dislocating his collarbone. This injury was serious enough that Johnson was subsequently sent ashore, 10 June 1812, to the naval hospital at Brooklyn and was not able to rejoin *Hornet* before the declaration of war. It was also considered a sufficient basis for Johnson to be awarded a pension of three dollars a month in August 1839, even though the permanent disability, if any, was not serious enough to have kept him from an active-duty career at sea in the intervening twenty-seven years.

Just when Johnson was discharged from the hospital is uncertain, but he joined *United States* in April 1813 and served in the blockaded frigate for twelve uneventful months with the rating of seaman. Here follows a seven-month hiatus in Johnson's service record until he reenlisted in *United States*, once again rated seaman, on 13 November 1814. This enlistment was mysteriously short; Johnson was discharged six months later, on 12 May 1815, with no reason for his early release from service stated. Events in his next recorded service in the U.S. Navy hint at what may have happened.

That service was in the frigate *Guerriere* on the Mediterranean station. Johnson joined her on 9 May 1818, was promoted from seaman to quarter-gunner in less than three weeks, served in that capacity until 15 January 1819, then was disrated to seaman. Eight months later, on 22 September, Michael Johnson was in big trouble. Because Johnson was creating a disturbance with a patient in *Guerriere's* sickbay, Midshipman Walter F. Jones was instructed to apprehend and confine the disorderly Johnson. The latter responded by physically attacking Midshipman Jones. Here was a violation of command and order that could not be tolerated. Johnson was court-martialed, received fifty lashes with the cat-of-nine-tails, and was summarily discharged from *Guerriere* on 6 December 1819. The most interesting aspect of Johnson's court-martial record was his defense of his behavior. He asserted that he had sustained a head injury at some earlier date; that this made him crazy (his word) when he drank; and that he had on an unspecified earlier occasion—most likely the unexplained 1815 early departure from *United States*—been discharged from the Navy as insane (again his word). At the court-martial *Guerriere's* assistant surgeon, John W. Peaco, testified that he had examined Johnson's head and found evidence of several old wounds, one of them "pretty severe." Johnson never explained how he received these head injuries, but it was probably in some shoreside brawl from his merchant-service days, as he did not claim them as service-related in his later application for a Navy pension. Although these old head wounds are never again mentioned in the records of Johnson's life, it is likely that a combination of the old brain injury and alcohol explains his dangerously violent behavior when he drank.

For the eleven and a half years of Johnson's life following his discharge from *Guerriere*—an event that he concealed in his autobiographical statement—no official record has been found. The sole source is his own old-age story of his life. Johnson claimed to have served in *United States* during Commodore Isaac Hull's 1824–27 command of the U.S. squadron on the Pacific coast of South America. This may have been so, but several searches of the rolls of *United States* during these years have failed to find his name. If he did serve, it could have been under a false name, one assumed to hide his court-martial and punishment in *Guerriere*.

According to Johnson, his enlistment expired while *United States* was still in the Pacific, and he was discharged at Callao, Peru. Thereafter, he said he served in a series of Latin American navies during their wars of independence from Spain, culminating in service in Mexico's navy. Johnson reported that he was in the 22-gun Mexican brig *Guerrero* during her February 1828 battle with, and capture by, the Spanish 54-gun *Lealtad*, a bloody conflict which he recalled in sufficiently accurate detail to convince this historian that Michael Johnson really was there.[2]

Capture in *Guerrero* was followed by several months in a Cuban prison, after which Johnson made his way to New Orleans, where he served for a year and a half in that station's revenue cutter, presumably in the *Louisiana*, but possibly in her replacement, the *Ingham*, or perhaps in both. From New Orleans Johnson eventually made his way back to the east coast; thereafter the narrative of his life can be verified from sources other than his own recollections. On 7 June 1831 Johnson joined the sloop-of-war *Falmouth*, Commander Francis H. Gregory, with the rating of quarter-gunner. Johnson was once more bound for familiar waters along the west coast of South America. There, at Callao, after a year and a half of service, he was discharged from *Falmouth* and loaned, together with two other men from the sloop-of-war, to a short-handed French ship bound to Bordeaux with a high-value cargo. One cannot help wondering if Captain Gregory's choice of Johnson for this duty might have been a convenient opportunity to rid *Falmouth* of a difficult sailor—but the truth of that can only be a guess. Back in the United States by 10 June 1832, Johnson joined the frigate *United States* as quarter-gunner, was almost immediately promoted to boatswain's mate—his highest career rating and a reflection of his competence as a seaman—and held that post until 15 February 1833, when he was transferred to the frigate *Brandywine* at the lower rating of quarter-gunner. The following July, Johnson— still rated quarter-gunner—was again transferred to the Boston-based receiving ship *Franklin*, from which he was discharged on 12 August 1833 as "unfit for service"—whether for health or behavioral reasons the roll does not state.

During the next twenty-eight months Michael Johnson returned to the merchant service, in which he said he made three voyages before rejoining the U.S. Navy for his final active-duty cruises: first, eleven months, December 1835–November 1836, with the rating of seaman, in the sloop-of-war *Warren* in the West Indies and, second, in the sloop-of-war *Levant*, Commander Hiram Paulding, again in the West Indies. Neither Johnson's rating, nor his dates of service in *Levant*, can now be verified; the sloop-of-war's surviving rolls are too badly water-damaged to determine with total certainty whether his claim to have been a member of the ship's company is an accurate one.

In 1839, as mentioned earlier, Johnson applied for, and was granted a pension of three dollars per month for the injury in *Hornet*. The documentation that Johnson was disabled by this old injury was rather flimsy, but the more realistic bases of the award were his long service in the Navy, his age—he claimed to be fifty-seven, but was more likely around fifty—and his allegedly decrepit health, which had caused his rejection at his most recent attempt to reenlist. Because the pension, awarded on 29 August 1839, was retroactive to 31 January 1812, Johnson would have received a lump-sum payment of nearly one thousand dollars. Whether he spent this sailor's small fortune wisely or squandered the money is not known. He apparently did a bit of double-dipping during this time as well, since—by his own account—he worked at the Norfolk Navy Yard for a year and served for a year in the revenue cutter which operated out of Norfolk. Johnson reported that he lost the use of one of his eyes during this time, though how that happened he did not say, but by March 1843—when he was in his mid-fifties—he said that he was no longer fit for demanding physical work and applied to commute his pension for admission to the Naval Asylum. (Note that these claims of decrepitude and inability to perform demanding physical work are at odds with the previously quoted 1845 court-martial testimony that he was still a powerful man for his size. However, pension applications typically over-represented the applicant's physical decay.) A permit of admission to the Asylum was granted on the twenty-third of the month and Michael Johnson began his equally stormy—or, if one prefers, colorful—career as a resident of old-age refuges for mariners.

It took just two months for Michael Johnson to get into trouble and less than six months to be kicked out of the Asylum—for the first time. On 22 May he was reported for drunkenness, apparently a serious first offense, as he was consigned to the cells for four days. Two months later he was back in the cells for another four days, this time for being drunk, behaving in a riotous manner, and smuggling liquor onto the grounds. Finally, on 1 September 1843, came the patience-breaker for Governor William W. McKean. Johnson had gone into Philadelphia, came back intoxicated, assaulted the gatekeeper, then grabbed at McKean or his jacket when the governor came to investigate the disturbance. McKean had Johnson expelled from the grounds with orders not to return until sober. Johnson had not gotten far from the gate when he came upon one of his fellow beneficiaries, a shaky old man, on whom he vented his rage by knocking him to the ground. That was more than enough for McKean, who secured Johnson's 4 September dismissal from the Asylum.

He was not gone for long. Johnson apparently made his way to Washington, where—through his subterfuge and someone's carelessness in the Navy Office—he was able, on 25 September, to obtain a new permit of admission to the Asylum as though he had never been there. Governor McKean was hardly pleased. Johnson's behavior "has been worse than that of any other attached to the institution," and now he was back. Things rocked along for two years, with Johnson keeping his behavior just this side of dismissal, although he was confined in cells seven times for periods up to nine days for his customary misbehavior. Finally, at some point between his 7 May 1845 tussle with Gunner Asa Curtis, Master-at-Arms John Fitzmorris, and Lieutenant Robert Johnson and the opening of Lieutenant Johnson's court-martial on 20 August, Michael Johnson slipped quietly away—no one knew where. He had already suffered hard punishment at the hands of one court-martial in his naval career; perhaps he was apprehensive of being called as a witness at Johnson's trial and what might come out under cross-examination.

It is not clear whether anyone at the Asylum learned what had become of him, but Michael Johnson had gone to Sailors' Snug Harbor, the Asylum's privately funded sister institution in New York, which served merchant mariners, and had been admitted there on 9 August 1845. From Snug Harbor's records one learns for the first time that the "infirm" Johnson had a wife and one son living in Boston and another son at sea. He managed to hang on at Snug Harbor for nearly four years, finally being expelled on 23 July 1849 for "intemperance and absenting himself from the institution all night and for his insolent language to the Governor [Snug Harbor's chief administrator] on his return to the institution"—still the same old Michael Johnson.

Out on his own once more, Johnson lost little time before attempting to return to the U.S. Naval Asylum. Supervision of the Asylum had by now been transferred from the office of the Secretary of the Navy to the Bureau of Yards and Docks. At this point the Bureau seems to have had little or no institutional memory of the Asylum's beneficiaries or their behavior before the change of responsibility. Johnson applied to commute his now six-dollar-a-month pension—"insufficient for my support"—for admission to the Asylum, a place he never mentioned that he had ever been before. The ruse worked; on 1 September 1849, Michael Johnson had a new permit of admission.

Johnson's behavior over the next three years and two months was about what could have been expected: drinking, smuggling alcohol, fighting, striking beneficiary John Anderson with a cane, kicking beneficiary William Hull. The culminating misdeed took place on 1 November 1852, when Assistant Surgeon James McClelland caught Johnson smuggling liquor to patients in the hospital. Johnson's response was to declare McClelland a "damned villain" and a "damned son-of-a-bitch"—behavior that insured his dismissal from the Asylum on 6 November.

One way or another Johnson eked out an existence on his pension until the summer of 1853, when he persuaded Commodore Joseph Smith, probably against the latter's better judgment, to admit him to the Asylum yet one more time on account of his "long service in the Navy and advanced old age." (Johnson was almost certainly now around sixty-four years old, though he represented himself to be seventy-two.) This, Johnson's fourth residence at the Asylum, lasted something less than eighteen months, at which point—late December 1854—Governor George W. Storer threw up his hands and requested Johnson's removal from the Asylum. He is "the most insubordinate and troublesome man here and [is] entirely regardless of the regulations. . . . He will not be controlled by any means at my disposal." And out he went on 17 January 1855. Joseph Smith had keen misgivings about turning Johnson away in the middle of winter, but he need not have worried. Johnson soon made his way to the Blockley alms house across the Schuylkill, where he identified himself as "single." What, one wonders, had become of his wife and two children? Johnson remained snug, if far from luxuriously comfortable, at Blockley until 4 April, when the arrival of spring weather lured him out and on his way.

But to where? The next twenty-nine months are another void in the discovered record of Johnson's life. In August 1857 he managed to secure readmission to Sailors' Snug Harbor, where he survived something short of four years before being expelled as drunk and disorderly on 11 May 1861. This dismissal may just have been a short-term cautionary one, as he was readmitted on 24 July of that same year. By now Michael Johnson was a man about seventy-two years old—eighty by his own account—and he may not have had much fight left in him. At least there are no demerits recorded against him between that July 1861 readmission and his death at Snug Harbor on 21 March 1869—perhaps a quiet end to a life of violence.

GETTING PICKLED

Drinking to excess and its follow-on effects—accidental self-injuries, interpersonal violence, defiance of authority—were far and away the most common and the most challenging beneficiary behavior problems with which those who administered the Naval Asylum had to cope. Why this was so is a complex story.

The Asylum was officially a totally dry institution. The initial 1834 regulations provided that a ration, "similar to that now used in the naval service," but "omitting spirits and substituting for it tea, tobacco, and pickles," would be provided for the beneficiaries. Secretary Abel P. Upshur's 1843 revision of the regulations did not specifically mention *no spirits*, but implied as much when it said that, in addition to the beneficiaries' pocket-money allowance of eleven cents per week, they would receive cash compensation in lieu of a spirit ration. When Commodore Joseph Smith took over the supervision of the Asylum in 1849, he cleared up any lingering ambiguity in the regulations in his usual no-nonsense fashion. Smith's revision of the rules provided, in Article XI: "No liquors of any kind will be allowed the inmates of the institution; nor will they be allowed to bring them into the building. A violation of this regulation will be deemed a sufficient cause for dismissal from the Asylum."

Beneficiaries who on arrival were transitioning to a totally dry environment had spent their active-duty years in a navy with a quite different tradition. From its earliest days the U.S. Navy had provided its enlisted force with alcohol as an integral part of the daily ration—half a pint of *spirits* per man per day. Initially, following the Royal Navy tradition, spirits were provided in the form of imported rum. In 1806 whiskey was substituted for rum to support the home-grown distilling business of states such as Pennsylvania and Kentucky. A typical Navy contract from the 1820s specified: "copper distilled whiskey, full first proof according to the United States Standard, made wholly from grain, at least one-third of which shall be rye." Full first-proof whiskey by the United States Standard was 50 percent alcohol and 50 percent water.[3] By tradition the half-pint of spirits was divided in two and served at two different times of day. Also, by tradition, the half-pint was diluted with water. But how much water? The Navy Department never issued a directive on that matter. The degree of dilution was left to the discretion of each ship's commanding officer. Evidence is scanty. One reliable source reports a ratio of equal parts of water and whiskey, which was probably typical, resulting in a tot which was 25 percent alcohol. However, when then-Captain Joseph Smith commanded the ship-of-the-line *Ohio*, he used the one-to-one whiskey-to-water ratio, but had the grog ration divided into three servings a day rather than two.[4]

Commencing in 1831, U.S. Navy sailors who chose to forego the daily spirit ration were compensated by adding six cents per day to their pay. This reflected the growing temperance movement in the United States. That movement itself was a response to the high per-capita consumption of alcoholic beverages in the United States in its first forty years as a newly independent nation—a widespread culture of indulgence and overindulgence skillfully chronicled in W. J. Rorabaugh's classic, *The Alcoholic Republic: An American Tradition* (1979). Congress rewrote the specifics of the Navy ration in an act of 29 August 1842. This new law reduced the daily spirit ration to one-quarter pint per day, but it also lessened the incentive to commute the spirit ration by cutting the cash compensation to two cents per day. The daily spirit ration in the U.S. Navy was totally abolished as of 1 September 1862, by which time the greater part of the five hundred forty-one Naval Asylum beneficiaries who are the subject of *Ungentle Goodnights* had retired from active duty.

The spirit ration in the nineteenth-century U.S. Navy had its advocates and its critics among the officer corps. In January 1850 Secretary of the Navy William Ballard Preston asked the Navy's senior officers whether the service could dispense with the spirit ration. Two of the replies came from men having substantial experience with the veteran Marines and sailors at the Naval Asylum— Commander Henry A. Adams, then serving his second tour as executive officer at the Asylum, and Commodore Joseph Smith. Their opinions could not have diverged more widely:

> COMMANDER ADAMS: The present allowance of grog, served out as it is, cannot hurt men who have been accustomed all their lives to much greater quantities. The certainty of getting it regularly is a strong inducement to seamen to enter the service. It is not this ration that makes them drunkards. Men very rarely get drunk at sea. It is in port, where the utmost vigilance of the officers cannot always prevent liquor from being smuggled on board, that all drunken excesses occur. Sailors have many ingenious ways of getting rum on board which will always be tried whether whiskey is allowed in the ration or not. Above all, it is the chief—almost the only—pleasure of the sailor's life at sea. He looks forward through the stormiest day to grog time as one moment of happiness. That draught repays him for hours of labor and exposure, and I think no one who has watched, as I have, the cheerful faces of a ship's company when the drum rolls to grog would ever wish to deprive them of the single pleasure of their lives.
>
> COMMODORE SMITH: The use of ardent spirits has been undoubtedly the primary cause of a very large proportion of the crimes and punishments in our Navy, and the daily use of grog on shipboard keeps alive the desire and thirst for its use. It is the *Grog Tub* which presents a strong inducement to the low and dissipated seaman to enter the service and, when daily paraded before the crew, offers temptation to those who might otherwise escape its baleful influence.[5]

When visiting a lovingly preserved and restored nineteenth-century sailing warship—whether the frigate *Constitution* at Boston or the sloop-of-war *Constellation* at Baltimore—it is difficult to avoid seeing these beautiful vessels through a rosy haze. One requires

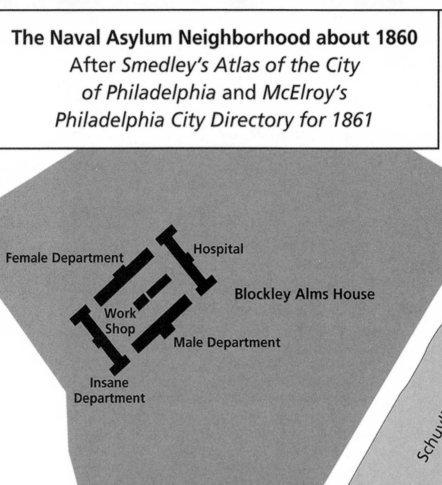

The Naval Asylum Neighborhood about 1860
After *Smedley's Atlas of the City of Philadelphia* and *McElroy's Philadelphia City Directory for 1861*

Female Department

Hospital

Blockley Alms House

Work Shop

Male Department

Insane Department

Schuylkill River

Sutherland

Schuylkill Ars

N

● Places known to sell alcoholic beverages

Thirtieth

Twenty-Ninth

Twenty-Eighth

Twenty-Seventh

0   1/16   1/8   3/16   1/4 Mile

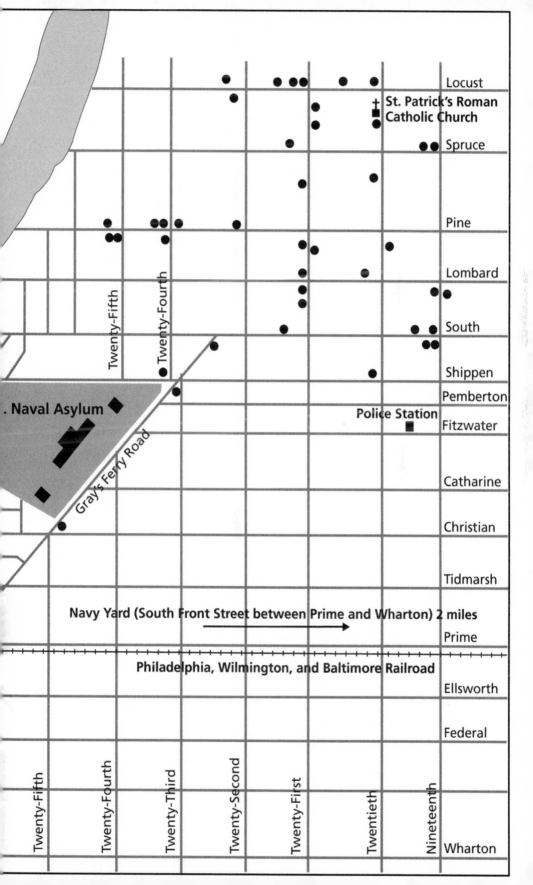

a hard-nosed realism to remember that life at sea in these ships was no romantic ocean cruise for the men of the vessel's lower deck. Living spaces were damp and often cold. Food—unless supplemented by a fortuitously caught fish or tasty seabird—was monotonous. One slept and ate next to sweaty men who bathed infrequently. Opportunities for leave ashore in foreign ports were scarce. Death or wounding from enemy action was far less of a danger than a shipboard accident or some strange disease in a remote part of the globe. Discipline and vigilance were constant and strict to maintain efficiency against unforeseen contingencies. Under such conditions is it any wonder that when a ship's sailors or Marines had a chance for shore leave or reached the end of an enlistment, the natural response was to forget it all temporarily through a deep plunge into shoreside alcohol in taverns and brothels?

By declaring the Asylum a dry institution the Navy made alcohol forbidden fruit, desirable if it could be obtained by any means—and especially so to men accustomed to its daily consumption for most or all of their working lives. And this was low-hanging forbidden fruit. The map of the Naval Asylum's neighborhood shows all of the known taverns and stores where alcohol could be purchased, fully justifying Governor Frederick Engle's lament: "The rum-shops around this place are so numerous that the great good which all are desirous [the beneficiaries] should enjoy is defeated. There never was a more perfect place for old men if rum could be kept from them." What are not marked on the map are the clandestine unlicensed places, such as private homes, where alcohol might be available for sale on the sly or the South Street taverns and brothels, popular with the beneficiaries, but located off the eastern side of the map. Confronted with an enemy ship or an approaching storm, a naval ship's company typically became a cohesive, disciplined unit, focused on a common goal. But in more routine hours the lower decks of the United States and British navies shared a tradition—usually good-natured, but sometimes not—of actively testing the boundaries, with the ship's officers in the role of rule-enforcers. What could the lower deck get away with and not be caught in the act? As Commander Henry Adams said, nowhere was this can-we-get-away-with-it tradition stronger than in the ingenious attempts to smuggle alcohol on board ship to supplement the grog ration.

Contemporary sociological and medical studies of alcohol use and abuse among the elderly and retirees provide insights which are useful in understanding the Naval Asylum's greatest behavioral challenge.[6]

To begin with the basic physiology: the same quantity of alcohol will produce a higher concentration of blood alcohol in an older person than it would have done in the same person in younger years. Because one's lean body mass has decreased in relation to fat, there is a parallel shrinkage in the volume of body water. The consequence: there is less fluid to dilute alcohol consumed. Aging also appears to diminish the older person's ability to metabolize alcohol, which lingers in the blood awaiting distribution to the brain. Simultaneously, aging weakens the barrier between blood and the brain, increasing the sensitivity of the receptors to which alcohol binds in the brain. All this adds up to intensify the effect of alcohol on the older individual. Compounding the problem, the aging body's natural repair processes for damaged cells and tissue have diminished with time, making recovery from overindulgence a slower and more difficult process.

Equally relevant to the Asylum beneficiaries' situation are certain psychological-sociological findings. Social networks have the effect of validating how much alcohol consumption is tolerated or sanctioned. Blue-collar occupations typically have permissive drinking cultures, tending to legitimatize heavy drinking among peers. Drinking to fit in socially with one's peers at work and drinking to deal with stress in the workplace are two powerful motivations for alcohol consumption. Men who drink heavily tend to drink in groups, a habit which can create an ambiance in which interpersonal conflicts flourish. Although the term blue-collar was not in use or applied to mariners in the nineteenth century, it is easy to see how these insights fit naval sailors from that era to perfection. In civilian life, alcohol consumption may decline after retirement and separation from the drinking culture of one's friends at work. But in the case of the Naval Asylum beneficiaries, these men transitioned into retirement alongside their hard-drinking shipmates from active-duty days. Add to this the hypothesis that individuals follow relatively stable patterns of alcohol consumption through life—at least until severe ill health curtails the ability to drink— and it is not difficult to see why the Naval Asylum's attempt to establish a temperate or dry culture at the institution was a set-up for chronic problems with beneficiary behavior.

WHAT *SHALL* WE DO?

Coping is the single word that best describes the response of the Navy's leadership—whether it was the more remote authorities in Washington or those charged with the immediate administration of the institution—to the problem of alcohol abuse at the Naval Asylum. They never solved the problem, but it was managed.

Joseph Smith was a resigned realist: "That the old salts will get drunk when liquor is . . . placed before them is not at all surprising, and that they will be unruly and insubordinate when so is always the case." What should be the response to these ingrained habits? The philosophy articulated by Secretary Abel P. Upshur in 1842 was one that was shared by Smith and the governors of the Asylum late into the nineteenth century—even if none of them went back through the files to find Upshur's original articulation. The Asylum had been created with money deducted from the beneficiaries' pay while they had been on active duty, Upshur wrote, and it was intended as their refuge in old age. Consequently, while "it is undeniable that some degree of discipline must be maintained at the Asylum and punishment awarded for a violation of its regulations," the nature and extent of that punishment was left to the discretion of the governors, subject to any applicable laws and the final authority of the Secretary of the Navy. Dismissal from the Asylum always required the Secretary's approval. But before turning to that ultimate sanction, Upshur continued, "the mildest and most forbearing course seems to be most proper towards men in the decline of life and who have devoted their best years to the service of the country."

Short of dismissal, four sanctions were available to, and used by, the governors and their executive officers: (1) restriction to the grounds for a period of time; (2) suspension of the monthly allowance of pocket money; (3) suspension of the tobacco allowance; and (4), in the case of extreme drunken behavior, confinement in cells overnight or for a few days, occasionally on a diet of bread and water. These sanctions created their own follow-on problem: men who were entitled to leave the grounds would smuggle alcohol in for their peers who were restricted—"an offense," said Governor David Geisinger, "considered here to be the worst of all that are committed," and one that frequently led to a recommendation of dismissal from the Asylum. More often than not such dismissals were followed by a period of repentance for the offender, living in a sailors' boarding house or rough on Philadelphia's streets; by an appeal for forgiveness to Joseph Smith or the Secretary of the Navy, often seconded by the Asylum's governor or executive officer; by a stern *don't-do-it-again-or-face-another-dismissal* warning from Smith; and by eventual restoration to the Asylum.

This practice, in turn, brought its own set of problems. Beneficiaries quickly detected how the system worked and figured that, unless their offense was so serious that it resulted in a dismissal without any possibility of readmission—and that *did* happen—they could misbehave in a major way, get kicked out, then appeal to soft-on-old-sailors Joseph Smith for a lecture and eventual readmission. The case of Thomas Reynolds provides an extreme example of how the system—and Joseph Smith—could be manipulated to advantage.

Officers who had been Reynolds' shipmates remembered him as a skilled member of the carpenter's crew and carpenter's mate, one who had served in the Navy more or less continuously since, as a young man of twenty, he joined *Constitution* in 1824 with the rating of ordinary seaman. Recruiting records from the height of Reynolds' active-duty career in the mid-1840s describe a man just short of seventy inches tall, with gray eyes, red hair, and a ruddy complexion. Once Reynolds was admitted to the Naval Asylum, on 16 May 1859, the good reputation he had earned at sea became only a memory. Between his admission and 12 August of that same year Reynolds was on report no fewer than eight times for drunkenness and unauthorized absences. This behavior pattern had begun just two days after his admission to the Asylum when, drunk, he forced his way out the gate in spite of the best efforts of the gatekeeper to stop him and disappeared for three days. On Sunday, 7 August, while he was restricted to the grounds for violation of the rules, Reynolds informed Governor William W. McKean that his mother—Reynolds was a native of Philadelphia—was seriously ill and requested special permission to visit her. He did not return until the following Friday, when, either hung over or still drunk from a multi-day spree, he announced that he wanted to resign his appointment at the Asylum, collected his belongings, and said he was going back to sea.

Reynolds got no closer to the sea than the receiving ship *Princeton*, from which he wrote Joseph Smith at the end of February 1860, requesting permission to return to the Asylum. Smith checked the records, then responded with a firm denial of his request. Nothing daunted, Reynolds turned in early May to Philadelphia Congressman Thomas B. Florence, reported that he had broken his leg while on leave from *Princeton*, that he was "poor and hard up," and asked Florence to intercede for him with Smith. The commodore was not about to say *no* to a congressman, so—whatever his concealed misgivings—Joseph Smith accepted Reynolds' remorse at face value and gave him a new permit of admission. The old sailor's arrival at the Asylum's gate on 15 May did not vouch well for his promise of changed ways and future good conduct; the daily log notes that "when presenting himself [Reynolds] was intoxicated with blacked eyes and face bruised." A month and a day later he was on report for drunkenness and confined to the grounds for thirty days.

That remained the pattern for the next year and a half. Reynolds was placed on report and punished no fewer than nineteen times for drunkenness, staying out after hours, and absences without leave, culminating on 4 January 1862, when he jumped the wall and disappeared. But not for good. In early April Reynolds asked Philadelphia attorney A. Dekalb Tarr to appeal to Florence's successor in Congress, William E. Lehman, on Reynolds' behalf. Tarr did not spare the pathos: "He is too old and crippled to go to sea again. He is very penitent and promises, if allowed to return, to observe and keep the rules of the institution. If you can get Commodore Joseph Smith, Chief of the Bureau of Docks and Yards, to let him return to the Asylum, I think he will be faithful and keep his promise. . . . He is now without a home and money." Then, switching from pathos to flattery, Tarr added: "Commodore Smith is a kind-hearted, noble gentleman, and I have no doubt, if you ask it, he will allow Mr. Reynolds to return to his old quarters in the Asylum." Once again, Joseph Smith was not going to refuse a member of Congress; on 12 April 1862 Thomas Reynolds was readmitted to the Asylum.

In September Commodore Frederick Engle succeeded the late Commodore George C. Read as governor. Reynolds had once served in the same ship as Engle and the latter, recalling the old carpenter's better days, was—by his own admission—inclined to cut Reynolds more slack than he deserved. But, by December, even Engle's good nature was worn out: "He has again been drunk, turbulent, insolent, and has conducted himself so badly that it cannot be overlooked." Engle summoned Reynolds to his office on 6 December with the intention, under a standing permission from Joseph Smith, of dismissing him from the Asylum. Sensing what was coming, Reynolds asked to be discharged rather than dismissed, and Engle complied.

It took just twelve days for Engle to regret his decision. December was no time for an old man to be roaming Philadelphia's streets, and Reynolds appealed to Engle for readmission. "With your permission," Engle wrote Smith, "I will try Thomas Reynolds again. . . . He has been a good man, [but now] he is a poor, miserable creature and cannot take care of himself." Reynolds had an advocate at the Navy Department in the person of John Lenthall, Chief of the Bureau of Construction, Equipment and Repair, who strongly seconded Engle's appeal. On 19 December 1862 Joseph Smith admitted Thomas Reynolds as a beneficiary for the fourth time in less than four years. If only that were the happy ending of Reynolds' life story. But, no, in early April 1863, with the return of pleasant spring weather, Thomas Reynolds walked away from the Asylum, never to return. Even Governor Engle's goodwill was exhausted: "His conduct has, of late, been so recklessly defiant of all regulations and so subversive of good order that I consider him utterly unworthy of the support of the government and that his longer stay here would be the source of incalculable annoyance and injury."

There is no record of yet another appeal for readmission from Reynolds. Perhaps he recognized that he had terminally exhausted his options. In any event his life had almost reached its end. Thomas Reynolds died of "natural causes" on 18 September 1863 and is buried in an unmarked grave in Gloria Dei (Old Swedes') churchyard in Philadelphia.

THE PLEDGE: EASY TO TAKE, HARD TO KEEP

Just how pervasive was alcohol abuse at the Naval Asylum? The surviving records do not permit an accurate quantitative answer, but a sense of the dimensions can be gained from the testimony given by John Ward, an eighteen-year Navy veteran, now sixty-two, at the court-martial of Executive Officer Robert E. Johnson in the late summer of 1845.

> WARD: There are nine drunkards to one sober man
> among the [beneficiaries].
> JOHNSON: Do you mean that out of the eighty
> [beneficiaries] there are not more than ten sober men
> in the house? Or do you mean there are more men
> given to drunkenness than sobriety?
> WARD: That is my idea. I do not believe there is
> more than eight or ten sober men—teetotalers. All the
> rest get drunk sometimes.

Before proceeding further, it is necessary to puncture gently a balloon of well-established myth. According to Andrew Hull Foote's first biographer, James M. Hoppin, Foote told or wrote his brother John, "When I came here [as executive officer at the Asylum in November 1841] I found these old sailors dreadful drunkards. Whenever I gave them any privilege, they invariably got drunk. I could do nothing with them." No argument there! "At last," Foote continued, "I signed the [temperance] pledge myself, and then they followed me." Hoppin goes on to quote a petition from the beneficiaries to the Secretary of the Navy in which they reported that Lieutenant Foote "has done us a great deal of good in making us all sober men. We once thought that old sailors could not do without grog. Now there is not a man in the house who draws his grog, and we feel like human beings and hate the sin of getting drunk."

This is misleading. Foote's most recent biographer, Spencer Tucker, does not swallow Hoppin's story unquestioningly—nor should he.[7] The United States Naval Asylum hardly became overnight an island of sobriety in a civil society steeped in alcohol. The institution's daily log and the governors' correspondence provide ample evidence to the contrary, even during Foote's tenure. The reality seems to have been that, as noted earlier, the initial 1834 regulations for the Asylum did not permit alcohol in the form of grog as part of the daily ration served the beneficiaries. Somehow, between 1834 and Foote's appointment, this regulation had come to be ignored, and a daily grog ration was served. The chaotic condition at the United States National Archives of the settled accounts of the pursers assigned to the Naval Asylum makes it impossible to determine when this practice began, how widespread consumption of the grog was among the beneficiaries, or when the daily grog ration was finally halted. Note that the just-quoted beneficiaries' petition refers only to the *grog* ration—not to any off-grounds alcohol consumption.

The reality here seems to be that Foote, setting the example himself, persuaded the beneficiaries to accept the voluntary eleven-cents-per-week cash compensation, which was instituted Navy-wide around this time, in lieu of the grog ration. Andrew Hull Foote deserves high admiration as a lifelong advocate of temperance, one who served in a Navy with a quite different tradition. But he was no pied piper, miraculously able to lead the Asylum's beneficiaries and the crews he later commanded at sea and on the Western rivers to lives of total abstinence. Foote had work cut out for him which demanded strength of personality, resolution, persistence—and painful willingness to see his efforts fail with many.

In January 1843 Foote endorsed beneficiary George Wilson's request to leave the Asylum and live with his family in Philadelphia, "having now, as he believes, acquired sufficient mastery over his appetite to discontinue the use of intoxicating drinks." A year later, on 18 January 1844, George Wilson returned to the Asylum. The hospital journal provides a grim narrative of the next ten days of his life: 19 January: "Had the 'horrors' all night in his room; removed into hospital at 8 a.m. At 9 had an epileptic fit. Pulse after fit soft and slow. Shaking continues." 22 January: "Want of sleep and delirium continued all yesterday." 23 January: "Yesterday about 11 a.m. became much worse. In constant motion; delirium and tremors increase, eyes wild, pulse small and frequent, copious perspiration rolling off his face and trunk." 27 January: "Don't improve any. Is comatose and a little delirious at times." 28 January: "Continued sinking and died at 1 a.m." George Wilson was only forty-five years old.

The deck was heavily stacked against successful total rejection of alcohol at the Asylum. To abstain, a beneficiary would have needed a powerful motivation, such as something demanding sobriety, which he hoped to accomplish in his remaining life. The end-of-life enclave on Gray's Ferry Road offered few such motivations. Neither were there support groups, such as the latter-day Alcoholics Anonymous, with the reinforcing camaraderie of mutual struggle. Any support groups available at the Naval Asylum were likely to encourage drinking, not sobriety. Temperance lectures by visiting clergymen and lay abstinence advocates would have been listened to politely by the assembled beneficiaries, but they produced no collective behavioral changes and were abandoned almost as soon as they were initiated.

So far as the surviving record shows there is little evidence of beneficiaries who overcame the addiction to pursue a life of total sobriety. One who did was a former quarter-gunner named John Peterson, a native of Prussia, who was born in the first half of the 1790s. Peterson spent about ten years in the merchant service—whether before or after he came to the United States is not known—then joined the U.S. Navy in May 1832 as a seaman in the frigate *United States*. On 18 or 19 April 1846 (records differ as to the date) Peterson, physically described only as a stout-built man, fell from the spar deck ladder of the frigate *Cumberland* into the ship's chain locker, sustaining severe incised wounds to his head and lacerated wounds to a lower leg. The leg healed completely, but Peterson's more serious head wounds left him with dizzy spells that made another active-duty enlistment out of the question. He was pensioned on 10 August 1847 and almost immediately surrendered his pension for admission to the Asylum. In less than two years Peterson became a problem beneficiary, "intemperate and troublesome." Between 16 August 1849 and 19 May 1856 he was hospitalized for alcohol abuse sixteen times for a total of one hundred twelve days. Then, in the late 1850s, John Peterson changed his ways completely, became a model beneficiary, and was appointed to the responsible job of gatekeeper, a post he held until his death from a stroke on 11 February 1869. Never once between 21 May 1856 and the day of his death was John Peterson put on report or sent to the hospital for drinking.

The story of a beneficiary who almost duplicated Peterson's achievement, Marine Corps veteran Francis Wilson, is known in greater detail. On the night of 14 May 1854 four Philadelphia policemen showed up at the Asylum's gate with a wheelbarrow and its contents—a hopelessly intoxicated Wilson. This was the typical practice with Philadelphia's police: haul offending beneficiaries back to the Asylum and let the institution's authorities deal with them rather than confining them to the city's jail or the drunkards' ward at the Blockley alms house. In Wilson's case it was the culmination of a long list of alcohol and absent-without-official-leave offenses stretching back to May 1849. Even Andrew Hull Foote's reforming instincts and patience were exhausted: "So far from evincing any disposition to reform his habits, it is said on reliable authority that he often has declared that he didn't care for any officer in the Asylum from the Commodore [David Geisinger] down; that, if turned out [of the Asylum] even, he had such influence at Washington as would readily secure an order for his readmission." Nothing daunted, Foote recommended Wilson's dismissal from the Asylum and out he went on 16 May 1854.

Wilson, who was probably born in 1798 or 1799, was an atypical beneficiary in two ways. He was a Southerner, born in Augusta, Georgia, and—according to Geisinger's successor as governor, George W. Storer—"being a person of superior intelligence to most of the beneficiaries, he was considered especially offensive on account of his dangerous influence over them." Following his dismissal from the Asylum Wilson spent almost all of the next sixteen months at the Blockley alms house, which he left in late September 1855. A few days later he turned up at the Navy Office in Washington, seeking readmission to the Asylum. Because this had been Wilson's first expulsion, Commodore Smith followed his usual practice of granting one more chance, 5 October 1855, conditioned on Wilson's agreement to sign the usual pledge. The signed copy of Wilson's pledge survives in the archives:

> In consideration that I be once more admitted to the Naval Asylum I hereby pledge myself to conform strictly to all the rules of that institution and to abstain from all intoxicating liquor and that, on the first violation of this, my sacred pledge, I will submit without complaint or remonstrance to be summarily ejected from the Asylum and never again ask to be admitted to, or receive any of the privileges of, said institution. Signed this fifth day of October 1855.
>
> FRANCIS WILSON

Those good intentions, however sincere they may have been, lasted just short of two months. On the night of 2–3 December

Wilson arrived at the gate too intoxicated to stand or walk by himself and had to be carried into the building. Joseph Smith confirmed that Wilson's pledge was binding; the Marine veteran was ejected for the second time on 5 December. At that point, Wilson decided to exercise his self-proclaimed political influence and enlisted the aid of the beneficiaries' friend-in-power, Congressman Thomas B. Florence of Philadelphia. This time Florence's usually successful intercessions failed to work. Joseph Smith advised the congressman that Wilson's reputation was so bad that readmission was out of the question: "Wilson is represented as an *intelligent* man and, instead of appropriating this virtue to some wholesome purpose," Smith reported, "he has perverted it into a weapon of mischief by setting an example of frequent and flagrant acts of insubordination and disrespect to the inmates of the institution, which deserves the severest reprehension."

What happened in the next sixteen months is not known in detail, but Wilson eventually made his way to Norfolk. There he did some serious soul-searching and decided to make the tough effort to kick his alcohol habit. He was successful—at least in the short run. From Norfolk he petitioned Secretary of the Navy Isaac Toucey in March 1857, asserting that he had undergone a "thorough and permanent reformation" and asking to be readmitted to the Naval Asylum on the grounds that he was old, his physical strength exhausted, and he had no means with which to support himself. The petition came with an endorsement from Finlay F. Ferguson, the mayor of Norfolk, who certified that Wilson "has been an inmate of the alms house of this city for some time back and, I believe, has entirely broken off from his intemperate habits." G. F. Anderson, president of the Norfolk Young Men's Christian Association and two Navy lieutenants, shipmates of Wilson in the frigate *Brandywine*, added their support, with the result that the old Marine was quickly restored to beneficiary status, effective 4 April.

There can be no question of the sincerity or the reality of Francis Wilson's effort to change his ways. He seems to have been completely successful for fourteen months. When Wilson did fail, he must have had the sympathetic support of the Asylum's administration, as the condition attached to his readmission—immediate dismissal on the first offense—was never invoked. After readmission, Wilson was on report only three times. On 28 June 1858 he went AWOL, reappeared at 2 a.m. on 1 July, and was committed to the cells for forty-eight hours. Three and a half months of apparent sobriety passed before Wilson was in trouble again; then, on 12 October, he disappeared, to be carried through the gate four days later, and immediately consigned to the hospital with a diagnosis of alcoholism, and kept there nine days. Once again Wilson tried hard to fight his addiction; he remained off report until the following June. Francis Wilson's last hurrah began on the sixteenth of that month. He and a fellow beneficiary, James Quinn, walked off the grounds, with Wilson not reappearing until 9:30 the following night. Although he was consigned to the cells for two days on bread and water, it quickly appeared that the old Marine was a sick man in need of medical attention—not punishment. Wilson was admitted to the hospital on 20 June, with a diagnosis of alcoholism, his age recorded as fifty-nine, and died there five days later. The medical staff was content with the verdict of death from alcohol abuse; no autopsy was undertaken to discover in clinical detail how drinking had destroyed Wilson's health.

THE DOCTORS COPE

Alcohol abuse at the Naval Asylum. To this point, *Ungentle Goodnights* has told the story primarily as a behavioral problem, one seen through the eyes of the institution's officers and the records they created. There is another perspective, that of the Philadelphia Naval Hospital's surgeons and assistant surgeons. They sought to restore to health, as best they could, the elderly and disabled sailors and Marines whose drinking problems were serious enough to require hospitalization. It has been possible to compile health histories for 269 of the 409 beneficiaries who died while they were residents of the Asylum. Among those 269 men, 124—or 46 percent—were hospitalized one or more times to be treated for the results of alcohol abuse. That number—46 percent—should not be regarded as appropriate for carving in stone. There are enough holes in the hospitalization records to justify a serious caution, but the number is another strong indicator of the extent of the problem of alcohol abuse among the Asylum's beneficiaries.

A closer and more detailed examination of the doctors' rescue mission is provided by eight-and-a-half years (1 July 1868 through 31 December 1876) of detailed case records compiled by the hospital's medical team. These records offer the insight of reliable numbers on the dimensions of alcohol abuse at the Asylum. One hundred and one of the 541 beneficiaries whose lives are recorded in *Ungentle Goodnights* were alive on 1 July 1868. Among these 101 veterans, 28 have been identified as being hospitalized during these years one or more times for alcohol abuse. From the most positive perspective, these numbers mean that nearly three-quarters of the resident beneficiaries did not, during the years on record, abuse alcohol to an extent which required hospitalization. That is not to imply that these 73 men were all abstainers; far from it, to judge by the Asylum's behavioral records. But those among the 73 non-hospitalized beneficiaries who *did* drink managed to keep indulgence within limits which avoided medical intervention. One note of caution: By 31 December 1876 some 62 among the 101 beneficiaries resident on 1 July 1868 had died or left the Asylum, which may make the three-quarters not-hospitalized proportion less positive than it appears at first encounter. If all 101 had still been around eight and a half years later, a larger number than 28 might at some time have drunk to excess to a degree that would have sent them to the hospital.

The records also show wide variation in the number of times the twenty-eight beneficiaries were hospitalized for alcohol abuse. Five men among the twenty-eight were hospitalized only once; four men twice; five men three times; two men four times; two men five times; three men six times; and one man seven times. Fourteen of these twenty-eight men died before 31 December 1876, so it is impossible to know how many of them would have experienced more hospitalizations if they had lived the full eight and a half years. Beyond the one man who was hospitalized seven times the pattern of medical confinement changes dramatically: two beneficiaries were hospitalized on twelve occasions and one each fourteen, eighteen, twenty, and twenty-six times. All six men were chronic alcoholics.

The Philadelphia Naval Hospital records use various terms to diagnose the condition of their alcohol-abusing patients, notably *debauch, incipient delirium tremens,* and *delirium tremens,* before settling on *alcoholism* as the standard diagnosis toward the end of the eight and a half years. The frequency with which cases are diagnosed as incipient delirium tremens and delirium tremens is misleading. In his book *Rum Maniacs: Alcoholic Insanity in the Early American Republic* (2014), Matthew Warner Osborn shows that the Philadelphia medical community and the city's population at large were fascinated—perhaps *obsessed* is a better word—with the phenomenon of delirium tremens. It appears to be over-used in the Philadelphia

Naval Hospital's records for cases in which *alcoholism* would usually have been the more appropriate diagnosis. In the present chapter *delirium tremens* will be restricted to the few instances in which the hospital's case file specifically mentions hallucinations.

Typically beneficiaries seem to have reported to the hospital on their own initiative, seeking to dry out after an extended drinking spree which left them in a condition such that they could no longer cope with their lives. A few were brought to the hospital by the master-at-arms, when they were physically unable to get there on their own. Edward Sanderson, an Irishman from County Cork, who entered the U.S. Navy in the late 1830s and was now somewhere in his mid-sixties, was so delivered in October 1872 "in a beastly state of intoxication." He had just fallen and rolled down the main marble staircase inside the Asylum. Luckily for Sanderson, his body was apparently so relaxed from alcohol that he avoided real injury. A few scratches and some skin wounds to his scalp were all he had to show for what could have been a serious accident.

On reporting to the hospital, the beneficiary was first asked by the assistant surgeon on duty how long he had been drinking. Answers ranged from two or three days, through "some time" and "several days" to a week or ten days and (occasionally) two weeks. Just-mentioned Edward Sanderson once asserted that he had been drinking for eighteen days, but this is perhaps one more sailor's tall tale embroidered to show his prowess as a drinker. The assistant surgeon on duty then moved on to the beneficiaries' symptoms, recording a spectrum of feel-bad afflictions which will be familiar to anyone who has experienced a serious hangover or been on a multi-day drunk—headache, anxiety or depression, nervousness, trembling, vertigo, wandering mind and incoherent speech, nausea, vomiting, loss of appetite and failure to eat, constipation or diarrhea. Among the one hundred seventy-four case files for hospitalizations for alcohol abuse between July 1868 and December 1876, only a half-dozen or so mention hallucinations. No descriptions of any of the hallucinations were recorded, although one was tantalizingly called "terrifying," leaving the sensation-seeking historian hungry for details.

One assistant surgeon, John L. Neilson, noted the physical appearance of the beneficiaries he admitted. His sketches are suffused with Neilson's elitist attitude of superiority toward these alcoholics, but they still have value as word-pictures of the Asylum's residents for whom regrettably few physical images survive: "An obese old man, not much broken down by his great age [recorded as eighty-three in the hospital case file] and continual excesses."—"A florid, fleshy man, [with] small, red, ferrety eye—loquacious."—"Presents in his countenance evidence of habitual use of alcoholic liquors; face flushed . . . pupils contracted, uneasy motion of eyes, tremulousness of voluntary muscles."—"A weak . . . tremulous old drunkard, with the signs of his recent debauch showing in his bleared countenance, tremulous hands, sodden skin and watery red eyes."

Upon hospitalization patients were immediately treated with a variety of medications designed to relieve the symptoms of their condition. Tincture of opium (or laudanum) and chloral hydrate were among the most commonly used sedatives, as well as potassium bromide. Jalap, tincture of capsicum, bismuth subcarbonate, magnesium sulfate, and castor oil, as well as an occasional enema or a mustard plaster applied to the stomach, were brought into play to deal with the stomach and intestinal problems consequent upon excessive drinking. Once the immediate symptoms were alleviated, the patient was placed on a liquid but nourishing diet. Here a favorite component was beef tea. Although there were several recipes for beef tea, the one most commonly used involved cutting juicy beef into thin slices; these, sprinkled lightly with salt, were placed in a closed jar which was set in a pan of boiling water for an hour or more; the resulting essence was strained into a bowl and served to the patient. Thereafter the recovering patient was moved through a bland diet until he was ready to eat the standard daily hospital ration.

Medications and an appropriate diet aside, time for alcohol-abused bodies to heal themselves was the major component of hospital treatment. The most common stay among the 174 cases was three or four days (22 percent of the hospitalizations). Slightly over half (54 percent) of the admissions lasted between three and eight days, while hospital stays of anywhere from one to thirteen days accounted for 84 percent of the cases. Those beneficiaries hospitalized longer than thirteen days for alcohol abuse (16 percent) typically had other health conditions which complicated their treatment. "Discharged to Asylum. Has regained his usual health." Such was a typical final notation among these 174 case files. But, in too many instances, the assistant surgeon entered those words with a resigned expectation that his recovered patient would be back all too soon: "Is an inveterate drinker, it being only one month since he was in the hospital with a similar attack."

With four beneficiaries there would be no discharge back to the Asylum. They died as a direct result of alcohol abuse. Angus Wheeler's death from cirrhosis of the liver was mentioned in chapter 8. Another beneficiary died as a result of a fracture incurred in a fall while intoxicated; the not-uncommon problem of beneficiary falls and fractures will be explored in chapter 14. The remaining two deaths were remarkably similar. That of beneficiary Samuel Smith will be here related, because a detailed record of his final hours was created and an autopsy performed on his body.

Smith was well known to the hospital staff. He was admitted there seventeen times—twelve of them for alcohol abuse—between 31 December 1870 and his terminal admission on 7 March 1876. Smith was a resident of Philadelphia, where he was born, probably in 1805; his naval service stretched back to July 1829, when he joined the sloop-of-war *Peacock*. He was first admitted to the Naval Asylum in October 1860 from the sloop-of-war *Falmouth* on the grounds that a recent attack of remittent fever had left him much weakened, added to which he exhibited palpitation of the heart. With the outbreak of the Civil War, sitting around the Naval Asylum quickly lost whatever appeal it may have had for Samuel Smith. In May 1861 he volunteered for service as a quarter-gunner in the screw-steamer *Union* of the Potomac Flotilla. (Fellow beneficiary James F. Dunbar was a shipmate.) By November Smith's health was again a problem, and he asked to return to the Asylum. Shipping for active duty while a beneficiary, as Smith had done in *Union*, was a violation of the Asylum's rules, but Commodore Joseph Smith decided to overlook the infraction this time. He sent Samuel Smith back to the Gray's Ferry Road campus without sanction or other formality.

Beneficiary Smith stuck it out there until 14 June 1862, when he departed on an approved leave of absence from which he failed to return. In fact he had headed straight to New York where he joined the screw sloop-of-war *Adirondack* with the rating of seaman. Joseph Smith was not about to be indulgent a second time. On 30 July Samuel Smith was formally dismissed as a beneficiary. Shortly thereafter his service in *Adirondack* came to an abrupt end when she struck a reef in the Bahamas on 23 August, bilged, and was abandoned as a total wreck. This mishap involved no casualties to *Adirondack*'s crew; Smith was transferred to the sidewheel steamer *Florida*. He ended his active-duty career afloat as a quarter-gunner in the sidewheel steamer *Ella*, performing patrol and dispatch-boat duty in the Potomac during the latter years of the war. *Ella*'s muster roll offers a snapshot of Smith when he joined her in June 1863— fifty-eight years old, sixty-eight inches tall, with hazel eyes, a sun-darkened complexion, and brown hair still without any significant threads of gray. Following his discharge from *Ella*, Smith worked at the New York Navy Yard, then—late in 1870—traveled to Washington to apply in person for readmission to the Naval Asylum on the grounds of chronic rheumatism. Smith's 1862 dismissal was forgotten or forgiven, almost certainly on the basis of his Civil War service afloat. The requested readmission was granted on 7 December.

However valuable he may have been on shipboard, Samuel Smith was a problem beneficiary during all three of his residencies at the Asylum. The problem was always the same, recorded time after time in the log and the conduct book: alcohol abuse. Smith's final spree began on 3 March 1876 when he went absent without leave. He returned some time on the night of the sixth, still badly intoxicated, and was confined in one of the cells. By morning it was apparent that Smith belonged in the hospital, not a cell, and at 9:30 he transferred there in an alarming condition: "Tongue swollen, dry and covered with a brownish fur; pupils contracted and only slightly responding to light; pulse 140 per minute and very weak; abdomen distended and tympanitic and painful upon pressure; and skin dry. He was apparently conscious of all going on about him, as he understood to answer all questions put to him, tho' he could not make himself understood owing to the swollen condition of his tongue." The old sailor was placed in bed and medicated, but things rapidly got worse, not better. At 10:45 he "began to vomit and ejected a large quantity of dark and very offensive fluid and then began to sink very rapidly. His skin was covered with cold perspiration, his pulse exceedingly rapid and scarcely perceptible, and he died in five minutes, rapidly and quietly, without any exertion."

During the morning of 8 March a formal autopsy was undertaken, but with inconclusive results. Nothing appeared seriously out of order in the upper half of Smith's body; attention focused next on his stomach, which was found to be denuded of mucous membrane in several small spots and a cyst observed. The colon was next explored, where the examining assistant surgeon found "several small projecting masses of liver-like substance which, upon section, has the appearance of adipose tissue infiltrated with blood. . . . The entire colon is very dark and much thickened from extravasated blood apparently. The stomach and intestines distended with offensive gas, but otherwise almost empty." In the final analysis, Smith's death was a medical puzzle: "There was no postmortem evidence sufficient to account for the rapid death, but the history of the case renders it evident that the patient died from the effects of a prolonged debauch and confinement following it"— thus passing the responsibility back to the Asylum's authorities for committing Smith to a cell overnight instead of sending him to the hospital for immediate medical care. The official death certificate filed with the City of Philadelphia was short and to the point: "*Cause of Death*: Debauch."

There remains one final way that the hospital records can help assess the extent of alcohol abuse at the Naval Asylum. This is by comparing the hospital's records of admissions involving alcohol abuse with behavioral records maintained by the Asylum's administration. The eight and a half years covered by the hospital's sick tickets—July 1868 through December 1876—have surviving behavioral records as well: a conduct-book covering 1 July 1868 to 31 March 1873 and, when that stops, the Asylum's daily log from 1 April 1873 through 31 December 1876. The comparison is surprising and puzzling. Slightly more than 80 percent of the 174 incidents which led to beneficiaries being hospitalized for alcoholism do not appear in the behavioral records. Why this was so is difficult to fathom, but this puzzling number certainly suggests that the documents created to keep track of beneficiary behavior greatly under-record the extent of alcohol use and abuse at the Asylum—at least for the years during which it is possible to compare the medical and the behavioral records. This historian can only guess that there was a lot of looking the other way when it came to keeping the behavioral records. The institution was cutting its elderly residents ample slack.

A MORE SOBER FUTURE?

Whether alcohol abuse remained as great a problem for the generations of Marines and sailors who entered the United States Naval

Asylum after 1865 is a question whose answer lies beyond the scope of *Ungentle Goodnights*. Perhaps the abolition of the Navy's tradition of the daily grog ration in 1862 did, as admirals Joseph Smith and Andrew Hull Foote fervently wished, led to more sober lives for the men of the Navy's enlisted corps in the later years of the nineteenth century. However that may be, the ugly reality is that, for an unmeasurable majority of the elderly and disabled veterans who came to the enclave on Gray's Ferry Road before 31 December 1865 and who are the subjects of *Ungentle Goodnights*, alcohol consumed in excess negatively affected their lives, their behavior, and their health—and in some cases led directly to their deaths— to an extent that the Asylum's historian should neither conceal from history nor romanticize as colorful behavior.

TEN

"A House of Refuge
for Exotic Malefactors"

Everyone caught up in the turbulent life of beneficiary Richard B. Randolph, whose story will be told in chapter 12, agreed that he was insane—possibly dangerously so. Insane though he might have been, Randolph was perhaps not that far from the truth when he once described the United States Naval Asylum as "a house of refuge for exotic malefactors."[1] As a historian turns page after page of beneficiary behavioral records, it sometimes seems that Randolph was right on target.

So pervasive was the culture of alcohol abuse at the Naval Asylum that it is difficult to find censured beneficiary behaviors that did not have their roots in intoxication or in which intoxication was not a major component. It would be seriously misleading for *Ungentle Goodnights* to draw a sharp line and put alcohol-fueled offenses on one side of that line and non-intoxicated misbehavior on the other. There can be no such line, only a cloudy horizon where the two types of offenses merged with one another. When, on 6 November 1855, beneficiary Thomas Huntley burst into the office of William W. S. Dyre, clerk to the Asylum's purser, and announced "I want my pay—$800! If I do not get it, I will kill you," and then proceeded to attack Dyre physically, it sounds like a simple case of assault. But the story is more complicated.

Thomas Huntley was born in New London, Connecticut, apparently in 1798. He went to sea in the merchant service when he was eighteen, if not earlier, and entered the U.S. Navy on 5 June 1818 in the frigate *Guerriere*, bound for the Mediterranean under Thomas Macdonough. Twenty years and five months later, on 8 November 1838, Huntley was discharged from active duty because of a hernia, plus "disease of colon," and placed on the pension roll at half-disability—three dollars per month. During his active-duty service, Huntley rose to petty officer, serving in the sloop-of-war *Vandalia* as captain-of-the-foretop for thirty-two months and as quarter-gunner for six.

In July 1846 Huntley, whose employment in the intervening years is not known, relinquished his pension for admission to the Naval Asylum. His stay was brief; he departed "at his own request" on 8 February 1847. In 1852–53 Huntley sought reinstatement as a beneficiary. Joseph Smith, with his usual caution in these matters, inquired of Governor David Geisinger about Huntley's "general character and habits" during his previous residence at the Asylum and was told that "there is nothing on record as regards his character and habits whilst an inmate of the Asylum." Actually, a little research in the Asylum's log would have revealed that Huntley had been confined in the cells for a total of sixteen days between 29 December 1846 and 28 January 1847. This historian cannot prove it, but he is convinced that the Asylum's governors used the discharged-at-his-own-request formula to offer a problem beneficiary a choice between giving up his position voluntarily and being reported for dismissal.

When Huntley returned to the Asylum in March 1853 he quickly showed his true colors. By June 1855 Governor George W. Storer was appealing for Huntley's dismissal: "In defiance of all discipline he scales the walls or runs the gate, remains at times out all night and returns drunk, abusive and riotous to the great annoyance of all the inmates here." The log's record provides colorful details. On 19 August 1853 Huntley was "drunk, noisy, and breaking windows; he resisted the master-at-arms and had to be dragged to the cell." He returned to the Asylum on 15 October 1853 after three days of absence-without-leave, during which he had been confined for the second time to Philadelphia's Moyamensing Prison. On this occasion it was by order of Mayor Charles Gilpin, who now asked—without success—that Huntley be permanently restricted to the Asylum grounds. On 30 June 1855 Storer was given authority to dismiss Huntley the next time he offended.

At this point there is an extended silence about Huntley and his behavior in the Asylum's records. Possibly he was absent without leave; perhaps, with dismissal hanging over his head, Huntley was on his good behavior. All that is now known is that around noon on 6 November 1855 Huntley appeared at the northeast gate, somewhat (but not greatly) intoxicated and demanded admission to the grounds, which the gatekeepers stationed there refused him. One of the gatekeepers hurried off to report to Executive Officer Henry K. Thatcher. The latter was heading toward the gate to deal with the situation when he met gatekeeper John O'Leary. The gatekeeper reported that Huntley had forced the gate in spite of O'Leary's best efforts to keep him out and was in fact now following O'Leary onto the grounds. Thatcher allowed Huntley to enter the Asylum building, where the executive officer directed Master-at-Arms William Kane to confine Huntley in one of the cells. At this point Huntley became so violent that Kane had to go in search of the Asylum's laborers to help him subdue the beneficiary. Huntley took advantage of the master-at-arms' absence to enter Dyre's office, threaten him orally, throttle him, and force Dyre up against a wall. Dyre broke Huntley's grasp, but the enraged beneficiary then got an arm around the purser's clerk's neck. Dyre, who must have been a fairly strong man, forced Huntley toward the office door—Huntley's arm still around Dyre's neck—at which point the assault was broken up by three or four men who had heard the noise of the fight. Governor Storer now had Huntley where he wanted him. Thomas Huntley was immediately and permanently ejected from the Asylum under the provisional authority granted Storer on 30 June.

Fluid as are the boundaries among the categories of disapproved beneficiary conduct, it is possible to distinguish two types of unsanctioned behavior in which alcohol abuse was not the primary factor—theft and sexual offenses.

NOT TO BE TRUSTED

Theft from a fellow beneficiary was a rare occurrence at the Naval Asylum, but when it was discovered the outcome was typically draconian—dismissal without hope of readmission. "Though I am a friend to old sailors," said Joseph Smith, "I am an uncompromising enemy to thieves. Once found guilty, they are not to be trusted." Smith's aversion to thieves was shared by the mass of the Asylum's beneficiaries, who did not hesitate to report suspected thieves to the institution's authorities, no matter how much they may have protected fellow beneficiaries from detection for other infractions of the rules. Though never explicitly stated, the basis for the reprehension

with which thieves were viewed is easily surmised: it violated com-
radeship among the beneficiaries; the only sure remedy was expulsion from the group.

In late December 1843, Governor William W. McKean
reported to Secretary of the Navy David Henshaw that he had dismissed a beneficiary named John Ewing, a former seaman about
forty-five years old, for stealing a new pea coat belonging to a fellow beneficiary. Ewing had been a resident of the Asylum for less
than a year, but in that brief time he had compiled quite a record.
"The conduct of this man has always been bad," McKean wrote,
"scarcely ever leaving the building without returning drunk and
riotous. He has been twice apprehended by the civil authorities,
once upon a charge of stealing and once as a vagrant. I have long
suspected his stealing from the [beneficiaries] but never could fix
it upon him until yesterday, when it was *fully proved* by some of
them and the man to whom he sold the jacket. He also admitted
his guilt." Secretary Henshaw quickly agreed to Ewing's dismissal.

Ewing was still young and healthy enough to reenlist in the
Navy, but by March 1849 it was a different story. Carefully conceal-
ing his previous admission to, and history at, the Naval Asylum,
Ewing applied to Secretary of the Navy William Ballard Preston:
"Having been invalided home from the *Brandywine* in the *Congress,* I have reached [Baltimore] where I am now sick, and having
exhausted all my funds, I am obliged to appeal to you for a permit
to the Asylum, to which I am entitled." The secretary's office replied
with the standard letter, asking the details of Ewing's service. Presumably because doing so would necessarily have revealed his earlier misdeeds at the Naval Asylum, Ewing never answered this letter
and disappears from the historical record.

SEXUAL ENCOUNTERS: EXUBERANT AND OTHERWISE

Save for three solitary cases, almost nothing is known about the sex
lives of the Asylum's beneficiaries. This lack of information about
sexual activity in the Asylum's voluminous records—the stories here
related aside—is readily explained. Asylum beneficiaries were typically men in their fifties, sixties, and seventies. Some of them were
seriously ill. There is no way of determining how many of them were
still sexually active. Married men, absent any surviving evidence to
the contrary, may be presumed to have satisfied their sexual desires
at home. As for the single men and the widowers, if they sought

sexual encounters, it would have been in the taverns and brothels of Philadelphia. There was no administrative reason to enter such information in the Asylum's records. Were it not for newspaper stories, James Forten Dunbar's involvement with the bawdy house in Brown's Court (chapter 7) would be totally unknown to the Asylum's historian.

A colorful character named John Underwood will have to stand as the sole representative for the sexually active heterosexual beneficiaries. Underwood was born in Baltimore around 1792 or 1793, learned the carpenter's trade, and served in the Maryland militia during the War of 1812.[2] Combat participation in repelling the British attack on Baltimore in 1814 was one of the notable memories of his life. In the brief autobiographical statement which he contributed to "Biography of Beneficiaries United States Naval Asylum Philadelphia" (chapter 6) Underwood drew particular attention to his fathering of eight children. Whether all eight were with the same woman he did not say. His statement also implied (but did not explicitly record) that Underwood was a widower at the time he gave it. Underwood worked in the merchant service "about ten years," then transitioned to the Navy when he joined the sloop-of-war *Fairfield* as a carpenter's mate on 19 April 1833. On 1 May 1844—while Underwood was serving in the same rating in the sloop-of-war *Vandalia*—he was driving an iron bolt when, recorded *Vandalia*'s medical journal, "some substance flying from between [the bolt] and the hammer" struck his left eye. This was long before the era of mandatory protective eyewear. The accident permanently blinded Underwood's left eye and impaired the vision in his right eye as well. Pensioned for this injury in September 1844, Underwood did what work he could find to supplement his nine-dollar-and-fifty-cent-per-month pension until September 1852, when he surrendered his pension to enter the Naval Asylum.

On Christmas Eve of 1853, as Master-at-Arms William Kane was making his usual rounds, he sensed that there was a woman in John Underwood's room. Kane at once notified Lieutenant Louis C. Sartori. The two of them entered Underwood's room to discover the beneficiary half intoxicated, but apparently satiated sexually, and the woman—now identified as "a notorious prostitute"—hurriedly getting dressed. Underwood's female companion, whom he had snuck into the building during the supper hour while Sartori's and Kane's attention was diverted elsewhere, was immediately expelled from the grounds and Underwood confined to a cell. He went neither quietly nor willingly. Nearby beneficiaries were entertained by Underwood using "the most indecent language towards all the officers" attached to the Asylum. He employed either brute strength or his carpenter's skills to break through the door of his cell, whereupon Sartori had Underwood clapped in single irons. What irritated Lieutenant Sartori the most was that, instead of expressing regret and begging forgiveness the next morning, Underwood "seems to exult in his conduct."

Governor David Geisinger recommended Underwood's dismissal from the Asylum on the grounds, not only of this incident, but because "Underwood has repeatedly violated the rules and regulations and has at times been very troublesome." At least on the basis of the surviving record, that seems a rather unfair characterization of the man, as only two relatively minor offenses are recorded against Underwood in the Asylum's log before his Christmas Eve sex frolic. Joseph Smith forwarded Geisinger's recommendation to Secretary of the Navy James C. Dobbin, who ordered: "Let him be dismissed from the institution and never again admitted."Underwood was publicly turned out on 28 December.

Never turned out to be just eight days long. Underwood seems to have had something of the bad-boy charmer in his makeup. He immediately traveled to Washington to appeal his dismissal directly to Commodore Smith. The latter wrote Geisinger that "John Underwood . . . has made a full confession of his faults and begged to be readmitted under a solemn pledge that he will never touch intoxicating liquor again or violate any one of the regulations of the institution. Under these pledges he may be admitted, but on condition that he shall be summarily dismissed by the governor on a violation of his pledge without reference to the department." Draconian as that condition sounded, it was never enforced. Between Underwood's return on 10 January 1854 and his voluntary withdrawal from the Asylum on 12 July 1860 the log records ten offenses against Underwood, most of them involving intoxication, but none of them resulting in the promised dismissal.

When Underwood withdrew from the Asylum in July 1860, it was with the intention of moving in with his only son, newly married and living in New Orleans. That plan did not work out. By 28 September he was back in Washington, alleging that "domestic disaffection and discontent forced me to leave my son's house"—

was the new wife unwilling to have a disruptive John Underwood in her home?—and appealing for reinstatement at the Asylum. Joseph Smith checked Underwood's record during his previous residencies; the commodore was distinctly unenthusiastic about a third admission. However, Underwood had the savvy to make his appeal through Philadelphia Congressman Thomas B. Florence, who often acted as an intermediary between beneficiaries in trouble and the Navy Department. Characteristically, Smith grumbled but consented, once again with the condition that, if Underwood did not "deport himself properly" he was to be dismissed "forever."

John Underwood returned to the Asylum on 6 October. Disciplinary infractions are not recorded in the Asylum's log between 9 November 1861 and 30 June 1866. Consequently, this history cannot say how well Underwood observed the mandate. But on 18 February 1861, before the recording of behavior in the log stopped, it notes that Underwood came in drunk, abused the gatekeeper orally, was restricted to the grounds for sixty days, and forfeited a month's pocket-money allowance. One more time Underwood had charmed his way around the dismissal sanction which was supposed to be immediately invoked. By now he was a man approaching seventy, his health was beginning to deteriorate, and the Asylum authorities were prepared to be lenient. John Underwood died from unspecified ailments of old age on 11 June 1865.

On 4 June 1856 the Asylum's log recorded that John Smith, the seventh beneficiary of that name since June 1838, was expelled by Governor George W. Storer for "the crime of *Sodomy* with a boy named Henry Myers, an inmate of the hospital." More is known about Smith than might be anticipated when the life details of seven different men with the same non-distinctive name need to be untangled in the records. He was born in Richmond County, Virginia, in April 1793, and had spent forty-four years of his life at sea. Twenty-two of those forty-four years were in the U.S. Navy, from which he was discharged in February 1855 and admitted to the Asylum. About half of Smith's naval service was as a petty officer, concluding as captain of the forecastle in the steamer *Saranac*. "His constitution is completely broken down," reported the surgeon who examined Smith, "and I do not believe he will ever sufficiently regain his health to be able to support himself by manual labor." He was just a half-inch short of six feet tall, his eyes blue, his hair still brown.

No details are known about John Smith's sexual encounter with Henry Myers—the sole case of homoerotic activity discovered in the records of five hundred forty-one Asylum beneficiaries examined for *Ungentle Goodnights*—other than it appears to have been consensual. Myers was sixteen years old, a typical age for beginning adult careers at sea. A native of Philadelphia, Myers—his rating was *apprentice boy*—had been sent to the hospital from the receiving ship *Union* on 21 December 1855 to be treated for dislocation of an unspecified bone. The reason for assuming that the encounter was to some degree consensual is that Myers was kicked out of the hospital and sent back to the receiving ship the day after Smith was expelled from the Asylum. This would almost certainly not have been the response if Myers had been an unwilling victim, raped by Smith.

One can imagine the revulsion and anger Governor James L. Lardner felt on 31 May 1871 when he received a note from the Asylum's chaplain, the Rev. John K. Lewis, reporting that, three days earlier—presumably the delay in reporting is accounted for by the time required for Chaplain Lewis or his wife to discover what had happened—one of the beneficiaries "took my little girl, three years and five months old, to a retired quarter of the grounds and there removed her drawers from her and looked at and fingered her person; he then exposed his private parts to her and made water before her and talked to her obscenely. The particulars I can give you more in detail in a personal interview. I lay the case before you as being a most flagrant one, demanding your attention." The beneficiary in question was Orin Galusha, and Lardner's attention he certainly got. Nothing in the record of Galusha's life before 1871 warned of this ugly turn in his behavior, although an incident two days after Chaplain Lewis' letter, and while the child-molestation incident was under investigation, suggests he was experiencing some kind of psychological crisis. Galusha, who was not confined in the cells in spite of the seriousness of the allegations against him, turned up at the northeast gate, drunk, and "abused [an] old woman at [the] gate," as recorded in the Asylum's book of disciplinary infractions. "She has a stand for the sale of cakes and candies. He threw her cakes on the ground."

Orin Galusha was born in Albany, New York, in November 1804. Nothing is known about his life before the 1840s. He said that he served in the frigate *Guerriere* for eighteen months around the year 1829. This service cannot be verified in *Guerriere's* rolls for 1828–31. Either Galusha had the ship wrong, his years of service wrong, or he enlisted (for some now unknown reason) under a false name. Beginning in June 1842, when Orin Galusha appears in the rolls of the ship-of-the-line *Delaware*, his naval career is well authenticated. Galusha signed on *Delaware* with the rating of *seaman*, evidence of substantial seafaring experience in the merchant service. Thereafter his career in the Navy was continuous, culminating in Civil War service in the screw steamer *Norwich* and the screw gunboat *Ottawa*, by which time he was described as a man in his late fifties, five-and-a-half feet tall, with grayish hair, gray eyes, and a dark complexion. During almost all of this and his earlier service Galusha was rated as signal quartermaster or boatswain's mate, an indication of above-average efficiency and intelligence. It was in *Norwich* and later in *Ottawa* that Galusha experienced a painful and crippling hernia which, together with his age, justified his admission to the Naval Asylum on 23 May 1865.

At the Asylum, Galusha was one more restless beneficiary. He was granted a leave of absence in November 1865 and immediately enlisted on board the frigate *Sabine*, Commander Reigart B. Lowry, as signal quartermaster, even though such an active-duty reenlistment was strictly against Asylum regulations. (This return to active duty was probably made possible and appealing because of the hernia-supporting truss with which Galusha had been fitted in *Ottawa* in 1863 or 1864.) During Galusha's service in *Sabine* she was based at New London, Connecticut, and served as a training ship for apprentices and landsmen. Commander Lowry, with whom Galusha had apparently served in the past, reported that "Galusha's services while in [*Sabine*] have been very valuable." He rated Galusha as "a faithful man, an excellent seaman, and well adapted to this service . . . [who] has performed his duty, at sea and in port, as well as any man." Not until late 1867 did age and that old hernia compromise Galusha's performance, leading him to seek reinstatement at the Naval Asylum. Joseph Smith, after some customary grumbling about Galusha's reenlistment having forfeited his right to the Asylum, let the signal quartermaster back in on 7 April 1868.

On hearing Chaplain Lewis' shocking May 1871 allegation, Governor Lardner immediately recommended Galusha's dismissal from the Asylum. Captain Daniel Ammen, who had succeeded Admiral Joseph Smith as chief of the Bureau of Yards and Docks

in 1869, forwarded the Secretary of the Navy's approval of Galusha's dismissal on 3 June. The Asylum's beneficiaries were mus-
tered on 7 June and Galusha formally expelled in their presence.
Whether the specifics of Galusha's criminal action were announced
at his dismissal is not known, but his behavioral record was noted:
"The evidence of the shocking offense for which Galusha was dismissed is filed in the Governor's office."

What became of Orin Galusha after his dismissal? That is an
unsolved mystery. On 26 June 1873, from a post office box in Philadelphia, he filed an application for a pension on the basis of twenty
years of service. His papers passed back and forth among the Commissioner of Pensions, the Fourth Auditor of the Treasury, and the
Secretary of the Navy until 21 November, when a blank form was
sent Galusha to be completed. He never returned the form. Orin
Galusha's pension application file is stamped "Abandoned," sug-
gesting that he was dead by November 1873, but no record of his
death has yet been found.

"The Bureau [of Yards and Docks] can but congratulate the
beneficiaries in freeing them from a messmate whose degradation
will not allow any association and should place him in solitary confinement during life," Daniel Ammen had written Governor James
Lardner in dismissing Orin Galusha. "You will be good enough to
say to the beneficiaries that it is believed that no such instance of
depravity has ever before exhibited itself at that institution." So far
as the discovered records of the old sailors and Marines at the United
State Naval Asylum reveal, Captain Ammen was entirely correct.

ELEVEN

Hard Lives,
Tolls Collected

In June 1843, when he had been chief of the Navy Department's newly created Bureau of Medicine and Surgery for nine months, Dr. William P. C. Barton issued a general order requiring that the senior medical officer of each ship and shore establishment keep a journal that would record, for every patient he treated, his name; rank or rate; age; time and place where taken ill; nature of the injury or disease; the history, symptoms and daily progress of the injury or disease; and the date of the patient's discharge by cure, desertion, or death.[1]

Dr. Barton's directive regularized to the degree possible what the U.S. Navy's medical men had been doing since the service's earliest days—keeping written records of their practice. These pre-1843 records varied in the completeness with which they were created and even more in the extent to which they survived among the Navy's archives. But those earlier records, and the newer ones created under the direction of the Bureau of Medicine and Surgery, are of the greatest importance. Surviving documentary records concerning the lives of the Navy and Marine Corps' nineteenth-century enlisted forces are far from ample. The one great exception to that statement are the records compiled by the Navy's medical corps about the health of Marines and sailors. These survive as a vast archive of information about the physical and mental health of nineteenth-century seafarers—an archive that historians have only begun to explore and exploit.[2]

What is true about the seagoing services as a whole is equally so for the portion of that force that found its way to the Naval Asylum. The surviving medical records for the Asylum's beneficiaries, added to the better-known pension files, are daunting in their volume. In an attempt to manage the archival mass, this chapter will exclude from the 541 beneficiaries who entered the Naval Asylum before January 1866 the 132 men who left the Asylum and died elsewhere; they are the subject of chapter 13. That leaves a total of 409 men who ended their lives at the Naval Asylum; usable medical records exist for 234 of them. The present chapter will examine the physical well-being of these 234 individuals as they came to the ends of their active-duty careers and sought admission to the Asylum as beneficiaries. Chapter 14 promises a look at the declining health of these elderly men and the causes of the deaths that terminated their once active and physically demanding lives.

Do not anticipate here tables with neat columns recording in percentages discrete categories of disability under which the beneficiaries labored when they were admitted to the Naval Asylum. Human disabilities are not that tidy. The same man's body might be experiencing the loss of physical strength that came with advancing age, plus rheumatism, plus impaired vision. Nor are the records of admissions all that tidy either. Much of what is known about the health of just-admitted beneficiaries must be taken from a survey of beneficiary health conducted in 1849—a survey in which the results are reported in brief summary phrases: "Infirm and injured leg" or "Wounded side." For a smaller number of men much more is known, either from earlier pension applications or from written appeals for admission describing the applicants' disabilities. From these records it is possible to collect a sense of the toll that active lives took on the bodies of two hundred thirty-four of the U.S. Navy's sailors and Marines. Particular attention will be directed to three categories of declining health and incapacitating disability—age, service-related injuries, and combat wounds.

OLD IN A YOUNG MAN'S WORLD

"Inclination would induce me to go another cruise or two, but old age and impaired health will be much against me." So wrote quarter-gunner Henry Smith, who claimed to be sixty-three, in appealing for admission to the Naval Asylum. "His general health seems to be good," reported Surgeon Samuel Jackson when he examined sixty-two-year-old quartermaster Abram Jennings. "His decrepitude, which renders him unfit for further service, as well as unable to obtain his livelihood by manual labor ashore, is but the natural consequence of advanced age and the vicissitudes and exposure incident to a seaman's life." Seafaring was a young man's profession. Some fortunate sailors might be able to prolong their active-duty years with less physically demanding assignments in navy yards or in receiving ships, but the most common reason offered by applicants seeking admission to the Asylum—106 out of 234 men—was that they no longer had the stamina and health to get the job done day after day at sea. (Approximately half of the 106 cited one or more specific disabilities in addition to age and general infirmity.)

As readers of *Ungentle Goodnights* must be well aware by this point, basing any kind of assessment on sailors' self-reported ages is building a sandcastle in a swamp. That caution noted, statistical evidence clearly confirms the anecdotal testimony that the sea was a young man's world. Among 838 sailors who passed through the receiving ship *Ohio* during the year between 1 July 1843 and 30 June 1844 only 45 (5.4 percent) said they were in their forties, with 7 (0.8 percent) of the men reporting ages between 50 and 62. Something more than a decade later, during the months of July through September 1858, 1,463 men are recorded as passing through all the Navy's recruiting rendezvous. Of them, 86 (5.9 percent) asserted to being between 40 and 49 years of age; 30 (2.1 percent) said they were 50 to 59; and a negligible 3 men reported being 60, 62, and 67 respectively.[3] To repeat the earlier warning: an unknown number of the men who said they were 38 or 39 were actually in their forties, and an equally unknown number of the 48s and 49s were actually 50 or older. It was obviously in a middle-aged recruit's self-interest to represent himself as younger than he was. That said, these are as reliable data as are ever likely to be obtained for an age profile of the pre–Civil War naval enlisted force.

If each beneficiary had been given, on entering the Naval Asylum, a complete physical examination of the type that would have been routine a century later, history would have far better information on the toll that twenty or more years at sea and in garrison duty took on nineteenth-century sailors and Marines. What such a thorough physical might have found is suggested by the examination that Surgeon Charles Chase gave one would-be beneficiary in October 1864. "I have subjected William Sennott, seaman, aet. 60, to physical examination and find him unfit for further active duty," Chase recorded. "He has chronic rheumatism affecting the back, hips, and right shoulder, swelling of the right knee joint, and hemorrhoids. He is also enfeebled by age and suffers with stilli-cidium [incontinence of] urine." This is, incidentally, one more warning about the lack of trust to be placed in self-reported sailor ages and seafarer veracity. Nineteen days before the obviously unfit Sennott told Dr. Chase that he was sixty, he had sought reenlist-ment with the assurance: "I am 51 years old, but as good a man as I was ten years ago."

DANGER IS MY SHIPMATE

Unless they died in distant waters from diseases to which their bodies did not have immunities or served in ships that went down with all hands, the greatest danger that the Marines and sailors of the early nineteenth-century naval establishment faced was on-the-job injury. This is hardly news to those who know much about the maritime world, but it is confirmed yet one more time by the health records of the Naval Asylum's beneficiaries. The second most common health reason, one cited by 82 of 234 would-be benefi-ciaries seeking admission to the Asylum, was complete or partial disability incurred through shipboard and navy yard dangers.

More frequently cited than any other injury was the single or double hernia, which was reported by thirty-five of the eighty-two men who recorded service-incurred disabilities. Indeed, hernias were so widely recognized as an occupational hazard in lives that involved almost daily lifting, pushing, and hauling that the sur-geons' reports were typically limited to reporting the fact of the hernia being incurred plus a brief statement of the circumstances: "Was disabled during the month of March 1856 while endeavor-ing to secure a tackle on the main yard of [the frigate *Savannah*] with which to hoist in the boats by being ruptured in the right groin, producing *hernia*," reads a typical statement of disability. That was enough to justify at least a partial pension for the injury, even though many sailors and Marines continued to serve after incurring such damage to their bodies.

No accounts of the circumstances of these injuries, more detailed than the one just cited, are on record for any of the thirty-five men. As complete as any is the story of Henry Powell. His record has the added advantage of coming embedded in a longer health history cov-ering the years from Powell's first enlistment until his admission to the Naval Asylum. There are gaps in the record, but Powell is unique among the five hundred forty-one Asylum beneficiaries in having a compiled health dossier covering almost the entire span of his active-duty career. He was born in Baltimore, most likely at some date between 1813 and 1816. Although his age data are problematic, there exists a detailed and verified accounting of Powell's naval service, which began in February 1836 when he joined the frigate *Hudson* as an ordinary seaman. Within a month *Hudson's* surgeon was treating him for gonorrhea, a disease he probably contracted before he entered on board *Hudson* and of which there is no further mention in his medical record. The most serious event in Henry Powell's medical life occurred in the frigate *Macedonian* on 5 February 1840—in his own words, "a fall from the foretop yard of nearly a hundred feet, and striking on the hammock netting, which ruptured the right groin so that the intestines protrude and hang down in a large bunch." He failed to mention that the fall also resulted in a contused testicle. Powell was treated for his injuries on shipboard through 3 April, then sent ashore to the Pensacola Naval Hospital, where he remained until 11 July. He rejoined *Macedonian* for her passage to Boston, was there transferred to the naval hospital, 4 August, and discharged two weeks later.

Although there are no recorded details of Powell's recovery from his injury, the disability was serious enough that his next three duty assignments, August 1840 until March 1843, were to the receiving ships *Columbus, Ohio,* and *North Carolina.* Powell attempted sea duty again in the sloop-of-war *Vandalia,* but after five months he was transferred to the receiving ship *Pennsylvania,* August 1843, seemingly because of limitations arising from his old injury. The hernia aside, his only recorded medical problem during these three years was a cold serious enough to require five days of treatment in *Columbus.* Henry Powell finally got some significant sea duty again with a twenty-six-month posting to the sloop-of-war *Dale* during the Mexican War. *Dale's* medical journal lists Powell as being treated for a boil, dysentery, gastric irritation, diarrhea, a cold, a severe headache, and an inflammation of one of his testicles. It makes no mention of his being wounded in the leg during a boat landing from *Dale* at Guaymas. This, his second most serious service injury, is, however, well verified by an 1892 medical examination that states that Powell displayed a "wound of left leg below the knee, six inches above ankle, entering at this level over spine of tibia and emerging in the position of posterior part of leg in median line on same level. Leg [is] considerably bowed," the report continued, "and lines of union of old fracture of both tibia and fibula [were observed], evidently due to the gunshot."

Service in the frigate *Congress*, June 1855 through April 1856, was punctuated with serious upper respiratory infections, which— together with his old hernia—led to a medical survey dispatching Powell back to the United States as "unfit for the service." He then spent something less than a month at the Philadelphia Naval Hospital. After his July 1856 discharge from that institution, Powell had no further naval service until 1858, when he passed through the receiving ships *Ohio*—where he experienced another brief upper respiratory infection—and *North Carolina* before being assigned to the leased screw gunboat *Atlanta* or *Atalanta* (Navy records differ as to her correct name) in November. Here Powell's old hernia began to give him serious trouble again. The ship's medical journal for 25 December 1858 reveals that Powell had worn a truss ever since the original injury in *Macedonian* in 1840, but had stopped using it about five months earlier. The surgeon easily manipulated the intestines into a more comfortable situation, then sent Powell ashore to be fitted with a new truss. That seems to have alleviated the hernia problem for the immediate future; Powell's only other medical treatment in *Atalanta* was for a boil on his right arm just above the wrist.

After spending the summer of 1859 in the receiving ship *North Carolina*, Powell did a four-month tour in the screw steamer *Mohawk* as boatswain's mate, during which he experienced two brief spells of colic and diarrhea. After he left *Mohawk* in January 1860 Powell worked in the merchant service until April 1862, then turns up in New Orleans in June 1862 without any explanation of how he got there. The badly extended Union Navy needed any experienced sailor it could find, even one with a disability; Powell had no difficulty in signing on the screw sloop-of-war *Brooklyn* at the rate of seaman. But now the hernia came back to haunt him. Powell landed in the New York Naval Hospital in August 1862, was transferred to the Philadelphia Naval Hospital in October, and discharged to the receiving ship *Princeton* in November. Following a three-month stint as master-at-arms in the monitor *Patapsco*, Powell was back in the Philadelphia Naval Hospital, 30 March 1863, where the examining surgeon noted: "He is unfit for active duty and likely so to remain during his natural life." That verdict notwithstanding,

Powell was able to join the monitor *Lehigh* in April 1863, but he turned himself in on 11 May, saying that he was unable to perform any duty, and was sent ashore to the Norfolk Naval Hospital two days later. There he remained until 27 June, when he joined the steam gunboat *Allegheny*. In her, or possibly ashore at the Washington Navy Yard, Powell incurred a second hernia—this one on the left side—while lifting shot in late October 1863. That put an absolute end to Powell's shipboard service. The Navy still needed him, though. Powell worked in the mould loft at the Washington yard until almost the end of the Civil War, when he finally packed it in—"I am not fit for active service any more"—and applied for a permit to the Naval Asylum. He was admitted on 25 March 1865.

The second most common source of service-incurred injuries, one cited by twelve of the eighty-two duty-injured beneficiaries, was a fall. The twelve include Henry Powell, already counted under hernias, but whose injury was sustained when he fell from aloft. Powell's hernia was a bad injury. How much more serious it could have been if the hammock netting had not broken his fall can be seen in the story of Thomas Coleman. The latter, an experienced seaman in his mid-thirties, volunteered for the United States Exploring Expedition under Lieutenant Charles Wilkes, perhaps in hopes of some exotic adventures in the distant reaches of the Pacific, and was assigned to the sloop-of-war *Vincennes*. Sadly, instead of sex with eagerly compliant Polynesian women, a different future was in store for Coleman. Before the expedition sailed, "whilst aloft on duty on the topsail yard, your memorialist accidentally fell from thence to the deck," he—or, more correctly, the person who wrote in his name, because Coleman was illiterate—petitioned the Secretary of the Navy, "and broke his arm in two places, fractured several of his ribs, and dislocated several of his joints, which entirely disabled him at that time for further service." All this was confirmed by John S. Whittle, then *Vincennes'* junior assistant surgeon, who reported that Coleman had broken his left arm and injured his head, chest, and back. "The fracture of the arm was a compound one and of a very bad kind and the limb is now very much disabled." With a stint in the hospital, Coleman recovered sufficiently by the spring of 1839 to serve a two-year, eleven-month enlistment as cooper in the frigate *Constitution*, but then came ashore for good. "In consequence of the injuries received on board the *Vincennes*," Coleman's amanuensis continued, adding a touch of calculated pathos to the appeal, he "finds himself unable to procure a livelihood and reduced to the lowest depths of poverty and is now dragging out a miserable existence in the House of Industry (or almshouse) at South Boston." A member of the Board of Overseers of the alms house—eager, of course, to shift the expense of supporting Coleman to the national government—endorsed the decrepit sailor's appeal; he was admitted to the Asylum on 9 April 1849.

Coleman's bodily injuries must have damaged his spirit as well. Following a serious disciplinary incident in which he directed "threats and curses" at Asylum Executive Officer Henry A. Adams, the latter described Coleman as "a poor wretch, always drunk when he can get liquor." Only the fact that he was so badly disabled and unable to work in any way for his own support spared Coleman from dismissal. What might have happened had he lived longer can only be guessed. In one of his voyages Thomas Coleman had apparently contracted malaria or some other recurring fever with which he was repeatedly hospitalized during his brief Asylum residence. He died there just seventeen months after his admission.

STOP THAT—RIGHT NOW!

Hernias and falls aside, the other injuries sustained during their active-duty service by the eighty-two beneficiaries are so diverse— an arm injured in the bursting of a gun, a foot crushed when a tank being lifted from the hold dropped on it, a hand disabled when caught on a hammock hook, an eye blinded when struck by a swinging block during a storm—as to forbid other generalizations about the specific dangers of sea life as experienced by these men. One unique injury *is* worth mentioning, because it offers some light on a vexed subject in naval history: shipboard homoerotic activity. Historians diverge as to the extent of such relations in the nineteenth-century U.S. Navy, but they agree that the behavior was subject to a broadly held cultural taboo of the time.[4]

This attitude explains seaman William Downing's self-appointed role as a lower-deck sexual policeman in the sloop-of-war *Plymouth*: "On the 13th February 1849, between seven and eight bells in the evening, I saw James Bennett in another person's hammock," Downing later reported. "I went over to see what they were doing, and I found that they were 'frigging' each other. Bennett had his trousers unbuttoned and down below his seat, and I thought it my duty to make him get out of the hammock and go to his own hammock." Bennett thought otherwise: "He told me to go to hell, and I put my hand on his foot. Then he opened his knife and cut me on the arm. Then he got out of the hammock and buttoned up his trousers. I took him by the collar and told him to go to his own hammock, and with that he cut me across the wrist." Downing's intervention cost him the use of his right wrist, for which he was granted a pension for half-disability in 1850. More immediately, Bennett and his partner, Peter Peppinger, were punished two days later with twelve lashes each, Bennett for wounding Downing and Peppinger for "filthiness."[5] Both Bennett and Peppinger were rated as *landsmen*, that is, novices to seafaring life. What bearing that may have had on their encounter can only be a matter of speculation. Perhaps experienced sailors found more private spaces than berth-deck hammocks to act out homoerotic impulses.

COMBAT'S LEGACIES

Among the Naval Asylum's 234 applicants whose health is analyzed in this chapter there stands, as best as they are able, a detachment so small that it might easily be overlooked. That would be a mistake. These were five men, wounded in battle, who elected to surrender their pensions in exchange for admission to the Asylum. Their individual histories run the gamut of the naval establishment's combat experience from the War of 1812 through the Civil War.

Joseph Dalrymple was born somewhere in Virginia, probably in the late 1770s, depending on which of his self-reported ages one chooses to accept. Nothing has been discovered about his life before his early thirties.

In September 1811, Dalrymple joined the sloop-of-war *Hornet*, with the rating of seaman, evidence that he was already an accomplished sailor. During *Hornet*'s battle with the British brig sloop *Peacock*, 24 February 1813, Dalrymple sustained a wound to his ankle. Master Commandant James Lawrence, *Hornet*'s commanding officer, dismissed Dalrymple's wound as "slight" in his official report of the action.[6] However, pain is in the body of the wounded man, not in the prose of his uninjured captain. In the 1830s Dalrymple asserted that after the battle he remained partially incapacitated by the wound. This claim was confirmed by Surgeon Bailey Washington, who rated the injury at three-fourths of a total disability; Dalrymple was accordingly granted a pension of four dollars and fifty cents a month. But this is getting ahead of the story. Seaman Dalrymple was discharged from *Hornet* at the expiration of his enlistment in April 1813. After the War of 1812 he did a second tour in the Navy, joining the schooner *Prometheus* as seaman in November 1817; from her, Dalrymple was transferred to shoreside duty at the New Orleans Navy Yard when *Prometheus* was decommissioned in October 1818. According to his brief autobiographical statement, Dalrymple next moved up-river to Kentucky in 1821. There he remained until May 1837, when he moved once more—this time to Hallett's Cove, on the Long Island side of the East River, in New York. The New York residency, whatever may have been its purpose, did not last long. In January 1839 Dalrymple, by now a man pushing—if not past—sixty, showed up at the Naval Asylum and asked Governor James Biddle if he could commute his pension, the certificate for which he had lost in his travels, for admission as a beneficiary. Commodore Biddle checked the published list of Navy pensioners, verified that Dalrymple was telling the truth, and recommended his admission. As a beneficiary Dalrymple soon succumbed to the Asylum's prevailing culture of alcohol abuse. Between 1 October 1842 and 28 November 1846 he was put on report twenty-one times for alcohol-related offenses and earned the questionable distinction of being named one of the three "most disorderly" beneficiaries resident at the Asylum in 1842. So far as the institution's disciplinary record shows, Dalrymple stopped drinking to excess after November 1846. His health began to decline in the 1850s. On 15 March 1853 he was admitted to the hospital with a diagnosis of "debility" and died there seven hundred twelve days later, on 25 February 1855.

Proceeding chronologically by the date of combat, the next two beneficiary-veterans were both wounded during Florida's Second Seminole War, 1835–42. Marine Peter Foley's life story is a puzzle of contradictory information. His enlistment records all claim that he was born in Northampton, Montgomery County, New York, but his death certificate lists his place of birth as Ireland. His birthdate is equally ambiguous. According to the various ages he self-reported, Foley could have been born anywhere between 1804 and 1811. More trustworthy is the description of Private Foley's appearance at his first Marine Corps enlistment at Gosport, Virginia, on 17 June 1828—blue eyes, sandy hair, light complexion, and sixty-eight and a quarter inches tall. That five-year enlistment produced a mixed record: Foley deserted on 9 July 1832, perhaps under the influence of alcohol, was picked up three days later, but was still promoted to corporal on 1 November. Foley reenlisted, this time for a four-year hitch, in June 1833, was almost immediately reinstated as corporal, then promoted sergeant in May 1834. All this looks like the record of a capable Marine with a promising future in the Corps—that is, until 11 January 1836, when he was reduced to private, though there is no record of the misdeed that led to his reduction. As Private Foley he was wounded on 27 January 1837 in the inconclusive battle of Hatcheelustee Creek with the elusive Seminoles.[7] While he was loading his musket, a ball struck Foley in the left arm just below the elbow, passed along the ulna, lodged deep in the muscles of his forearm, and produced a partial fixation of his elbow joint.

His Marine Corps enlistment up on 24 June 1837, Foley decided to give the United States Army a try, signing up at New York on 15 July 1837. Although Navy Surgeon John A. Kearney rated Foley's Hatcheelustee Creek wound a total and permanent disability, entitling him to a full pension, the wound was apparently no obstacle as far as the Army recruiter was concerned. Foley's Army service record is, if possible, more puzzling than his one in the Marine Corps. He later reported that he participated in the battle with the Seminoles at Lake Okeechobee on 25 December 1837.[8] On that his Army enlistment record is silent, but it does list Foley as deserting on 17 June 1838, apprehended on 1 March 1842, and deserting a second (and successful) time on 18 June of that same year. When Foley had later to account officially for these Army years he covered them by saying: "I was with my friends"—*friends* was then typically a term for family—"in the South."

In April 1843 Foley joined the sloop-of-war *Vandalia* for a two-year enlistment as her master-at-arms, then verified the adage that there is no such thing as an ex-Marine by reenlisting as a private in the Corps in July 1845. That enlistment seems to have passed with no black marks to Foley's record; he reenlisted for a final time on 1 October 1849, and was promoted to his old rank of corporal on 18 December 1851. In May 1855 Marine Corps Commandant Archibald Henderson recommended Foley for admission to the Naval Asylum, a recommendation strong enough to insure Foley's immediate appointment.

At the Naval Asylum Peter Foley's record is as puzzling as that for the earlier portions of his life. Obviously a capable man, he was soon appointed, 1 September 1855, to the responsible beneficiary job of watchman, transferred to the equally responsible job of messenger two months later, and then disrated without explanation on 17 November. By June 1856 he was back in his job as watchman at the Asylum's front door, a post he held until 31 March 1860. This time there can be no question why he lost his job. At 8 a.m. on 22 March Foley was reported as absent without leave; 3:30 the next afternoon he was brought—by whom the record does not say—onto the Asylum campus totally drunk. When he behaved himself Peter Foley was really good at his job, so he got another chance as watchman on 1 June 1860 and held the post for almost a year—until 11 May 1861 when he lost it for the final time because of unspecified "misconduct."

Peter Foley's life course was about run. He died on 7 January 1863 with the cause of death listed as delirium tremens. One more puzzle! Foley's behavioral record at the Asylum shows only two instances of alcohol abuse (those noted above) and only two hospitalizations, of six and five days each, for alcoholism. His monthly behavior evaluations were typically "good" and "very good." By Asylum standards that was a pretty clean slate. There is no record of a final hospitalization that preceded Foley's death. At his life's end, history is left to puzzle about the place and the circumstances of the wounded veteran's demise.

On 15 January 1838 the wily Seminoles lured Lieutenant Levin Powell, USN, commanding a mixed force of soldiers and sailors, into attacking a fiercely defended position near the head of the Jupiter River. Powell's force suffered a clear defeat, with five dead, including the detachment's medical officer, and fifteen wounded.[9] Among the latter was John Clark, acting as boatswain's mate with Powell's force, who was struck by a rifle bullet or musket ball that totally destroyed the vision in his right eye and badly impaired that of the left as well.

According to his brief biographical statement, Clark was born in Baltimore, Maryland, around 1788 or 1789, and served twenty-two years in the merchant service in addition to several naval enlistments. He said he had seen action in both the Army and Navy during the War of 1812—several John Clarks served in the Maryland militia during that conflict—but his earliest naval service that can be independently verified was in the ship-of-the-line *Franklin*, Commodore Charles Stewart, in 1818–19. Clark's loss of eyesight was, obviously, a total disability, entitling him to a full pension. He seems to have lived on this—and perhaps on such work as he could pick up—first in Baltimore and then in New York City until the late 1840s. In 1846, basing his claim on his twenty-two years of merchant service, Clark twice applied for admission to Sailors' Snug Harbor, but his entries in Snug Harbor's admission book are incomplete, suggesting that he never took up residence. The Naval Asylum was a more attractive option; Clark surrendered his pension in exchange for admission as a beneficiary there on 18 July 1848.

By November Clark had worn out his welcome with Executive Officer John P. Gillis, to whom he denounced the Asylum's "tyrannical government," and with Governor Jacob Jones, who described Clark as "*habitually* intemperate and disorderly—and apparently well able to earn his living." How Commodore Jones could judge a man blind in one eye and partially blind in the other as *well able* to earn a living is puzzling, but Jones was clearly at the end of his patience. Although Jones did receive authority to dismiss Clark from the Asylum, the elderly governor apparently had second thoughts and declined to act. Clark, then a man of sixty himself, remained a beneficiary for the balance of his life.

Not that it was an easy life. Given the psychological burden he must have carried from the near-complete destruction of his vision, one can perhaps cut John Clark some slack for resorting to drink to ease the pain. During the ten years from November 1851 to July 1861 he was put on report at least nine times for alcohol-related infractions. Even more tellingly, Clark was hospitalized for alcoholism no less than twenty-five times between 4 June 1849 and 12 May 1858. In his seventies Clark seems to have tapered off, if he did not completely stop, his drinking. By then severe respiratory problems were sending him to the hospital time after time; to them he finally succumbed on 15 June 1865.

A private who lost his arm by amputation when he sustained a gunshot wound during the Marines' legend-building participation in the September 1847 attack on fortified Chapultepec, that blocked the approach to Mexico City, is the only Mexican War casualty among the five battle-wounded beneficiaries. He was born Morten Berg Fog in Copenhagen, Denmark, somewhere between 1799 and 1804. Fog was trained as a shoemaker, presumably in Denmark. When he immigrated to the United States is unknown. The first firm record is that of his enlistment at Rochester, New York, as a private in the U.S. Army, 11 December 1837—standing just over sixty-five inches tall, with blue eyes, fair skin, light brown hair, and aged (he said) thirty-three years. Three years of the Army were apparently enough; he reenlisted—this time with his name Americanized to Martin B. Fogg—in the Marine Corps, in which he continued to serve as a private until he was awarded a full pension for his amputated arm. Fogg received his pension certificate on 1 June 1848 and commuted it, on the twenty-sixth of that same month, for admission to the Naval Asylum. There he kept an unusually low profile. Fogg's behavior was uniformly recorded as "very good"; he was never put on report for a disciplinary infraction; and he was hospitalized only once, on 14 February 1855, with typhoid fever from which he died on 31 March.

The final combat-wounded beneficiary has already been met in chapter 1—William Thompson, the Civil War medal-of-honor quartermaster who had his leg shot away during Flag Officer Samuel F. Du Pont's 7 November 1861 attack on Port Royal, South Carolina. Following his admission to the Naval Asylum on 7 January 1863, Thompson proved to be a model beneficiary, never put on report for incorrect behavior, and scarcely surfacing in the Asylum's voluminous records until his final illness and death.

On 26 July 1872 Thompson reported to the hospital, complaining to the assistant surgeon who admitted him that he was "suffering very much with pain in left side in the region of heart—pain extending down through the hip-joint to the left leg and to the left shoulder and arm." Thompson added that he had been experiencing some pain in his left side for several months, worse in the last fifteen days, and for two days past "violent and of rheumatic character, extending to the leg and arm." The problem was diagnosed at intake as acute rheumatism, for which Thompson was treated with slow but steady success until 12 September, when he told the doctor that he felt "a good deal better" and asked to be discharged to his Asylum room. This was done at 1:30 p.m.

At about 8 that same night, thinking that he was experiencing the need for a bowel movement, Thompson headed to the water closet. Minutes later a fellow beneficiary found him, "leaning over the bathtub with blood issuing from his mouth in a stream. He called to a friend and desired him to go for the doctor, saying that he was bleeding to death." By the time the duty medical officer arrived Thompson had somehow made it back to his room, where the doctor found him lying on a lounge "in an unconscious and moribund condition, with great pallor of surface, cold extremities, and a slim, feeble and compressible pulse; eyes widely open and pupils responding sluggishly to light; his mouth filled with clotted blood, and liquid blood issuing from the angles; his respiration slow, labored and gurgling." Within three to five minutes of the doctor's arrival, William Thompson was dead. Given the state of medical knowledge and surgical practice in 1872, there was nothing anyone could have done to save Thompson's life. An autopsy the following morning revealed that the old hero had died from a ruptured aneurysm of the aorta.

TWELVE

Minds Decayed, Minds Disordered

Bodies in pain and in decline. Bodies damaged and worn out by hard work, by times of intense stress, by health-threatening living conditions, and by the pleasures and antidotes pursued to compensate for or deaden them. These decaying bodies were the principal professional challenge confronting the Philadelphia Naval Hospital's medical staff. But they also had to encounter and treat, as best they could, minds decaying with advancing age—and other minds, not necessarily those of elderly men, but ones seriously disordered and often pregnant with dangers to others. Not to suggest that bodies and minds are distinct entities. Far from it. The failing and disordered minds and the sick bodies were in reality individual human beings, each unique in his own way; it would be seriously misleading to suggest a sharp division between ill bodies and sick minds in their real-life settings. Still, it is convenient to look separately at the mental health issues of the Asylum's beneficiaries. One hopes it can be done without forgetting that the minds in distress were those of men whose bodies were often impaired as well. Nor will a sharp boundary be drawn here between cases of mental illness and the Asylum's culture of alcohol abuse. Current scientific research discovers strong links between excessive alcohol use, dementia, and other forms of acute mental illness, findings strongly seconded by the life stories in this chapter.[1]

Ungentle Goodnights cannot say with certainty the number of Asylum beneficiaries for whom psychological ailments were the primary medical issue. Health records for the residents of the Naval Asylum run the gamut from none, through sketchy and suggestive, to voluminous. However, some thirty cases have been identified through which it is possible to explore the United States Naval Asylum's encounter with the problems of sailor and Marine mental health.

The Asylum administration and the Naval Hospital medical staff typically used the term *insanity* to describe all forms of psychic behavior that deviated from their perception of the healthy norm. Under that umbrella term one can discern two broad streams of behavior. The first, often called *senile dementia* in the Asylum's records, was characterized by the progressive loss of mental faculties among some beneficiaries as they aged. The second was marked by behavior that deviated widely from accepted norms and typically involved the potential for physical harm to others. That is not to suggest that the two streams of "insanity" were always sharply distinguished. There was an ambiguous middle-ground between them that makes some cases difficult to assign to one category or the other. This challenge of classification is present in the first two cases of "insanity" with which the Asylum had to cope in 1842. They involve a Marine Corps beneficiary, John Stratton, and a Navy veteran named Godfrey Winslow. Because the two cases were similar, Winslow's story will be told here, but he will represent both men.

"I do not consider John Stratton and Godfrey Winslow proper persons to be inmates of the Naval Asylum," Assistant Surgeon Joseph Beale reported to Commodore James Barron, the governor, on 30 May 1842. "Both of them are incurable cases of insanity and require at all times, as well for their own welfare as for the comfort of those about them, seclusion and frequently bodily restraints— the former of which is entirely impracticable in this institution and the latter so nearly so as to be, if possible, more painful than the necessity which justifies it. They are, besides," he continued, "liable, in the usual paroxysms of their diseases, to become violently excited and there is great reason to apprehend they may, in one of these moments, inflict serious injuries on those who are the innocent causes of their rage." Were Stratton and Winslow permitted to mingle with the other beneficiaries, Beale concluded dramatically, "no one can venture to predict what their fury may prompt them to do." If that were the only document to survive about Godfrey Winslow's mental state, it would be easy to classify the case—behavior that departed from the Asylum's accepted norm and was a danger to others. However, if one works backward through Winslow's life, peeling the layers of documentation in succession, a more complex story is found.

Winslow was admitted to the Asylum on 15 January 1840, but he had been trying unsuccessfully to get there for the two previous years. He enlisted for shoreside service at the New York (Brooklyn) Navy Yard in October 1836, wound up in the hospital sixteen days later, and was discharged from the Navy on 7 December 1837. All sympathetic officers who tried to get him into the Naval Asylum agreed that Winslow was, at this point in his life, old, destitute and helpless. The problem was that, even though he had evidently served more than twenty years in the Navy, his memory was so feeble that he could not produce a list of the ships and dates of his service which was accurate enough to be verified against the rolls on file in the office of the Fourth Auditor of the Treasury. Pending a resolution of this problem—an effort that had run out of momentum and stalled in Washington—the commandant of the New York Navy Yard authorized, in February 1838, Winslow's readmission to the hospital. There Winslow remained nearly two years later, to the mounting frustration of Surgeon Stephen Rapalje, whose patience was finally exhausted. Winslow, he complained in early December 1839, "has become entirely unmanageable and his present condition, being almost an imbecile from dotage, places him beyond the pale of all restraint and authority. His facilities for procuring intoxicating liquors are unlimited unless he is kept confined constantly in a cell, which will require an extra fire and a person to attend to him. The evil resulting from his use of liquors is not confined to himself, but he is made the means of procuring it for the invalids and convalescents of the hospital to their great injury, and our utmost vigilance cannot prevent it." Rapalje's letter finally broke the bureaucratic stalemate. Winslow was admitted to the Naval Asylum a month later.

However, there was one more layer, apparently unknown to Winslow's advocates in New York, that can be peeled back to find (perhaps) the root cause of his psychological problems. Godfrey Winslow was born in Freetown, Massachusetts, almost certainly in 1780 or 1781. (Because Winslow's birth year is known with reasonable accuracy, one might here note that he was at most a man in his late fifties when Dr. Rapalje described him as "almost an imbecile from dotage.") At seventeen, Winslow went to sea in the merchant service, sailing out of Providence, Rhode Island. His earliest recorded naval service was in the brig *Hornet* in 1809–10. By this time Winslow was clearly an experienced and valuable seaman, as he was rated quarter-gunner throughout his enlistment. During the War of 1812 Winslow served first in the frigate *United States*, with the rating of seaman, and participated in Stephen Decatur's capture of the British frigate *Macedonian*, then—after a fortnight's run shoreside—he reenlisted for *Constitution* in time to fight as a sponger (and potential boarder) at Carronade Number 8 during Charles Stewart's defeat of *Cyane* and *Levant*. This 1812–15 combat experience was an asset when Winslow sought admission to the Naval Asylum on the basis of a poorly remembered service record that did not appear to add up to the twenty years required to become a beneficiary. After the war Godfrey Winslow made cruises as seaman and quarter-gunner in the frigate *Congress* until his sea service was cut short by an event known only from a single sentence in a letter that the illiterate Winslow had someone write in his name to the Secretary of the Navy: "I was wounded by lightning and never have recovered." That happened during *Congress'* 1819–21 cruise to China, under Captain John D. Henley. *Congress'* medical journal for this cruise does not survive, so it is not possible to learn the details and extent of Winslow's injury. What *is* known is that Winslow was thereafter unfit for the demands of sea-service and enlisted for less strenuous assignments in various navy yards. Even this type of work came to an end with his time at the New York Navy Yard, where Winslow's inability to perform the most routine duties led to his hospitalization in 1836–37. One can certainly wonder whether being struck by lightning was a contributing factor—or even the fundamental cause—of Godfrey Winslow's psychic and behavioral problems on such dramatic display at the Naval Asylum.

STAY-AT-HOMES

What was to be done with Godfrey Winslow and John Stratton? The solution was to send them on a journey that would take them away from the Naval Asylum for the rest of their lives. But before following Stratton and Winslow to that destination, a brief look at those—about one-third of the thirty psychically impaired beneficiaries—who ended lives at the Naval Asylum is in order. These men are typically referred to in the institution's records as "idiotic," though occasionally the terminology used is "childish" or "imbecile." The decision to keep such cases in residence at the Asylum appears to have been a pragmatic one. They could be cared for there with the available staff and facilities.

Some spent the majority or the entirety of their Asylum residencies in the hospital wing, receiving palliative care from the medical staff until their deaths. Typically, quarter-gunner Charles Collins was sent to the hospital, where he was classified as "insane" or "idiotic" on the day after his admission to the Asylum and he remained there until his death on 30 October 1852—a total of 1,704 days. Others, although mentally impaired, continued to live among their fellow beneficiaries in the Asylum's portion of the building. Of the three, the most is known about Jeremiah ("Jerry") Miller.

Miller gave the compilers of "Biography of Beneficiaries United States Naval Asylum" (chapter 6) one of the longest and most-detailed life stories in the entire volume—tales of merchant voyages, shipwrecks, naval battles, impressment, escape from impressment, and romance with two beautiful sisters while hiding out in Ulster or the North of England. Perhaps the officer who took down Jerry Miller's stories should have been warned by the monthly entries in the Asylum's muster rolls and other records in which Miller is reported as "insane," "crazy," and "deranged." There is no way to verify most of the life narrative that Miller told, but some parts that can be checked against other records are fabrications. A case in point is Miller's circumstantial account of his participation in the frigate *Constellation*'s 1799 capture of the French frigate *L'Insurgente* during the Quasi-War with France. It all sounds convincing until the cautious historian checks *Constellation*'s muster roll, and discovers that Jerry is nowhere to be found in that carefully kept record. He possibly concocted his participation narrative from one or more books about the Navy's history known to be available on the shelves of the Asylum's library. Other Miller stories contain a kernel or two of fact buried in webs of distortion and unverifiable anecdote. Thus his story of refusing to serve in the 74-gun HMS *Montagu* at the beginning of the War of 1812: In this version, Miller defiantly gives himself up as an American and is dispatched to Dartmoor prison, where his fellow American prisoners inexplicably threaten to tar and feather him as a traitor. The facts, recorded in the British prisoner-of-war records are rather otherwise and make more sense. In late May 1813, almost a year into the war, Miller, who is serving as a seaman in HMS *Scipion*, gives himself up as a U.S. citizen. Incarcerated as a prisoner-of-war at Chatham on 9 August, Jerry takes only five and a half weeks to change his mind and agree, on 16 September, to reenlist in the Royal Navy. He continues to serve until

25 January 1815, when, with the war almost over, he declares himself as an American to *Montagu*'s officers. This time Miller is sent to the infamous Dartmoor Prison, where he arrives on 17 February and is released, with the return of peace, on 6 April 1815.[2] Whether they really had tar and feathers on their agenda, and whether the incident took place at Dartmoor or earlier at Chatham, is it any wonder that sailors from United States ships-of-war and privateers, who had been captured and imprisoned for fighting against the British, considered Jeremiah Miller a traitor to his country?

By October 1867, Miller—who claimed to be one hundred three years old, though almost all Asylum records would make him about ten years younger than that—had become a problem beneficiary. "On account of extreme age [he] has entirely lost his mind and is in every way unable to care for himself," Governor Hiram Paulding reported to Admiral Joseph Smith. "I cannot describe to you the disgusting practices of this man, but they render the corridor in which he has his room unfit for other men to occupy." Paulding wanted to relocate Miller to some other institution, but Surgeon George Maulsby of the Philadelphia Naval Hospital, recognizing that a long-distance transfer might well kill Miller, offered to provide a room for him in the hospital. His assessment of Miller's mental condition differed in some ways from Paulding's. "Owing to his extreme age," Maulsby wrote in conjunction with Assistant Surgeon J. Albert Hawke, "we find Miller quite helpless in his lower extremities and unable to leave his bed without assistance. . . . His mind appears to be rational in a general sense of the term, though it is depraved to such an extent that in his personal habits he is exceedingly filthy." Provided with whatever palliative comforts the medical staff could offer, Jerry Miller lived in the hospital for the months of December 1867 and January 1868, returned to his Asylum room for the months of February and March 1868—no record exists of how he was cared for there—went back to the hospital on the first day of April 1868, and died there on the fourth of the month.

DR. WILLIAMSON'S PATIENTS

To return to the interrupted story of Godfrey Winslow and John Stratton, in June 1842 Secretary of the Navy Abel P. Upshur decided that the two beneficiaries should be sent to the naval hospital at Norfolk, the Navy's primary facility for treating patients with mental health issues. There they would be under the care of

Dr. Thomas Williamson, one of the Navy's senior surgeons. The Norfolk hospital had been constructed contemporaneously with the Naval Asylum. Although designed by a different architect, the two buildings had much in common. With their monumental classical porticoes, solid stone construction, ample proportions, and capacities in excess of immediate needs, both expressed the nation's and the Navy's post-1815 expansive exuberance. At the same time they seemed to ask—or perhaps demand—that other nations recognize the U.S. Navy as a rising maritime power.

In the ten and a half years between June 1842 and December 1852 seven Naval Asylum beneficiaries, including Stratton and Winslow, were sent to Norfolk to be housed and treated alongside mental health patients from the active-duty Navy. To judge from the language that Dr. Williamson used to describe his mentally ill charges it would seem that the doctor found them a distasteful part of his responsibilities. They were "at times refractory, boisterous, and quarrelsome—easily excited by the most commonplace remark." Added to those problems were "their incoherent remarks, the peculiar odor from a maniac, [and] the unsightly and disgusting appearance of them at times ... as they are with great difficulty kept clean." Repugnance notwithstanding, Dr. Williamson did the best he could for his mentally ill patients, to whom he routinely referred as *maniacs*. Given the state of medical science with respect to impairments of the mind in the mid-nineteenth century, his record was a respectable one. During the eight years ending with May 1844, twenty-three mentally ill members of the Navy and the Marine Corps had been sent to Norfolk for treatment. Ten were released as cured, four died, one escaped and disappeared, and eight were still confined to the hospital.[3] Godfrey Winslow was among those in the latter category—a mentally ill man who was going to be at Norfolk for the remainder of his life.

Following the treatment of Winslow for the six years and eight months of his residence at Norfolk Naval Hospital, from his admission on 9 June 1842 until his death on 31 January 1849, gives a good idea of what could and could not be done for the more difficult cases among the Navy's mentally ill. His care was essentially custodial and palliative. Williamson's only recorded diagnosis of Winslow was "chronic insanity." He provided no description of the behavioral manifestations of this insanity. In one note he seems to have described Winslow as "a morose character." But

Williamson's handwriting can be a challenge to read, and the word that looks like *morose* may possibly be *nervous*. The daily instructions for Winslow's care, recorded in the hospital's medical journal, reveal Williamson's approach to his mentally ill charges: keep Winslow comfortable. See that he gets regular light exercise within the hospital grounds. Watch him. See that he is not annoyed by anyone. Give great attention to his personal cleanliness. The frequency with which instructions to attend to Winslow's cleanliness appear in the medical journal suggest that he may have often, or even habitually, soiled himself. As Winslow's obviously impending death approaches, Williamson's concern for Winslow's physical well-being mounts. Make him as comfortable as possible. Let him be carefully nursed.[4]

Williamson was aware of—and trying to follow so far as he could—the *moral treatment* method of working with the insane, which was considered the best practice of his time. Moral treatment rejected the older methods—imprisonment, physical restraints, and coercion—the latter sometimes employing whips. It held instead that the insane were still, in some degree, rational human beings; it sought to reach and encourage that fragment of rationality within the patient. The asylum for the insane, an institutional home, preferably in a rural setting, was the best site for practicing the moral treatment. Physical constraints were to be used only to the degree necessary; the ideal was for patients to learn to control themselves. This was promoted by a humane and caring environment characterized by kindness and indulgent attention, exercise, and sharing in the work of the institution.[5]

Trying to achieve this ideal in a general naval hospital, with a full spectrum of sick and injured officers and enlisted men, fell short of the ideal—a deficiency graphically described in a report that Williamson prepared in July 1844: "As you have requested my opinion in relation to the keeping of the chronic cases of mania at a hospital appropriated for the sick," Williamson wrote Commodore Jesse Wilkinson, commandant of the Norfolk naval station, "I would beg leave to remark that great injury results to both [classes of patients], as it is not possible to isolate them in such a manner as to prevent them from at least hearing each other. The incessant ravings of the maniacs, day and night, and the impossibility of preventing it without resorting to harsh means, are amply sufficient, without assigning any other cause, why they should be removed to a regular insane establishment, where the moral curative means in their cases called for might be resorted to with a greater chance of success than if kept where they can so much annoy and where they can be so much excited at all times by the most ordinary conversation of the unthinking and those convalescent from disease. We have only twelve cells, and they upon the basement story, calculated only for temporary cases of insanity or the acute forms of it, [and] but illy adapted to the chronic induration and character [of cases] which for years have been pronounced as incurable."[6] Secretary of the Navy John Y. Mason, whose desk Williamson's report eventually reached, promised to see if the Navy Department had the power to act on Williamson's request to move these men to an asylum for the insane or—lacking that—to refer the problem to Congress at its next session.

INTENT ON HARM

Williamson's promised relief was not soon in coming. The act of 3 August 1848, making appropriations for the Navy for the fiscal year 1849, authorized the Secretary of the Navy "to cause persons in the naval service or Marine Corps, who shall become insane while in the service, to be placed in such lunatic hospital as in his opinion will be most convenient and best calculated to promise a restoration of reason." But the Naval Asylum, for reasons undiscovered by this historian, continued to send mentally ill beneficiaries to Norfolk into the 1850s, when the new U.S. Government Hospital for the Insane (more popularly known as St. Elizabeths Hospital) opened in Washington in 1855 with a mission to care for mentally ill members of the Army, Marine Corps, and Navy, as well as for indigent psychically impaired residents of the District of Columbia. Beginning with that year, nine pre-1866 beneficiaries were eventually dispatched to the Washington facility. The history of one man sent there, James Morris, provides a good transition to the other class of mentally ill beneficiaries with which the Asylum authorities had to concern themselves: those whose illness and behavior made them dangerous.

Morris was born in Ireland in 1795, according to his own account. A person of good education, he listed his earlier occupations as schoolmaster on one occasion and apothecary on another. Why and how Morris came to the United States, where he became a naturalized citizen, is unknown. He enlisted as a private in the

Marine Corps in July 1827 and served, with brief intermissions and an apparently clean record, until he was discharged because of chronic rheumatism in February 1852 and was immediately admitted to the Naval Asylum.

Whether and to what extent drinking had been a problem in Morris' earlier years is not known, though his abandonment of two careers for the life of a Marine Corps private offers the suggestion of a downward spiral. Once he was at the Asylum, Morris' addiction blossomed into full flower. Between 1 February 1853 and 14 September 1861 Morris was put on report no fewer than twenty-eight times for alcohol-related offenses: "Very drunk—attacked the master-at-arms with a cane and resisted him some time" (3 October 1853). "Brought into the grounds this morning for assaulting persons in the city and insanity" (16 July 1857 and the first mention of "insanity" in his record). "Came in quite drunk and was so boisterous that it became necessary to confine him with the gloves in one of the upper rooms" (8 September 1860). All this culminated on the night of 13–14 October 1862. Morris had been delivered to the Asylum, presumably by the Philadelphia police, for riotous conduct in the city and locked up in one of the cells. There he continued to be excessively noisy. In an attempt to deal with the situation, the Asylum's executive officer, Commander Peter Turner, opened the cell door and was physically attacked by Morris, who simultaneously showered Turner with a torrent of oral abuse. Inevitably, this resulted in Morris' expulsion from the Asylum on 18 October. Striking an officer was an offense that could not be tolerated, violating as it did the Navy's fundamental hierarchy.

By 29 October Morris had made his way, almost certainly involuntarily, to Blockley alms house across the Schuylkill, where he was lodged in the drunkards' ward, and from which he escaped on 11 January 1863. He then began hanging around the Asylum "in a most destitute condition," according to Governor Frederick Engle, "and imploring aid from us." Commander Turner favored forgiving Morris and urged his readmission to the Asylum—a request seconded by Morris' former fellow beneficiaries. "It is feared that he may be frozen to death," Engle continued, "as he has no place to eat or sleep." With misgivings Admiral Smith consented to Morris' readmission. This only set the stage for more serious problems.

In April 1864 Morris suffered an attack of typhoid fever, which confined him to the hospital for nineteen days; in August he was back in the hospital with delirium tremens; and in mid-September "mania" led to his transfer, on 16 April, to the Government Hospital for the Insane. Nothing in his surviving record indicates whether Morris' attacks of "insanity" were a consequence of excessive drinking or whether he was drinking to anesthetize deeper psychological problems. But at Washington Morris had no access to alcohol and became a rational and model patient who wandered the grounds at St. Elizabeths freely and peaceably. By October 1865 Dr. Charles H. Nichols, the superintendent of the hospital, pronounced him recovered and ready to return to life in the outside world. The doctor did caution, however, that "should [Morris] get to drinking, he would be likely to have another maniacal attack, but it seems justifiable to me to run some risk of that in an effort to promote the old sailor's happiness." Morris attempted to get a pension, but was told that was not possible because he had sustained no pension-justifying injury while in the Marine Corps. His only alternative was to return to the Naval Asylum, which permission Admiral Smith granted on 13 October.

Nichols should have listened more seriously to his nagging misgivings than he did to his cautious optimism. Morris set off on his own for Philadelphia, arriving at the Asylum on 23 October. Presumably he had returned to his old alcohol-fueled life along the way. When Commander Turner met Morris at the northeast gate he was, Commodore Engle reported to Admiral Smith on 25 November, "Judging from his conversation, crazy and has so continued on the increase until we have been compelled to place him in the cells." Just the previous morning, Morris had somehow armed himself with a hickory axe handle with which he said he intended to kill (among others) the governor, the executive officer, the master-at-arms, and the ship's corporal. "The short of it is," continued Engle, "that Morris is crazy and a dangerous man and should be removed from amongst the old men, who fear him. I had a long talk with him"—presumably without the presence of the axe handle. "He was civil but crazy. I agreed to all he said, which pleased him." No surprise there. Smith quickly surmised that Morris had gotten his hands on alcohol, which had led to his precipitous relapse, and authorized the Marine veteran's speedy return to the Government Hospital for the Insane. Morris would never again leave, no matter how good his apparent behavior. James Morris died at St. Elizabeths on 25 February 1875.

THE MANIAC

The United States Naval Asylum was lower-deck turf. Although the institution's founding legislation specified that it was to provide a home for "disabled and decrepit Navy officers, seamen, and Marines," only three former officers where admitted as beneficiaries before the end of 1865. All three had risen no higher in rank than midshipman before leaving the service. One ex-midshipman, George Douglass Dods, reinvented himself as a seaman, a petty officer, and in other shipboard rates below the rank of commissioned officer; he seemed more or less comfortable among his beneficiary peers. Another, Lewis Charles Francis Fatio, became a revenue cutter officer after leaving the Navy. Fatio decided the accommodations for him at the Asylum did not measure up to his self-perceived status as a gentleman, and soon departed. The third was a different person altogether. His name was Richard Bland Randolph, and his mind was seriously disordered.

Randolph's story is not unlike a three hundred piece jigsaw puzzle with a third of the pieces missing.[7] The portions that can be reconstructed are segments from a deeply troubled life. Large empty spaces remain. How much and what crucial information is lost? Richard was the second child and second son of John Randolph and Anne (Poythress) Randolph. Throughout his life Richard gave consistent information about his age, data that almost certainly place his birth sometime in 1781. He was also consistent in giving his place of birth as Prince George County, Virginia, although his father's thousand-acre plantation, Bloomsbury, was in adjacent Chesterfield County. Nothing is known about young Richard's education, but the documents he wrote in later life demonstrate that it must have been a good one. An 1846 newspaper article about Randolph's life, reportage not particularly noted for its accuracy, asserted that he was at sea in the merchant service between 1796 and March 1798. That may be doubted, because the earliest firm record of his life states that on 21 May 1798 he entered on board the frigate *Constellation*, Captain Thomas Truxtun, as an ordinary seaman—a rather low rate for a young man with two or more years at sea under his belt. During that enlistment Randolph participated in *Constellation*'s capture of the French frigate *L'Insurgente* on 9 February 1799 and, his one-year enlistment expired, was discharged on 26 May 1799. Two weeks later Randolph was appointed a midshipman (10 June 1799) and ordered back to *Constellation*'s prize, now incorporated into the Navy under the Americanized version of its name, *Insurgent*. Why had a young man from an elite background been serving as an ordinary seaman? How did he make the transition to midshipman? There is a missing story here; it falls in one of the blank spaces in the jigsaw puzzle of Randolph's life.

The pieces are all there for the next recorded event in Richard Bland Randolph's life. About 4 in the morning on 25 January 1800, *Insurgent*, cruising the West Indies under the command of Captain Alexander Murray, fell in with and recaptured a United States merchantman, the schooner *Aurora*. Randolph was ordered to lead the boarding party to *Aurora*, where he was met by the schooner's enraged French prizemaster, who took a swing at Randolph with a cutlass, cutting off the forefinger of the midshipman's left hand. About the same time some unknown member of the prize crew fired a pistol at Randolph, lodging a ball in his right ankle. In later life Randolph was inclined to play up the extent of these wounds. More realistically, an examination by two Navy doctors in 1842 noted the missing finger, but made no mention of any permanent damage from the pistol shot to the ankle. Randolph was easily patched up by *Insurgent*'s surgeons and dispatched to the United States as prizemaster in the recaptured *Aurora*. He rejoined *Insurgent* after her return to the United States, but was later sent on shore on sick leave and was unable to make it back to the frigate before she sailed again in July 1800. Missing his ship was a bit of good luck for young Randolph. *Insurgent* was lost with all hands in a September 1800 hurricane in the West Indies. In the reduction of the Navy's officer corps at the end of the Quasi-War with France, Midshipman Randolph was, for whatever reason, not considered an officer of sufficient promise to be retained in the downsized force and was discharged in early May 1801.

By then Randolph was long gone from the United States, having joined the ship's company of the American merchant brig *William* in a capacity that is not recorded. On 8 March 1801, off Santiago de Cuba, *William* was boarded by the 18-gun British sloop HMS *Osprey* and Randolph was pressed into the Royal Navy as an ordinary seaman. Along with a number of other sailors from *Osprey*, Randolph was briefly loaned (4 July–10 July) to HMS *Malta*, then discharged from *Osprey* by Admiralty order at Spithead on 14 July 1801. Randolph later said that his discharge from the British service was secured by U.S. diplomatic representatives in London, but independent verification of that claim has not been found by *Ungentle Goodnights*.[8]

Randolph returned to Virginia at some point before the morning of 27 December 1803, when his father, John Randolph, was found shot to death in his bed at Bloomsbury. The finger of suspicion immediately pointed at son Richard, though why is not known. In later life Richard B. Randolph had a vicious dispute with at least one authority figure, Asylum governor William W. McKean, and it may be that he and his father were seriously, violently, or publicly at odds—but that can only be speculation. A preliminary inquiry was immediately launched in Chesterfield County. This concluded that sufficient evidence against Richard Randolph existed to justify lodging him in jail until the district court met in Richmond in April and could try his case. That trial went badly for Richard Randolph. The jury appeared to be agreed on a verdict of willful murder, which would have entailed a death sentence for Randolph, when one of the jurors changed his mind at the last minute and announced that he did not agree with the guilty verdict. In view of the hung jury, the court ordered a new trial at its September 1804 term and sent Randolph back to jail pending the new trial. After his close escape, one can only imagine the gloom and anxiety with which the accused awaited his second court appearance on a charge of murder, but—to everyone's surprise—the second trial acquitted him entirely and Richard Bland Randolph was once again a free man. Forty years later Randolph asserted that insanity was hereditary in his family and that his father, a victim of the disease, had killed himself. Presumably the jury at the second trial accepted that defense and any evidence produced to support it, clearing the way to acquit the accused son. Because the records of the district court no longer exist, these events are known only from brief newspaper stories, which leave many important questions: Who accused Randolph? On what evidence? They are unanswerable.[9]

However this murder *versus* suicide business affected Richard B. Randolph's reputation, it did not keep him from marrying, on 4 May 1805, twenty-one-year-old Jerusha Anderson, with whom he eventually had two sons, Richard and Edmund. Almost nothing is known about Jerusha, but she may have been a good soulmate for Richard. Skipping ahead to 1821 finds her indicted and convicted for maintaining an illegal tavern in the Randolph-Anderson family home in Chesterfield County. Now that Richard was a husband and father, he had an urgent need to make a respectable living. He tried rejoining the Navy, entering as a quartermaster in the Mediterranean-bound frigate *Chesapeake* on 4 April 1807, but his return to the active-duty Navy was a brief one. On 21 May *Chesapeake*'s captain, Master Commandant Charles Gordon, discharged Randolph from the ship. Why, history will probably never know, but one can surmise that Gordon had seen or heard something; he wanted Randolph out from under his command.

If the Navy did not need him, perhaps the merchant service was a better choice after all. Randolph had kept that option open. On 2 April, just before the beginning of his short-lived *Chesapeake* experience, Randolph took out a seaman's protection certificate at the custom house in Norfolk. From this one catches a snapshot of a young man of twenty-five, sixty-eight inches tall, with a light complexion, hazel eyes, and red hair. Thereafter Randolph reported that he commanded "several" merchant ships in both the West Indian and the European trade, but gave no details, and research for *Ungentle Goodnights* has failed to verify this assertion. From Richmond in March 1814 he wrote now-Commodore John Rodgers, who was senior lieutenant in *Constellation* when Randolph had been an ordinary seaman in her, offering to serve as a master's mate in *President*. He reported his pressed service in *Osprey* and *Malta* to Rodgers, but inflated his 129 days in the British warships to two and a half years. Randolph further asserted that he had never served in the Royal Navy in a rating lower than master's mate, although he was in reality rated ordinary seaman for the entire period. Rodgers—who seems to have kept a cautious distance in his later-in-life dealings with Randolph—apparently filed Randolph's letter without reply. Frustrated there, Randolph turned to the war-expanded Army, enlisting as a private on 18 July 1814 and describing himself as a farmer. Predictably perhaps, this strange career move turned out badly. Randolph soon tired of Army life, and deserted on 20 August. Recaptured on 19 December, he was sentenced to be shot, then pardoned, and—with the return of peace—discharged on 23 March 1815.

For the next three decades of Randolph's life the record has more holes than solid data. It is clear that he was in financial difficulties. His older brother was by now dead, leaving Richard the master of Bloomsbury, but Richard seems to have had little interest in the life of a planter. In 1819 he sold off part of Bloomsbury, no doubt to raise cash, and in 1822 he conveyed the rest of the property to his two sons. Perhaps Jerusha's 1821 run-in with the law over her unlicensed home tavern was a response to the couple's money problems. Two years later Richard was arrested and detained until he could be tried for an unspecified felony; however, the jury released him with a not-guilty verdict. The none-too-accurate 1846 newspaper story about Randolph's life, which says that "he was three times tried for horse stealing and twice convicted an[d] pardoned," may refer to (and possibly exaggerates) events from these years. Money problems were the motivation for Randolph's 1824 petition to Congress in which he claimed he had never received his pay for his service in *Insurgent* or any prize money from the several ships captured or recaptured during his time in that frigate. He further requested a pension for the injuries sustained during the recapture of *Aurora*, a combat which he improbably implied had also resulted in a hernia from which he now suffered. Because Randolph could produce no documentary evidence that he had never been paid, because the prize-money matter was a private transaction between *Insurgent*'s ship's company and Captain Alexander Murray's prize agent, and because there were regular channels through which Randolph could apply for a pension if he was entitled to one, the House Committee on Naval Affairs declined to act on the petition.

Now the puzzle pieces of Randolph's life become even more scarce. He may have resorted to serving in non-officer capacities in the Navy, but the lack of Navy-wide recruiting records before the 1850s makes finding this service a matter of serendipity rather than systematic research; no such documentation has been discovered in writing *Ungentle Goodnights*. Randolph, who tended to be quite accurate about dates, says that his last discharge from the Navy was in February 1841, but he gives no indication in which ship or ships he had been serving. Jerusha had apparently died at some undiscovered date, because on 22 January 1835 Richard married Sally Andrews in Chesterfield County. This was no May-December romance. Sally, who was fifty-six at the time the marriage was recorded, was Richard's contemporary and probably someone he had known for many years.

In the decade of the 1840s information about Richard Bland Randolph becomes much richer. Crucial holes in the picture are still there, but they are smaller, and the larger image is more developed.

As mentioned, Randolph said he received his last discharge from the Navy in February 1841. Fourteen and a half months later he was admitted, 17 May 1842, on the strength of his merchant marine service, to Sailors' Snug Harbor on Staten Island. That institution's records describe Randolph as a widower—when did Sally die?—a man with two living children, who asserted forty-two years at sea, and who suffered from one or more hernias. Randolph lasted a little more than two weeks at Snug Harbor before he checked himself out on the third of June.

By December 1842 he was in Washington where he resubmitted his 1824 petition to Congress, strengthened with the report of a medical examination by two Navy surgeons: "He is afflicted with a very large scrotal hernia of the right side, with a lesser one on the left side. He has also a prolapsus ani attended with hemorrhoidal tumors, and has lost the forefinger of the left hand. He is, in our opinion, totally disabled from age and disease to support himself." Although the basis of Randolph's petition was his service in *Insurgent*, except for the missing forefinger, none of his physical problems was documented as deriving from his service in that frigate; they were probably all incurred later in his life. Randolph's renewed petition was referred to the House Committee on Naval Affairs, which passed it along to the Pension Office for action. At this point either there is a gap in the documentary record or the relevant documents have eluded this historian's search. The ever-restless Randolph returned to Snug Harbor for less than a month—6 April to 1 May 1843. Meanwhile, one can surmise that there was communication about Randolph's application between the Pension Office and the Navy Department, the upshot of which was a decision to admit Randolph to the Naval Asylum on 9 October 1843 in lieu of granting him a pension.

Randolph's life at the Asylum seems to have run along smoothly enough for a while—at least as far as the record shows. On 7 February 1844 Governor William W. McKean gave him permission to visit Washington to pursue his claim for the pay and prize money allegedly due from service in *Insurgent*. Then things fell apart. On 25 February McKean wrote Secretary of the Navy Thomas W. Gilmer to report that Randolph, "who is insane," had begun to behave so violently that he had been placed under restraint, and asked Gilmer to remove Randolph from the Asylum. This is the first time in the discovered record of Randolph's life that the word *insane* is used to describe him. That word is, of course, a subjective descriptor that has been perceived, defined, and applied in a variety of ways by different societies at various times. By the time McKean used it to describe Randolph, the latter was a man in his mid-sixties. How long had others thought of him as "insane"? Had perceptions progressed from "normal," through "eccentric," to "insane"? The record is silent.

No answer to McKean's letter came from the Navy Department, undoubtedly because Gilmer was killed by the notorious explosion of the experimental gun "Peacemaker" in the screw steamer *Princeton* on 28 February. McKean waited a decent interval, then tackled the subject again with interim Secretary of the Navy Lewis Warrington. Randolph was calmer now, McKean reported, and no longer under restraint, but the Asylum's civilian employees and some of the beneficiaries were afraid of him; he was constantly making threats, and there was no way of knowing when he might again turn violent. Randolph had written McKean to warn him of a plot (in reality non-existent) to poison the Asylum's officers, their families, and the beneficiaries by putting prussic acid in the tea water. Soon thereafter he gave one of McKean's daughters a bottle of vitriol, which he told her was lemon extract which could be used to make lemonade. Fortunately, before the girl and her friends could brew the poisonous drink they spilled some of the "lemon acid" on their dresses, in which it immediately burned holes. McKean asked: Could not Randolph be transferred to the naval hospital at Norfolk, where the Asylum's dangerous-to-others mentally ill beneficiaries were normally dispatched?

That letter got Warrington's immediate attention. By 29 March Randolph was on his way to Norfolk, escorted by Midshipman James H. Moore. Surgeon Williamson checked in Randolph and another mentally ill beneficiary on 30 March, recorded that Randolph's diagnosis was *chronic insanity*, that he had a double inguinal hernia for which he wore a truss, and noted "These maniacs must be watched very closely." In line with his effort to apply the moral treatment to the Navy's insane, Williamson began by encouraging Randolph to assume as much responsibility for his own actions as possible, permitting him to leave the grounds unescorted on 7 and 13 April, excursions from which he returned as promised. However, on the Fourth of July holiday Randolph left the hospital without permission and did not return for two days.

This led Williamson to ratchet up the security. Randolph was confined in one of the basement cells, and the doctor's instructions to the hospital staff now began an almost daily litany of "Watch him closely" or "Be very careful at all times that he does not escape." Confinement was mitigated by daily exercise on the grounds under close surveillance, and Randolph was allowed to have a cot frame, chair, and table in his cell.

The table and chair were soon in active use, as Randolph's pen was far from idle during confinement. From the hospital he bombarded the Secretary of the Navy, Congress, Commodore Jesse Wilkinson (commandant of the Norfolk station), Julia Tyler (wife of President John Tyler), and almost certainly others with letters and petitions demanding his release from the hospital, complaining that the way he was being treated was not appropriate for a former officer of the Navy, and asserting once again his claim to the $160,000 allegedly owed him by the United States.[10] Unlike Randolph's 1824 petition to Congress, which—whatever its merits as a legitimate claim—was a cogently argued, clearly written document, these letters and petitions are long, rambling, difficult-to-follow rants, laced with Randolph's resentment against William W. McKean. Most of them were probably received with a sigh of "Oh, God, another one!" and filed under *Ignore*.

The written word having failed his purpose, Randolph moved from paper to action during the night of 4–5 August 1844, when he broke out of the cell where he was lodged and made his escape over the wall which surrounded the hospital grounds. "It is most important that this man be taken as soon as possible," a frustrated and alarmed Williamson wrote Commodore Wilkinson in the morning. "His deadly dislike to the President of the U. States [John Tyler], yourself and others renders it so very necessary to adopt measures immediately for his apprehension." Then, revealing that he knew important facets of Randolph's history that are hard to recover more than a century and a half later, Williamson added: "He has been so often the inmate of a penitentiary that locks, bolts, bars, etc., cannot keep him."

"The maniac Randolph," as Williamson habitually referred to him, was not on the loose for long. He was soon found, lodged temporarily in the Norfolk alms house, and was back at the naval hospital by 10 August. Williamson immediately clapped Randolph in a cell in hand irons, then appealed to Commodore Wilkinson to send a blacksmith over from the Navy Yard to see what could be done to increase security. "The notorious bad character of this man is such that every possible effort must be made to keep him where he cannot injure anyone and to prevent him from annoying the community." Did Wilkinson have any recently patented irons for the hands and feet at the yard? If so, he should send them with the blacksmith, "as I have no doubt, from the many crimes committed by this man, that he is most familiar with those we have here." Here is a second tantalizing suggestion from Williamson that he might have been able to fill in some of the now-present holes in the puzzle of Randolph's life. Or was this a case of oral lore about Randolph that exaggerated reality?[11] Not content to rely solely on the irons to keep Randolph secure, Williamson instructed his staff to confiscate all Randolph's clothing except for his shirt each night and to inspect the cell to ensure that he had not hidden replacement clothing in his bed or somewhere in the room. "A great scamp," "a vile fellow," and "a worthless scamp" were Williamson's less-than-clinical evaluations of his patient, scattered through the hospital's daily journal.

In spite of all the precautions, Randolph made an attempt to escape during the night of 6–7 November 1844, but was caught in the act and again locked up with his hands and feet in irons. Thereafter the doctor managed to keep Randolph confined until 6 April 1845, when he finally made good his escape from the hospital. Williamson never explained, at least in writing, how Randolph had managed to get away in spite of the doctor's daily injunctions that he was "Ever to be closely watched." Williamson only noted that Randolph "Escaped yesterday afternoon from the hospital," without providing any details. One cannot help suspecting that the doctor was happy to be rid of his troublesome patient and not about to ask too many questions.[12]

Determined not to repeat the mistake of his August 1844 escape, Randolph avoided Norfolk and headed—where? It was not until the twenty-eighth of the month that Commodore Wilkinson learned that Randolph had somehow made his way to Washington. "He is represented by [Dr. Williamson] as very dangerous," the commodore alerted Secretary of the Navy George Bancroft. "He imagines the government to be largely indebted to him and the President the cause of his not getting it; therefore, with his abandoned character, he might make an assault upon him or some of the high officers of the government." Then, lest Randolph be sent back to Norfolk to become Wilkinson's problem once more, he added: "I do not consider he has any claims whatever upon the Navy as a pensioner and ought to be placed in the lunatic hospital of Virginia, of which state he is a citizen."[13]

Actually, the greatest danger Randolph posed to official Washington was a case of aggravated annoyance, since the applicant visited the Navy Office on an almost daily basis, pestering the staff about his alleged $160,000 claim against the United States. Bancroft passed Wilkinson's letter along to Washington Mayor William W. Seaton on 30 April, leaving it up to Seaton to decide what to do about the Randolph problem: "The [Navy] Department has no control over the individual nor the means or power to place him in confinement again," Bancroft wrote. Seaton decided to have Randolph picked up. When this was done on 1 May, Randolph was offered the choice of posting a one-thousand-dollar bond for future good behavior or going to jail. A one-thousand-dollar bond was beyond Randolph's means, so to jail he went. He immediately found an attorney, who appeared before the Circuit Court for the District of Columbia on 3 May and sought to have his client released. If Randolph really was a dangerous lunatic, his attorney argued, it was not proper to keep him in a jail; rather, he ought to be transferred to a hospital for the insane and correctly treated. The court decided that it was back to jail for Randolph, but ordered that the Secretary of the Navy be informed of the decision and asked to take appropriate action for his future care.

At that point someone seems to have dropped the ball, because in late December 1845 Richard Bland Randolph was still sitting in the Washington jail when a new attorney sought his release under a writ of *habeas corpus*. The Criminal Court of the District of Columbia took up the matter on 2 January 1846, at which time—according to the reporter for Washington's *Daily National Intelligencer* who observed the proceedings—"It appeared from the statement made in court [by Randolph] . . . and the prisoner's conduct that he is a person of unsound mind and has committed sundry acts of violence." The court continued the case until 8 January, when it again took up the matter of Randolph's requested release. Randolph handed Judge Thomas H. Crawford a written statement—long, rambling, and more incoherent than anything he had produced to that date—which the judge read and ordered to be filed with the court proceedings as evidence of Randolph's insanity. Asked by Crawford if he wanted to make any oral statement, Randolph launched into another attack on Governor William W. McKean. He had, he said, told McKean, "I will take a cattleskin knife and cut your tarnished uniform into sack cloth and read a newspaper through your hide." For this insult McKean had "imprisoned" Randolph at Norfolk, from which assertion Randolph moved on to a bitter and emotional tirade against the Norfolk Naval Hospital and its medical staff. Once Randolph had finished, Judge Crawford told him that he would take his case under consideration and let him know the outcome "in a few days." However, no sooner had Randolph been removed from the courtroom than Crawford—who had earlier consulted the grand jury on the case—read an order to the effect that it was evident from Randolph's behavior and statements that he was a lunatic pauper. He ordered the marshal to have Randolph sent to "the lunatic asylum in Baltimore or any other public lunatic asylum in the U.S. at his discretion" and at the public's expense.[14]

What happened next is one more missing puzzle piece. If the authorities found a place for him in a nearby asylum, Randolph might have used his well-honed escape skills to give confinement the slip. Whatever occurred, the "dangerous lunatic" was no longer the City of Washington's problem, and he disappears from those records. On 31 March 1846 Randolph turns up at the Blockley alms house, across the Schuylkill from the Naval Asylum, says that he is sixty-five years old, born in Virginia but a legal resident of Philadelphia, a married man with two living children, and a former officer in the Navy. He appears to have been picked up off the streets and dispatched by city authority to Blockley, where he was lodged in the old men's ward. Randolph left Blockley three weeks later, on 22 April, and disappears once again. He next turns up in New Orleans on 15 November 1847. He arrived that day from Memphis—had he perhaps been working on some riverboat on the Western waters?—and was confined the next day to the lunatic asylum of New Orleans' Charity Hospital. Randolph identified his occupation as seaman and reported that he was a sixty-seven-year-old widower. Charity Hospital's diagnosis: mania. Randolph was released on 12 December, but he was back two days later with a fractured rib—how incurred not recorded—and discharged again on 8 January 1848.[15] Here follows a year-long hiatus in the record of Randolph's life, which ends in late January to early February 1849 when he was readmitted to the Naval Asylum as a beneficiary.

For this, Randolph's second admission to the Naval Asylum, there is a good record—a petition that Randolph addressed to Secretary of the Navy John Y. Mason on 26 January 1849. Although the document is signed by Randolph with his customary copperplate signature, the text is in someone else's handwriting, possibly an attorney who assisted in its composition. It incorporates three counterfactual assertions. First, Randolph had been deprived of his pension. (Fact-check: Randolph was never granted a pension; his application was turned down.) Second, he was sent to Norfolk Naval Hospital "for an act of indiscretion ... to be attributed more to a hasty temperament, rather than to any wish or desire to injure anyone." (Fact-check: Randolph was transferred to Norfolk because he had been behaving violently, because the Asylum's civilian employees and some of the beneficiaries were afraid of him, and because he had tried to poison Governor McKean's daughter.) Third, he is no longer insane. (Fact-check: The authorities at New Orleans' Charity Hospital considered Randolph insane fourteen months earlier.)

Warmed to their task by these distortions of reality, Randolph and his amanuensis launched into purple prose behind which can be discerned the grim realities of a sick man's life. Randolph had "escaped from that wretched abode of insanity [Norfolk Naval Hospital] after a confinement of fifty-two weeks and has been a wanderer over the world since that period—living upon the charity of those who might deem him a worthy object. Whithersoever he has traced his course," the petition continued, "this stigma has followed him. Everywhere suspected and repelled, he has tasted the wretchedness of misery and want. His old age has no asylum where it might rest—forsaken by friends, deserted by kindred, and shunned by all!" Secretary Mason had his office check with the Commissioner of Pensions, learned that Randolph had never been granted a pension, and decided to send him back to Philadelphia and the Naval Asylum.

This residence at the Naval Asylum was shorter than Randolph's first and equally problematic. He was admitted on 4 February 1849. Little more than a week later Governor Jacob Jones was reporting to Secretary Mason that Randolph has "exhibited evidences of insanity since his admission" and urging that he be transferred elsewhere—to some institution with appropriate accommodations for treating the mentally ill. And, added Jones, "particularly where he can be prevented from obtaining liquor, which tends very seriously to increase his malady"—the first surviving indication that alcohol abuse was a factor in Randolph's behavior. When Jones' letter went unanswered in the transfer of the Navy Department from Mason to his successor, William B. Preston, Jones tried again a month later and ramped up the urgency, writing that Randolph's malady has "very much increased" in the past month, and warning that "He has made various threats which endanger the safety of the officers connected with the institution, and I fear that he will perpetrate some great outrage, should he be permitted to remain at the Asylum." Jones' preference was to relocate Randolph, at government expense, to the Pennsylvania Hospital for the Insane in Philadelphia. The Navy's hospital at Norfolk was, in Jones' mind, a far less appropriate destination for Randolph than the Philadelphia institution. At Norfolk "there are no suitable arrangements for the accommodation of such cases, [and Randolph] would necessarily be subjected to a close confinement [there], which would doubtless very seriously increase his malady." Jones opened negotiations for a transfer to the Pennsylvania Hospital for the Insane, but his efforts were moot; Randolph escaped or walked away from the United States Naval Asylum on 22 March 1849, never to return.

Where he went immediately is unknown, but on 29 August of that same year he was admitted—or more likely committed— to the lunatic asylum section of Blockley alms house. On admission he slightly exaggerated his age to seventy and identified himself as a mariner by profession and a widower, with one living child. Randolph remained at Blockley until 9 November, when he was discharged. And with that discharge the story of Richard Bland Randolph's life reaches the last missing piece or pieces of the puzzle. A man in his late sixties, not in the best of health, could have died not long thereafter. But where? When? The elusive answers are almost certainly there, in some record waiting to be discovered.

THIRTEEN

LEAVING ASYLUM

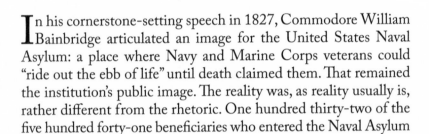

In his cornerstone-setting speech in 1827, Commodore William Bainbridge articulated an image for the United States Naval Asylum: a place where Navy and Marine Corps veterans could "ride out the ebb of life" until death claimed them. That remained the institution's public image. The reality was, as reality usually is, rather different from the rhetoric. One hundred thirty-two of the five hundred forty-one beneficiaries who entered the Naval Asylum before 31 December 1865—almost exactly one-quarter of them— ended their lives elsewhere than at the home on Gray's Ferry Road.

Why did they leave? What became of these one hundred thirty- two elderly or disabled men? The first question can easily be answered. The second is a different matter. Men with non-distinctive names mostly blend into the records of the general population and cannot be positively identified. Some may have returned to the sea and died abroad. Others were perhaps quietly and quickly interred in unre- corded graves. Some city poorhouse records that may have noted the ends of certain lives apparently no longer exist.

CLEARING THE DECKS

Before meeting some representative beneficiaries who pursued post- Asylum lives, it is desirable to eliminate those among the one hun- dred thirty-two who do not strictly belong in that group. Among them are the sixteen men classified as *insane*, already met in chap- ter 12, who were transferred either to the Norfolk Naval Hospital or to the U.S. Government Hospital for the Insane in Washing- ton, and who died in those institutions. Such men remained in the care of the federal government, but at a different location. To them should be added Henry D. Tucker, a mid-fifties Marine from Portsmouth, New Hampshire, who entered the institution in December 1834 with a severe case of senile dementia. Within a few weeks of Tucker's arrival Superintendent James B. Cooper was complaining that Tucker is "an idiot incapable of taking care of himself, so much so that all his evacuations are made in his trousers or in his bed. He requires one person to be constantly with him, and this duty at present is performed by the invalids of the institution, one of whom is nearly blind, one with but one leg, one with one arm, and one that is here in consequence of old age and other infirmities. Their comfort and happiness are destroyed since his arrival amongst them. They are daily complaining to me that they have to perform the duty of nurses, an employment they are unacquainted with and did not expect to perform when they came here." The Asylum and its affiliated naval hospital were not prepared to cope with dementia this extreme. A contractual arrangement was negotiated to house Tucker at the Philadelphia alms house. He was transferred across the Schuylkill to Blockley on 31 January 1835 and died there a week later, on 6 February.

To these seventeen men can be added five who departed for unrecorded reasons and four who were dropped because they had accepted outside employment, typically at the Philadelphia Navy Yard. Four other men left for unique individual reasons. A veteran Marine sergeant and naval master-at-arms went to live in the National Home for Disabled Volunteer Soldiers at Dayton, Ohio; a former Marine was returned to Blockley when it was discovered that he was an escapee from the alms house lunatic ward; still another Marine, now totally blind, chose to go to the Pennsylvania Institution for the Instruction of the Blind; and an ex-midshipman and dismissed revenue cutter commander, already mentioned in chapter 12, judged that his accommodations at the Asylum were not appropriate for what he perceived as his elite status and departed, on 1 April 1850, to Boston, where he died of dropsy at Massachusetts General Hospital on 14 August of the same year. When these thirty men have been deducted, there remain one hundred two former beneficiaries whose post-Asylum lives fall under one of three rubrics—twelve men who left to live on their pensions; thirteen who departed on approved leaves of absence but never returned; and seventy-seven expelled men who could not or did not try to gain readmission.

YOUNG AND DISABLED: A SURVIVOR'S STORY

There was one small group among the twelve beneficiaries who left the Asylum to live on their pensions whose members could unfailingly be predicted to make an early departure from the institution. They were young men who had been admitted because of serious disabilities rather than age. None of them ever stated a reason for leaving, but one can easily be inferred. Typically in their twenties or thirties, they just did not fit in comfortably at a home dominated by weatherworn Jack Tars and aging Leathernecks in their fifties, sixties, and seventies. Governor William W. McKean confirms this inference: "By the present regulations for the Asylum a man is entitled to admission after fifteen years faithful service, so that one who enters [the Navy or Marine Corps] very young may be entitled to admission when in the vigor of life," he told Secretary of the Navy David Henshaw in 1843. "There is but little probability that a good man accustomed to an active life would wish to avail himself of it."

The future looked grim for twenty-four-year-old Thomas Dennis. An Englishman by birth and an experienced seafarer, Dennis came to the United States in June 1844, enlisted in the Navy at Baltimore on 18 June 1847, and was detailed to the screw steamer *Princeton*. He served as ship's coxswain, with the rating of seaman. On 5 September of that same year, while *Princeton* was at Gibraltar, an expatriate Russian aristocrat, Count Anatoly Nikolaievich Demidov, Prince of San Donato, who was on his travels through Spain, asked to visit *Princeton*. As Demidov was leaving the ship, her commander, Frederick Engle, ordered a thirteen-gun salute in the Prince's honor. The eleventh gun of the salute went off prematurely, apparently while being reloaded, and tore off both of Thomas Dennis' arms just below the elbow.[1]

Dennis was transferred to a British hospital ashore in order to receive more expert care for his grievous wounds than would have been possible in *Princeton*'s sick bay. Prince Demidov, deeply mortified that the accident was an outcome of his visit to *Princeton*, immediately offered to provide a lifetime annuity for Dennis. Captain Engle protested—or so he later said. The United States was proud to support its injured sailors and did not need to accept assistance from a foreigner. Dennis would have a lifetime home at the Naval Asylum. Yet, either Engle's protest was not as vigorous as he later asserted, or Demidov politely chose to ignore him, because the Russian did arrange an annuity of about eighty dollars per year to be paid to Dennis. As soon as Dennis was able to travel, Demidov sent a member of his entourage to escort Dennis to Paris and London; in both places, the Prince attempted to have prosthetic arms made for the disabled sailor. The arms, heavy and awkward, were not a success, although in later life Dennis used improved prosthetic hands with great élan.

Thus far the surviving official contemporary record. The first pages of *Princeton*'s pay roll for the cruise—pages that would have contained Thomas Dennis' data and might have shown reliably the dates of his absences from the ship—are now missing. Consequently, what happened next is known only from Dennis' later-in-life interviews with the press and may have been subject to the distortions and elaborations of time. He was apparently not all that eager to rejoin *Princeton*; his half-hearted attempts managed to miss her port calls. Instead, he seems to have spent much of the next two years traveling as a member of Demidov's entourage, living at the Prince's expense, or residing as a guest at Demidov's estate in Italy. It was the first, but far from the last, evidence of Thomas Dennis' ability to charm and ingratiate himself with the right people. And his gratitude to Deminov was certainly genuine, as he was to name one of his future sons Anatole. However, this luxurious idyll could not last forever. Dennis finally rejoined *Princeton* in time for her June 1849 return to Boston.

Dennis' application to become a beneficiary was processed briskly; he arrived at the Naval Asylum with his permit of admission on 30 July. But there was a problem. The Asylum authorities did not know how to cope with a man without arms, one who required an assistant at all times, so they transferred Dennis to the naval hospital section of the institution. There he was a most unhappy patient. Except for his disability, Thomas Dennis was a young and otherwise healthy man. On 12 August he somehow managed to leave the Asylum and took up residence at a private boarding house in Philadelphia, where he remained in mid-November 1849, presumably living on his small federal pension, money from Prince Demidov, and possibly his accumulated back pay.

The highest pension that a seaman could receive under the applicable law was six dollars per month—clearly not enough to support an armless man. Arms or no arms, however, throughout his life Thomas Dennis showed an amazing ability to land on his feet. By January 1850 he was in Washington where, citing the precedent of a War of 1812 sailor who had lost both arms in a similar accident, he petitioned Congress to grant him a monthly pension of thirty dollars. "I was," wrote Dennis or more likely the person who drafted his petition, "by this accident, in the bloom of life, blasted in a moment from all future prospects and at once not only restricted upon the threshold of actual usefulness and [in]dependence, but [am] inexpressibly uncomfortable in my condition. Few can fully appreciate my gloomy feelings and despondence." The Senate Committee on Naval Affairs, which was demonstrably capable of dragging its feet or pigeonholing special pension requests, moved this one along expeditiously. On 29 March 1850 Thomas Dennis was granted a lifetime pension of thirty dollars per month, a sum which was increased to fifty dollars per month in 1874, to seventy-two dollars per month in 1878, and finally to one hundred dollars per month in 1889.

By July 1850 Thomas Dennis was living in Washington, with a twenty-year-old wife named Sarah Ann. Other than that her family name was Leibengerth and that she was born in Lehigh County, Pennsylvania—probably in or near Allentown—little is known about Sarah. Perhaps she and Thomas met in Philadelphia. When the census taker came around, Dennis listed his occupation as "none," but he did not intend to remain unemployed and idle for long. On 24 May 1854 he was naturalized as a U.S. citizen, a prerequisite for seeking government employment. By June of 1860 his family had been enlarged by two children, Henrietta (seven) and Anatole Bennett (four)—another child, Manual B., born in October 1857, had died on 1 July 1859—and Thomas listed his occupation as "watchman," in which capacity he worked in the copper-rolling mill at the Washington Navy Yard. Dennis was busy on a number of other fronts as well. He worked for a time as an advertising solicitor; he served as agent for several landlords, collecting rents on residential properties they owned in the vicinity of the Navy Yard; he operated a livery stable on Capitol Hill; and he owned two small frame houses on G Street, between Sixth and Seventh streets Southeast, in one of which he lived with his family. His neighbors knew him as a good-looking man, sixty-four and a half inches tall, with blue eyes, an oval face, light complexion, and straight nose; as one endowed with an outgoing personality that enabled him to gain the friendship and trust of others; as an honest, hard-working man; as a strong temperance advocate; and as an individual respected for having overcome a major disability so successfully.

On Thursday, 5 October 1865, to their shock and surprise, his neighbors learned that Thomas Dennis may have been something else as well—a confidence man. The previous evening, about 7, Dennis left his job at the Navy Yard, hailed a for-hire carriage, and asked to be driven to the railroad station. There Dennis ran into someone he knew and explained that he was going to take the night train to New York. Alerted by his mysterious disappearance, creditors and others began comparing notes and discovered that Dennis, depending apparently on his supposedly spotless reputation and popularity, had in the past two or three years borrowed upwards of ten thousand dollars from various individuals, and had used the money to speculate in gold. About a year earlier he had conveyed title to the two G Street houses to a third party; consequently, they could not be seized by his allegedly defrauded creditors without extended litigation. These facts, quickly verified by Washington's newspaper reporters, were immediately inflated by rumor and speculation: Dennis had booked a passage on a steamer that left New York for Liverpool on Thursday before he could be apprehended; he was accompanied, so it was said, by "two young men," not otherwise identified; the actual losses might run as high as twenty thousand dollars. At that point Thomas Dennis disappeared.

Then, on Saturday, 15 September 1866, Washington's *Evening Star* reported that, "much to the surprise of some of his neighbors and creditors," Dennis had suddenly reappeared "a few days ago" at Sarah's home near the Navy Yard, telling those who asked that he had not run off to Europe, but had spent the last eleven months in Pennsylvania. Or at least that is what they thought they heard him say. Over the weekend Thomas Dennis contacted someone at the *Star* to get his corrected version of the story on the record. On Monday the paper duly reported that Dennis said that "he has not been in Pennsylvania all the time he was absent from the city"—but he carefully avoided saying where he *had* been. Dennis assured the *Star*'s readers that his unpaid debts amounted to no more than six thousand dollars, and that he expected to pay "or otherwise secure" his creditors.

Thomas Dennis went back to work, using his persuasive sales-man's skills in his old occupation as a newspaper advertising solici-tor. Dennis' brave promises of repayment notwithstanding, he could not fulfill them. In 1868 he filed for bankruptcy under the provi-sions of the new federal bankruptcy act of 2 March 1867. When the court had collected and verified all the claims against Dennis, it turned out that his total defaulted debt was neither as large as the newspapers reported nor as small as he said, but actually came to $8,243.50. How much of this amount the creditors were able to recover is not clear from the surviving bankruptcy documents; however, a second and later list in the file reduces the number of creditors from ten to six and the remaining debt to $6,762.70, sug-gesting an out-of-court settlement with the other four creditors.

With his financial crisis resolved through bankruptcy, Thomas Dennis managed once again to land on his feet. Between 1869 and 1877 he worked as a watchman at the Treasury Department, immediately east of the White House, at an annual salary of $720 per year—in addition, of course, to his annual pension of $360 (increased to $600 in 1874) and his annuity of $80 per year from Prince Demidov. In 1870 the census taker found Thomas still married to Sarah, and with the addition of two more children to the family: Thomas B. (eight) and a one-year-old boy, Archie C. B. Dennis. There should have been a third young child in the home, John Bennett Dennis, but he had died on 27 September 1868 at the age of seven years and two months.

For a decade Thomas Dennis managed to keep his head down and his name out of the newspapers. Then Washington's *Evening Star* for 9 September 1878 reported on a messy real estate transac-tion involving the Dennis livery stable on Third Street Southeast, just below Pennsylvania Avenue. That business was now operating in Anatole's name as A. B. Dennis & Company, which presumably put this asset beyond the reach of Thomas' creditors. At the end of its story the *Star* noted that "Thomas Dennis, the father of A. B. Dennis, left the city last week for a visit to Fairview, Md.," then added: "The story of his having run away with a large amount of money and a woman not his wife it is believed [is] without foundation." The "large amount of money" cannot be verified, but—the *Star*'s disclaimer notwithstanding—the rest of the story was all too true.

About January 1879 Thomas Dennis moved to Chicago. On 8 July 1879 a child, George Edward Dennis, was born there to

Thomas and a woman who identified herself as "Frances Dennis."
In fact, the mother was Frances Elizabeth Pettis, a native of Virginia
and a woman thirty-four years younger than Thomas, whom he must
have impregnated in October or November 1878. In June 1880 the
census taker recorded Thomas (fifty-eight), Frances E. (twenty-four),
Thomas B. (eighteen), and George E. Dennis (eleven months) living
in Chicago, where Thomas reported his occupation as "speculator"—
possible evidence that he had indeed arrived with the "large amount
of money." The two oldest Dennis children, Anatole and Henrietta,
were by now adults and on their own, Henrietta being married to
Richard Bennett, a messenger (and later a clerk) in the Treasury
Department. (Clearly, there was a close relationship between the
Dennis and the Bennett families, but its exact nature has not come
to light.) Shortly before or just after Thomas' and Frances' scandalous departure to Chicago, Sarah, the real Mrs. Dennis, and Archie
removed from Washington to Allentown, Pennsylvania, presumably
to live with relatives. Sarah died at Allentown on 14 August 1879.
Her fortuitous death cleared the way for Frances and Thomas to
get legal. One year and one week after Sarah's death they slipped
quietly off to Milwaukee, where they were married in the chapel of
All Saints' Episcopal Cathedral on 21 August 1880 by Erastus W.
Spalding, dean of the cathedral.

Whatever may have been Thomas Dennis' activities as a "speculator," Chicago directories from 1879 through 1893 record that
he earned his living as a watchman or usher at the Cook County
office building and at the federal customs house and resided at
several different city addresses. In 1893 Dennis was given another
opportunity to display his agility at landing on his feet when he
was caught in a reduction of staff at the Chicago customs house.
One of two men had to go, and Dennis volunteered to be the one
in preference to the other man, who had a large family. It may well
be that Thomas and Frances wanted to leave Chicago and return
to Washington, where their scandalous relationship was old news
probably long forgotten, and Thomas' job loss provided a welcome
excuse. Be that as it may, one of Thomas Dennis' survival skills was
the cultivation of powerful acquaintances, and that skill was now
called into play. Walter Q. Gresham, judge on the U.S. Seventh Circuit Court (Illinois, Indiana, and Wisconsin) had been appointed
Secretary of State by President Grover Cleveland in March 1893.
Dennis appealed to Gresham for a Washington job and got one,

in October of that year, as a watchman in the State, War, and Navy building (now the Eisenhower Executive Office Building) adjacent to the White House. This post paid a salary of seven hundred twenty dollars a year which, in addition to Thomas's annual pension, now twelve hundred dollars a year, and the Demidov annuity, kept Thomas and Frances in decent, if not affluent circumstances.

Dark shadows there may have been in the earlier parts of his life, but Thomas Dennis returned to Washington as an interesting character, a survivor from an older era in the nation's history, and something of a media personality. Newspaper stories featured him as a successful federal employee who had overcome a disability. For the *Washington Post*'s reporter, Dennis demonstrated his Decker Tweezers—prosthetic hands invented by Samuel Decker, a Civil War double amputee—with which Dennis could easily pick up any necessary papers in the course of his daily duties. With his elbow he pushed a button to summon an elevator, and with his teeth he picked up a full glass of water and drank it without spilling any of it. Then came his proudest demonstration—the ability to sign his name "with a clearness of well-shaped letters that many a two-handed man cannot boast. To do this the pen, deftly picked up with the tweezers, dipped in ink, is then placed between his teeth and the signature written." Dennis dropped in at the White House once in a while to call on President Theodore Roosevelt, whom he had come to know when Roosevelt was Assistant Secretary of the Navy, and he never failed to visit the president on the birthday—27 October—that they both shared. Roosevelt, advocate as he was for the strenuous life to overcome one's physical limitations, must have admired Dennis' achievements.

In 1902 Dennis retired from his watchman post at the State, War, and Navy building to live on his pensions and a pot of saved money—somehow he always seemed to have money. "I am in my eighty-first year and expect to live out the full century," he told the *Evening Star*'s reporter. "The report that I gave up my place at the War Department on account of old age is untrue. I simply want to live quietly and enjoy myself the remainder of my life, and I am going to do it." His plan to live to one hundred was not to be fulfilled. Around 1904 Dennis began to manifest symptoms of dementia and thereafter declined slowly into old-age invalidism. He died on 23 July 1908, and his body is buried in Washington's Congressional Cemetery, his never-forgotten naval career commemorated in the carved anchor on the top of his tombstone. Frances outlived Thomas by a quarter-century, dying on 17 December 1932 at the age of eighty-five. For a man who had told Congress in 1850 that the loss of his arms "in the bloom of life" had "blasted in a moment . . . all future prospects," ex-seaman Thomas Dennis had proved to be an energetic and a crafty survivor.

I WAS COMING BACK, BUT . . .

Thirteen beneficiaries went on leaves of absence in good standing, but never returned. One of them, John W. Sims, a native of Pennsylvania, was born on 27 September 1791. When he was just short of twenty, Sims enlisted in the Marine Corps at Philadelphia. The most eventful part of his career was the campaign around Washington and Baltimore in 1814, when he participated in various engagements, including the battle of Bladensburg, and rose to the ranks of corporal and—by his own unverifiable account—sergeant. After he reenlisted in August 1816, Sims began a long period of service at sea, sailing in the frigates *Congress*, *Constellation*, and *Java* (twice), in the schooner *Decoy*, and in the sidewheel gunboat *Sea Gull*—the latter two during the 1820s campaign against West Indian piracy. In his later enlistments Sims typically served as a private, with occasional stints as corporal. He completed his final enlistment on 31 May 1841 and settled in Montgomery County, Pennsylvania.

There he met Catherine ("Kitty") Heflesdrager or Hefentrager—her family name is uncertain. They were married in February 1842 at the public house run by Enos Weiss in Spring House, Montgomery County, amid a party of their friends. The groom was a handsome man of fifty, nearly five feet nine inches tall, with hazel eyes and brown hair not yet tinged with gray. John was eking out a subsistence living for himself and Kitty as a farm laborer, but it occurred to him that, as a Marine with three decades of creditable service, he might be entitled to a pension to supplement his earnings. He asked Abiram P. Knapp, a prosperous gentleman farmer in the county, for whom John Sims may have been working, to see if he could help him with the authorities in Washington. Knapp tried, but without success. At this time pensions were awarded only for injuries received in service, not for length of service. The best that Secretary of the Navy John Y. Mason could offer was an appointment as a beneficiary at the Naval Asylum.

Sims accepted the offer, reported to the Naval Asylum on 2 November 1846, and left by permission the same day. Kitty was ill, she could not live with John at the Asylum, and she needed him at home to care for her. In 1849 John Sims made a second attempt to live at the Naval Asylum, arriving on 23 May. Within three days this still-vigorous man found that he "could not endure the confinement of the Asylum" and left a second (and final) time on an open-ended leave of absence. Thereafter John and Kitty, in the words of A. P. Knapp, "ganged along together so well as they could," with John working as a farm laborer, and Kitty, who could neither read nor write and was sometimes ill, doing laundry in the neighborhood. By 1867 John was in his mid-seventies (Kitty's age is uncertain); he was still working but age was taking its toll. The county poor house looked like the end of the road for the elderly couple. Luckily for John and Catherine Sims, the pension law had just changed. It was now possible to draw a pension for twenty years or more of service in the Navy or Marine Corps. Abiram Knapp went to bat for John Sims once again and secured him a pension of three dollars and fifty cents per month, later increased to eight dollars. John apparently continued to work some; this, with the pension, kept the wolf a safe distance from the Sims family door. He died on 1 September 1874, just shy of his eighty-third birthday, and was buried in the Friends Cemetery in Gwynedd Township, Montgomery County, where his body and gravestone remain to this day. Kitty died a few years later, but neither the date of her death nor her place of burial are apparently on record.

KICKED OUT AND THEN . . .

By far the largest group among the 132 beneficiaries who did not end their lives at the Naval Asylum were 77 men dismissed for unacceptable behavior or desertion from the institution and who either failed or did not attempt to gain readmission. Where could they go? What would become of them? In almost all cases the answer has to be: *Ungentle Goodnights* does not know. Still, enough can be discovered about a few to suggest the fates of the larger whole.

The Asylum's problematic first resident, Daniel Kleiss, last met in chapter 3, was dismissed from the institution for the fourth and final time when, on 19 December 1842, he broke through the door of the cell where he was confined for drunkenness and fled the grounds. Nine days later he was committed to the lunatic ward at the Blockley alms house across the Schuylkill with a diagnosis of mania a potu. He was either discharged or ran away—the records are contradictory—from Blockley on 4 January 1843. Within the month Kleiss made his way to Washington, where he appealed to Secretary of the Navy Abel P. Upshur for yet one more readmission to the Asylum. Executive Officer Andrew H. Foote, temporarily in charge at the Asylum, was willing to give him another chance, to which Upshur assented. But Kleiss never went back to Philadelphia. Instead, he decided to stay in Washington and clean up his act. The catalyst for his behavior change appears to have been a woman, Agnes Ellen Haggerty, whom he married on 30 September (some records say 1 October) 1843. Whether Daniel Kleiss gave up drinking entirely is unknown, but he became a naturalized United States citizen, lived with Agnes at 477 South M Street, between 10th and 11th Streets, and held down a job in the Navy Yard.[2] He died on either 21 or 22 July 1854—again the records differ—from the results of a fall at work in the Navy Yard. Daniel Kleiss had become a practicing Roman Catholic by the time of his death—perhaps another influence of Agnes'; his body lies in an unmarked grave in Washington's Mount Olivet Cemetery.

Seven former beneficiaries are on record as having successfully managed to reenlist in the Navy. The real number is surely much larger. This was the life that the ex-beneficiaries had known; it was natural for them to return to it. Unfortunately for sleuthing historians, the Navy's centralized recruiting records only begin in the mid-1850s. Before then there is no way to follow such men as they attempted to resume their lives afloat.

For those who can be traced, these second naval careers were short and typically ended in death on active duty. Edward Fowler was born in Salem, Massachusetts, probably about 1806. His family was apparently low enough on the social scale that his birth went unrecorded in Salem's elaborate demographic record compiled in the early twentieth century. Fowler joined the Navy when he was twenty or thereabouts and served, a few short leaves between voyages aside, continuously until 1849, when—still a man in his early forties—he began to complain of physical disabilities and started angling to get admitted to the Naval Asylum. He had, he told the Secretary of the Navy, recently shipped as a coal-heaver for the sidewheel steamer *Mississippi*, but "my age and infirmities induces me to ask you for support, as I am advanced in years [and] as I have no one that I could call on for a subsistence. . . . I would like to go to the Asylum." Although Fowler was granted admission to the Asylum on the basis of this application, he changed his mind and enlisted for the sloop-of-war *Marion* on a cruise to the East Indies. On his return Fowler renewed his application for admission to the Asylum, this time to Commodore Joseph Smith. With Smith he could play the always effective old-shipmate card by reminding the commodore that he had served under him in the ship-of-the-line *Ohio* and had never been on report for any infractions during that cruise. (He spoke truthfully, as *Ohio*'s punishment record verifies.) From Lynn, Massachusetts, Fowler wrote that he was "broken down by long service and exposure in the naval service in different parts of the world and am now no longer able to follow the sea." During his service in *Marion* he had suffered a severe attack of dysentery, "which has left me with the piles, rheumatic pains, and otherwise much debilitated." Admission granted, Fowler arrived at the Asylum on 8 December 1852.

Although Fowler claimed to have had an excellent record in all the ships in which he had served, at the Asylum it was a different story. A series of disciplinary run-ins culminated in early February 1856, when Governor George W. Storer reported to Joseph Smith that Fowler "has again been guilty of setting at defiance the rules and regulations of this institution. Returning from liberty drunk a day or two since, his liberty was again restricted, but he escaped from the grounds by scaling the fence! After a long search he was brought in very drunk and riotous." Contrary to Fowler's self-portrayal as a broken-down old man, Storer reposted that "he is not an old man [Fowler was about fifty], does not complain of any disability, and is as capable, I think, of supporting himself by labor as anyone." Because Fowler "has always been troublesome and insubordinate and his example here is exceedingly pernicious," Storer recommended his dismissal without the possibility of readmission.

Perhaps remembering that Fowler was an old shipmate, Smith was loath to come down hard on him: "The Department is reluctant to inflict the penalty [of dismissal] due to the violation of the rules of the institution and generally forbears to visit with severity ordinary infractions of its regulations," he wrote Storer, "but in

Fowler's case there seems to be no mitigating circumstance to extenuate his gross misconduct.... Kind warnings and wholesome counsels have failed to correct his perverse habits, and the only alternative remains to dismiss him." And out he went.

Fowler had no trouble being accepted for reenlistment at the Philadelphia rendezvous less than a week after his expulsion from the Asylum, but by October of the same year he was writing from an active-duty station, pleading with Commodore Smith for another chance at the Asylum and claiming that since he shipped "I have been incapable of performing any duty." Smith reviewed Fowler's record and turned him down. In spite of his assertions of ill health, Fowler served out his three-year enlistment and reenlisted successfully, when the recruiter described him as a man sixty-seven and a half inches tall, with hazel eyes, gray hair, and a dark complexion. But the end was near for this seemingly perennial hypochondriac. It came in the form of all-too-real illness. In 1859 Edward Fowler was serving as a seaman in the sloop-of-war *Germantown*, then anchored in the harbor at Manila in the Philippines. He had been on liberty ashore in Manila a few days before he reported himself to *Germantown*'s sick bay on 12 January with a severe case of diarrhea. He was treated for that condition for two days, but by the fourteenth the medical staff recognized the symptoms of cholera, which he probably contracted during his run ashore. Heroic efforts were made to save Fowler's life, but without success, and he died at 11:20 that night.[3]

Five former beneficiaries lived the remainder of their lives at Sailors' Snug Harbor, the privately funded institution on Staten Island for elderly and disabled members of the merchant service. A veteran Navy petty officer named Lewis Brown is the best-documented of the five.

Actually, "Lewis Brown" is probably an Americanized version of his birth name, since he was born in Gothenburg, Sweden, sometime between 1801 and 1803. By 1821, if not earlier, Brown had emigrated to the United States; on 12 July of that year he enlisted as an ordinary seaman in the ship-of-the-line *Franklin*, Commodore Charles Stewart, and served until September 1824. At the rendezvous Brown covered up his foreign birth and explained away his accent with the threadbare ploy of claiming to have been born in German-speaking Lancaster, Pennsylvania. Thereafter, Lewis Brown served in the Navy more or less continuously, possibly with one or two brief interruptions for merchant voyages, until he was admitted, presumably on the basis of long service, to the Naval Asylum on 13 December 1847.

The 1850s were a restless decade for Brown, then a man five feet, six and a half inches tall, with blue eyes, gray hair, and sun-darkened complexion. He was in and out of the Asylum on leaves of absence. The first ended badly when Brown developed a severe case of varicose veins in the left leg while serving as seaman in the sidewheel sloop-of-war *Saranac* and was discharged from the Navy as "unfit for the service" on 26 May 1853. He requested a later leave on the grounds that he was inclined toward alcoholism, but thought he could control the habit more easily while working away from the Asylum. Brown's final readmission to the Asylum occurred in September 1860, endorsed by Governor William C. Nicholson on the grounds that "he has served for a long time in the service and has always borne a good name," added to which Nicholson assured Joseph Smith that, during Brown's earlier stays, "I believe his character was good."

Lewis Brown's good reputation quickly evaporated. By August 1862 the Asylum's executive officer, Commander Peter Turner, char-acterized Brown as "one of the worst men in this house"—a hotly competitive dishonor, as readers of *Ungentle Goodnights* know—"continually drunk and insubordinate." The final incident came on 5 August of that year when Brown, allegedly without provocation, attacked Peter Ackerman, "a good, unoffending man," beating him over the head with a chair leg until it appeared that Brown had killed him. Actually, Ackerman was not dead, only unconscious, but he was hospitalized from 5 August through 13 August to recover from the beating. This was Brown's third assault on a fellow beneficiary. Com-mander Turner judged enough was enough; he urged Brown's dis-missal from the Naval Asylum. Secretary of the Navy Gideon Welles approved Turner's recommendation, and Brown was out, effective 14 August 1862.

Three weeks later a letter arrived on Welles' desk from Hannah Barnard, proprietor of a sailors' boarding house on Sansom Street in Philadelphia: "I write to you to see if you will not have some pity for a poor old sailor in regard of being turn out of the Naval Asy-lum. This old man [Brown] is an old boarder of mine," she reported. "I always found him to be a[n] honest kind-hearted old man. In regard to the Naval Asylum, I am well acquainted with near all the old men. They all will drink and fight occasional. I have near one dozen to come to my house for shelter, having been turn out for different offenses, and they all got back, and why not look over his offense? He is not able to work and, having served the country 30 years, I think it is very hard. He has no friends, and he will have to go to the [Blockley] Alms House. I am a sailor's widow. I feel for him. I hope you will allow him to go back. I think he will do better, and I hope God will reward you." Welles forwarded the appeal to Joseph Smith, but the admiral was for once unmoved: "The Asylum was instituted for worthy men who will deport themselves as worthy of this great privilege," he told Mrs. Barnard. "Brown's conduct was such as to make the example necessary for the proper administration of the Asylum."

Hannah Barnard's prophecy notwithstanding, Blockley was not Lewis Brown's next refuge. Rather, it was a Navy hard-pressed for experienced sailors to man its Civil War fleet. Brown was able to enlist in the sloop-of-war *Jamestown* as a quarter-gunner in September 1862, was discharged in the first months of 1863, then found employment as coxswain in the revenue cutter *Varina*. She was Brown's last service afloat; he was discharged from the cutter in 1864.

Somehow Lewis Brown was able to keep body and soul together, possibly on the small pension awarded for the varicose veins in the left leg, until 15 May 1867. He was then admitted to Sailors' Snug Harbor on the basis of his claim of twenty years' service in the merchant marine, plus his thirty years in the Navy. His Snug Harbor papers noted that thirty-four of Brown's fifty years at sea had been under the U.S. flag. Brown's behavioral record at Snug Harbor was hardly spotless. He overstayed his liberty twice and came in drunk; another time he returned intoxicated, quarreled with a roommate, struck him, and tore his clothing. But Lewis Brown managed to hang on without expulsion until 6 a.m. on 17 November 1875, when he was found dead in his room from heart disease. His body lies beneath Staten Island's soil in the old Sailors' Snug Harbor cemetery.

FOURTEEN

VOYAGE'S END

Death. Naval Asylum beneficiaries had seen enough of it during their active-duty careers: battle—accidents—fatal illnesses—ships lost with all hands. Sooner or later, each had to confront the reality of his own death—certainly frightening for some, perhaps welcome to others.

Of the 541 beneficiaries whose life stories are the basis of *Ungentle Goodnights*, 132 left the home on Gray's Ferry Road for one reason or another and died elsewhere; they were the subject of chapter 13. The remaining 409 former sailors and Marines ended their lives as residents of the Naval Asylum. Among these 409 beneficiaries, almost all—385 of them—died from what will here be termed *natural causes. Ungentle Goodnights* will not attempt to analyze the deaths of all 385 beneficiaries who succumbed to natural causes. Before July 1868 the Philadelphia Naval Hospital did not maintain a consolidated record of each beneficiary's hospitalization. Instead, admissions, treatments, and discharges (including deaths) were recorded on a day-by-day basis in the hospital's medical journals. To follow any individual's terminal illness, one would have to track the daily journal entries for days, weeks, months, or (in some cases) years. If the historian had a team of skilled research assistants, working through nearly four decades of the Philadelphia Naval Hospital journals could provide a rich harvest of health information on a substantial cohort of aging Marines and sailors.

Significant though the results of this tedious work might be, such an effort is beyond the scope of *Ungentle Goodnights*. Instead, the book's examination of beneficiary death will narrow its focus to one subgroup within the 385. Beginning in July 1868 the

Philadelphia Naval Hospital started keeping consolidated medical histories for each individual beneficiary admitted there; these documents are available through July 1886—eighteen years and one month of detailed information.[1] During the 217 months between July 1868 and July 1886 some 73 beneficiaries died from natural causes; consolidated hospital records exist for 65 of the 73. These medical histories of terminal illnesses are the source from which this chapter is constructed. Based on the diagnoses of the Philadelphia Naval Hospital's medical staff, the five biggest killers were old age or debility (24 percent of deaths); heart disease (21 percent); stroke and paralysis (18 percent); respiratory ailments (17 percent); and digestive or intestinal disorders (14 percent).

FADING AWAY

The category at the head of the list of causes of beneficiary death during 1868–86—old age, debility, and the latter's alternative name, *adynamia*—is one that will not be found in any twenty-first-century table of mortality. Deaths assigned to this category were typically those of older men, their cases presenting a variety of symptoms not limited to any particular disease—men who experienced long periods of terminal hospitalization during which they grew progressively weaker before finally succumbing to death. No autopsy was usually conducted in such cases to identify the immediate cause of death; the official certificate simply recorded the cause as *old age* or *debility* or *adynamia* and let it go with that.

According to his own account, John McGinley was born in Ireland in 1801. As a teenager he was apprenticed to a firm in Londonderry, but ran away from his apprenticeship when he was sixteen and somehow made his way to the United States. Young McGinley worked ashore in New York City for about four years, then tried his hand at sea by joining the merchant service, as was typical of many future naval sailors. His merchant service experience must have been strangely limited, because when McGinley transitioned to the Navy by enlisting in the brig *Spark* in 1823 it was at the rating of *boy*. That was an unusual rating for a young man who said he was in his early twenties and had working experience at sea. He was still rated *boy* when he was discharged from *Spark* in September 1825. McGinley's farthest-ranging cruise occurred in the early 1830s when, by now rated a skilled *seaman*, he joined (18 June 1831) the sloop-of-war *Falmouth*, Commander Francis H.

Gregory, for a cruise in Pacific waters, with occasional detached service in the schooner *Dolphin*. Around 1840, while he was serving in the sloop-of-war *Ontario* in the Gulf of Mexico, McGinley's health began to fail and he was hospitalized at Pensacola.

Unfit for further blue-water duty, McGinley did one final shoreside enlistment at the New York (Brooklyn) Navy Yard before seeking (and securing) admission to the Naval Asylum in January 1843. That appointment started off badly; between March and October 1843, John McGinley was confined in the cells no fewer than four times for drunkenness and absence-without-leave. Then his behavior underwent an abrupt and total change. McGinley became a model beneficiary—a man without a single behavioral infraction recorded for nearly three decades—held the responsible job of Asylum messenger for more than ten years, and regularly joined the party of Roman Catholic beneficiaries who filed off to St. Patrick's church for Sunday Mass.

McGinley's health seems to have remained sound until 1871–72, when he was hospitalized three times with a diagnosis of dyspepsia. On 22 August 1872 he checked himself into the hospital for the last time. The admitting medical officer entered a diagnosis of adynamia and noted that McGinley was partially paralyzed on the left side, though there is no record of when this paralysis occurred. McGinley told the doctor that his stomach was "very weak," that he could hardly keep any food down, and that he was experiencing chills followed by sweats at night. The next morning the patient was much more upbeat: he had slept well, had experienced no chills, and he was looking forward to a hearty breakfast. But then, about mid-afternoon, the chills and heat-flashes returned. At the end of August, McGinley's medical record noted that he "complains of feeling cold—hands are very cold—is feeble and greatly emaciated [but] says appetite is pretty good."

So John McGinley's final hospitalization would go—up and down, with more downs than ups. By 5 September he was complaining of soreness over his entire body, especially through his hips, his left thigh, and the back of his head; he was unable to urinate or get out of bed. On 8 September he clearly felt better; much of the pain had abated, his appetite had returned, and he was able to leave his bed. Eight days later he was recorded as weak, losing flesh and strength, and complaining of numbness and loss of power in his lower extremities. Come 24 September he was complaining of pains in his right side. During the night of 24–25 September severe pain struck in the left hip joint and ran down his left leg. On the record goes: "States that he could not possibly feel much worse" (27 September); "Feels sore and miserable" (1 October); "Severe pains all over his body—intense at back of head" (5 October); "Confined to bed greater part of time; complains of general soreness; unable almost to move hands or feet" (10 October); "Feels miserable. To have oyster soup for dinner. Could not eat much of it" (12 October). Then, one day later, an apparent turnaround: "He is stronger than he was a week ago, as shown by the expression of his countenance, tone of voice, and an increase in energy."

On through October and into November, the same rhythm of downs and occasional small ups continued. By 18 October McGinley was groaning with pain all the time, pain made even more intense by any attempt to move. Two days later he told his doctor: "I can't tell you how I feel, I am so miserable." On 26 October he said that he thought he was dying, but this was followed by two weeks or more during which his spirits improved and he appeared to be feeling better. By 20 November McGinley was down again, confined to his bed and claiming, "My legs are dead." From there, it was all down and no ups. Between 22 and 27 November the hospital recorded him as: "Moaning all the time. Very much emaciated. Does not often get out of bed now." "Eats very little." "Very weak. Constantly in bed." Early December brought incontinence of urine and feces. "Moans constantly this morning. Cannot articulate distinctly any more." The end came on 5 December: "Only moans in reply to questions. Sinking very rapidly," was the hospital's morning summary. Just before midnight John McGinley, finally quiet, died.

Atypically for a case of old age or adynamia, the hospital staff *did* conduct an autopsy on McGinley, but offered no conclusion on the cause of his final illness and death, simply recording "general debility" in the official death certificate filed with the City of Philadelphia. Whether McGinley received the sacraments for the dying from the priest at St. Patrick's is not recorded, but his Roman Catholic heritage was honored in death. After a funeral service at the Asylum John McGinley's body was turned over to his niece and her husband, James Mullin, who lived on Philadelphia's North Second Street, for burial in the Cathedral Cemetery.[2]

EXIT QUIETLY—AND KEEP YOUR SECRETS

Around 6 in the morning on 25 September 1868 someone knocked on the door of beneficiary James Doran's room. When he failed to respond, the would-be visitor opened the door to find Doran sitting in a chair—dead. The end had come suddenly, and possibly with little pain or distress, early the previous evening, between supper and bedtime. An immediate autopsy revealed that although all of Doran's other organs were healthy, his heart was badly enlarged. The medical team noted that the dead man had been hospitalized for five days in early August, complaining of asthma. "[His] chest was examined [then], but nothing abnormal about the heart could be detected."

Doran's was a quiet end to an elusive and contradictory life. A short autobiographical statement, taken down as part of Governor George W. Storer's project to record beneficiary lives, is the only source for his first two-and-a-half decades. James Doran reported that he was born in Dublin, Ireland, sometime between 1788 and 1794, depending on which of his self-reported ages one chooses to accept. In 1804, when he had reached the time of life at which young men typically began their adult working careers, Doran made his first voyage in a merchantman. That—or a subsequent voyage soon thereafter—was interrupted, said Doran, when he was pressed into HMS sloop-of-war *Cyclops*, in which he served about nine months before *Cyclops* was captured by a French squadron and Doran was taken to Rochelle as a prisoner-of-war. A good story, but the problem with it is that there was no sloop-of-war *Cyclops* in the British navy to have pressed Doran or to have been captured by the French. At this point in his life, again according to his own narrative, James Doran switched sides without qualms of conscience and joined the French service for about four years. Thereafter, in some manner that he never explained, Doran signed on a vessel bound for New York, sailed in the American merchant service for about five years, and enlisted in the U.S. Navy in time to fight in the climactic battles of the War of 1812 that repelled the British assault on New Orleans in December 1814–January 1815. Here, at last, is an opportunity to do a fact-check on Doran's life story. The Navy's well-maintained New Orleans muster rolls survive complete. They reveal that Seaman James Doran did not join the station until 6 April 1816—more than a year after the British defeat—and that he deserted the station and the Navy less than a year later, on 11 February 1817. The old tar had spun quite a story, and the Naval Asylum officers who wrote it down never suspected how phony much of it may have been.

The balance of James Doran's life is more easily followed and reliably verified in the records. On 30 April 1822 he enlisted as a private in the Marine Corps at Brooklyn, New York. He self-reported his age to be twenty-eight—almost certainly younger than he really was—and is described in his enlistment papers as five feet, six inches tall, with gray eyes, brown hair, and a fair complexion. Doran added that he had been trained as a clerk, a believable assertion inasmuch as he appears to have been fully literate. Doran made two cruises as a Marine—in the frigate *Congress*, Captain James Biddle, and in the sloop-of-war *Hornet*, Commander Edmund P. Kennedy, advancing to corporal in *Hornet*'s Marine detachment. One five-year tour in the Corps seems to have exhausted Doran's enthusiasm for that branch of the service. He returned to the Navy for his next five enlistments, with the rating of either seaman or yeoman—one enlistment in the sloop-of-war *Natchez*, two in the frigate *Brandywine*, one in the frigate *Columbia*, and one in the frigate *Constellation*.

Admitted to the Naval Asylum in June 1844 on the basis of his apparently unverified claim of twenty-five years of active-duty service, Doran soon began a frequent-drinker career that lasted into the early 1850s. Boredom hanging around the Asylum was probably a major motivator for his alcohol abuse; in 1851 and 1852 Doran obtained leaves-of-absence to make voyages in the merchant service, ventures from which he returned a changed man, sober and responsible. In the mid-1850s Doran held a succession of key Asylum jobs as watchman, gatekeeper, petty officer, and ship's corporal, until he began drinking again toward the end of the decade and lost his last in-house job in August 1862. For Doran the 1860s were marked by seven brief hospitalizations for alcoholism, but he appears to have sobered up again during the last two years of his life. Somewhat surprisingly for a before-the-mast sailor James Doran ended his life with a personal library of ninety books. What were they? No list survives. Did he embroider the alleged story of his early life from some of them? *Ungentle Goodnights* can only wonder. Equally surprisingly, James Doran died with $1,050 in cash savings, which surely made him the wealthiest beneficiary in the Asylum. The secret of how Doran—a drinking man—had managed to accumulate and retain such a stash died with him. But of his generosity there could be no question. He left three hundred dollars apiece to three Philadelphia institutions—St. Joseph's Orphan Asylum, St. Joseph's Hospital, and the Hospital of the Protestant Episcopal Church. There was a further bequest of one hundred dollars to one Latitia Conner—who had she been in his life?—plus fifty dollars and a watch to fellow-beneficiary and executor George Rogers.[3]

PAIN UNBEARABLE

Monday, 2 April 1877, was the last day of William Lewis' life. He had reported to the hospital on 12 January of that year, complaining that he had not felt well for the past four or five months. He was losing weight and strength, his appetite was poor, his bowels were irregular, and he was nauseated and vomited often, complaining of pain in the region of his stomach. Lewis added that he had been a habitual tobacco chewer for many years, but had lost any desire for tobacco about two months earlier and was no longer a user. As to why he waited so long to seek medical help, Lewis left no record.

The morning after Lewis' admission, the hospital staff had an opportunity to observe an attack of vomiting. About half an hour after breakfast, the patient's stomach ejected a dark, stringy substance, streaked with a small amount of blood. And so it went for the next seventy-nine days. Lewis vomited periodically, sometimes more than once a day, and was tormented by attacks of hiccups, four or five in succession, each attack lasting five to ten minutes. Some days Lewis seemed to be improving—"feels rather better" or "doing well," the hospital record noted. Then would come another spell of vomiting—perhaps a sour, greenish liquid or a partially digested meal—and more hiccups. Not surprisingly, Lewis' mental health was affected; he complained that he was experiencing depression each afternoon.

When Passed Assistant Surgeon J. Albert Hawke made his morning rounds on 2 April, Lewis reported that he felt about as well as usual, except for a slight discomfort around his stomach. Suddenly Lewis was seized with excruciating pain, accompanied by great physical prostration and a feeble and frequent pulse. Perspiration covered his skin and color drained from his face, which expressed the most intense suffering. The pain, said Lewis, was constant and agonizing, worse when he attempted to lie down. A dose of tincture of opium helped somewhat, but the pain was still severe. Next, morphine sulfate and some type of warm applications to his abdomen were tried. These reduced, but did not eliminate, the pain, although Lewis was finally able to lie down. By 5 in the afternoon he was immediately vomiting everything he tried to swallow, the rejected matter showing no evidence of blood. A clammy sweat covered Lewis' face, his hands and feet were cold, and his voice was failing—but not failing so badly that he could not (around 8 p.m.) ask for and receive a brandy and water. (During earlier weeks Lewis had been allowed sherry and, later, red wine as part of his diet.) The dying man's stomach refused the brandy, which he quickly vomited; indeed, Dr. Hawke noticed that the brandy seemed to make Lewis' suffering worse. Around 9 p.m. Lewis lost consciousness, but by 10:30 he roused himself enough to answer Dr. Hawke's query, "Do you have any pain?" "Yes," he replied, putting his hand on his stomach. "Right here." With that, William Lewis lost consciousness and died at ten minutes before midnight. Small wonder that the brandy intensified Lewis's pain: the post-mortem autopsy revealed that the old sailor died of a gastric ulcer that had perforated his stomach.

LETHAL FUMES

Stroke was sometimes followed by a quick (and perhaps merciful) end, but more typically it resulted in some degree of paralysis that led to extended periods of hospitalization and a slow decline to death. Among the seventy-three beneficiaries who died between July 1868 and July 1886 the man who was hospitalized the longest with a form of paralysis—5,917 days—was also the only one diagnosed with Parkinson's disease or, as it was then more commonly known, *paralysis agitans*. Much as the typical sailor may have disliked a ship's master-at-arms—for that was the rating Francis Sullivan had held—none would have wished him this dreary end to his life.

Sullivan, one more of the many Irishmen in the U.S. naval service, was born in Cork between 1812 and 1814. It was probably at home in Ireland that he was apprenticed to the trade of morocco (goatskin leather) finisher. Just when young Sullivan came to the United States is unknown, but he committed himself to four years' service as a private in the Marine Corps in June 1837, then reenlisted for a second tour, also as a private, July 1842–October 1846. The greater part of these years were spent on sea duty in sloops-of-war *Ontario*, *Vincennes*, and *Portsmouth*, and in the frigate *Constitution*. Service in *Constitution* was followed by eleven months on the beach at the end of which Sullivan switched career tracks and did five U.S. Navy enlistments (1847–58) as a master-at-arms, beginning with service in the sloop-of-war *Albany*. The highpoint of these enlistments must have been his three years in the sidewheel steamer *Mississippi* during Commodore Matthew C. Perry's expedition to Japan. In his next ship, the screw frigate *San Jacinto*, Francis Sullivan's successful and respected career as a senior petty officer came to an end.

In August 1856 he was directing, as was part of his official duties, the fumigating of *San Jacinto*'s lower decks with charcoal and sulphur to free them of rats and other vermin. A conscientious supervisor, the master-at-arms lingered too long among the noxious fumes and was overcome by them. Sullivan was hospitalized in *San Jacinto*'s sickbay for only five days, but before the end of the cruise he experienced the onset of Parkinson's disease through the partial paralysis of his left arm. This was sufficient to secure him a pension for complete disability in August 1859, twelve months after his discharge from *San Jacinto*. For the next five years Francis lived as an invalid with his brother John and John's wife, Anna, in Brooklyn, New York. Then the Civil War intervened to destroy family harmony. Brother John, a captain in the 90th Infantry Regiment, New York State Volunteers, died of yellow fever at Key West on 16 August 1862. This threw the burden of managing a family of four children plus an invalid brother-in-law onto Anna. It was too much to ask of one woman. Francis sought to commute his pension for admission to the Naval Asylum. This met with some initial resistance from Joseph Smith: Francis Sullivan had not quite served the full twenty years usually required for Asylum admission. However, the former master-at-arms had some heavy-hitters— Commodore Henry H. Bell and Chaplain George Jones—on his advocacy team. Admiral Smith soon crumpled and issued Sullivan the requested permit of admission.

Francis Sullivan arrived at the Asylum on 1 August 1864, went immediately to the hospital and never left for the next sixteen years, two months, and thirteen days. The periodic medical examinations required for all pensioners record the unstoppable progress of Sullivan's illness:

January 1868: Paralysis, which originally incapacitated only Sullivan's left arm, now incapacitates his right arm as well, with his head and legs affected to a lesser extent.

February 1874: "Both upper extremities so much affected that he cannot feed himself. Walks with uncertain dragging gait. Needs constant attention." Weight 138 pounds.

September 1875: "Is helpless and incurable. Needs constant attention. Will never recover."

September 1877: Weight 104 pounds. "His motions are a constant series of irregular twitchings. Both upper and lower extremities involved. His speech is uncertain. This man can neither dress nor feed himself and is unable to sit still, needing constant attention from another person."

On 2 October 1880 the hospital noticed that Sullivan had been growing noticeably weaker for the past few days and was now unable to leave his bed. From there he went downhill rapidly. The muscular spasms became even more evident and were especially violent in his face. By the twelfth the invalid could hardly expectorate the mucus which collected in his throat. That proved to be the last full day of his life. At 2:30 a.m. on 13 October Francis Sullivan's extended torment was at last over.

JACK FALLS DOWN AND BREAKS . . .

A total of 409 of the beneficiaries ended their lives at the United States Naval Asylum; 385 of them died of illnesses of one type or another. What of the other 24 beneficiaries? They met death, sometimes without warning, in one of five ways: falls, accidents stemming from Philadelphia's increasing urbanization and industrialization, drowning, suicide—and one beneficiary-on-beneficiary homicide.

The Naval Asylum was home to aging and increasingly feeble men. It is no surprise then that falls and similar injuries, classified by the medical staff as *contusions* or *fractures*, led to slightly more than half—thirteen—of the twenty-four deaths. The details of all thirteen injuries are not on record, but *Ungentle Goodnights* assumes, on the basis of those injuries for which full medical records survive, that all deaths resulting from fractures and contusions were the consequence of falls. Given the Asylum's pervasive culture of alcohol abuse, drinking was often a factor in such injuries. Current scientific research has shown that alcohol can exacerbate aging's natural diminution of the body's ability to maintain its balance.[4]

The story of Charles Lindsay's fatal fall under the wheels of an ice wagon—a typical case of the toxic marriage between alcohol abuse and falls—was related in chapter 6. In fairness to the beneficiaries who did not abuse alcohol, let it immediately be noted that not all falls were the outcome of intoxication. James McFarland's well-authenticated naval service began in April 1833 as an ordinary seaman in the sloop-of-war *Fairfield* and ended in June 1862 as captain of the hold in the steam sloop *Brooklyn*. Much as he may have wanted to finish out the Civil War on active duty McFarland was invalided ashore from *Brooklyn*, suffering, reported Surgeon Lewis B. Hunter, from chronic rheumatism, deafness—a common problem for those, be they seamen or officers, who had passed their careers with inadequately protected ears amid loud and frequent gunfire—and partial blindness of unspecified origin. With a service record like that, and with his various disabilities, McFarland's admission to the Naval Asylum was assured and granted on 15 December 1862.

When he presented himself at the Asylum's gate with his permit of admission James McFarland was five feet, eight inches tall, with blue eyes, gray hair, and the florid complexion of an active-duty seafarer, who asserted to be fifty-eight years old. At the Asylum his behavior was uniformly recorded as "good" and "very good." His record shows only two (unspecified) disciplinary infractions. McFarland was certainly not spending his money on alcohol or selling his clothing to purchase it. He was something of a natty dresser. The wardrobe in his room was well stocked with fourteen linen shirts, three coats and vests, five pair of linen pants, four neckties, a pair of gloves, a scarf, and numerous other articles of clothing.

Fourteen years after he entered the Naval Asylum James McFarland's health took a sharp turn for the worse. Following breakfast on 22 April 1877 he experienced an episode of hemiplegia which hospitalized him for forty days. When he returned to the Asylum from the hospital, at his own request, his recovery was far from complete, but probably as good as could be expected under the medical and rehabilitation knowledge of the day. Passed Assistant Surgeon Henry C. Eckstein, who created the record of

McFarland's case, noted: "He has regained considerable use of right arm and leg. He is able to walk about with a cane. His speech is a little thick, and he drags the right foot a little in walking."

Stroke, and especially hemiplegia, increases the risk of subsequent falls and hip fractures. On 9 February 1878 McFarland caught his dragging right foot on one of the mats that covered the hallways of the Asylum building and tumbled. He landed hard on his right hip, incurring a fracture at the neck of the femur. It was the beginning of a protracted end, brought about by what in twenty-first century medical terminology is called *comorbidity*—that is, existing ailments of age are exacerbated by the broken bone that leaves the patient permanently disabled and consequently inactive. James McFarland was still a tough man. Admitted to the hospital that same day, he never left, dying 396 days later, on 12 March 1879. At admission McFarland's general health was rated as good, but he was unable to walk and gradually succumbed to albuminuria, or Bright's disease—probably a symptom of kidney dysfunction. He had not been an easy patient. Sometimes he refused to take his medications and resisted efforts to help him; at others his mind was incoherent and subject to delusions; by the end he was totally helpless and required the constant attention of three nurses. No autopsy was conducted. The hospital staff was content to record: "The disease to which his death [is] due was chronic albuminuria."

WATER FINALLY WINS

Drowning was a major occupational hazard for nineteenth-century sailors, whether by falls from the rigging into turbulent oceans from which they could not be rescued, violent storms that occasionally washed men overboard, shipwrecks, and vessels lost at sea without a trace. Beneficiaries who made it to the Naval Asylum had dodged that danger successfully, but the water at last claimed two of them— one a member of the Asylum's small cohort of sailors of color.

"Like most colored folks, [he] is wholly ignorant of his age," Frederick Engle, then commandant of Philadelphia's navy yard, told Joseph Smith. The man for whom he was soliciting admission to the Naval Asylum was a long-service sailor named Isaac Harman. His approximate age is no mystery: the seaman's protection certificate, which he took out in 1817 records that he was born in Philadelphia around the year 1797, although Engle guessed him to be at least eight years older than that, surely evidence of a hard life at sea. Harman enlisted in late October 1823 for the frigate *United States*, Commodore Isaac Hull, bound for the Pacific coast of South America. In *United States* he was initially rated as ordinary seaman, but was promoted to seaman on 1 January 1827. Harman subsequently served as seaman in the sloop-of-war *Falmouth*, June 1827 to April 1830, then reenlisted immediately for the frigate *Brandywine*, in which he served, rated seaman, from April 1830 to July 1833. The senior officer who recommended Harman for admission to the Naval Asylum asserted that Isaac Harman had served as a cook at some point during his sea career. But even when Harman was in his forties and fifties, the Navy's surviving muster and pay rolls show him filling active, responsible roles as an equal of his white shipmates—captain of the hold (but disrated to seaman for unknown reasons) in the screw steamer *Princeton*, June 1844 to January 1846; seaman and captain of the hold in the sidewheel steamer *Susquehanna*, November 1850 to November 1853; and seaman during his final service afloat in the sloop-of-war *St. Louis*, June 1855 to April 1858. There, in April 1858, the Navy drew the line—Isaac Harman was too old (about sixty-one) and too infirm to pass the recruiting officer for active duty at sea. He was admitted to the Naval Asylum on 23 June of that year.

Isaac Harman's behavior record at the Asylum was hardly a model one. By 1 October 1859 he was restricted to the grounds thirty days for drunkenness, but was released on 11 October in order to exercise his right to vote. Harman and a fellow beneficiary-voter came back the next day so violently drunk and noisy that they had to be confined in the cells. In mid-November Harman was drunk again; the sanction: another thirty days' confinement to the grounds and no pocket money for a month. On 19–20 December he was out all night without permission and, though still confined to the grounds for that offense, he managed to get drunk on 6 or 7 January 1860. By 9 February, Isaac Harman was once more in trouble for being "drunk, noisy, and kicking the corporal"—an offense that landed him in cells for forty-eight hours, stopped his pocket money for one month, and confined him to the grounds until 2 April.

The entry in the Asylum's log on 21 September 1860 was short and entirely factual: "Received intelligence of the death by drowning on the 19th instant (at the mouth of Smyrna Creek in New Jersey [actually in Delaware], about 70 miles below Philadelphia) of Isaac Harman, colored, a beneficiary of this institution, having fallen overboard from the deck of a shallop; at that time his body had not been recovered." On 2 September Harman had come off a thirty-day confinement to the Asylum grounds for drunkenness. The Bureau of Yards and Docks did not ask, and the Naval Asylum did not explain, what a beneficiary, whose absence from the Asylum had not been noted in the daily log, was doing on a shallop seventy miles downriver. Obviously he was pursing outside income as a member of the shallop's crew. Did the official failure to account for his absence reflect a lower value set on the life of an African American beneficiary? Or was the Asylum just silently glad to be rid of another behavior problem? There is no way to answer that question, although the frequent practice of noting that Harman was "Negro" or "colored" in the Asylum's records may tip the balance in favor of the former supposition.

THE CITY KILLS

When the United States Naval Asylum accepted its first beneficiaries in the 1830s the institution had a quasi-rural setting. Philadelphia was near, but separated by a wide band of undeveloped land. The city's population growth, spurred in part by rapidly developing industrial technology, soon ended this isolation. The horse-drawn Philadelphia & Gray's Ferry Passenger Railway was running past the Asylum's front gates by the 1860s. It claimed its first beneficiary-victim when, on the afternoon of 25 April 1862, James Alexander Jordan, sixty-two, tried to duck across Gray's Ferry Road, stumbled, and fell so close to the oncoming street railway car that it could not be stopped in time. It passed over his body, killing him instantly. When Executive Officer Peter Turner reported the fatal accident to Washington, he tried to put the best face he could on the incident, saying Jordan's death was "the result of his own carelessness." Jordan's behavior record at the Asylum reveals that he was a heavy and frequent drinker, and the likelihood is that alcohol had impaired the beneficiary's judgment and led to his death. It was one of four beneficiary deaths that can be attributed to the nineteenth century's diverse and rapidly expanding industrial technology.

The most sensational of those four deaths was that of Seaman John C. Munroe, who was born in New Orleans, probably in 1803. He entered the Navy in 1826 and served—one hiatus in the 1830s aside—continuously until 1859. On 26 May of that year he was admitted to the Naval Asylum. A little more than two months later he received a leave to travel to Norfolk to collect, he said, money and clothing he had left there. Munroe had been gone about two weeks when Governor William W. McKean received a letter from him reporting that, because he had no money to pay his way back to Philadelphia, he had signed on board his old ship, the sidewheel steamer *Fulton*. Doing so was a violation of Asylum regulations. Age and years of hard service had long since caught up with Munroe. Already in February 1852 he had been described by an examining surgeon as "a short, old man, with prominent forehead." As often happened to beneficiaries who tried to return to active duty too late in life, Munroe was soon invalided from *Fulton* and eventually made his way back to Philadelphia. From there he appealed to Joseph Smith for readmission to the Asylum, claiming that he had been "persuaded against my will" to ship in *Fulton*. It is doubtful that Commodore Smith, plagued as he was by Asylum beneficiaries reshipping against the rules, believed Munroe's story of coercion for a minute, but he was in a forgiving mood, and sent Munroe a permit for readmission. When Munroe showed up at the Asylum's northeast gate, permission in hand, the Asylum log noted disapprovingly that he was intoxicated. This was hardly an auspicious omen for Munroe's future behavior as a beneficiary; he was restricted to the grounds until such time as the executive officer saw fit to cancel the restriction.

That restriction was apparently lifted by 14 June 1860, on which day Munroe and a fellow beneficiary, Andrew Tunnell, left the Asylum to watch a balloon ascension farther to the south along the Schuylkill. Although the record is silent on this point, it is safe to assume—based on subsequent events—that the excursion included some significant drinking as well. Munroe and Tunnell decided to walk back to the Asylum on the tracks of the Philadelphia, Wilmington, and Baltimore Railroad. They were near the Schuylkill Arsenal when Tunnell heard a Philadelphia-bound train approaching. Tunnell was trying, apparently with some difficulty, to get an intoxicated Munroe off the tracks when the locomotive came round a bend at top speed, blowing its whistle and ringing its bell. The locomotive's cow-catcher hit both men, throwing them off the track. Munroe, the more seriously injured, lost a foot in the accident. The city police transported both beneficiaries to the Asylum's hospital. John C. Munroe died there in less than three hours, from the severed foot, other injuries, loss of blood, and shock. Philadelphia's *Public Ledger* assured its sensation-seeking readers that "no hopes were entertained" for Tunnell's life, but he made a speedy recovery from his injuries and was released from the hospital in just eleven days. A fate different from death-by-locomotive was in store for Andrew Tunnell. In April 1865 he began to display alarming symptoms of mental illness, was transferred to Washington's Government Hospital for the Insane in September 1866, and died there on 12 July 1868.

THE FATAL ACT

Four beneficiaries ended their lives by suicide. The early life of one of them, Rudolph Bernard, is obscure. He was born in Switzerland, probably in the early 1790s, though he once asserted his age to be some fifteen years younger than that. When Bernard enlisted as a private in the Marine Corps on 29 January 1839, he represented himself as a native-born citizen and explained away his accent with the standard recruiting excuse of native German speakers—birth in German-speaking Lancaster, Pennsylvania. He almost certainly lied about his age, and got away with it because his hair was still black and his complexion fair. Less than three years of service showed that this seemingly fit exterior concealed inner decay. On 19 January 1842 Rudolph Bernard was discharged from the Marine Corps and dispatched to the Naval Asylum, where his medical record noted that he was deaf and suffered from unspecified "injuries."

The puzzle in all this is that Rudolph Bernard was admitted to the Asylum on the basis of six years of service, three in the Marine Corps and another three—in which service?—of which *Ungentle Goodnights* has found no record. (At his 1839 enlistment, Bernard stated his trade or occupation to be that of *soldier*, strongly suggesting European military experience before immigration to the United States.) Six years of service was far too short for a typical Naval Asylum admission, but is explained by a letter from Colonel Archibald Henderson, commandant of the Marine Corps, to Secretary of the Navy Abel P. Upshur of 23 December 1841. With that letter Henderson forwarded a report from Surgeon John A. Kearney that listed a number of Marines—including Bernard—who were unfit for service, but who did not meet the twenty-year rule for admission to the Naval Asylum. "The strict application [of this requirement] will," argued Henderson, "exclude many disabled soldiers from the Asylum who would have to be discharged the service in a helpless condition or continued in it at a greater expense to the government than would be incurred by their admission into that establishment." Would bending the rules lead to an unwelcome influx of short-service but disabled Marines? Not so, thought Henderson. "There is little probability of soldiers making a convenience of the Asylum, as there is great reluctance on their part to avail themselves of this comfortable home provided for them by the government."[5]

Once Bernard arrived at the Asylum, his record is more complete, but still not without its puzzles. In March 1850 his character and habits were rated as "very good," but by that date his behavior record indicated that he had been reported at least twenty times for drunkenness or absences without leave. On 6 August 1851 a loaded pistol was found in Bernard's room and he was confined to the grounds indefinitely. Already, in 1850, he had been hospitalized twice for dementia. No one in authority seems to have connected these clues or, if they did, took any cautionary action. "He has been partially deranged for some time past," Governor David Geisinger explained to Joseph Smith, "but [was] inoffensive and has been accustomed to pass in and out the grounds as other men." Then, around 1 p.m. on 28 October 1852, the sound of a loud pistol shot was heard in Bernard's room. The coroner was hastily summoned; the *Public Ledger*'s reporter was not far behind. This was the kind of news for which Philadelphians read the *Ledger*, and they were not disappointed. Under the headline "Horrid Case of Suicide," they were informed the next day that Rudolph Bernard, a German and resident of the Naval Asylum, had ended his life "by blowing his brains out by the discharge of a pistol. The weapon was very heavily charged, shattering his head in the most awful manner and causing instant death. He . . . is supposed to have been insane when he committed the fatal act." By the time the story appeared, Rudolph Bernard's remains had been hastily buried in the Asylum's cemetery.

MURDER. OR WAS IT?

Thomas Taylor is a beneficiary about whom even less is now known than about Rudolph Bernard. His last recorded active-duty rating was as a seaman, and he was reported to be fifty years old in 1845.

Taylor was admitted to the Naval Asylum on 14 June 1843, and, at some unknown date thereafter—or perhaps immediately—was sent to the hospital with a diagnosis of consumption. He died there on 12 March 1845. Surgeon Benjamin F. Bache thought Taylor's symptoms appeared suspicious during his final days, but it was not until after Taylor's death that Bache was able to search Taylor's room, where he found a pair of vials containing 2 ounces of laudanum, a box with 185 grams of solid dry opium, a bottle of port, and an empty bottle that had once contained port, all of them well hidden. On investigation Bache discovered that, with the connivance of hospital nurse James Burns, two beneficiaries—John White and Richard Jones—had been visiting Taylor, who was in great physical distress. White and Jones were clandestinely administering wine and opiates to Taylor, over and above the amounts he was supposed to receive as part of his regular medication, thus hastening his death. All of this was confirmed by the coroner and by the Asylum's own internal investigation. Suspicion was deepened by the discovery of Taylor's will, which bequeathed his personal belongings to Burns, Jones, and White. The will was said to have been drafted by White and signed by Taylor under the influence of alcohol and drugs.

Burns was immediately fired, and Governor Charles W. Morgan's suspicion and ire were focused on John White as the alleged ringleader in this supposedly nefarious plot. Morgan clearly had it in for White, whom he described as "a mischievous person [whose] influence is very injurious among the men generally," commenting that "the part he took in contributing to the death of Thomas Taylor is but one of many instances which might be mentioned of his misconduct. He is dishonest, having several times stolen articles from the Asylum, and his character is generally bad and has been repeatedly so reported by all of the officers. Indeed, I am persuaded that such men do an incalculable amount of evil in an institution of this kind." Governor Morgan had no trouble in securing White's highly public dismissal as a beneficiary, effective 26 March 1845. Richard Jones received no recorded punishment.

Why, based on the evidence thus far, is the death of Thomas Taylor recorded here with the Asylum's suicides? To this historian, it appears more likely to have been a case of assisted suicide than one of homicide. Taylor, who may have been in great pain, took the ultimately fatal drugs willingly, hid his stash from the authorities, and almost certainly encouraged White to procure them. In all probability, the dying Taylor would have willed his few possessions to his friends, whatever the circumstances. Finally, if the case against White was as strong as Dr. Bache and Commodore Morgan said it was, why did they not turn White over to the civil authorities for a homicide investigation? In the twenty-first century assisted suicide is still controversial. Rather than confront that troublesome ethical issue directly, Bache and Morgan, firmly entrenched in nineteenth-century Christian morality, may have preferred to sweep the whole business under the rug by scapegoating troublemaker White and getting him off the scene with a quick and supposedly final dismissal.

REDEMPTION

Considering the finality of John White's dismissal in disgrace from the Asylum and his non-distinctive name, one would expect him to join the roll of ex-beneficiaries whose later lives cannot be traced. Not so in White's case. It is worthwhile to detour briefly from the stories of beneficiaries' deaths by accident and violence and discover what became of a man portrayed by Governor Morgan as so thoroughly corrupt.

Five months after his expulsion White applied to Secretary of the Navy George Bancroft for readmission to the Asylum, but his request was summarily rejected on Charles W. Morgan's advice; the governor's negative opinion of White had not mellowed in the intervening time. Thereafter, White disappears from the recoverable record until the early 1860s, when he decided to make a determined attempt to regain the security of the U.S. Naval Asylum. The documents White created in support of that effort reveal most of what is now known about the man.

John White was born in England in 1798 or 1799, but came to the United States as a young child with his father, who was a United States citizen, and grew up in New York City. White's first naval service was in the ship-of-the line *Franklin*, Commodore Charles Stewart, which he joined as an ordinary seaman in July 1817. He then alternated among naval service at sea, merchant voyages, and work in navy yards until, in October 1840, he was detailed as a seaman to the sloop-of-war *Boston*, Commander John C. Long. This proved to be his last active-duty sea service. A back injury—whether sustained in *Boston* or earlier is not clear—invalided him

from *Boston* to the naval hospital at New York in February 1841.
From there White was recommended as a candidate for the Asylum, to which he was admitted on 14 May 1841. He arrived there
as a man in his early forties, five feet, six-and-a-half inches tall,
with brown hair, blue eyes, and a light complexion somewhat disfigured by scars from smallpox. White was relatively young for a
beneficiary, which may partly explain his penchant for getting into
trouble and thereby earning, deservedly or not, Governor Morgan's
low opinion.

As noted, little is known about White's life in the seventeen
years following his March 1845 dismissal from the Asylum. Governor Morgan reported that White held a pension for his injury
on which he could fall back for support. But the governor was
wrong. None of the John Whites whose pension records survive
matches the ex-beneficiary. He appears to have returned to the
New York City area, was turned down for employment at the New
York (Brooklyn) Navy Yard because of his disability, worked as
best he could, and was employed for a time in some capacity in the
tobacco trade. The former beneficiary is almost certainly this man
recorded in the federal census of 1860—John White, a resident of
New York City, age sixty-one, self-identified as a laborer, born in
England, married to a woman whose first name was Sarah, thirty-two years old, a native of Ireland, the couple having two children,
Mary (nine) and John (seven).

It was through his residence in New York that White became
reacquainted with Commander Andrew Hull Foote, who had been
executive officer at the Asylum during White's residence, and who
served as executive officer in the Navy Yard at Brooklyn beginning
in October 1858. Foote was a deeply religious man. White had
at some point experienced conversion himself and repented his
younger, wilder days—a life change in which his wife may have
played a role. Shared faith somehow brought Foote and White
into association. By September 1862, when White decided to
make that one more attempt to return to the Asylum, Foote was
an admiral, the victorious commander afloat on the Western rivers during the early years of the Civil War, and was attempting to
regain his duty-impaired health in a Washington desk job as Chief
of the Navy Department's Bureau of Equipment and Recruiting.

White's initial appeal was to Secretary of the Navy Gideon
Welles, who passed the request along to Joseph Smith. In addition

to being fellow bureau chiefs, Smith and Foote were longtime personal friends, and Foote assured Smith in conversation that White was now a man of "improved habits." Things were looking up for White. Send in the required proof of service, Smith told him, and your case will receive favorable consideration. White quickly submitted the required papers, but in the interval Smith had apparently done some deeper research into White's 1845 dismissal. He now decided that White's "gross misconduct" and the fact that he lacked by a year or two the twenty years of service required for admission to the Asylum were sufficient reasons to deny White's request without a special exemption. That special exemption could only be granted by the Secretary of the Navy. White appealed directly to Foote: "God forbid I should tell an untruth to you." His role in Taylor's death had, he asserted, been greatly misrepresented. "Dear Sir, I still have a ray of hope that pardon may be found and, though my repentance has been at the eleventh hour, I have bitterly repented of all my past misconduct, of which I hope Almighty God, in his infinite mercy, will forgive me. . . . I am deeply and sincerely grieved when I think of my past actions." If reinstated at the Asylum, "I sincerely promise not only to behave myself but to do all the good I can through God's help to bring others that have erred to the path of duty." Were these White's real feelings? Or was he telling the genuinely religious Foote what he thought the admiral wanted to hear? Only White would have known the true answer. However, Foote was a hard-headed naval veteran, with ample—if sympathetic—experience of sailors and their failings. He knew White personally, and he must have judged his plea of a reformed life had some acceptable measure of reality. On 1 November 1862, twelve days after White's letter to Foote, he was at last readmitted to the Asylum.

Once there, White compiled a relatively clean record. His behavior was rated as "good" and "very good" into 1864. He was hospitalized five days with delirium tremens in September of that year, and in January 1866 his behavioral record was noted "intemperate." A year later his habits were reported to be "improving." Drinking aside—it was hard for any old sailor to give up a life-long source of pleasure—there were no official complaints about him. On 10 July 1868 John White entered the hospital for the first time since his delirium tremens episode four years earlier; the diagnosis was "acute diarrhea." One day later he was dead, leaving behind

Sarah to collect and dispose of, as best she could, the extensive inventory of clothing found in John's room.

HOMICIDE AT THE NAVAL ASYLUM?

It was about 5 p.m. on 16 November 1854. Outside, dusk was darkening into night, and several of the beneficiaries had gathered in the sitting room near the dining hall on the lowest floor of the building. A quarrel broke out between beneficiaries Anthony Prussock and William C. Riggs. Harsh words degenerated into blows with fists—or, in some accounts, with Riggs striking Prussock with a walking stick. Prussock left the sitting room. Riggs followed, still orally abusing Prussock, until they reached the door of Prussock's room. Riggs tried to follow him inside, whereupon Prussock turned, blocked the doorway, and told Riggs, "Clear out! For God's sake, clear out!"—or words to that effect. To make his point, Prussock pushed Riggs, a large man, away. Riggs fell backwards, struck his head against the opposite wall, and lost consciousness. A fellow beneficiary, Andrew Stephenson, witnessed the encounter and immediately demanded, "What did you knock that man down for?" Prussock's response was to knock Stephenson down as well, but without causing any recorded injury. About this time Executive Officer Andrew H. Foote arrived to break things up and had Riggs carried to his room, where he died from a concussion to his brain in about fifteen minutes. The coroner was summoned, collected testimony, and rendered his verdict: death resulting from the shove by Prussock, who was thereupon taken into custody.

That was the generally agreed-upon narrative of this sad incident. But there was more to the story and, typical for this kind of incident, not all the witnesses were in agreement, even under oath.

Anthony Prussock was born in Warsaw, Poland, sometime in the 1780s. When he came to the United States is not on record, but he apparently worked as a laborer for a time before enlisting in the Marine Corps at Philadelphia on 25 July 1825. That day he told the recruiter that he was thirty-eight years old, and the recruiter noted that Prussock was five feet, six inches tall, had blue eyes, sandy hair, and ruddy complexion. With some interruptions, Prussock served in the Corps until May 1849, when he was admitted to the Naval Asylum on the grounds of "long and faithful service," although he was "now worn out and no longer able to perform the duties of a soldier." Most of his Marine Corps duty appears to

have been at sea. At the Asylum Prussock was an unpopular beneficiary. He had a particularly annoying habit, when he saw two of
his fellow beneficiaries in conversation, of standing close by and
eavesdropping. He was suspected (correctly) of being a snitch to
the Asylum authorities.

Prussock's version, under oath, was that he had informed the
executive officer that a fellow beneficiary, whom he identified as
"Black Sam," regularly smuggled liquor into the Asylum, a tattle that
led three beneficiaries—one of them Riggs—to attack Prussock
orally, and Riggs to hit Prussock with a walking stick as well. As
the inquest into the incident unfolded before Alderman John B.
Kenney it appeared that "Black Sam" was the African American
beneficiary Samuel Howard, already met in chapter 7. Prussock's
attorney, John Hamilton Jr., asked Howard to identify himself:
"Are you a Marine or a sailor." "Me, Sir," replied Howard. "I am
cook for the bluejackets. I always cook for them." Attorney Hamilton
probed to discover whether Howard, a witness to the incident,
had reason to be prejudiced against Prussock. Howard replied that
Prussock had reported him to Executive Officer Foote for bringing liquor into the building. "He called me a damned n----r and
[said] that I ought not to be in the country," but Foote had refused
to believe Prussock's accusation. Then, just to make sure that the
record was straight, Howard added: "I have been a little groggy,
but . . . I always got my liquor outside, because it is against the
rules to have it inside."

Why had Riggs, among the three men who quarreled with
Prussock in the smoking room, been so persistent and violent in
his pursuit of the self-admitted snitch? Not much is known about
Riggs, his life, or his service in the Navy. He was apparently born
in Virginia and asserted he was seventy-four years old when he
was admitted to the Naval Asylum in 1852. Philadelphia's *Public
Ledger* reported that "it is said" that Riggs had been a participant
in Stephen Decatur's burning of the captured U.S. frigate *Philadelphia* during the Tripolitan War, but this claim is not borne out
by the roll of the heroic crew that carried out the deed.[6] The Asylum's records suggest a motive for Riggs' hostility to Prussock. On
7 May 1853 Riggs was caught smuggling a flask of liquor into the
Asylum. Governor David Geisinger had reason to believe that Riggs
had done this more than once, but this was the first time he had
been caught. Normally this offense would have merited dismissal

from the institution, but Geisinger recommended a lesser punishment on the grounds of Riggs' age and long naval service. That had been a close call for Riggs. Whether Riggs suspected Prussock of a role in his own apprehension or whether he was coming to Sam Howard's defense because Sam was being accused of a similar offense—or whether both suppositions are true—Riggs, an easily belligerent man, clearly had it in for Prussock. That hostility cost him his life.

Two days after the incident Anthony Prussock was, as previously mentioned, arraigned before Alderman Kenney, who took extensive testimony, then committed Prussock to jail on the charge of killing William C. Riggs. A grand jury considered the matter on 12 December 1854, heard additional testimony from six beneficiaries, and indicted Prussock for homicide. That trial took place on 29 January 1855, but the outcome was a surprise. After all the testimony had again been heard, the prosecutor, Deputy District Attorney William B. Mann, addressed the jury. This was, said Mann, "a case in which the evidence left a doubt on his mind, and he supposed on the minds of the jury also, as to the guilt of the defendant. From the testimony submitted," he continued, "the defendant may have acted entirely, at this period of the quarrel at least, in self-defense. It was the duty of the Commonwealth [of Pennsylvania] to present a case clear, beyond a reasonable doubt, before they could ask for a conviction. In this case there was a doubt, and it was for the benefit of the defendant." Mann asked the jury to acquit the defendant, a request with which they at once complied.[7]

Anthony Prussock was a free man. He returned to the Naval Asylum that same day. From Washington, Joseph Smith hoped that "the ordeal through which [Prussock] has just passed may be a salutary lesson to him and others." That was not to be; acquittal and freedom were not the happy ending of Prussock's life story. He had never been a model beneficiary. Prussock's conduct record shows a pattern of drunkenness, quarreling, and noisy, disruptive behavior between 1849 and 1853. Tellingly perhaps, his dossier reveals that Prussock himself had been caught, and punished for, smuggling liquor back in 1850. Not too long after his return to the Asylum, Prussock's behavior took an alarming turn. Between 31 May and 18 June 1855 he was hospitalized for dementia. By the end of June Surgeon James Cornick concluded that Prussock's symptoms of insanity were unmistakable; Governor George W. Storer recommended that Prussock be removed to the newly opened Government Hospital for the Insane in Washington. Joseph Smith checked into the possibility, and discovered that the hospital was already at capacity. Prussock could not be admitted before September at the earliest.

While this recommendation was being made, considered, and action deferred, events had taken their own direction at the Naval Asylum; on 10 July, as Governor Storer reported to Commodore Smith: Prussock "escaped from his room [where he was confined] by cutting out the fastenings of his door with a small knife which he had secreted in spite of search and by his violent conduct caused considerable alarm among the officers' families." The Asylum's corporal and his assistants set off in pursuit of Prussock, who was finally caught and subdued inside Governor Storer's official residence. "The noise he makes," a seemingly unruffled Storer continued, "disturbs the inmates of the Asylum night and day, and as he is impressed with the idea that he *must* kill certain two of the old men [unfortunately not identified], no one here can feel secure so long as he remains among us." Storer again urged transfer to the Government Hospital for the Insane, and Smith again reported that Prussock could not be accommodated right now. Lock him up in one of the Asylum's cells for the present was the best solution Smith was able to discern. This was apparently done, but Prussock's condition must have continued to deteriorate, because he was admitted to the Asylum's hospital on the first day of November with a diagnosis of "mania." Not until 20 December was it possible to transfer him to the Washington facility, escorted by Assistant Surgeon Andrew A. Henderson and the Asylum's carpenter—the latter's role presumably being to supply any muscle the task required. The records of the Government Hospital for Insane simply state that Prussock's mental illness was "chronic mania," with no indication of what role, if any, the death of William C. Riggs may have played in his descent into insanity.

Anthony Prussock died at the Washington hospital on 18 April 1861. By then he was probably unaware of the world outside the institution's walls and the rapid collapse of his adopted country into the trauma of civil war.

FIFTEEN

Safe Harbor— Finally Found

When, in 1834, the United States Naval Asylum received its first residents, it was to be anticipated that, sooner or later, the beneficiaries—men in their fifties and sixties and some older than that—would die at the institution. However, no decision had been made about their burial—nor, indeed, is there evidence that anyone had thought about the matter—when a beneficiary died on 3 August 1835.

He was a Marine named Jacob Dehart, born in Richmond, New York, probably late in the 1770s or early in the 1780s. Dehart trained as a blacksmith and presumably followed that trade until war was declared against Great Britain in 1812. On 13 July of that year he abandoned blacksmithing and enlisted as a private in the Marine Corps. At the time of his enlistment, he asserted he was thirty-seven years old; he stood five feet, seven inches tall, and had blue eyes, brown hair, and a florid complexion. Soon thereafter Dehart was dispatched to Sacket's Harbor, New York, where he served as part of the base's Marine detachment for the rest of the War of 1812. With the return of peace, Dehart was reassigned to the Boston (Charlestown) Navy Yard. Shortly thereafter he experienced his first recorded sea duty as a member of the Marine detachment in Commodore William Bainbridge's *Independence*, during that ship's 1815 cruise to the Mediterranean. With *Independence*'s return to Boston, Jacob Dehart came ashore and—as far as is known—never went to sea again; the remainder of his Marine Corps career was spent as a private in detachments at navy yards or on board ships in ordinary there. Dehart was stationed at the Boston Navy Yard until his five-year initial enlistment expired in August 1817. He then left the Marine Corps for about four years—what he did during that time is as yet undiscovered—but reenlisted in January 1821 and remained in the Corps until his final discharge in July 1835, serving that entire period at the New York (Brooklyn) Navy Yard.

In mid-1823 Dehart got into serious disciplinary trouble, and was sentenced by court-martial to wear a ball and chain for what appears to have been nearly a year. The transcript of Dehart's trial has disappeared, so the exact nature of his offense or offenses is not known. Neither are the full details of his punishment on record. These months with the ball and chain aside, the most memorable event of Dehart's postwar service was the explosion of the magazine of the receiving ship *Fulton* at the Brooklyn Navy Yard on 4 June 1829, destroying the ship in which he was stationed as a member of the Marine guard. Dehart was severely injured, with burns to his head and hands that kept him hospitalized at the New York Naval Hospital until mid-March 1830. Upon recovery he returned to duty, reenlisted in August 1831 after a one-month stint of civilian life, and resumed the round of routine guard duty at Brooklyn. By this time, however, Dehart's health had begun a serious decline. In December 1834 he was admitted to hospital where he remained, a terminally ill man in his mid to late fifties, until he was transferred to the Naval Asylum on 23 July 1835. He died just thirteen days later. The cause of his death is recorded as vomiting of blood, but this was only a symptom of some underlying illness not identified in any surviving record.

Absent any provision for the burial of dead beneficiaries, Commodore James Barron—in 1835 the Naval Asylum still reported to the commandant of the Philadelphia Navy Yard—coped and arranged for Dehart to be buried in "consecrated ground." Presumably this was the graveyard of one of Philadelphia's churches. Which one it is not possible to determine, because Philadelphia's register of deaths does not record cemeteries of burial for the year 1835. With the lack of any place of interment for the Asylum's beneficiaries brought forcefully to his attention, Barron immediately referred the problem to Secretary of the Navy Mahlon Dickerson. Secretary Dickerson passed the matter on to the Board of Navy Commissioners, which at that time had oversight of the physical facilities at naval shore establishments such as the Asylum. Commodore Charles Morris, speaking on behalf of the board, proposed that the question be deferred until the board made its annual tour of inspection of the Navy's bases and shipyards. At that time, the commissioners and Commodore Barron would seek a site within the Asylum's premises for a burial ground.

At this time the Asylum property still included the peninsula tract that extended from the compact central site in a northerly direction to South Street. It was on this space that the commissioners and James Barron decided to locate the burial ground. Little is known about this facility; it appears to have been a simple, no-frills space, similar to the churchyard burial grounds of the eighteenth and early nineteenth centuries—closely spaced rows of graves with wooden headboards painted with the name of the sailor or Marine who was buried there, his age at death, and possibly his rank as well. The wooden headboards endured about three or four years of Philadelphia's rain, snow and sun, at which point they had to be replaced with new ones. Eventually, fifty-three men were buried at this site. Not all fifty-three were Asylum beneficiaries, because it was also the practice to bury in the same ground sailors and Marines who died at the Philadelphia Naval Hospital which shared building space with the Asylum.[1]

BURIAL GROUND TO CEMETERY

Within a decade, several problems with this initial burying ground were all too obvious. The soil was clay. This meant that it did not drain well, but retained water—leaving the graves, coffins, and bodies wet or damp for much of the year. The burying ground was fast running out of space for new interments. Then there was the matter of Shippen Street. The City of Philadelphia had a legal right to open the already-platted Shippen Street through the peninsula extension, although it did not actually do so for a number of years. Whenever opened, Shippen Street would leave the burying ground cut off from the rest of the Asylum property by steep, high embankments on either side of the roadway, since the ground level of the Asylum property was considerably above the grade of the planned street. The Navy Department and the Asylum authorities engaged in a certain amount of wishful thinking that the city could be prevented from cutting the street through, but they got no encouragement for these hopes from the U.S. District Attorney, who said that sooner or later Shippen Street would be opened; legally, it could not be stopped. This threat had already caused the

Asylum's stable to be relocated, and a number of the existing graves were now within the yard of the new stable. Finally, there seems to have been an important psychological issue only hinted at in the surviving record. The burial ground was in plain sight from the Asylum building, and this all-too-visible reminder of the end of life was apparently distressing to some of the elderly beneficiaries. A new burial place was urgently needed.

On the northwest side of the Asylum grounds the land fell off rather steeply toward the Schuylkill River. Governor Charles W. Morgan chose a site for the new burial space at the foot of this incline—well out of sight from the Asylum's main building—and at the junction of Sutherland Avenue and the proposed Shippen Street. The soil here was gravel, thus eliminating the problem of the water-retaining clay at the old burial ground. None of the surviving professional surveys of the Asylum's grounds shows the new burial site and its measured dimensions. The latter must be estimated from two hand-drawn sketches which, although generally reliable, may not be to scale. From these it would appear that the site chosen measured about 135 feet by 90 feet—that is, a space of approximately 12,000 square feet. A handsome "dead house" was to be constructed in the middle of this site for the immediate reception of bodies before burial. The new site would be enclosed on three sides by brick walls. On the fourth side—the one nearest to the Asylum's main building—where the ground was to be excavated to provide a flatter surface for the burials, the resulting steep bank would be sodded and topped with a hedge to create the final enclosing physical and visual barrier of the site.

Ever the enthusiastic booster of the merits of his numerous construction projects at the Asylum, Commodore Morgan confidently predicted that the new site would accommodate "about" eight hundred burials. A quick calculation will demonstrate that, conservatively assuming that each grave would require a space of at least three by seven feet, and deducting space for the dead house and walks, there was no way Morgan was going to get eight hundred individual graves into 12,000 square feet. His solution to this problem was to dig the graves down to a depth of ten feet and bury two coffins, one on top of the other, in each grave.

Construction of the new burial site got under way in the late spring or early summer of 1845. By September the work was sufficiently advanced (though still in progress) to permit John Ward, a former purser's steward who died on the fourth of that month from, according to the Asylum's log, "delirium tremens and inflammation of the lungs produced by intemperance" to be buried there that same afternoon. The Rev. John W. Grier, the Philadelphia Navy Yard chaplain, and the Rev. Thomas Porter, seamen's missionary, performed the graveside service. Early burials such as Ward's excepted, moving the fifty-three bodies from the old burial ground to the new site was deferred until construction was complete. By then it was December of 1845, Philadelphia's winter and no time, Commodore Morgan thought, to be digging in wet, cold clay. The transfer was finally carried out the following spring in two days (10–11 April) by William H. Moore, a Philadelphia undertaker, at a cost of two dollars and eighty-six cents per body.

There are no surviving images of the 1845 burial site. One can infer from hints in the records that it was more landscaped than the old burial ground. But the most significant clue about the character of the new place of interment was the language used to refer to it. The old site had always been called a *burial ground*, conjuring up images of the churchyard burials of an earlier time; the new site was uniformly referred to as the *cemetery*. That term, *cemetery*, derived from the Greek word for sleeping chamber, was replacing the older terminology everywhere in the United States by the 1840s. Language at the Naval Asylum mirrored that of the broader society in which the Asylum, its staff, and its residents lived. Cultural historians see in the new terminology a changing view of death as sleep, the body in repose until the day of resurrection, when it would join the soul in heaven. This upbeat view of death—far fewer sinful humans in terror of the angry God they would meet upon death—reflected both the more optimistic theology of the times and the exuberant nationalism of the post–War of 1812 United States.

MORE PERMANENT MEMORIALS

Changing culture is a slow business. The new cemetery continued the old burial ground's use of painted wooden headboards to mark the graves. The wooden markers cost about a dollar and ten cents each and needed to be repainted or replaced every three or four years. There is evidence that at least some of the beneficiaries were unhappy with these transitory markers for their graves. As early as

1858, Asylum resident John Fauss purchased an elaborate and expensive stone memorial to mark a fellow beneficiary's grave:

DEDRICK SMITH
Born in Hamburg Germany
Died Nov. 4 1858 aged 68 [*stone broken*]

Erected by his friend
JOHN FAUSS

That a sailor-beneficiary at the Naval Asylum could afford to do this should not be a surprise, though it probably will be. The popular image of the nineteenth-century sailor as an improvident spendthrift was just that—a stereotype. Yes, there were many impoverished men among the Asylum's beneficiaries with little to show for lifetimes of sailing and drinking. But there were also men who saved their money carefully and left impressive sums at their deaths.

Whether the request originated with the beneficiaries, or whether he thought of it himself, in 1859 Governor William W. McKean included in his budget request for the fiscal year 1860–61 a proposed expenditure to replace the wooden headboards with small stone markers. Money for that purpose was allocated by Congress in its annual appropriation for the Naval Asylum. As for future burials, at about this time the beneficiaries and the governor made an informal agreement: when a beneficiary died two dollars and sixty-two and a half cents would be deducted from the proceeds of the sale at auction of his remaining possessions to his fellow beneficiaries—or from any cash that he left—and used to purchase a stone marker for his grave.

Captain McKean's informal agreement with the beneficiaries for the purchase of permanent grave markers remained in effect until July 1864. By that time Civil War–driven inflation had pushed the cost of the individual tombstones up to seven dollars. Only ninety-one dollars and seventy cents remained in the collective Tomb-Stone Fund, and thirty-five stones were needed to mark recent graves. To address the problem the beneficiaries and the then-governor, Commodore Frederick Engle, negotiated a new and more formal agreement. Thereafter seven dollars would be deducted from the physical or cash estates of dead beneficiaries for the purchase of their gravestones. As for those beneficiaries who died without making a will—

A typical stone grave marker in the Naval Asylum's cemetery. PHOTOGRAPH BY SHARON MCKEE

or who had no relatives to claim their personal property—the entire proceeds from the sale of their belongings and any cash they left would go to the Tomb-Stone Fund.

Inflation continued to take its toll. By late 1867, the Tomb-Stone Fund was depleted and thirty-four graves still lacked head-stones. Pending funds to purchase permanent stone markers, these thirty-four graves were marked only by wooden slabs painted with a number to identify the beneficiary buried beneath. Where was the money to come from? That question was passed up the line and eventually reached the desk of Secretary of the Navy Gideon Welles, who decided the time had come for the Navy to be respon-sible for purchasing a permanent marker for the grave of each Naval Asylum beneficiary. Although there is no record of the basis for Welles' decision, it seems likely that he was influenced by the national cemeteries then being developed for the nation's Civil War dead, sites at which the federal government assumed respon-sibility for placing a marker at each grave.

TO MOUNT MORIAH
Secretary Welles' decision to use government funds to mark the beneficiary graves has run a bit ahead of the story, because by 1867 the Asylum's cemetery had moved—again. Commodore Morgan's

forecast of space for eight hundred burials in the new cemetery established in 1845 proved to be hopelessly optimistic. In the latter months of 1861 the Asylum's then-governor, Commodore George C. Read, reported that three-quarters of the cemetery space had already been used for graves. The cemetery was still expected to accommodate both the Asylum beneficiaries and patients who died at the Philadelphia Naval Hospital. Add to this, the commandants of the Philadelphia Navy Yard were in the habit of sending the bodies of sailors who died at the yard, or on one of the ships based there, out to the Asylum cemetery for burial. It was a practice much resented and vigorously, if unavailingly, resisted by the Asylum's governors, haunted as they were by the finite limits of the existing cemetery.

Two and a half years after Read's pessimistic report the situation was worse. Read's successor as governor, Commodore Frederick Engle, had been compelled by lack of room for additional burials to start a new line of graves in space that had been intended as a walkway through the cemetery. To complicate the situation further, a separate building had recently been authorized for the naval hospital; the site selected would impinge on the 1845 cemetery. Rather than attempting to expand the cemetery parallel with Sutherland Avenue, Engle suggested that the government purchase a burial site away from the Asylum grounds, one which would provide ample space for the Asylum beneficiaries, as well as the dead from the hospital and ships at the Navy Yard. Admiral Joseph Smith authorized Engle to explore the options.

What happened next is not part of the written record and can only be inferred. Commodore Engle would have moved in the same social circles in Philadelphia as members of the board of directors of the Mount Moriah Cemetery Association. Some off-the-record conversations clearly must have occurred, because three months later Engle, without any preliminaries, sent Admiral Smith a formal proposal to purchase a portion of Mount Moriah Cemetery as a new burial site. Mount Moriah, established in 1855 by an act of the Pennsylvania General Assembly, was typical of a new type of cemetery being founded all across the United States in the early and mid-nineteenth century. It was not owned by a church or government body, but by a corporation set up for the express purpose of providing a burial facility. These new cemeteries departed from the old burial grounds, with their densely packed and regimented rows of graves, by featuring a picturesque setting for burials—winding roads and paths, elaborate landscaping, and a variety of artistic (and expensive) monuments and memorials designed to advertise the socio-economic status of those buried beneath them. The cemetery had become a park and a destination. On a Sunday one or one's family might stroll or drive through the cemetery to admire the landscaping and the monuments; pause to picnic on the grounds; or, for those of more morose disposition, to reflect on human mortality and its implications.

Although such cemeteries are often referred to generically as *garden cemeteries*, cemetery historians would more accurately classify Mount Moriah as a *lawn-park cemetery*, descended in design inspiration from Cincinnati's Spring Grove Cemetery. The *lawn-park* cemetery departed in plan from the earlier so-called *rural* cemetery, of which Cambridge's Mount Auburn was an inspirational example. The latter—the *rural* cemetery—was densely landscaped with many trees and shrubs, featured sharply curving roads and surprise vistas. The newer *lawn-park* cemetery displayed a more open and manicured appearance, although the winding roads and status-advertising mausoleums were prominent features of both types of cemeteries.

After some haggling over the price, the Bureau of Yards and Docks agreed to purchase ten-plus acres of Mount Moriah Cemetery for $9,500. Mount Moriah is a large cemetery of 380 acres straddling Cobbs Creek, the boundary between Philadelphia and Delaware Counties. The Asylum's plot, now officially known as the Mount Moriah Cemetery Naval Plot, is located at the far northwestern edge of the Delaware County portion of the cemetery. Its open ground falls off at first gradually and then, when it reaches the wooded bluff along Cobbs Creek, more steeply toward the water. This nearby creek initially alarmed Admiral Smith, who imagined grave robbers ascending it in search of fresh beneficiary cadavers to supply Philadelphia's numerous medical students. Not so, replied Commodore Engle: shallow and rock-strewn Cobbs Creek was not navigable even with small boats; moreover, there were many and less well-protected cemeteries much nearer Philadelphia that would be more attractive sites for cadaver hunters in search of fresh burials.

Admiral Smith authorized Engle to select a competent person to lay out the new Asylum plot. Engle chose G. M. Hopkins, a Philadelphia civil engineer who also worked at Laurel Hill Cemetery. Hopkins produced a plan in the fashionable lawn-park cemetery tradition, with winding roads, ornamental trees, and a summer house on the bluff overlooking Cobbs Creek. All this was more than Admiral Smith, the frugal New Englander, was prepared to accept. (It might be noted here that Smith had given Engle complete discretion in selecting an engineer and developing a plan—discretion that, when exercised, failed to meet Smith's after-the-fact approval.) The winding roads, the new trees, and the summer house on the bluff were all rejected by Smith. The admiral grudgingly authorized an "arbor or resting place" on the bluff, but it appears that this was never constructed. A much simpler plan was thereupon adopted, calling for the beneficiary graves to be clustered in an angle in the southern boundary of the naval plot.[2]

With the ground purchased and its internal layout determined, Commodore Engle's next administrative challenge was to move the bodies from the 1845 cemetery to the new site at Mount Moriah. That move would not occur without further interventions by Joseph Smith. Timing of the move was one concern. The old cemetery needed to be cleared during the winter of 1865–66 in anticipation of the construction of the new naval hospital building, but rain, snow, and freezing temperatures might then complicate the task. In mid-December 1865, Engle spent two days at Mount Moriah staking off the lines of graves. They were to be three feet apart, center to center, with a separation of three feet between the foot of the graves in one row and the tombstones in the next adjacent row.

That, of course, presumed that Engle would be moving individual bodies, the identities of which could be verified. Someone—perhaps one of the long-term residents of the Asylum—told the governor that when the bodies were moved from the old burial ground in 1846, the disarticulated skeletons had been placed in one large common grave and markers set up to give the faux impression of individual graves. Was this the case? Engle could not be sure. "I am working in the dark," he complained. No record exists of what was found when the graves were actually opened. The best inference to be drawn is that the report of the large common grave was erroneous, because when the bodies were reburied at Mount Moriah each was placed in an individual grave with an individual tombstone.

Engle proposed to use Philadelphia undertaking contractors to move the bodies, and sought competitive bids. These came in higher than suited fiscally conservative Admiral Smith. Could not the Asylum staff just hire some low-wage Irish laborers and do the job themselves without a contractor? Commodore Engle priced this option out, but he was clearly not enthusiastic. After some haggling back and forth, Engle proposed (and Smith agreed) to accept the bid of one John Hutcheson, whom Engle had negotiated down to a price of seven dollars and seventy-five cents for each body moved.

Repeated searches at the National Archives have failed to turn up the executed version of Hutcheson's contract. The terms must be inferred from the surviving preliminary drafts. These required Hutcheson to dig trenches along the line of the graves at the Asylum cemetery, remove the bodies, repair damaged coffins (or provide new ones in case the existing ones were completely decayed or bodies had been buried without coffins), and load the coffins, each accompanied by its tombstone, on wagons for transportation to Mount Moriah Cemetery, approximately three miles away. At Mount Moriah Hutcheson was to dig the individual graves, place the coffins in them, and lay the tombstone on each grave. After six months, the ground, which would have settled over the individual graves, was to be filled, leveled, and sodded, and the tombstones set upright. Meanwhile, back at the Asylum cemetery, the old graves were to be refilled and ground leveled.

The contractual requirements are clear, but little is known about the actual move of the bodies. The Asylum's log, which is typically a rich source for all which was going on about the institution, is uncharacteristically taciturn during this period. There is not even a mention of when the work began or was concluded. The event was also a great opportunity for any enthusiast in the burgeoning popularity of glass-plate photography, but if any photographs were taken, they have either not survived or they have eluded research for *Ungentle Goodnights*. What is known is this: the bodies did get moved to, and reinterred at, Mount Moriah. The work was apparently carried out in late January and early February of 1866. There turned out to be 351 bodies: 298 beneficiaries and 53 sailors and Marines who had died at the hospital or had been sent out to the Asylum from the Navy Yard. Some graves at the Asylum cemetery contained two coffins, one placed above the other. What had not been anticipated was that many of the graves were deeper than expected. Engle had assured Hutcheson that none of the graves went more than seven feet below ground level, but 132 were found, on actual excavation, to be ten feet deep. In the long tradition of

low-bid contractors, Hutcheson claimed that the additional excavation caused him to lose money on his contract, and he billed an
extra two dollars and twenty-five cents for each ten-foot grave.

By 1866 the remains of some of the earlier beneficiaries had
been exhumed and reburied twice. The removals to Mount Moriah
and the new burials there were meant to be permanent interments.
However constrained their lives may have been by circumstance,
however rough and sometimes eccentric had been their responses
and their adaptations to the lives in which they found themselves,
these veterans had done an essential, often difficult and dangerous, job for the country of their birth or their adoption. Sailor and
Marine, they deserved to be buried with respect and their burial
place to be maintained with care by the nation. They themselves
expected no less.

SEEKING THE OLD MEN TODAY

By the time I first visited Mount Moriah in 1990, the once beautiful and fashionable cemetery had fallen upon evil days, and I watched its continued deterioration each time I visited there over the next two decades. Mount Moriah had been in a slow death spiral since around the middle of the twentieth century. As with many formerly popular and well-maintained private cemeteries established in the nineteenth century, Mount Moriah had suffered from changing times. Reserved capital, in the form of perpetual-care funds, proved inadequate to meet rising costs of cemetery maintenance. Income from new burials, money that might have been used to fill the gap, declined as the demographics of the neighborhood changed. Neglect and vandalism were rampant. Mausoleums that once had had grillwork gates and stained-glass windows had been bricked up for their protection. Statues and monuments stood mutilated and defaced. Gravestones had toppled or were missing. Some sections were so overgrown that it was impossible to find the graves, even if one were willing to risk the ticks and the poison ivy that lay in wait. Under-protected Mount Moriah was a convenient spot to dump old tires and other unwanted waste. The bodies of at least two murder victims had been found on the grounds—one in the trunk of a burning car. Prostitutes judged the place a convenient spot to meet their clients.

More recently much has changed for the better. Mount Moriah Cemetery formally ceased operation as a business in March 2011. Horatio Jones, the last known member of the Mount Moriah Cemetery Association, has been dead since 2004. The Friends of Mount Moriah Cemetery—an organization of individuals and

families who have relatives buried there and others who are concerned about the preservation of Philadelphia's historic burial
places—serves as the chief advocate for the cemetery. Prompted by
community outrage over Mount Moriah's deplorable condition,
volunteers under the vigorous leadership of the Friends' president,
Paulette Rhone, meet on-site regularly to work at the daunting task
of rolling back the decades of neglect and restoring the place to a
presentable appearance. Much remains to be done. Certain burial
plots were sold outright to Philadelphia churches and fraternal
organizations. Some of these organizations continue their responsibility and keep their plots well maintained. In 2014 the Orphans'
Court Division of Philadelphia's Court of Common Pleas declared
Mount Moriah Cemetery Association to be defunct and the property in receivership. The not-for-profit Mount Moriah Cemetery
Preservation Corporation—created in December 2012 by the City
of Philadelphia and the Borough of Yeadon (in which the portion
of Mount Moriah west of Cobbs Creek is located)—is the
court-appointed receiver for the property. The long-term legal and
preservation fate of Mount Moriah Cemetery is a continuing story.

There are few, if any, signs to help find the way, but if one is
interested, intuitive, and adventurous enough, he or she can wind
through the cemetery's rutted roads to reach a well-groomed and
peaceful place—the Mount Moriah Cemetery Naval Plot. These
are the ten-plus acres purchased by the federal government in the
1860s and maintained today as part of the national cemetery system administered by the U.S. Department of Veterans Affairs.
Graves that are the last resting places of men who died in the
Philadelphia Naval Hospital and of other Navy veterans occupy
the larger part of the site. The tomb of Commodore Jesse Duncan
Elliott, the most prominent officer buried at Mount Moriah, sits
isolated in an open field, almost as if the much-maligned and
enigmatic man were being shunned by the other dead.

In one pleasant tree-shaded corner is the destination that I
seek on my field trips—the Asylum burials. Here are six hundred
forty-four graves in twenty-four rows. Most are marked by tombstones, although the identities of some of the individuals in particular graves have been lost and these burials are marked by stones
with the single word *Unknown*. Other stones have been so eroded
by time and acid rain that names and dates legible in 1990 no longer can be deciphered. The site presents the customary regimented

The Naval Asylum Plot at Mount Moriah Cemetery. PHOTOGRAPH BY SHARON MCKEE

appearance that one associates with national cemeteries. Still, there is sufficient diversity among the tombstones—a few with privately erected markers, others a record of changing styles in government-issue tombstones—to catch the eye and arouse the interest of the visitor. Given the number of times the earlier burials and their associated markers have been moved, one cannot be absolutely certain that the body under a particular stone is that of the sailor or Marine whose name is on the marker, but collectively the Asylum's dead are all present and accounted for at this, their final muster, their graves carefully and respectfully tended.

The well-maintained condition of the Asylum burial plot is no accident. Another energetic and dedicated volunteer, Samuel A. Ricks, leads a corps of interested individuals who have discovered unmarked Asylum graves, identified correctly many of the men buried under stones marked *Unknown*, insured that the graves of Medal of Honor recipients are appropriately marked, compiled an accurate listing of all burials in each row of the site, and sustained vigorous citizen oversight on the Department of Veterans Affairs to make sure that the agency fulfills its responsibilities to the long-dead sailors and Marines buried here.

On a warm spring or fall day, one with a bright blue sky, I like to walk among the graves. The grass is neatly mowed. Peaceful quiet belies the Naval Plot's urban location, although the tallest buildings of Philadelphia's skyline are visible through gaps in the trees. Mount Moriah's Naval Plot is a good place to sit and think about what is important in the individual human experience. While writing this book, I have often come here to do so. I meet old acquaintances whom I know only from the archived paper records of their eventful lives. The thought is hardly original to me, but no one is truly dead so long as someone remembers that person. My hope is that *Ungentle Goodnights* will introduce these men who served their country long and well to those who—now and in the future—explore with keen interest the story of the nineteenth-century United States Navy.

Sailors of Color in the Pre–Civil War U.S. Navy

The specific numbers for estimates of men of color—persons of African and African-mixed ethnicity—in the pre–Civil War U.S. Navy and their sources are:

- U.S. War of 1812 general enlisted naval force: 9.7 percent. Ira Dye's computer tabulations of maritime prisoners of war in England (now at the USS *Constitution* Museum, Boston) as revised by Christopher McKee.
- U.S. War of 1812 naval enlisted force on the Great Lakes: 21.1 percent. Public Archives of Canada, British Military Records, "C" Series, Record Group 8, Volumes 694A and 694B, "General Entry Book of American Prisoners of War at Quebec."
- Naval recruits at Boston, June 1837–April 1839: 9.1 percent. United States National Archives in Washington, DC, Record Group 45, Subject File, Class NR, Surgeon Robert J. Dodd, USN, Examination reports on naval recruits at Boston, 28 June–14 August 1837, 22 December 1837–3 January 1838, 14 January–18 April 1839.
- Sailors in receiving ship *Ohio*, 1843–44: 6.6 percent. United States National Archives in Washington, DC, Record Group 45, Muster Rolls (Loose), "Semi-Annual Return and Descriptive list of Recruits received from the Naval Rendezvous at Boston and other Stations on board the U.S. Rec'g Ship 'Ohio,'" 1 July–31 December 1843, 1 January–30 June 1844.

- Service-wide naval enlistments, summer 1858: 5.2 percent. United States National Archives in Washington, DC, Record Group 24, Weekly Returns of Enlistments at Naval Rendezvous, July–September 1858, with returns for the week ending 3 July 1858 missing for these recruiting stations: Baltimore, Boston, New York, and Philadelphia.

Because of the fragmentary nature of the sources cited, these figures should be regarded as indicative rather than definitive.

NOTES

CHAPTER ONE. REFUGE ON THE SCHUYLKILL

1. Suellen Hoy, *Chasing Dirt: The American Pursuit of Cleanliness* (New York: Oxford University Press, 1995), especially pp. 13–15.
2. Dennis Clark, "'Ramcat' and Rittenhouse Square: Related Communities," in *The Divided Metropolis: Social and Spatial Dimensions of Philadelphia, 1800–1975*, ed. by William W. Cutler and Howard Gillette, pp. 125–140 (Westport, CT: Greenwood, 1980); Emma Jones Lapsansky, *South Street Philadelphia, 1762–1854: "A Haven for Those Low in the World"* (Ann Arbor: University Microfilms, 1975).

CHAPTER TWO. LIFE'S EBB TIDE

1. *Niles' Weekly Register*, 7 April 1827.
2. Library of Congress, Rodgers Family Papers, box III:2: Charles W. Goldsborough to John Rodgers, 9 April 1815.
3. Charles W. Goldsborough, *The United States' Naval Chronicle* (Washington, 1824), p. 301; Jeffrey A. Cohen and Charles E. Brownell, *The Architectural Drawings of Benjamin Henry Latrobe* (New Haven: Yale University Press, 1994), 2:538–551.
4. Harold D. Langley, *A History of Medicine in the Early U.S. Navy* (Baltimore: Johns Hopkins University Press, 1995), pp. 284–289; Leonard D. White, *The Jeffersonians: A Study in Administrative History, 1801–1829* (New York: Macmillan, 1951), pp. 292–296.
5. Reuel Robinson, *History of Camden and Rockport, Maine* (Camden: Camden Pub. Co., 1907), pp. 300–301.
6. The onset of Chase's stroke is well described in United States National Archives in Washington, DC, Record Group 52, *South*

Carolina Medical Journal, 25 May 1861–17 August 1866, at 4 February 1864.

7. United States National Archives in Washington, DC, Record Group 45, Letters Received by the Secretary of the Navy from the Chiefs of Navy Bureaus, 1842–1885: Joseph Smith to William Ballard Preston, 14 August 1849; United States National Archives in Washington, DC, Record Group 71, Letters Received by the Chief, Bureau of Yards and Docks, from Other Persons Connected with the Naval Asylum: A. O. Dayton to Preston, 18 August 1849.

CHAPTER THREE. A ROCKY START

1. Kleiss' pension file is United States National Archives in Washington, DC, Record Group 15, Old Wars Navy Invalid Application #895, but his name has been accidentally omitted from all the indexes to the Old Wars series of pension applications.

2. United States National Archives in Washington, DC, Record Group 45, Letters Received by the Secretary of the Navy from Captains: John Downes to Mahlon Dickerson, 30 June 1836; *Daily Atlas* (Boston), 30 June 1836; *Saturday Morning Transcript* (Boston), 2 July 1836.

3. *Public Ledger* (Philadelphia), 28 March 1838.

4. John H. Schroeder, *Commodore John Rodgers: Paragon of the Early American Navy* (Gainesville: University Press of Florida, 2006), pp. 198–199, 208–209; United States National Archives in Washington, DC, Record Group 45, Area File of the U.S. Navy, 1775–1910, Area 7: John R. Goldsborough to Louis M. Goldsborough, 1 November 1837 and 29 November 1837.

5. *Charleston Daily Courier*, 3 June 1853; *Pennsylvania Inquirer* (Philadelphia), 7 February 1854; *State Gazette* (Trenton), 8 February 1854.

CHAPTER FOUR. THE SHIP COMES ASHORE

1. The most interesting and useful obituary notice of Joseph Smith is in *The New York Times*, 25 February 1877, reprinted from a local Massachusetts paper.

2. Jedediah Dwelley and John F. Simmons, *History of the Town of Hanover, Massachusetts, with Family Genealogies* (Hanover: Town of Hanover, 1910), pp. 31, 34, 35, 57, 154, 167–168, 175, 246, and "Genealogies," pp. 347–349.

3. *Niles' Weekly Register* 7 (1814–15), Supplement, p. 136.

4. Navy Department Library, Hiram Paulding Manuscripts (microfilm): Joseph Smith to Paulding, 10 February 1873.

5. *The Annals of the War, Written by Leading Participants, North and South, Originally Published in the* Philadelphia Weekly Times (Philadelphia: Times Publishing Co., 1879), p. 18; Gideon Welles, *Diary*, edited by Howard K. Beale (New York: W. W. Norton, 1960), 1:214.

6. Richard F. Grimmett [historian of Saint John's] to Christopher McKee, 13 June 2013.

7. *Annals of the War*, pp. 25–26.

8. For the railroad accident—sensational news of the day—Harriet's death, and Joseph's injury see: *Daily National Intelligencer* (Washington), 3 September 1855; *Public Ledger* (Philadelphia), 3 September 1855; *Philadelphia Inquirer*, 3 September 1855; *Charleston Daily Courier*, 3 September 1855; *Centinel of Freedom* (Newark, NJ), 4 September 1855; *Alexandria Gazette*, 4 September 1855; *Worcester Daily Spy*, 5 September 1855.

9. William L. Clements Library, University of Michigan, Smith-Geisinger Collection: Joseph Smith to David Geisinger, 16 and 22 October 1855.

CHAPTER FIVE. A CURIOUS CHARACTER

1. *Maryland Gazette* (Annapolis), 16 February 1797; Dan W. Olds, *William Henry Ridgely (1786–1859): His Ancestors and Descendants* (electronic edition; Spartanburg, SC, 2007), pp. 7–17.

2. Maryland State Archives, Annapolis, Special Collections: St. John's College Matriculation Book, 1789–1860; there are no records for the period 12 December 1804–15 September 1822.

3. William M. Marine, *The British Invasion of Maryland, 1812–1815* (Baltimore, 1913), pp. 196, 418.

4. United States National Archives in Washington, DC, Record Group 45, Letters Received by the Secretary of the Navy from Captains: Thomas Williamson, James M. Greene, and Lewis B. Hunter to Isaac Hull, 28 March 1840.

5. Author's database of punishments in *Ohio* during her Mediterranean cruise under Isaac Hull.

6. *The Sun* (Baltimore), 20 August 1862; Ancestry.com "Civil War Prisoner of War Records, 1861–1865," Roll of Political Prisoners of War at Fort McHenry; *They Died at Fort Delaware, 1861–1865: Confederate, Union and Civilian*, compiled by Jocelyn P. Jamison

(Delaware City, DE: Fort Delaware Society, 1997), pp. 89–90; civilian deaths were not recorded before 1863.

CHAPTER SIX. DESERVING OLD MEN, ONCE YOUNG

1. Christopher McKee, *A Gentlemanly and Honorable Profession: The Creation of the U.S. Naval Officer Corps, 1794–1815* (Annapolis: Naval Institute Press, 1991), pp. 59–65.
2. *The Independent Chronicle* (Boston), 26 January 1815.
3. Morris' pressed service in *Fury* and *Zephyr* cannot be verified in British naval records; possibly he gave a false name the better to avoid recapture if he succeeded in deserting, a recourse at which he seems to have been adept. For *Saratoga's* cruise see *Baltimore Patriot & Evening Advertiser*, 22 November 1814; John A. McManemin, *Captains of the Privateers of the War of 1812* (Spring Lake, NJ: Ho-Ho-Kus Publishing Co., 1994), pp. 316–319; George Coggeshall, *A History of American Privateers and Letters-of-Marque* (New York: C. T. Evans, 1856), p. 307.
4. United States National Archives in Washington, DC, Record Group 233, HR25A–G13.1: Petition of Thomas Scantling to the House of Representatives, 13 January 1837 [i.e., 1838].

CHAPTER SEVEN. THE FEW, THE FORTUNATE

1. *Skin & Bones: Tattoos in the Life of the American Sailor* (Philadelphia: Independence Seaport Museum, 2009), pp. [26]–27; Julie Winch, "'No Common Lot': An African-American Sailor's Half-Century at Sea in the Age of Sail," in *Perspectives on Race, Ethnicity, and Power in Maritime America: Papers from the Conference Held at Mystic Seaport, September 2000*, edited by Glenn S. Gordinier, pp. [38]–49, 156–158 (Mystic, CT: Mystic Seaport, 2005).
2. Dunbar's merchant voyages from United States National Archives at Philadelphia, Record Group 36, Crew Lists for the Port of Philadelphia, 1793–1901, and Record of Arrivals and Clearances, Port of Philadelphia, 1789–1910.
3. David F. Long, *Gold Braid and Foreign Relations: Diplomatic Activities of U.S. Naval Officers, 1798–1883* (Annapolis: Naval Institute Press, 1988), pp. 281–283.
4. U.S. Navy Department, *Official Records of the Union and Confederate Navies in the War of the Rebellion* (Washington, 1894–1922), Series One, 11:535–536.
5. *The Philadelphia Inquirer*, 3 September, 7 September, 21 September 1869; *North American and United States Gazette* (Philadelphia),

4 September, 6 September 1869; *Public Ledger* (Philadelphia), 3 September, 1 October 1869.

6. This behavior is fully documented in Marcia Carlisle's Ph.D. dissertation, *Prostitutes and Their Reformers in Nineteenth Century Philadelphia* (Ann Arbor: University Microfilms, 1982) and in her subsequent article, distilled from the dissertation, "Disorderly City, Disorderly Women: Prostitution in Ante-Bellum Philadelphia," *The Pennsylvania Magazine of History and Biography* 110 (1986): 549–568.

CHAPTER EIGHT. SHIPMATES

1. Louisiana, Secretary of State, Vital Records Office: J. J. Steeg, Birth Certificate for John Francis Strain, 6 November 1865; Family Search, Louisiana, Parish Marriages, 1837–1957; Louisiana, Secretary of State, Vital Records Office: J. J. Steeg, Birth Certificate for Elizabeth and Mary Ellen Strain, 6 November 1865.

2. For typical quarterly accounts of the clothing issues to beneficiaries see United States National Archives in Washington, DC, Record Group 217, Settled Accounts of Navy Paymasters and Pay Agents, 1798–1915, Box 2092 (Robert Pettit), 30 June 1841, 31 December 1841, 31 December 1842.

3. Marcus Rediker, *Between the Devil and the Deep Blue Sea: Merchant Seamen, Pirates, and the Anglo-American Maritime World, 1700–1750* (New York: Cambridge University Press, 1987), pp. 158, 307, says that "as many as" three-quarters of the seamen in the Anglo-American shipping industry, 1700–1750, were literate, "if judged by the standard of the ability to sign one's own name." He then adds an important caution: "There is reason to suspect that the actual proportion of the literate may have been considerably smaller, because not all who could sign their names could read and write." Harry R. Skallerup, *Books Afloat & Ashore: A History of Books, Libraries, and Reading among Seamen during the Age of Sail* (Hamden, CT: Archon Books, 1974), pp. 22–23, 204–205, cites three pieces of evidence that would give a literacy rate of 87 percent to 90 percent among seafarers. Ira Dye, "Early American Merchant Seafarers," American Philosophical Society *Proceedings* 120 (1976):331–360, has a complex analysis of literacy "among early American merchant seamen" (pp. 340–344) based on seamen's protection certificates issued at Philadelphia, 1796–1803, 1812–15. Dye concludes that "functional literacy," defined as the ability at least to sign one's name, ranged between 63 percent and

70 percent of applicants for protection certificates during these years. Rediker's and Dye's are the two conclusions on the subject based on careful statistical analysis. Hester Blum, *The View from the Masthead: Maritime Imagination and Antebellum American Sea Narratives* (Chapel Hill: University of North Carolina Press, 2008), pp. 5, 26–32, conducts no data-analysis of her own, tends to favor Rediker and Skallerup, and asserts a rate of 75 percent to 90 percent literacy among sailors. She then adds an impressionistic factor to support her optimism about lower-deck literacy: the "range and vibrancy" of the "written narratives of sailors themselves," that "testify to the pervasive and powerful cultures of reading and writing at sea."

4. Daughters of the American Revolution, Washington: Ellen M. Howard Bloedorn, Application for Membership, 29 August 1908; Georgetown University Archives, Washington: Alumni Directory card for Angus Wheeler and Ellen M. Howard to David H. Buel, 8 August 1908; *Federal Republican* (Georgetown), 5 August 1814; *Daily National Intelligencer* (Washington), 14 August 1815.

5. *Commercial Advertiser* (New York), 12 May 1829; *Baltimore Patriot & Mercantile Advertiser*, 30 April 1830; *City Gazette and Commercial Daily Advertiser* (Charleston), 25 June 1831; *Alexandria Gazette*, 26 August 1831; *New York American*, 31 May 1833.

6. U.S. Bureau of Naval Personnel, *The History of the Chaplain Corps, United States Navy*, compiled by Clifford M. Drury [and others] (Washington, 1948–), 1:249–250.

CHAPTER NINE. WHAT SHALL WE DO WITH THE DRUNKEN SAILOR?

1. United States National Archives in Washington, DC, Record Group 125, Records of General Courts-Martial and Courts of Inquiry of the Navy Department, Case 981 (Robert E. Johnson).

2. For newspaper accounts of this battle see *Cabinet* (Schenectady), 5 March 1828; *Baltimore Gazette and Daily Advertiser*, 6 March 1828; *National Gazette* (Philadelphia), 11 March 1828; *New-York Daily Advertiser*, 8 April 1828.

3. United States National Archives in Washington, DC, Record Group 45, Contracts, 1794–1842, 13:251–253; "Remarks on the United States Standard of Specific Gravity for Indicating the Strength of Alcohol and on the Official Hydrometer," *The American Journal of Pharmacy* 28 (1856):209–212.

4. George Jones, *Sketches of Naval Life* (New Haven, 1829), 1:101; private collection: Joseph Smith, "Standing Orders," *Ohio*, 24 December 1838.

5. United States National Archives in Washington, DC, Record Group 45, Corporal Punishment and the Spirit Ration: Reports of Officers, 1850, National Archives Microfilm Publication T829: 451.

6. The following paragraphs are summarized from a recent meta-analysis of a large body of specialized studies: Peter A. Bamberger and Samuel B. Bacharach, *Retirement and the Hidden Epidemic: The Complex Link between Aging, Work Disengagement, and Substance Misuse—and What to Do about It* (New York: Oxford University Press, 2014).

7. James M. Hoppin, *Life of Andrew Hull Foote, Rear-Admiral United States Navy* (New York: Harper, 1874), pp. 56–57; Spencer C. Tucker, *Andrew Foote: Civil War Admiral on Western Waters* (Annapolis: Naval Institute Press, 2000), pp. 42–44.

CHAPTER TEN. "A HOUSE OF REFUGE FOR EXOTIC MALEFACTORS"

1. United States National Archives in Washington, DC, Record Group 233, HR28A–G14.3: Petition of Richard Bland Randolph, referred to the Committee on Naval Affairs, 30 December 1844.

2. William M. Marine, *The British Invasion of Maryland, 1812–1815* (Baltimore, 1913), p. 467.

CHAPTER ELEVEN. HARD LIVES, TOLLS COLLECTED

1. General Order, 6 June 1843, pasted in United States National Archives in Washington, DC, Record Group 52, Medical Journals of Shore Stations, Philadelphia Naval Hospital, 1 July 1843–8 February 1844.

2. Research on nineteenth-century sailor health has tended to focus on medical histories of individual voyages or on categorizing admissions to hospitals serving mariners. Examples of these approaches include: Guenter B. Risse, "Britannia Rules the Seas: The Health of Seamen, Edinburgh, 1791–1800," *Journal of the History of Medicine and Allied Sciences* 43 (1988):426–446; J. Worth Estes and Ira Dye, "Death on the *Argus*: American Medical Malpractice *versus* British Chauvinism in the War of 1812," *Journal of the History of Medicine and Allied Sciences* 44 (1989):179–195;

Estes, "Stephen Maturin and Naval Medicine in the Age of Sail," in Dean King [and others], *A Sea of Words: A Lexicon and Companion for Patrick O'Brian's Seafaring Tales* (New York: Henry Holt, 1995), pp. 37–56; Estes, *Naval Surgeon: Life and Death at Sea in the Age of Sail* (Canton, MA: Science History Publications, 1998); G. C. Cook, "Disease in the Nineteenth-Century Merchant Navy: The Seaman's Hospital Society's Experience," *The Mariner's Mirror* 87 (2001):460–471; Cook, "Medical Disease in the Merchant Navies of the World in the Days of Sail: The Seaman's Hospital Society's Experience," *The Mariner's Mirror* 91 (2005):46–51. More attuned to life-span health issues is Merja-Liisa Hinkkanen, "When the AB Was Able-Bodied No Longer: Accidents and Illnesses among Finnish Sailors in British Ports, 1882–1902," *International Journal of Maritime History* 8 (1996): 87–104. William D. Stevens and Jonathan M. Leader, "Skeletal Remains from the Confederate Naval Sailor and Marines' Cemetery, Charleston, SC," *Historical Archaeology*, vol. 40, no. 3 (2006): 74–88, documents what can be learned about sailor health when one has forensic access to the bodies of deceased seafarers.

3. United States National Archives in Washington, DC, Record Group 45, Muster Rolls (Loose), "Semi-Annual Return and Descriptive list of Recruits received from the Naval Rendezvous at Boston and other Stations on board the U.S. Rec'g Ship 'Ohio,'" 1 July–31 December 1843, 1 January–30 June 1844; United States National Archives in Washington, DC, Record Group 24, Weekly Returns of Enlistments at Naval Rendezvous, July–September 1858, with returns for the week ending 3 July 1858 missing for these recruiting stations: Baltimore, Boston, New York and Philadelphia.

4. Harold D. Langley, *Social Reform in the United States Navy, 1798–1862* (Urbana: University of Illinois Press, 1967), pp. 172–174; Christopher McKee, *Edward Preble: A Naval Biography, 1761–1807* (Annapolis: Naval Institute Press, 1972), p. 153; McKee, *A Gentlemanly and Honorable Profession: The Creation of the U.S. Naval Officer Corps, 1794–1815* (Annapolis: Naval Institute Press, 1991), pp. 438–439; Paul A. Gilje, *To Swear Like a Sailor: Maritime Culture in America, 1750–1850* (New York: Cambridge University Press, 2016), p. 32. The most recent comprehensive examination of the subject is B. R. Burg, "Sodomy, Masturbation, and Courts-Martial in the Antebellum American Navy," *Journal of the History of Sexuality* 23 (2014):53–78.

5. United States National Archives in Washington, DC, Record Group 24, *Plymouth* Log, 13 and 15 February 1849.

6. *The Naval War of 1812: A Documentary History*, William S. Dudley [and others], editors (Washington: Naval Historical Center, 1985–), 2:71.

7. John K. Mahon, *History of the Second Seminole War, 1835–1842* (Gainesville: University of Florida Press, 1967), pp. 198–199.

8. Mahon, *Second Seminole War*, pp. 226–230.

9. Mahon, *Second Seminole War*, p. 232.

CHAPTER TWELVE. MINDS DECAYED, MINDS DISORDERED

1. Peter A. Bamberger and Samuel B. Bacharach, *Retirement and the Hidden Epidemic: The Complex Link between Aging, Work Disengagement, and Substance Misuse—and What to Do about It* (New York: Oxford University Press, 2014), pp. 126–127, 130.

2. Ira Dye's War of 1812 prisoner-of-war database, now at the USS *Constitution* Museum, Boston.

3. United States National Archives in Washington, DC, Record Group 52, Letters Received by the Bureau of Medicine and Surgery, 1842–1856, Surgeons and Assistant Surgeons: Thomas Williamson to Thomas Harris, 3 June 1844.

4. United States National Archives in Washington, DC, Record Group 52, Medical Journals of Shore Stations, Norfolk Naval Hospital, 28 February 1842–11 September 1842, 12 September 1842–13 March 1843, 15 March 1843–24 July 1843, 8 August 1843–25 April 1844, January 1848–December 1849.

5. Andrew Scull, *Madness in Civilization: A Cultural History of Insanity from the Bible to Freud, from the Madhouse to Modern Medicine* (Princeton: Princeton University Press, 2015), pp. 160–161, 202–208.

6. United States National Archives in Washington, DC, Record Group 45, Letters Received by the Secretary of the Navy from Captains: Jesse Wilkinson to John Y. Mason, 6 July 1844, enclosing Thomas Williamson to Wilkinson, 6 July 1844; for the location and dimensions of the twelve basement cells at the extremities of the Norfolk hospital's two wings see United States National Archives at College Park, MD, Record Group 71, Architectural & Engineering Plans of Naval Shore Facilities: 551–31–154.

7. Sources for Randolph's life are scattered in many places; for that reason, they will be cited in the notes that follow in more detail than for most beneficiaries whose lives are sketched in *Ungentle*

Goodnights. General sources include: Wassell Randolph, *Henry Randolph I (1623–1773) of Henrico County, Virginia, and His Descendants* (Memphis: Crossitt Library, 1952), pp. 63–65, supplemented by Ancestry.com "Virginia Marriages, 1740–1850"; Library of Congress, Rodgers Family Papers, box III:22: Richard Bland Randolph to John Rodgers, 22 March 1814; United States National Archives in Washington, DC, Record Group 15, Old Wars Navy Invalid application, #774Rej; United States National Archives in Washington, DC, Record Group 45, Subject File of the U.S. Navy, 1775–1910, Class MC, where his file is incorrectly marked Richard *Roland* Randolph; United States National Archives in Washington, DC, Record Group 233, HR28A–G14.3: Petition of Richard Bland Randolph; "An Eventful Life," *Milwaukie Daily Sentinel*, 7 February 1846.

8. National Archives, United Kingdom, Admiralty Records 36/16398; National Archives, United Kingdom, Admiralty Records 36/16399; National Archives, United Kingdom, Admiralty Records 36/17150 (*Osprey* muster books); National Archives, United Kingdom, Admiralty Records 51/1373 (*Osprey* log); National Archives, United Kingdom, Admiralty Records 36/13809 (*Malta* muster book).

9. *Republican Advocate* (Frederick, MD), 27 January 1804; *The Farmer's Cabinet* (Amherst, NH), 7 February 1804; *City Gazette* (Charleston, SC), 30 April 1804; *Poulson's American Daily Advertiser* (Philadelphia), 13 September 1804.

10. College of William and Mary, Earl Gregg Swem Library, Tyler Family Papers: Richard B. Randolph to Julia Tyler, 29 June 1844.

11. United States National Archives in Washington, DC, Record Group 45, Letters Received by the Secretary of the Navy from Captains: Jesse Wilkinson to John Y. Mason, 12 August 1844, enclosing Thomas Williamson to Wilkinson, 5 August and 10 August 1844.

12. Details of Randolph's confinement: United States National Archives in Washington, DC, Record Group 52, Medical Journals of Shore Stations, Norfolk Naval Hospital, 8 August 1843–25 April 1844 and April 1844–April 1845.

13. United States National Archives in Washington, DC, Record Group 45, Letters Received by the Secretary of the Navy from Captains: Jesse Wilkinson to George Bancroft, 28 April 1845.

14. United States National Archives in Washington, DC, Record Group 45, Miscellaneous Letters Sent: George Bancroft to William

W. Seaton, 30 April 1845; United States National Archives in Washington, DC, Record Group 21, Criminal Court of the District of Columbia, Criminal Appearances, 1844–1861, Ex parte Richard B. Randolph, 2 January and 8 January 1846; J. H. Goddard to Marshal of the District of Columbia, 1 May 1845; Minutes of the U.S. Circuit Court for the District of Columbia, 3 May 1845; *Daily National Intelligencer* (Washington), 5 May 1845, 5 and 9 January 1846; *Sun* (Baltimore), 9 January 1846.

15. William L. Clements Library, University of Michigan: Charity Hospital (New Orleans), Lunatic Asylum admission book, 1841–48.

CHAPTER THIRTEEN. LEAVING ASYLUM

1. Principal sources for the life of Thomas Dennis: United States National Archives in Washington, DC, Record Group 15: Old Wars Navy Invalid Application #443; United States National Archives in Washington, DC, Record Group 233, HR31A-G12.2: Petition of Thomas Dennis to the House of Representatives, 5 January 1850; United States National Archives in Washington, DC, Record Group 46, SEN31A-H12.1: Petition of Dennis to the Senate, 5 January 1850; United States National Archives in Washington, DC, Record Group 21, Circuit Court for the District of Columbia: Dennis, Declaration of intention, 24 May 1854; United States National Archives in Washington, DC, Record Group 59: Dennis, Application for passport, 19 June 1900; United States National Archives in Washington, DC, Record Group 21, Bankruptcy Case File #45 (Thomas Dennis); Anatoly Demidov, *Étapes Maritimes sur les Côtes d'Espagne, de la Catalogne à l'Andalousie; Souvenirs d'un Voyage Exécuté en 1847* (Florence, 1858), 2: 180–182, 191–192, 371; *Register of Officers and Agents, Civil, Military, and Naval, in the Service of the United States* (Washington, 1853–77); *Official Register of the United States* (Washington, 1879–1905); Newberry Library, Chicago: Cook County Birth Index, 1871–1916; *The Lakeside Annual Directory of the City of Chicago* (Chicago, 1879–93); *The Union* (Washington), 25 October 1847; *Evening Star* (Washington), 2 July 1859, 20 September 1859, 6 October 1865, 15 September 1866, 17 September 1866, 9 September 1878, 4 January 1886, 7 October 1893, 30 September 1901, 26 July 1902, 18 July 1903, 27 October 1904, 24 July 1908; *National Republican* (Washington), 6 October 1865, 20 April 1868;

Daily National Intelligencer (Washington), 28 September 1868; *Washington Post*, 6 June 1899; *Washington Times*, 18 January 1903; *New York Tribune*, 19 July 1903; *Washington Herald*, 29 July 1908; Charles Brodine, photographs of Dennis family tomb, Congressional Cemetery, Washington, DC.

2. United States National Archives in Washington, DC, Record Group 21, Index to Naturalization Records of the U.S. Supreme Court for the District of Columbia, 1802–1909.

3. United States National Archives in Washington, DC, Record Group 52, Certificates of Death, 1852–62.

CHAPTER FOURTEEN. VOYAGE'S END

1. United States National Archives in Washington, DC, Record Group 52, Hospital Tickets and Case Papers, Boxes 141–151, conveniently available on Ancestry.com as "U.S. Naval Hospital Tickets and Case Papers."

2. Notice of funeral arrangements in the *Public Ledger* (Philadelphia), 7 December 1872.

3. Ancestry.com, "Pennsylvania Wills and Probate Records, 1683–1993": Philadelphia, 24 June 1867.

4. Peter A. Bamberger and Samuel B. Bacharach, *Retirement and the Hidden Epidemic: The Complex Link between Aging, Work Disengagement, and Substance Misuse—and What to Do about It* (New York: Oxford University Press, 2014), p. 8.

5. United States National Archives in Washington, DC, Record Group 127, Letters Sent by the Commandant of the Marine Corps, 13:21–22.

6. U.S. Office of Naval Records and Library, *Naval Documents Related to the United States Wars with the Barbary Powers* (Washington, 1939–44), 3:424.

7. *New York Daily Times*, 20 November 1854; *Public Ledger* (Philadelphia), 18 November 1854, 30 January 1855.

CHAPTER FIFTEEN. SAFE HARBOR—FINALLY FOUND

1. For the larger social and design contexts in which the Naval Asylum's successive burying grounds/cemeteries were situated see David Charles Sloane, *The Last Great Necessity: Cemeteries in American History* (Baltimore: Johns Hopkins University Press, 1991). A useful supplement to Sloane's work, particularly for its images, is Marilyn Yalom, *The American Resting Place* (Boston:

Houghton Mifflin, 2008). Thomas W. Laqueur, *The Work of the Dead: A Cultural History of Mortal Remains* (Princeton: Princeton University Press, 2015) offers a masterful synthesis of history, anthropology, sociology, theology, and literature which informs this chapter and the epilogue.

2. United States National Archives at College Park, MD, Record Group 71, Architectural & Engineering Plans of Naval Shore Facilities, 427–2–11 and 427–2–12.

BIBLIOGRAPHY

The Naval Asylum and Its Beneficiaries: A Survey of Sources

This book rests on a database of five hundred forty-one individual profiles for each Marine or sailor who was admitted to the United States Naval Asylum between 4 December 1831 (the first admission) and 4 December 1865 (the last admission of that calendar year). The profiles typically contain dozens of discrete bits of data about that individual, data culled from the Asylum's log, its hospital records, the reports of the institution's governors, pension applications, newspapers, and many other sources. To cite in this book all the sources on which the story of a beneficiary's life is sketched would result in a volume whose block of endnotes is as large as or larger than its narrative text. Because the same sources would be cited repeatedly, such notes would be deadeningly repetitious. To address such problems, this bibliographical essay will describe the principal sources on which this book is based, and the narrative text will contain unobtrusive citations that should enable anyone so inclined to pursue a particular individual or story back to the documentary origins. Endnotes will be used to cite sources unique to a particular story or situation.

The overwhelming majority of the sources for *Ungentle Good-nights* are located in three institutions: the United States National Archives in Washington, DC; the United States National Archives at Philadelphia, PA; and the Special Collections Department of the Nimitz Library, United States Naval Academy in Annapolis, MD.

A. GOVERNANCE
Until 1 July 1849, the leadership of the United States Naval Asylum reported directly to the Secretary of the Navy. During this period

documents relating to the Asylum were filed in one of several different ways. This can make the search for a particular letter or report a tedious process, and one that occasionally ends in failure. Before approximately June 1838, years when the Asylum was the immediate responsibility of the commandant of the Philadelphia Navy Yard, incoming correspondence from those in authority at the Asylum can typically be found in [A1] United States National Archives in Washington, DC, Record Group 45, Records of the Office of Naval Records and Library, Subject File of the U.S. Navy, 1775–1910, in the classes: MA, MC, PB, PN, and PS or in [A2] United States National Archives at Philadelphia, Record Group 181, Records of Naval Districts and Shore Establishments, Philadelphia Navy Yard, Letters Sent to the Secretary of the Navy, 1827–1900, volumes 1 and 2 (1827–1844). This latter series includes copies of the commandant of the Yard's letters to the Secretary of the Navy, but not the enclosures, which usually—but not always—can be found in [A1] the Subject File. Beginning in 1838, with the creation of the office of governor at the Asylum, correspondence from the governors is usually to be found in either [A3] United States National Archives in Washington, DC, Record Group 45, Letters Received by the Secretary of the Navy from Captains ("Captains' Letters"), 1805–1861, 1866–1885, National Archives Microfilm Publication M125 or (depending on the rank of the governor) in [A4] United States National Archives in Washington, DC, Record Group 45, Letters Received by the Secretary of the Navy from Commanders, 1804–1886, National Archives Microfilm Publication M147. In addition, there is a single volume of segregated incoming correspondence: [A5] United States National Archives in Washington, DC, Record Group 45, Letters Received by the Secretary of the Navy Relating to the Naval Asylum, 1848–1850, National Archives Microfilm Publication T829:428.

Outgoing correspondence from the Secretary of the Navy to the governors and others in authority at the Naval Asylum begins with [A6] United States National Archives in Washington, DC, Record Group 45, Letters Sent by the Secretary of the Navy Relating to the Naval Asylum, Naval Hospitals, and the Navy Hospital Fund, 1834–1840. Thereafter letters to the governors are to be found in [A7] United States National Archives in Washington, DC, Record Group 45, Letters Sent by the Secretary of the Navy to Officers ("Officers Ships of War"), 1798–1886, National Archives Microfilm Publication M149.

Not all letters sent by the Asylum's governors can be found among the correspondence received by the Secretary of the Navy [A3, A4, A5]. This is not a serious problem, because almost all of the governors' outgoing communications are also recorded in letterbooks maintained at the Asylum [A8] United States National Archives at Philadelphia, Record Group 24, Records of the Bureau of Naval Personnel, Correspondence with Naval and Federal Officials, Office of the Governor, 1838–1862, and [A9] United States National Archives at Philadelphia, Record Group 24, Letters and Endorsements Sent, Office of the Governor, 1862–1911. These two series, while inventoried separately at the United States National Archives at Philadelphia, actually are a continuum; the only difference between them is that the former series are transcribed copies in letterbooks and the latter series press copies. The former series includes copies of both outgoing and incoming letters until the beginning of the governorship of Charles W. Morgan; commencing with 25 May 1844, both series contain only copies of outgoing letters. No copies of the governor's letters written between 28 November 1860 and 10 May 1861 were entered in [A8], the only discovered gap in this extremely useful series. It should also be noted that enclosures to the governors' letters are not typically entered in these two series [A8, A9] but must be sought (not always successfully) among the original letters in the Secretary of the Navy's incoming correspondence [A3, A4, A5].

With the 1 July 1849 transfer of supervision of the Asylum from the Secretary of the Navy to the Bureau of Yards and Docks records relating to the Asylum become more straightforward and less challenging for the researcher. Incoming correspondence from the governors (including enclosures) is found in [A10] United States National Archives in Washington, DC, Record Group 71, Records of the Bureau of Yards and Docks, Letters Received by the Chief, Bureau of Yards and Docks, from the Governor of the Naval Asylum, 1849–1885. Outgoing communications are in [A11] United States National Archives in Washington, DC, Record Group 71, Letters Sent by the Chief, Bureau of Yards and Docks, to Commandants, 1842–1885, and [A12] Letters Sent by the Chief, Bureau of Yards and Docks, to Miscellaneous Correspondents, 1842–1885. The Asylum's copies of outgoing correspondence [A8, A9] remain useful for the occasional letter from a governor that cannot be located in the files of the Bureau of Yards and Docks [A10, A11]. [A13] United States National Archives at Philadelphia, Record Group 24, Letters Received by the Office of the Governor, U.S. Naval Asylum, from the Bureau of Yards and Docks, 1845–1890, although fragmentary for the earlier years, eventually contains most of the recipient's copies of the Bureau's letters that are also recorded in its letterbooks of outgoing correspondence to commandants [A11].

Other sources containing correspondence relating to the management of the Naval Asylum include [A14] Library of Congress, Washington, DC, Andrew Hull Foote Papers, Letterbook, 1842–1846, covering his first period as executive officer at the Asylum; [A15] Navy Department Library, Washington, DC, personal letters from Joseph Smith to Foote, 1847–1860, with the letters dated between 19 March 1854 and 5 June 1855 covering Foote's second tour of duty as executive officer; [A16] College of William and Mary, Williamsburg, Virginia, Swem Library, Special Collections, James Barron Papers, with a small number of documents from Barron's tenure as governor; [A17] United States National Archives in Washington, DC, Record Group 52, Records of the Bureau of Medicine and Surgery, Letters Received from Officers Not Medical, 1842–1856; [A18] United States National Archives in Washington, DC, Record Group 52, Letters Sent by the Chief, Bureau of Medicine and Surgery, 1842–1886; [A19] United States National Archives in Washington, DC, Record Group 217, Records of the United States General Accounting Office, Miscellaneous Letters Received by the Fourth Auditor of the Treasury, 1795–1897; and [A20] United States National Archives in Washington, DC, Record Group 217, Miscellaneous Letters Sent by the Fourth Auditor of the Treasury, 1800–1896.

The Asylum is rarely mentioned in the yearly reports of the Secretary of the Navy through 1848: [A21] U.S. Navy Department, *Annual Report of the Secretary of the Navy* (Washington, 1821–1948). Beginning with the report for 1849, information about the Naval Asylum is included in the reports of the Chief of the Bureau of Yards and Docks, appended to the Secretary of the Navy's annual report. The Bureau's reports become increasingly discursive and more useful to the historian until the Civil War years. From then on, the narrative content of the annual reports on the affairs of the Asylum is brief and stereotyped; the documents are useful primarily for statistical data such as the categories and numbers of civilian employees. This situation continues until the report for 1881, when the narrative and evaluative content of the document again becomes substantial.

The first regulations governing the Asylum were issued by Secretary of the Navy Levi Woodbury in May 1834. They can most conveniently be found in [A22] *Letter from the Secretary of the Navy, Transmitting Rules and Regulations, Recently Prepared, in Regard to the Naval Asylum Near Philadelphia*, 15 May 1834, 23d Congress, 1st Session, House of Representatives, Document 419 (Serial 258); but see also [A1] Subject File, MA: John Rodgers, for Board of Navy Commissioners, to Woodbury, 11 July 1833, for the Commissioners' contribution to the final document. A revised set of regulations was issued by Secretary of the Navy Abel P. Upshur on 20 March 1843: [A23] "Regulations, for the Naval Asylum at Philadelphia," in U.S. Navy Department, General Orders and Circulars, 1798–1862, National Archives Microfilm Publication M977. When supervision of the Naval Asylum was transferred to the Bureau of Yards and Docks in 1849 Commodore Joseph Smith, the bureau chief, immediately issued a new set of "Regulations for the U.S. Naval Asylum," 1 July 1849, a printed sheet, which can be found in [A1] Subject File, PB. Two years later Smith issued a revised version, dated 1 July 1851, copies of which can be found in [A1] Subject File PB, in [A10] Letters Received by the Chief, Bureau of Yards and Docks, from the Governor of the Naval Asylum, enclosure to J. L. Lardner to Daniel Ammen, 8 July 1869, and in [A24] Navy Department Library, ZE File, Philadelphia Naval Home (Naval Asylum).

The Asylum's governors issued their own sets of internal regulations for the institution, similar to the internal regulations they would have issued for ships they had commanded at sea. Although these are all similar in general content, each governor revised the internal regulations to suit his administrative preferences. Research for this book located four such sets of regulations, though it is virtually certain that other governors must have issued their own versions that cannot now be found or that have eluded this historian's search. Those found are: [A25] William W. McKean, "Regulations for the U.S. Naval Asylum," 29 March 1843, in [A8] Correspondence with Naval and Federal Officials; [A26] David Geisinger, "Internal Rules and Regulations of the United States Naval Asylum," 1 July 1851, in [A10] Letters Received by the Chief, Bureau of Yards and Docks, from the Governor of the Naval

Asylum; [A27] George W. Storer, "Regulations for the U.S. Naval Asylum," 28 October 1854, with additions to 14 August 1856, in [A24] Navy Department Library, ZE File, Philadelphia Naval Asylum (Naval Home); and [A28] "Internal Rules and Regulations of the United States Naval Asylum, established by Rear Admiral J. R. M. Mullany, Governor," July 1878, with revisions and corrections to 1 October 1886, in [E4] Edward Hooker, "The U.S. Naval Asylum, A Sketch of Its Origin and History and a Record of Useful Information Regarding It," pp. 307–367.

B. ENVIRONMENT

Fundamental documents for understanding the buildings and grounds of the Naval Asylum are the architectural plans and maps in [B1] RG 71, Records of the Bureau of Yards and Docks, Architectural & Engineering Plans of Naval Shore Facilities, 1820–1966, United States National Archives at College Park, MD. In the former category the floor plans of uncertain date prepared by William Strickland (427–30–1 through 427–30–6) and a set of floor plans annotated by Governor William W. McKean in July 1843 (427–30–8 through 427–30–10) are the most important. Filed with the latter plans is a sheet numbered 427–30–11, which is actually an enclosure to the letter from William C. Nicholson to Joseph Smith, 7 May 1860, in [A10] Letters Received by the Chief, Bureau of Yards and Docks, from the Governor of the Naval Asylum. As with any public building in active use, assignments of space within the structure changed over the years with which *Ungentle Goodnights* is concerned. No attempt is made in this book to track those sometimes difficult to follow reassignments, but only to locate features that remained constant throughout the period, such as the chapel, the dining room/kitchen, and the pensioner quarters. Among the various maps and surveys of the grounds those of 1836 (427–3-1), circa 1844–45 (427–3-2), and January 1878 (unnumbered) were the most useful for this book. *Smedley's Atlas of the City of Philadelphia* (Philadelphia: J. B. Lippincott, 1862) also provides essential and detailed coverage of the Asylum and its environs.

Of almost equal importance with the plans and maps from the archives of the Bureau of Yards and Docks are the records compiled by the [B2] Historic American Buildings Survey (HABS) in the Prints and Photographs Division of the Library of Congress, which can be accessed online at http://www.loc.gov/pictures/collection/hh/.

The HABS documented five structures on the Asylum site, of which the most important for present purposes is William Strickland's Naval Asylum building, identified in the HABS records by its twentieth-century name Biddle Hall. The extensive HABS file on this building includes measured drawings, photographs taken before and after the 3 February 2003 fire, and text documentation. In the latter category the report, "Addendum to U. S. Naval Asylum, Biddle Hall (U.S. Naval Home)," HABS No. PA-1622-A (2003) is the most complete examination of the architecture, construction, and history of the building. Another series of highly useful photographs of the Strickland building, taken by a U.S. Navy photographer in 1944, is found in [B3] U.S. Naval Academy, Nimitz Library, Special Collections and Archives, Transitional Picture File. Among the nineteenth-century artistic representations of the Naval Asylum those by Wild (1838), Köllner (1847), and *Harper's Weekly* (1878) are the most useful as historical records. The author has assembled a file of additional images—stereopticon views, postcards, and photographs—that document the physical appearance of the Naval Asylum into the early twenty-first century.

The correspondence of the Asylum's governors, described in detail in the previous section [A2, A3, A4, A5, A8, A9, A10] is rich with detailed information about the Asylum building, the grounds, and the adjacent areas. For example, the only floor plan showing the development of the Asylum's attic space as living quarters for the beneficiaries is to be found in [A3] Letters Received by the Secretary of the Navy from Captains, as an enclosure to Charles W. Morgan to George Bancroft, 6 July 1846. [A1] Subject File, PN and PS contain important records concerning the Asylum's site and the construction of the Strickland building. Histories of the Asylum by [E1] Shippen, [E2] Stockton, and [E4] Hooker, cited in detail in a later section of this bibliographic essay, include information about the Asylum physical site and facilities not to be found in other records. An early article, [B4] "United States Naval Asylum, near Philadelphia," in *Atkinson's Casket; or, Gems of Literature, Wit and Sentiment*, [Vol. 6], No. 12 (December 1832):553–554, contains information about the building that can only have come from William Strickland himself. The best scholarly assessment of the architect is [B5] Agnes Addison Gilchrist, *William Strickland, Architect and Engineer, 1788–1854* (Philadelphia: University of Pennsylvania Press, 1950). Strickland's work on the Naval Asylum is discussed, documented, and illustrated at pp. 7–8, 14, 41, 73–76, 87–88, 98–100, 105 and plates 15, 16, 17, 36, 37.

C. DAILY LIFE

Some information on day-to-day life at the Asylum can be collected from the correspondence and reports of the governors [A2, A3, A4, A5, A8, A9, A10], but the better sources for activities and routines (as well as unusual events not always reported in the governors' letters) are the governors' internal regulations [A25, A26, A27, A28] and especially [C1] United States National Archives at Philadelphia, Record Group 24, Station Logs, U.S. Naval Asylum/Naval Home, 1842–1942. During research for this book the author read in detail the first five volumes of the log, covering the period 1 October 1842 through 31 December 1876.

D. BENEFICIARIES

Five hundred forty-one residents of the Naval Asylum are the subject of *Ungentle Goodnights*. Consequently, this section of the bibliographical survey, covering information about the institution's beneficiaries and their lives, is necessarily the most complex.

Registers: The first necessary step was to establish a reliable roster of the men who were admitted to the Naval Asylum between 4 December 1831 and 4 December 1865. For this purpose two registers maintained at the institution were essential: [D1] United States National Archives at Philadelphia, Record Group 71, Record of Inmates, U.S. Naval Asylum, 1831–1865. This volume includes all the beneficiaries who are the subjects of this book. The information recorded in its neat columns—age, place of birth, rank at admission, length of service, vessels in which sailed and commanding officers, whether a pensioner, date of admission to the Asylum, date and cause of discharge from the Asylum—is far from complete and individual stories must be expanded (and occasionally corrected) from other sources described below. Each beneficiary in the "Record of Inmates" was assigned a serial number when he was admitted to the Asylum. If a beneficiary left the Asylum for some reason and returned at a later date, he was supposed to be reassigned his old number. This did not always happen. Returning beneficiaries were sometimes given a new number, a practice that occasionally demands some serious detective work by the historian to determine whether this beneficiary and another beneficiary with the same or closely similar name are actually an identical person. This historian has been successful in resolving all these ambiguous cases and can report that, although the Record of Inmates lists 566 numbered beneficiaries, this represents only 541 individual men. In 1866 a new register was begun: [D2] United States National Archives at Philadelphia, Record Group 52, Record of Admissions into the U.S. Naval Asylum, 1841–1898 (2 volumes). All the beneficiaries who were still alive and residents of the Asylum on 1 January 1866 were transferred to the new register (hence the 1841 start date, representing the senior living resident's admission) but were assigned new serial numbers.

Dates of discharge, leaves of absence, and death missing from the registers [D1, D2] can often be supplied from [D3] United States National Archives at Philadelphia, Record Group 71, Naval Asylum Muster Roll of Pensioners and Beneficiaries, 1850–1886, 1894–1897.

Biographies: During the winter of 1854–55 some of the junior officers at the Naval Asylum and Governor George W. Storer's secretary, working under the direction of Commodore Storer, compiled a volume of biographical sketches of 172 of the Asylum's beneficiaries: [D4] "Biography of Beneficiaries United States Naval Asylum Philadelphia," now in [A24] Navy Department Library, ZE File, Philadelphia Naval Home (Naval Asylum). The biographies in this manuscript volume vary widely in length and usefulness. Some sketches (primarily those of deceased beneficiaries) were compiled from the institution's internal records, including a volume or file of the early governors' letters recommending admissions that apparently no longer exists. The most valuable biographies are those taken from the oral testimony of the living beneficiaries themselves.

Applications: Each would-be sailor-beneficiary was required to submit an application that outlined the dates of his service, the ships and shore stations in which he had served, and the names of his commanding officers. These were supplemented by certificates from naval surgeons to the effect that the applicant was no longer able to earn a living by manual labor and sometimes by letters of recommendation from commanding officers or other third parties. These statements of service were then forwarded to the office of the Fourth Auditor of the Treasury (the auditor who handled Navy accounts) for verification of service from the muster rolls and pay rolls on file at that office. For members of the Marine Corps, the required information was typically submitted on a printed form by the adjutant of the Corps. It did not require verification by the office of the Fourth Auditor, as the adjutant's certification of dates of service was considered sufficient evidence.

Finding such applications for the Asylum's beneficiaries is not always an easy task. The earliest ones, through 1840, are in [A1] Subject File, MC. After that, until 1 July 1849, when supervision of the Naval Asylum was transferred from the immediate purview of the Secretary of the Navy to the Bureau of Yards and Docks, applications for admission are typically (but by no means always) to be found in [D5] United States National Archives in Washington, DC, Record Group 45, Miscellaneous Letters Received by the Secretary of the Navy, 1801–1884, National Archives Microfilm Publication M124. No Miscellaneous Letters survive for the year 1847. [A5] Letters Received by the Secretary of the Navy Relating to the Naval Asylum, 1848–1850, also is rich in applications for admission as beneficiaries. Beginning in 1849 applications will be found in [D6] United States National Archives in Washington, DC, Record Group 71, Letters Received by the Chief, Bureau of Yards and Docks, from Other Persons Connected with the Naval Asylum ("Miscellaneous Letters"), 1849–1885. The series of applications for these years is almost complete, although occasionally particular applications cannot be located. Letters from the Bureau to applicants are in [A12] United States National Archives in Washington, DC, Record Group 71, Letters Sent by the Chief, Bureau of Yards and Docks, to Miscellaneous Correspondents, 1842–1885.

If a would-be beneficiary's application was successful, he was given a formal permit of admission to the Asylum. For the Marines and sailors who are the subjects of this book, such permits survive only for the years 1834–1846 in [D7] United States National Archives at Philadelphia, Record Group181, Admission Permits, U.S. Naval Asylum, 1834–1910, with a gap in the series for the years 1847–1875. The admission permits are useful for identifying rank and branch of service of admitted applicants when these data are not on file in [D1] Record of Inmates.

Pensions: A high proportion of the Naval Asylum's beneficiaries either held pensions that they commuted to enter the institution, had applied unsuccessfully for a pension, or resumed (or applied for) pensions after they left the Asylum. Consequently, the pension files in [D8] United States National Archives in Washington, DC, Record Group 15, Records of the Veterans Administration, are a valuable source of biographical data about the Asylum's residents. Almost all of these are or formerly were part of the "Old Wars" series of pension dossiers that embraced military service between the end of the Revolution and the beginning of the Civil War—and occasionally service in the early years of the latter war. Some of these "Old Wars" dossiers have been moved (not always accurately) to the War of 1812 and Mexican War pension files. [D9] Virgil D. White, *Index to Old Wars Pension Files, 1815–1926* (Rev. ed.; Waynesboro, TN: National Historical Pub. Co., 1993) is the easiest—and usually the most reliable—way to determine whether a particular beneficiary has a pension file based on pre–Civil War (or early Civil War) Navy or Marine Corps service. Beneficiary pension dossiers based on Civil War service [D10] are in United States National Archives in Washington, DC, Record Group 15, Civil War and Later Pension Application Files, 1861–1934. This series also includes applications from beneficiaries who may have entered the Naval Asylum before the Civil War but who elected to take advantage of the law of 2 March 1867, which granted pensions—in lieu of residence at the Asylum—to aged or infirm veterans with twenty years of service in the Marine Corps or Navy. On-line searching of this series is available through http://ancestry.com (Ancestry.com) [D11] "U.S. Navy Pensions Index, 1861–1910." Whether a beneficiary's pension application is likely to be found in [D11] Civil War and Later Pension Application Files can be determined and the progress of the application traced in [D12] United States National Archives in Washington, DC, Record Group 24, Register of Pensions Given to U.S. Navy Personnel, 1867–1902. For more detailed information on pension applications and related papers, one should consult [D13] Chapter 7, "Pension Records," pp. 167–177, in United States National Archives and Records Administration, *Guide to Genealogical Research in the National Archives of the United States* (3d ed.; Washington, DC, 2000).

Applying for a Navy or Marine Corps pension was a relatively routine procedure so long as the commanding officer or one of the medical officers of the ship or station on which the injury occurred was still alive or could be located to certify to the service-related injury. Absent such testimony, the would-be pensioner had to apply to Congress in the hope—often vain—of a private law granting him a pension. Such applications from Asylum beneficiaries are found in [D14] United States National Archives in Washington, DC, Record Group 233, Records of the U.S. House of Representatives, and [D15] United States National Archives in Washington, DC, Record Group 46, Records of the U.S. Senate. Petitions could be referred to a variety of Congressional committees and can be elusive to locate. In those cases in which a would-be pensioner's petition is one of the sources for a life sketched in this book, an endnote provides a link to the House or Senate committee file in which the document is to be found.

Marine Corps service: As mentioned above, a record of an enlisted Marine's service was typically provided as a printed form filled in and certified in the office of the adjutant and inspector of the Corps and forwarded to the Navy Department for Asylum admission or to the Pension Office in support of a disability application. Copies of such forms can be found in the various series of Asylum beneficiary and invalid-pensioner applications described above. Absent such forms, Marine Corps service and demographics can usually be established from [D16] United States National Archives in Washington, DC, Record Group 127, Records of the United States Marine Corps, Service Records of Enlisted Men, 1798–1895. Occasionally one's search of this series will fail to locate a particular Marine, in which case the researcher can turn to [D17] United States National Archives in Washington, DC, Record Group 127, Size Rolls, 1798–1901, for much of the same information, though it will be more tedious to extract. Rolls of individual Marine detachments can be found in Ancestry.com [D18] "U.S. Marine Corps Muster Rolls, 1798–1958," an on-line database that can be searched electronically for individual names. This is the least useful of the three sources for Marine Corps service, as the rolls include no demographic data.

Army service: Beneficiaries who served in the U.S. Army as well as the Marine Corps and/or the Navy can be found and traced through Ancestry.com [D19] "U.S. Army, Register of Enlistments, 1798–1914." The on-line database is well indexed for electronic searching.

Demographics: The Asylum's registers [D1, D2] contain data on self-reported ages and places of birth. Variants (and more rarely confirmation) of these data as well as physical descriptions—eye and hair color, height, complexion, and occasionally scars and tattoos—were found in a broad variety of sources. These include, in addition to the just-described Marine Corps records and D55, D56, D57 below:

- [D20] Robert J. Dodd, Surgeon, USN, Examination Reports on Naval Recruits at Boston, 1837–1839, in [A1] Subject File, NR.
- [D21] "Semi-Annual Return and Descriptive list of Recruits received from the Naval Rendezvous at Boston and other Stations on board the U.S. Rec'g Ship 'Ohio,'" July 1843–June 1844, in [D36] United States National Archives in Washington, DC, Record Group 45, Muster Rolls and Payrolls of U.S. Navy Vessels, 1798–1860.
- [D22] United States National Archives in Washington, DC, Record Group 24, Descriptive Lists of Men Entered at the Naval Rendezvous at Baltimore, 1846–1852.
- [D23] United States National Archives in Washington, DC, Record Group 24, Weekly Returns of Enlistments at Naval Rendezvous, 1855–1891, National Archives Microfilm Publication M1953. This series is also available on Ancestry.com as "U.S. Naval Enlistment Rendezvous, 1855–1891."
- [D24] United States National Archives in Washington, DC, Record Group 36, Records of the U.S. Customs Service, Register of Seamen, Baltimore, Maryland, 1808–1867.
- [D25] United States National Archives in Washington, DC, Record Group 36, Abstracts and Copies of Registers of Seamen, Boston and Charlestown, Massachusetts, 1813–1868, 1875.
- [D26] United States National Archives at Boston, Record Group 36, Seamen's Protection Certificate Register, Gloucester, Massachusetts, 1796–1860.
- [D27] United States National Archives at Boston, Record Group 36, Seamen's Protection Certificate Register, New Haven, Connecticut, 1803–1841.
- [D28] United States National Archives at Boston, Record Group 36, Seamen's Protection Certificate Register, New London, Connecticut, 1803–1818.

- [D29] United States National Archives in Washington, DC, Record Group 36, Proofs of Citizenship Used to Apply for Seamen's Protective Certificates for the Port of New Orleans, Louisiana, 1800–1802, 1804–1807, 1809–1812, 1814–1816, 1818–1819, 1821, 1850–1851, 1855–1857, National Archives Microfilm Publication M1826.
- [D30] United States National Archives at Boston, Record Group 36, Seamen's Protection Certificate Register, Newport, Rhode Island, 1812–1834.
- [D31] United States National Archives in Washington, DC, Record Group 36, Register of Seamen's Protection Certificates, Norfolk and Portsmouth, Virginia, 1807, 1813–1869.
- [D32] United States National Archives in Washington, DC, Record Group 36, Proofs of Citizenship Used to Apply for Seamen's [Protection] Certificates for the Port of Philadelphia, Pennsylvania, 1792–1861, National Archives Microfilm Publication M1880.
- [D33] *Register of Seaman's Protection Certificates from the Providence, Rhode Island, Custom District, 1796–1870, from the Custom House Papers in the Rhode Island Historical Society* (Baltimore: Clearfield, 1995).
- [D34] United States National Archives at Boston, Seamen's Protection Certificate Register, Salem, Massachusetts, 1797–1832.

Muster and pay rolls: Essential in many cases for verifying service and ratings asserted by Navy beneficiaries, these records are maintained at the United States National Archives in Washington, DC, in three discrete and chronologically overlapping series, commencing with [D35] Record Group 45, Muster Rolls and Payrolls of U.S. Navy Vessels, 1798–1860. A complete listing of the available rolls can be found in [D36] National Archives and Records Administration, *Inventory of the Naval Records Collection of the Office of Naval Records and Library*, compiled by Geraldine N. Phillips and Rebecca Livingston (Washington, 2005), pp. 173–195. Most of the rolls in this group are reproduced in National Archives Microfilm Publication T829. For rolls from the 1840s and 1850s— and to a lesser extent in the 1860s—the researcher needs to consult

[D37] Record Group 217, Records of the Fourth Auditor of the Treasury, Muster Rolls and Pay and Receipt Rolls for Ships and Shore Units, 1820–1898. These records and the records in [D35] were once all held by the office of the Fourth Auditor. At some point the (mostly earlier) rolls in [D35] were turned over to the Office of Naval Records and Library and the mostly later rolls in [D37] were retained by the Fourth Auditor's office. Unfortunately, many of the latter group were heavily damaged by water before they were turned over to the National Archives; the more badly injured volumes are not accessible to researchers pending future conservation. Even the volumes that can be consulted are sometimes only partially legible because of the water damage. [D37] includes 10 volumes of pay rolls, 1 October 1840–31 December 1862, for the officers, beneficiaries, and civilian employees of the Naval Asylum; these are especially useful for determining the names and dates of employment of the civilians. Beginning with the Civil War years muster rolls of vessels are in a better state of physical preservation and easier to use as [D38] Record Group 24, Bureau of Naval Personnel, Muster Rolls of Ships, 1860–1900.

Behavior: The Naval Asylum began keeping a register of offenses by, and punishments of, beneficiaries—"conduct books"—in 1849. Only two of these volumes appear to have survived: [D39] United States Naval Academy, Nimitz Library, Special Collections and Archives, List of Beneficiaries: Offenses and Punishments, 1867–1875, and [D40] U.S. Naval Academy, Nimitz Library, Special Collections and Archives, Pensioners' Record, U.S. Naval Asylum, 1889–1905. This loss is not as serious as it might seem, because offenses and punishments were typically recorded in [C1] the Asylum's station logs. There are, however, two important exceptions: no offenses and punishments were recorded in the logs between 25 January and the end of May 1850 and from 9 November 1861 through the end of June 1866. Occasional surviving extracts from the now-missing conduct books in the correspondence of the governors suggest that the registers of offenses and punishments were more complete than the corresponding entries in the logs. Nevertheless, the logs' record is amply sufficient to give a rich picture of beneficiary misbehavior.

Single-word and short-phrase descriptions of beneficiary behavior can be found in the "Character, habits, &c." column of

[D3] Naval Asylum Muster Rolls of Pensioners and Beneficiaries. The roll for June 1875 is the latest one in which data are entered in this column.

By far the richest sources for beneficiary character assessments and behavior are the several series of letters from the Asylum's governors and executive officers to the Secretary of the Navy and the Chief of the Bureau of Yards and Docks [A1, A2, A3, A4, A5, A8, A9, A10]. Replies to these communications can be found both in the endorsements to the letters themselves and in the replies to the governor and executive officer letters in the correspondence of the Secretary of the Navy and the Chief of the Bureau of Yards and Docks [A6, A7, A11, A12].

Typical Philadelphia police practice appears to have been to haul offending beneficiaries back to the Asylum and let the authorities there deal with them. Consequently, [D41] City Archives, Philadelphia, Prisons System, Daily Occurrence Docket, 1811–1948, has only rare appearances by beneficiaries.

Health: During the latter years of the period covered by this book, health records for the Asylum's beneficiaries are exceptionally rich. Admissions, brief descriptions of illnesses or injuries, discharges or deaths, and duration of hospitalizations are recorded in a continuous series of [D42] Registers of Patients for the Philadelphia Naval Hospital at United States National Archives in Washington, DC, Record Group 52, 1843–1868, 1863–1882, 1878–1890, and 1888–1896. The apparently overlapping dates of these volumes are accounted for by patients whose earlier-dated admissions were transferred to new volumes as they were begun. These and—so far as they survive—the registers of other naval hospitals are available on Ancestry.com as "Registers of Patients at Naval Hospitals, 1812–1934." Much richer detail regarding illnesses or injuries and their treatments and outcomes will be found in [D43] United States National Archives in Washington, DC, Record Group 52, Hospital Tickets and Case Papers, Boxes 141 (1868) through 153 (1889) for the Philadelphia Naval Hospital. These records are available electronically as part of Ancestry.com "U.S. Naval Hospital Tickets and Case Papers, 1825–1889."

Details of shipboard injuries and illnesses of beneficiaries during their active-duty careers can often be found in [D44] United States National Archives in Washington, DC, Record Group 52, Medical Journals of Ships, 1813–1889, assuming one knows the approximate date of the injury or illness and the ship in which the sailor or Marine was serving.

Beneficiaries who were subject to insanity were typically not treated at the Philadelphia Naval Hospital, which lacked facilities for their care, but were transferred in the earlier years to the Norfolk Naval Hospital and later to the United States Government Hospital for the Insane at Washington. The post-transfer histories of these beneficiaries can be followed in [D45] United States National Archives in Washington, DC, Record Group 52, Naval Hospital, Norfolk, Virginia, Register of Patients, 1830–1861, available on Ancestry.com "Registers of Patients at Naval Hospitals, 1812–1934" and in [D46] United States National Archives in Washington, DC, Record Group 418, Records of St. Elizabeths Hospital, Register of Cases, U.S. Government Hospital for the Insane (St. Elizabeths Hospital), 1855–1941.

Death and burial: Most beneficiary deaths are recorded in the Asylum's two registers [D1, D2]. They were reported to the Secretary of the Navy and (later) to the Chief of the Bureau of Yards and Docks. Such reports are most commonly found in [A3, A4, A8, A9]. Deaths and subsequent burials are almost invariably noted in the Asylum's station logs [C1], while beneficiary suicides, accidental deaths, and others considered newsworthy or sensational were often noted in the "Local Affairs" column of Philadelphia's *Public Ledger.* Municipal death certificates of beneficiaries, in those cases for which such a record exists, are in [D47] https://familysearch.org "Pennsylvania, Philadelphia City Death Certificates, 1803–1915."

Wills and inventories of possessions of many deceased beneficiaries are located in [D48] United States National Archives at Philadelphia, Record Group 181, Correspondence [and other loose papers] Relating to Beneficiaries, 1838–1910. If it is known that a beneficiary made a will and it is not in [D48], the researcher should then check [D49] Ancestry.com "Pennsylvania, Wills and Probate Records, 1683–1993."

The most accurate record of the graves in the Naval Asylum plot at Mount Moriah Cemetery is the one being developed privately by Samuel A. Ricks, who has graciously shared several successive iterations of this file with the author. Deaths and burial places of beneficiaries who died after they left the Asylum can sometimes be found in [D50] United States National Archives in Washington, DC, Record Group 52, Certificates of Death, Disability,

Pension, and Medical Survey, 1842–1896; in [D51] Historical
Society of Pennsylvania, Philadelphia, Philadelphia Board of Health
Death Records, 1803–1860, Cemetery Returns; in [D47] "Penn-
sylvania, Philadelphia City Death Certificates, 1803–1915"; in
[D52] U.S. Department of Veterans Affairs, National Cemetery
Administration, "Nationwide Gravesite Locator" http://gravelocator
.cem.va.gov; and at [D53] the Find a Grave website http://www
.findagrave.com.

   Other sources: A few of the beneficiaries were court-martialed
at earlier times in their Navy or Marine Corps careers. Transcripts
of these trials can be found in [D54] United States National
Archives in Washington, DC, Record Group 125, Records of the
Office of the Judge Advocate General (Navy), Records of General
Courts-Martial and Courts of Inquiry of the Navy Department,
1799–1867, National Archives Microfilm Publication M273. [D55]
City Archives, Philadelphia, Blockley Alms House, Male Register,
circa 1808–1921, microfilm copy made by the Genealogical Soci-
ety of Utah, was searched through May 1868 for residences at
Blockley by beneficiaries either before their admission to the Asy-
lum or after expulsion from the institution. State University of
New York Maritime College, Fort Schuyler, Throgs Neck, New
York, Stephen B. Luce Library Archives, Sailors' Snug Harbor
Records, [D56] Register of Pensioners, volumes 1 and 2 (1833–
1874), Inmate Register A, and [D57] Inmate Records, 1869–
2005, were searched for residencies there by Asylum beneficiaries
either before or after their time at the Asylum. In some cases the
Blockley and Snug Harbor records provided demographic data on
Asylum beneficiaries not found in the sources listed as [D16]
through [D34] above.

E. HISTORIES AND BACKGROUND STUDIES
The United States Naval Asylum has received little attention from
historians. The earliest published work is an article by [E1] Edward
Shippen, "Some Account of the Origin of the Naval Asylum at Philadelphia," in *The Pennsylvania Magazine of History and Biography*
7 (1883):117–142. This was soon followed by a thirty-seven-page
pamphlet written at the direction of Commodore David B. Harmony,
then Chief of the Bureau of Yards and Docks: [E2] Charles H.
Stockton, *Origin, History, Laws and Regulations of the United States
Naval Asylum, Philadelphia, Pennsylvania* (Washington: Government Printing Office, 1886). Both of these contain unattributed but

valuable information about the Asylum, its grounds and administration—information presumably gathered orally from contemporaries or by personal observation—that cannot be found in the surviving Asylum documentation cited above. There is also a brief article by one of the institution's twentieth-century governors: [E3] Admiral Albert Gleaves, "The United States Naval Home, Philadelphia," United States Naval Institute *Proceedings* 57 (1931):473–484. United States National Archives at Philadelphia, Record Group 71, includes a manuscript volume [E4] Edward Hooker, "The U.S. Naval Asylum, A Sketch of Its Origin and History and a Record of Useful Information Regarding It." Although this volume has an abbreviated sketch of the Asylum's early years, derived in part from [E1] Edward Shippen's article, the primary focus is the governorship of Rear Admiral J. R. M. Mullany, 1876–1879.

Philadelphia has a rich and daunting historiography, which the author does not pretend to have mastered in preparing to write this book. A few works have proved particularly pertinent to understanding the larger urban and social setting in which the Asylum was situated. [E5] Roger Lane, *Violent Death in the City: Suicide, Accident and Murder in Nineteenth-Century Philadelphia* (Cambridge: Harvard University Press, 1979) is an inspiring example of inferring mentality from the records and statistics of mortality; it has deeply influenced this and the author's previous books. Lane's work is also a fine introduction to Philadelphia's *Public Ledger*, which catered to its readership's appetite for stories of the sensational and the macabre. [E6] Simon P. Newman, *Embodied History: The Lives of the Poor in Early Philadelphia* (Philadelphia: University of Pennsylvania Press, 2003) includes seafarers in its inspired treatment of those on the lower rungs of the city's social ladder.

[E7] David J. Rothman's classic *The Discovery of the Asylum: Social Order and Disorder in the New Republic* (Boston: Little, Brown, 1971) analyzes the larger movement to create institutions to care for, house, or cope with the nation's impoverished, disabled, workshy, and antisocial residents. Rothman's perspective is primarily that of the elites who promoted the establishment of these institutions. A different perspective—one that has influenced this book—is provided by [E8] David Wagner, *The Poorhouse: America's Forgotten Institution* (Lanham, MD: Rowman & Littlefield, 2005). Wagner argues that the alms house's savvy residents were often able to subvert the elite's intentions of social control and use the institutions to meet their own needs. Although it mentions sailors only rarely,

Marines never, and the U.S. Naval Asylum not at all, [E9] James Marten's *Sing Not War: The Lives of Union & Confederate Veterans in Gilded Age America* (Chapel Hill: University of North Carolina Press, 2011) with its history of war-disabled veterans, its account of public opposition to pensions, its rather negative assessment of institutional veterans' homes (pp. 159–198), and its analysis of the problem of alcohol abuse in the homes (pp. 100–111) provides a counter-narrative to *Ungentle Goodnights*, raising a cautionary flag about the generally positive view of the Asylum that has been offered here. This historian notes Marten's views with some trepidation, but *Ungentle Goodnights* presents Christopher McKee's judgment, based on three decades of intimate association with the Asylum and its residents, and he's sticking to his story.

Index

United States Naval Asylum is abbreviated USNA.

ABOUT THE AUTHOR

Christopher McKee is Samuel R. and Marie-Louise Rosenthal Professor Emeritus at Grinnell College. He is the author of *Edward Preble: A Naval Biography, 1761–1807*; *A Gentlemanly and Honorable Profession: The Creation of the U.S. Naval Officer Corps, 1794–1815*; and *Sober Men and True: Sailor Lives in the Royal Navy, 1900–1945*. Now a scholar-in-residence at the Newberry Library (Chicago), McKee continues to research and write about the lives and experiences of individuals serving in naval forces.